CW01019623

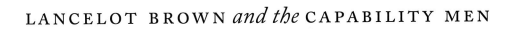

LANCELOT BROWN *and the* CAPABILITY MEN

LANCELOT BROWN
and the
CAPABILITY MEN

*Landscape Revolution in
Eighteenth-century England*

DAVID BROWN *and* TOM WILLIAMSON

REAKTION BOOKS

Published by Reaktion Books Ltd
Unit 32, Waterside
44–48 Wharf Road
London N1 7UX, UK
www.reaktionbooks.co.uk

First published 2016

Supported by a Publications Grant from the
Paul Mellon Centre for Studies in British Art

PAUL MELLON CENTRE
for Studies in British Art

Printed and bound in China

A catalogue record for this book is available
from the British Library

ISBN 978 1 78023 644 5

CONTENTS

1 Lancelot 'Capability' Brown, painted by Nathaniel Dance in 1773 at the height of Brown's career.

ONE

The World of Mr Brown

LANCELOT 'Capability' Brown is the most famous landscape designer in English history, in part perhaps because of his memorable moniker, and the broad character of his creations will probably be familiar to most if not all readers (illus. 1). Brown swept away walled gardens and geometric planting from around the homes of the rich, creating in their place compositions of studied 'natural' beauty. These comprised open expanses of turf, irregularly scattered with individual trees and clumps, which were surrounded in whole or part by a perimeter belt, ornamented with serpentine bodies of water and usually provided with, at best, a rather sparse scatter of temples and other ornamental buildings. Such 'landscape parks' did not, of course, spring from nowhere. Formal gardening had been in retreat long before the start of Brown's career. In the 1720s and '30s Charles Bridgeman and others had developed a simplified, less cluttered form of geometric landscape design and in the 1730s and '40s William Kent created gardens characterized by irregular planting and serpentine lines. But Brown, through the 1750s, '60s and '70s, took these tendencies to a new level, completely eschewing all forms of geometry and regularity and creating a type of natural, informal landscape that has been justly described as 'England's greatest contribution to the visual arts' (illus. 2).[1]

Such acclaim has not been universal. Brown had many critics even while his career blossomed, and following his death his work came under more sustained attack from the Picturesque theorists Uvedale Price and Richard Payne Knight.[2] Through the nineteenth century he fell still further from favour, with criticism coming in particular from the designer and writer John Claudius Loudon, as sweeping parkland landscapes were increasingly rejected as the prime setting for the mansion and as formal gardens and terraces, topiary and parterres came back into fashion. It was only in the middle decades of the twentieth century – first in the writings of Christopher Hussey, later through the research and publications of the great Dorothy Stroud – that Brown's achievements began to be acknowledged once again.[3] Stroud's book, *Capability Brown*, remains perhaps the most important text on Brown, although it was followed by studies by Hyams (in 1971), Turner (in 1985) and Hinde (in 1986).[4] And articles and books on Brown have continued to appear during recent decades, including the notable biography by Jane Brown, *The Omnipotent Magician*, and Laura

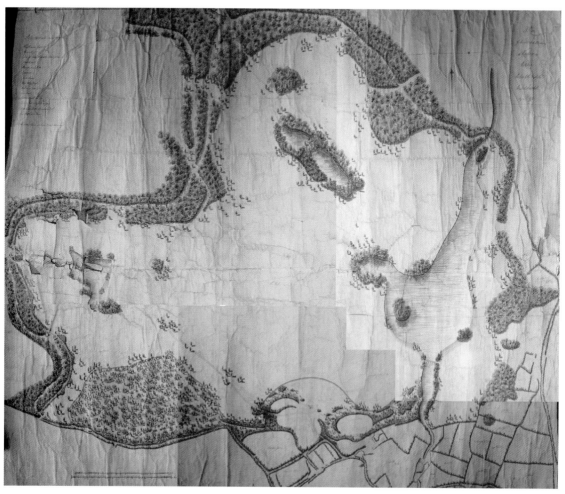

2 Brown's plan for Wardour Castle, Wiltshire, made in 1773, shows most of the principal features of his style: sweeping expanses of turf, clumps, a lake and a perimeter plantation belt with circuit ride.

Mayer's short but immensely informative *Capability Brown and the English Landscape Garden.*[5]

Brown was born in 1716 at Kirkhale in Northumberland, of modest although by no means impoverished parents. Modern scholars tend to exaggerate his lowly origins. In fact his father was a prosperous farmer, and his brother John married the daughter of the local squire, Sir William Lorraine, apparently without scandal or objection. Brown himself attended the local grammar school until he was sixteen, only then coming to work on Sir William's estate, where he remained for seven years. The precise character of his employment there remains unclear, although it is likely that he was involved in – and learnt much about – estate management and forestry. In 1739 he left Northumberland and moved south, initially to Lincolnshire, and notably to Grimsthorpe, where he gained an important reputation as an 'engineer' and became experienced in water management.[6] He may have designed lakes at Kiddington in Oxfordshire for Sir Charles Browne in 1740, and undertaken other work in the south Midlands, before taking up in 1742 a post at Stowe in Buckinghamshire, where Richard Temple, 1st Viscount Cobham, had been creating complex and elaborate gardens for over twenty years, initially with Charles Bridgeman and Sir John Vanbrugh, later with James Gibbs and William Kent. The latter had joined Cobham's design team in 1731 and, by the time that Brown arrived, was busy laying out a novel section of the grounds, the 'Elysian Fields', a serpentine garden containing a large number of ornamental buildings. The extent of Brown's own contribution to the design remains unclear, but it may well have been at Stowe that he first acquired the skills as an architect which were, as we shall see, to form so important a part of his practice. This, at least, was the common opinion in the eighteenth century, an article in the *Public Advertiser* for 1772, for example, describing how he designed the Temple of Concord and the Temple of Victory at Stowe, 'which raised him into some degree of estimation as an architect'.[7]

While still at Stowe Brown appears to have undertaken a number of commissions for other clients, principally friends or associates of Cobham himself, most notably the 6th Earl of Denbigh at Newnham Paddox in 1746 and Lord Guernsey at Packington in 1748.[8] After Cobham's death in 1749 Brown moved to Hammersmith and set up as an independent designer. His career took off with remarkable rapidity, and by 1760 he had undertaken perhaps thirty major commissions. But it was the 1760s and '70s that really brought success, and recognition by the wider public as the most important landscape designer of his day, 'the great Arbiter of British Taste'.[9] In

1764 he was made Master Gardener at Hampton Court and took up residence in the palace grounds. By the time of his death in 1783 he was the owner of a substantial estate at Fenstanton in Huntingdonshire and had probably worked on at least 250 sites. The precise number is uncertain because his single surviving account book contains only sixteen names, relating to commissions in the early 1760s (although some continued into the 1770s), while his bank accounts, which cover his entire career, mention in all a mere ninety commissions.[10] Many important and well-documented examples of his work do not appear there, payment having been made to Brown by some other means, usually in cash. George Lucy of Charlecote in Warwickshire described how, when he apologized for the late payment of money owed to Brown, the latter said that it did not matter 'as he did not want money: but upon my offering him a £100 note he pulled out his pocket book and carried it off with him'.[11]

Such a situation has allowed considerable speculation about the particular places where Brown may have worked. He has been identified as the designer of around 267 houses, gardens or landscapes by one authority or another, but suspicion surrounds many of these attributions: illustration 95 (p. 166), drawn by Jon Gregory and Sarah Spooner, is based on various published lists (especially those by John Phibbs) and includes both certain and less certain examples.[12] Even in the eighteenth century wealthy families were claiming he had designed places that he had never even visited. Ditchingham in Norfolk, for example (illus. 3), is often claimed as one of his works, but the 'Brown plan' supposedly kept at the hall does not appear to have been seen by anyone within living memory; the park was laid out around 1764 but no reference to its owners, the Bedingfields, appears in Brown's account book; and a map of this date apparently showing the proposed 'deformalization' of the grounds was surveyed by one Joseph Rumball, not known as an associate of Brown.[13] Other mistaken attributions have arisen due to misunderstandings on the part of researchers. Elveden in Suffolk is thus widely accepted as one of Brown's landscapes.[14] But the £1,460 he received in 1765 came from 'General Keppel': this was not Admiral Augustus Keppel, Elveden's owner, but rather his brother General William Keppel of Dyrham in Hertfordshire. Even where Brown *was* involved at a particular place the extent of his activities has often been exaggerated. Holkham in Norfolk is frequently cited as one of Brown's parks but its key designer in the

second half of the eighteenth century was unquestionably John Sandys, the head gardener, and Brown's contribution was limited to the pleasure grounds around the hall. Even here, according to Humphry Repton, the work was carried out by one of Brown's 'foremen', who had 'deservedly acquired great credit . . . by the execution of gravel walks, the planting of shrubberies, and other details belonging to pleasure grounds'.[15] Brown is similarly often credited with laying out the grounds of David Garrick's small villa at Hampton, but Garrick was an enthusiastic gardener in his own right and an article in the *Gazetteer and New Daily Advertiser* for 1780 described how he and his wife disposed the grounds themselves, 'without much, or indeed any regular help'. Brown's activities had been limited to the planting of a single weeping willow, albeit 'now a very fine one'.[16]

3 Ditchingham in Norfolk, although often claimed as a 'Brown' park, was almost certainly laid out by some other designer around 1765. The vast majority of landscape parks in eighteenth-century England were created by one of Brown's so-called 'imitators'.

Yet the opposite is also true. Many of the places where Brown worked still remain unknown to scholars, and research continues to turn up entirely new commissions, most of which have not yet reached the pages of the published texts on the subject, such as Overstone in Northamptonshire (1758).[17] Moreover, some of the commissions which past scholars had assumed remained unexecuted now appear to have been at least partly carried out. Brown thus drew up two plans for improving St James's Park in London and while his main proposal – turning the ruler-straight canal into a more naturalistic lake – was not effected until John Nash redesigned the park in 1826–7, other aspects of the landscape were transformed under Brown's direction, a newspaper report from 1770 noting how 'The principal Point intended is to give a full view of Whitehall to the Queen's Palace, and also of Westminster Abbey, to effect which almost all the Trees on that side will be taken away.'[18] A comparison of the anonymous *Plan of the Cities of London and Westminster, and Borough of Southwark* of 1767, with John Noorthouck's survey of 1772 and Carington Bowles's London map of 1775, shows that this plan was indeed carried out. Even allowing for a significant number of omissions from the accepted list of Brown's works, however, it is quite clear that the overwhelming majority of landscape parks created in England in the second half of the eighteenth century – over 90 per cent of them, at a conservative estimate – must have been designed by somebody else, one of those whom Humphry Repton was later to label 'the day labourers who became his successors', the 'illiterate followers' who allegedly diluted and corrupted Brown's style.[19] And it is the role of

such men, and their relationship with Brown himself, that are among the main topics addressed in this volume.

Although we still have much to learn about Capability Brown and the eighteenth-century landscape park, a great deal has been achieved by both professional and amateur researchers over the last few decades. In addition to the volumes noted above, important new light has been cast on Brown himself by John Phibbs in a series of scholarly and sometimes provocative articles.[20] There have been a number of important studies of eighteenth-century landscape design more generally, including the various volumes produced by Timothy Mowl (most notably his *Gentlemen and Players*).[21] Of particular importance are the studies of Brown's contemporaries and 'imitators' – most notably Fiona Cowell's biography of the designer Richard Woods – and the research by individuals like Kate Felus into the way that eighteenth-century landscapes were actually used, consumed and experienced by contemporaries.[22] This book draws extensively on all this work. But it is also the outcome of our own researches, carried out over many years, into various aspects of Brown's career, and into the development of eighteenth-century landscapes more generally. In particular, an extensive analysis of contemporary bank accounts – not just those of Brown, but of a broad section of wealthy individuals – allows us to understand rather better the working methods of someone who, whatever his claims to artistic genius, was above all a consummate businessman.

In this Brown was very much a product of his age, and fundamental to this book is the idea that the landscape park cannot be understood simply as the product of a single artist. In part this is because it is no longer clear that the landscape style was indeed invented or pioneered by Brown himself: it was, as we shall argue, simply the style of the times, and Brown's 'imitators' were no more and no less than colleagues – or rivals – in the business of landscape design. In part, however, it is because the landscape style's success indicates that it met a number of pressing contemporary needs, fitted in well with the aspirations and lifestyles of wealthy consumers. To understand the landscapes created by Brown we must therefore begin with a brief account, no more than a thumbnail sketch, of some of the key characteristics of eighteenth-century England. Some of this may seem to take us far from the world of gardens and landscapes, but landscape design was a serious business in the eighteenth century, and cannot be understood in isolation from the wider world or from politics, economics and social relations. Those seeking to learn more about Brown's 'place-making' will have to be patient: the character of this wider world needs first to be briefly, all too briefly, presented.

Politics

We will begin with politics and ideology, for styles of garden design in eighteenth-century England, together with styles of architecture, have often been explained as expressions of particular political ideologies, or as representations of the political system more generally.[23] Many of Brown's clients, moreover, like those of other designers, moved in the world of high politics. It was the air they lived and breathed. The Restoration of the monarchy that followed the political upheavals of the mid-seventeenth century, and which brought Charles II to the

throne, together with the 'Glorious Revolution' of 1688, when James II was ousted by a group of leading politicians in favour of William of Orange and his wife Mary, secured a political system in which power effectively lay with a parliament that broadly represented the propertied classes. The authority of the Crown, and the centrality of the court in the nation's political and cultural life, did not disappear, but they were less important than they had been.[24] Nothing, of course, that we would recognize as a 'democracy' yet existed. The franchise was limited to those owning property with a rental value of at least forty shillings a year. This said, such a qualification was possessed by a fairly wide swath of the population – probably around a fifth of male adults at the start of the century – and this figure increased steadily as, with inflation, the proportion of the population owning a house or land of the required value rose. Nevertheless, in both county and borough constituencies, contested elections were, in effect, clashes between local landed dynasties. The rewards of victory could be considerable, for entering the inner circles of power brought patronage and control over appointments to positions within the ever-increasing machinery of the state – in the armed forces, and in the excise or other government bureaucracies. The possession of a fashionable house, with a fashionable garden, was one way in which politicians advertised their success, attracting more people to their gang of supporters, or 'interest' – the more important of whom would themselves expect to be rewarded with a cut of the spoils, in terms of preferments, appointments, contracts and sinecures. To modern eyes, such a system appears corrupt and indeed, contemporaries were always keen to accuse their political opponents of corruption. But politics in the eighteenth century was not entirely devoid of genuine ideological debates, and for most of the eighteenth century these were usually described in terms of a clash between 'Whigs' and 'Tories'.

The Whigs originated as the faction that had successfully opposed the succession to the throne of James, Duke of York and brother of Charles II, in the Exclusion Crisis of 1679; the Tories, as the group who had supported him, and they continued to be supporters of the Stuart succession throughout the rest of the seventeenth century and into the eighteenth. But there were other differences between the two groups, which became more prominent in the eighteenth century.[25] In particular, the Whigs believed in a measure of religious toleration and became increasingly opposed to involvement in the wars which wracked continental Europe (largely because they raised levels of taxation), yet at the same time were keen on a foreign policy directed towards the promotion of trade. They were the party, in essence, of the social groups who had benefited most from the Civil War: great aristocratic families like the Cokes or the Townshends, the city interests of financiers and merchants. The Tories were in many ways a more diffuse group, but while led by major aristocrats like the Earl of Bolingbroke they drew much of their support from the countryside, from minor rural gentry. They were the party of the established Church, suspicious of increased religious toleration, initially at least supporters of the Stuart succession and widely suspected (in some cases, not without justification) of harbouring residual Catholic sympathies. But they were not simply a party of backwoods squires opposed to the erupting world

of commerce. One of their key members in the first decades of the century, Robert Harley, was among the founders of the South Sea Company, the dubious joint-stock venture that collapsed, spectacularly, in 1720. Nor were all minor country landowners supporters of the Tory cause, not least because – as explained below – this could bring serious personal and financial difficulties for much of the eighteenth century. While this description of the two groups is probably useful in very general terms, it masks a shifting pattern of aristocratic allegiances, and the meanings of the two terms were elaborated and redefined as the eighteenth century progressed.

Although William of Orange had effectively come to power because of the actions of the Whigs, he was prepared to favour the Tories on the understandable grounds that they were stronger supporters of royal authority, and many of his administrations contained individuals drawn from both groups. Anne, his successor, initially favoured the Whigs but she, too, came to prefer balanced administrations. Throughout the late seventeenth and early eighteenth century the two parties or factions were thus finely balanced, and there were numerous general elections. But on Anne's death in 1714 all this changed. The throne passed to the German George I, who brought in a government that consisted entirely of Whigs and which, from 1721, was firmly under the control of Robert Walpole, England's first 'Prime Minister'.[26] The 'Robinocracy' lasted until Walpole's resignation in 1742, and following the panic caused by the attempt of Charles Stuart (the 'Old Pretender'), with Scottish rebels, to gain the throne in 1715, political opposition was effectively suppressed. Tory lawyers could no longer become judges, Tory clergymen could not take the office of bishop and Tory army officers had their commissions removed. The Whigs won a string of general elections and survived the accession of George II in 1727, and Britain became, in effect, a one-party state. In the 1730s, however, Walpole's dominance was challenged by new political alignments, muddying the definition of already vague political labels. A loose group of disaffected Whigs – the 'Patriot Whigs', sections of which, young men associated with Lord Cobham, were described as 'Cobham's Cubs' – and Tories, associated with the Tory Sir William Wyndham and the Whigs William Pulteney and Lord Carteret, developed.[27] This group was to an extent centred around the household of George II's son, Frederick, Prince of Wales, and included several individuals who created innovative gardens, serpentine in layout and evocative in character, many of which were designed by William Kent. Lord Cobham laid out the great gardens at Stowe; Charles Hamilton created those at Painshill in Surrey; the Earl of Guildford (Lord of the Prince's Bedchamber) laid out Wroxton Abbey; and Charles Lyttelton, the prince's secretary, created Hagley.[28] The gardens at Stowe, as we shall see, carried complex political messages but that does not appear to have been the case with the other examples, and to a large extent the association of this group with these new landscapes probably reflects the fact that, out of government, they had the time and the energy to put into such projects. Retirement from public life, whether temporary or permanent, was often accompanied by an enthusiasm for gardening, in the eighteenth century as in earlier periods, not least perhaps because such men had time on their hands – and new gardens were much cheaper to establish than new houses were to build.

Walpole eventually left office in 1742, following a series of defeats inflicted by a combination of opposition Whigs and Tories, and a new government was organized by Pulteney: one that failed to live up to expectations regarding the investigation of the corrupt practices of the Robinocracy, or the impeachment of Walpole himself. The following year Britain became involved in a new European war, the War of the Austrian Succession, into which it was dragged by the king's continued role as Elector of Hanover. In 1745, with French encouragement and promised military support, which never materialized, the Young Pretender made a bid for the throne and marched south with a Scottish army, but failed to attract the hoped-for support of leading Tory families, and was easily defeated. In the wake of the '45 Rebellion, power passed from an administration led by Pulteney, now 1st Earl of Bath, and Carteret, now 2nd Earl Granville, to Henry Pelham, who earlier had been one of Cobham's faction. Peace was negotiated at Aix-la-Chapelle in 1748 and he and his brother, the Duke of Newcastle, led an administration that was exclusively Whig in character until 1756.

This, in brief, was the pattern of political history in the decades preceding the establishment of Brown as an independent designer in the 1750s. Brown's own career coincided not only with the effective eclipse of the Tories, and the rise of politicians who had originated as part of Cobham's group of Whigs, but with the disappearance of any close party affiliation. In H. T. Dickinson's words,

there were no organized political parties in Parliament between the late 1750s and the early 1780s. Even the Whigs ceased to be an identifiable party, and Parliament was dominated by competing political connections, which all proclaimed Whiggish political views, or by independent backbenchers unattached to any particular group.[29]

Party labels in the early and middle decades of the eighteenth century might be vague and shifting, but they were not devoid of meaning. They reflected, however imperfectly, underlying ideological realities. Whigs were, in broad terms, pragmatic, commercial, tolerant. But they were also closely associated with the kinds of free-market values which came to be articulated by Adam Smith in his *The Theory of Moral Sentiments* of 1759 and *The Wealth of Nations* of 1776, and subsequently in a rash of publications dealing with what was increasingly perceived as the 'problem' of the poor, including Bentham's *Observations on the Poor Bill* (1797) and Malthus's *Essay on the Principle of Population* (1798).[30] The improvement of society was to be achieved, not through acts of individual benevolence, but rather from what McCulloch in the early nineteenth century was to describe as the 'desire implanted in the breast of every individual of rising in the world and improving his condition'.[31] The Tories, as we have noted, were in essence the party of traditional values, the established Church, the old monarchy: of paternalism exercised by landowners in control of their own estates and localities. They were thus opposed to the centralization and monopolization of power under a Prime Minister in close alliance with London merchants and bankers, and suspicious of a large standing army. Centralized power threatened political liberty and allowed the unfettered growth of corruption. The broader opposition that developed against Walpole's one-party rule, involving the Whig Patriots, shows that some aspects of this Tory view of the world were more widely shared, especially perhaps the idea that local districts were being adversely affected by the dominance of London. Indeed, the usual labels were sometimes abandoned during Walpole's supremacy and a broader opposition described itself – reverting to terms widely employed in the previous century – as the 'country party', ranged against the politicians in power in London, the 'court'.

The development of the landscape garden, and the landscape park, has often been seen as an expression of Whig values, and was so seen by many at the time. The informal, serpentine lines combined art and nature, reflecting the balanced constitution of the nation, which incorporated the principals of both monarchy and democracy.[32] English gardens thus stood in marked contrast to those of less fortunate nations, especially France, where absolutism was expressed in the serried rows of trees, rigid parterres and disciplined topiary. But a more important connection between ideology and landscape can perhaps be identified: one concerning attitudes to land itself. To those with broadly Tory sympathies, land was the foundation of the nation, secure, dependable and real; and the long-established, traditional families who owned it, and who dominated their localities with paternalism and benevolence, were the nation's backbone. The Whigs, in contrast – and to simplify again a complex situation – were enthusiastic supporters of free-market principles and commerce, and thus tended to view land more as a commodity, as one of several kinds of wealth. Land could be bought and sold, and it could also be *improved*, its appearance, profitability and character changed through the application of initiative and capital.[33] Open fields could be enclosed, common land reclaimed, marshes drained. This is not of course to say that Tory landowners necessarily resisted enclosure, or were averse to making money from their landed estates. It was rather a matter of the enthusiasm with which these things were carried out, and of the manner in which they were justified. The ideological differences in eighteenth-century England are captured only partially and incompletely by labels first developed to describe political factions, but they existed nevertheless. To better understand them we need to delve into the deeper currents of social and economic life from which, and within which, these contrasting views of the world developed.

An age of expansion

The British domestic economy enjoyed steady expansion in the half century before Brown began his career. Following the Civil War, a new spirit of entrepreneurship was in the air: this was 'an age which . . . swarmed with projectors, adventurers, moralists and improvers of all sorts'.[34] Commerce thrived. Low population growth, and a steady expansion in the scale of production, helped ensure low levels of inflation; internal peace provided an atmosphere of financial confidence; while trading and manufactures were encouraged by the Whig party, with a foreign policy increasingly motivated by commercial considerations.[35] 'Our trade is our chief supporter,' Lord Carteret told the House of Lords in 1739, 'and therefore we must sacrifice every other view to the preservation of our trade'.[36] Of particular importance

was the fact that the first half of the eighteenth century saw a phenomenal expansion in trade with America and the Far East. It is true that, at the start of the Seven Years War in 1754, European markets still accounted for around 80 per cent of British exports, and for the majority of imports. But trade beyond Europe had been growing at a phenomenal rate. Imports from north America increased fourfold in value in the first half of the eighteenth century, while those from the West Indies more than doubled. Imports of tea from India grew from 67,000 lb in 1701 to around 3 million lb in 1750.[37] Trade, moreover, flowed the other way, especially to north America with its rocketing population. In Colley's words, 'In all, 95% of *the increase* in Britain's commodity exports that occurred in the six decades after the Act of Union was sold to captive and colonial markets outside Europe.'[38] By the 1750s re-exports of colonial goods made up some 40 per cent of total exports. One particularly important facet of this trade was the market in slaves, brought on an industrial scale from Africa to the New World by British ships; on average, around 23,000 per annum by the second decade of the century.[39] The Treaty of Utrecht at the end of the War of the Spanish Succession in 1713 gave the country control of the entrance to the Mediterranean and the notorious Barbary Coast through ownership of Gibraltar; and the *Assiento* contract gave control of the supply of slaves to Spain's South American colonies.

The increasing importance of foreign trade and imperial possessions is reflected in a number of ways in the design of gardens; in the enthusiasm for oriental and exotic, and especially Chinese, buildings and ornaments; and in the vast influx of foreign flowers, shrubs and trees. No fewer than 445 species of tree and shrub are said to have been introduced into Britain in the course of the eighteenth century, many in the early and middle decades, including Weymouth pine (1705), Indian bean tree (1722), weeping willow (1730), pitch pine (1743), ginkgo (1750), tree of heaven (1751), red maple (1755) and Lombardy poplar (1758): plants which Brown and his contemporaries were to use extensively.[40] Of equal importance was the fact that much of the wealth required for the creation of parks and gardens was based on trade at home or abroad, or on the

4 Harewood in Yorkshire. The house, by James Carr and Robert Adam, and the surrounding parkland, partly designed by Lancelot Brown, were largely paid for with income derived from the Lascelles family's sugar plantations in Barbados.

5 J.M.W. Turner, *Harewood House from the South*, 1798, watercolour.

financial system necessary to sustain it. The great house at Harewood in Yorkshire, with its grounds landscaped by Brown, was thus largely paid for with money derived from the Lascelles family's extensive plantations in Barbados (illus. 4, 5). By the 1790s these extended over more than 14,000 acres, were worked by nearly 3,000 slaves and were worth the incredible sum of £293,000.[41] The making of the new park at Chatsworth in Derbyshire, partly at least under Brown's supervision, was begun in 1759, almost certainly because of the promise of significant income from the Duke of Devonshire's copper mines at Ecton in Staffordshire: the lease on these was to run out in 1760, and ore deposits of exceptional quality had just been discovered.[42] In Christopher Christie's words, 'Landed society was shot through with money from trade and commerce, and many old and new county and aristocratic families who occupied magnificent houses acquired their wealth from non-agricultural sources.'[43]

Underpinning economic and military expansion was a well-developed system of credit that permeated all levels of society, from local shopkeepers selling goods to individuals with property but irregular incomes, to major merchants in London and Liverpool allowing long-term payment arrangements to exporters. Equally important was the organized, national credit system represented by the banknotes issued by the Bank of England, an institution established in 1694 to raise money for the government to provide for the rebuilding of the fleet after the disastrous defeat at the hands of the French at the Battle of Beachy Head in 1690, ultimately creating the most powerful navy in the world. The financial system thus developed in part out of the needs of the state to fight foreign wars, mainly against

the French, wars that in turn brought benefits to the nation's traders, thus ensuring the viability of the credit system. At the same time, a liberal Stock Exchange in London overtook the now more regulated Exchange in Amsterdam to become the largest and most active financial centre in the world. But all this financial complexity also had its downside. Speculation – in foreign adventures and other 'projects' – was rife in the half-century before Brown, and those with wealth invested freely in the investment markets provided by the two great joint-stock companies: the East India Company, first founded in 1600 but with monopoly trading rights to India from 1708; and the South Sea Company, founded in 1711 with a monopoly to trade with South America, and whose shares crashed disastrously ten years later, an institution which, together with the Bank of England, helped finance the War of the Spanish Succession, 'Queen Anne's War'.

The first half of the eighteenth century thus saw steady economic growth at home and abroad. But things changed significantly around 1750, and the start of Brown's career coincided with what might, without significant exaggeration, be described as Britain's take-off into the modern world. Following the great demographic decline of the later Middle Ages, the population had grown fairly steadily through the sixteenth and early seventeenth centuries, stoking up inflation and creating pressure on resources, which arguably contributed to the political crises and internal warfare of the mid-seventeenth century. The Restoration, perhaps significantly, came as population growth ground to a halt once again; thereafter population levels actually declined gradually until the end of the century, and afterwards remained comparatively stable, before rising fairly slowly to around six million by 1750. But thereafter growth was almost exponential, the population of England and Wales reaching around nine million by 1800 and nearly eighteen million by 1851.[44] Britain had, in effect, been released from the Malthusian trap, and thereafter the growth of its population never really slackened (illus. 6).

Demographic expansion had a direct impact on agricultural profitability, and especially bene-fited cereal growers. Whereas the period up to *c.* 1750 had been one of relatively sluggish prices, increasing demand thereafter stimulated agricul-tural innovation. This was the period of the classic 'agricultural revolution', in which the widespread adoption of new crops – especially turnips and clover – increased the amount of nitrogen being returned to the soil, raising cereal yields; and a

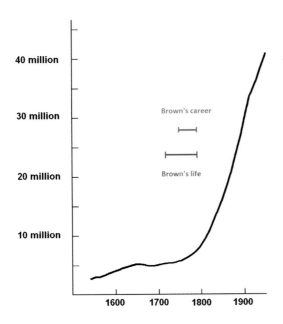

6 Brown's life and career, set against a graph showing the chronology of population growth in England and Wales since 1500. The emergence of the landscape park coincides with the country's take-off into modernity – with the start of the agricultural and industrial revolutions, and of unrestrained demographic growth.

range of other techniques, including large-scale land drainage and marling, boosted production. More land was brought into cultivation through the enclosure and reclamation of marginal 'waste', although in some regions (such as the Midland 'Shires') the area devoted to pasture increased at the expense of arable land, as improvements in transport encouraged new patterns of agricultural specialization. The scale of the achievement was astonishing. Even in 1851 imports only accounted for some 16 per cent of foodstuffs consumed in England and Wales. To feed an expanding popu-lation the volume of wheat produced more than doubled in the course of the later eighteenth and early nineteenth centuries, while that of barley may have risen by over two-thirds, and increases in the production of other foodstuffs were prob-ably of a similar order.[45] There was, at the same time, a dramatic improvement in what economic historians call 'labour productivity', that is, the number of individuals required to produce a given quantity of food.[46] In 1760 the work of each agricultural worker could feed around one other person, but by 1841 it could feed another 2.7.

This latter improvement was vital because it was also in this period that the nation experi-enced an industrial revolution, so that a higher and higher proportion of the workforce came to be employed full-time in mines, mills and fac-tories. Industrial growth was based on three key sectors: coal, iron and textiles. Coal production rose from perhaps 2.5 million tons per annum in 1700 to over 11 million by 1800;[47] there were fewer than twenty blast furnaces in England in 1700 but by 1805 there were 177. The production of textiles also saw much expansion, although this came a little later, from the 1770s, following the improvements in spinning machinery made by

7 Brown's career coincided with the development of the canal network. Here, near Watford in Hertfordshire, the main approach to The Grove, the home of the Earls of Clarendon, was carried across the Grand Junction Canal by an ornamental bridge, the canal effectively appropriated as an ornamental water body on the edge of the park.

Hargreaves, Arkwright and Compton.[48] The middle and later decades of the century saw the progressive improvement of the nation's roads through the proliferation of turnpike trusts, and from the early 1760s the growth and elaboration of its canal network, greatly facilitating the movement of bulk goods. In this take-off into modernity, demographic, industrial and agricultural expansion were all intimately connected. Better food supplies prevented the periodic dearths that had formerly served to check population growth, while the development of a more diversified economy encouraged earlier marriage, and

thus higher fertility rates. In addition, although it is true that living conditions in many industrializing and urbanizing areas were poor, encouraging disease, on the whole the population was warmer and healthier than it had ever been as a consequence of cheaper fuel and clothing. More people meant a greater demand for food and for manufactured products, further stimulating production in both the agricultural and industrial sectors. The concentration of industrial production in the north and west of the country, and improvements in transport infrastructure, encouraged a degree of de-industrialization in the densely settled south of England and East Anglia, regions in which many people had formerly been employed in small-scale cottage industries, thus providing a pool of underemployed labour that could be employed to make 'improvements'. There were innumerable other connections.[49] These great transformations of the country's social and economic life were well underway by the time Brown died in 1783. Their impact may still have been muted, compared with the situation in the middle of the nineteenth century, but all educated observers – and those not so educated – were aware that the country was changing fast (illus. 7, 8).

We do not need to deal here with the question of why this take-off into modernity occurred in

England earlier than in other countries. Suffice it to say that the dramatic economic expansion was a function of both long- and short-term trends. The factors that had encouraged economic growth in the first half of the century now stepped up a gear. Colonial trade, already substantial, received a further boost as a consequence of the Seven Years War (1754–63), which led to massive gains of territory from the French, and therefore access to raw materials for industrial production, especially cotton, and captive markets for exports in North America, India and the West Indies. Profits from foreign trade were ploughed back into mining and manufacturing to meet an expanding home market. The nation's

8 A 1758 print by Francis Vivares, 'A VIEW of the Upper Works at Coalbrook Dale in the County of SALOP' (after Thomas Smith of Derby).

place in the growing world economy was thus of fundamental importance. But in addition Britain possessed certain social characteristics which now helped to precipitate rapid economic growth. It had long been a society in which private property was established at almost all social levels, and in which a mercantile and artisan class was numerous and economically powerful in comparison with most other European countries. These characteristics had been exacerbated by the outcome of the Civil War, however, for in spite of the Restoration of the monarchy successive political settlements established a system that guaranteed the safety of private property from the arbitrary exactions of the Crown. The accumulation of capital could continue unhindered at the level of great landowners and merchants, but also among the larger farmers and petty industrialists. This group, the 'middling sort' in contemporary parlance, were crucial in economic expansion. It was composed of men who were 'intelligent but not always educated, well-to-do but not always wealthy, articulate but not always cultured, who owned property, manipulated money or followed one of the growing professions'.[50] Their numbers and wealth increased steadily in the course of the eighteenth century, and they were prepared to invest in new forms of industrial development. They also, alongside the wealthy elite, provided a ready market for sophisticated consumer goods, the production of which grew fast in the first half of the century. In 1749 the architect John Wood listed the many improvements in the domestic life of this group that had occurred since the accession of George II, including the proliferation of mirrors, the widespread use of furniture made of walnut and mahogany in place of oak, the use of leather and upholstery in

furniture and improved fireplaces.[51] The early eighteenth century also saw significant expansion in clock- and instrument making, and gunmaking, all of which utilized and further refined techniques such as precision boring and calibrating which were to prove essential for the development of industrial machinery, especially steam engines.[52] From the time of Brown, mass production of consumer goods – especially English porcelain – added further comfort to middle-class homes, while industrialization further enhanced the fortunes of their owners.

But the country's development as the world's first industrial nation had one last, fundamental ingredient. The nation enjoyed some of the most extensive and accessible coal reserves in the world, an 'underground forest' without which sustained economic growth would have been impossible. As Wrigley has observed, if coal had not existed England would, by 1815, have required at least 6 million hectares of managed woodland to meet its energy requirements – nearly half its total land area.[53] Industrialization represented, above all, the transition to a fossil fuel economy, and during Brown's lifetime the improvement in transport systems, a necessary concomitant of rapid economic growth, ensured that coal became the main domestic as well as industrial fuel across most parts of the country. The precise balance of factors that explain the nation's precocious take-off into modernity remains, it should be emphasized, a matter of debate. What remains clear, yet is seldom remarked upon, is the remarkable coincidence between Brown's career and these profound economic, technological and demographic transformations.

'Politeness'

One important consequence of the growing complexity of the British economy, and of the expansion in the size and economic importance of the middle classes, was a change in patterns of social behaviour on the part of the established elite. Protecting or expanding their incomes necessitated new ways of interacting with those who were most involved in finance, banking, commerce, industry and related activities. From the start of the eighteenth century, but especially from the time of George I's accession in 1714, it became fashionable to play down the scale of the gulf between the aristocracy on the one hand and the broader ranks of the propertied on the other. There was also a need to prevent political disputes from becoming too acrimonious and reopening the kinds of deep ideological fissures that had led to civil strife in the previous century. No internal wars should interfere with the safe enjoyment of property, or with the continuance of economic growth. There was thus a growing avoidance of overt discussions of religion and major ideological concerns at social gatherings. Strong political differences remained but the propertied were no longer sharply divided either on grounds of religion or, more importantly, by nuances of inherited status. 'Polite society', as Goldsmith described it, comprised all the members of the broader propertied classes – merchants, financiers and wealthy professionals, as well as gentry and aristocracy – associating without a keen awareness of rank. In Girouard's words, 'polite society' was made up of the people 'who owned and ran the country'.[54] Improved transport, especially the development of carriages with better suspension, allowed social interactions over a wider geographical area and encouraged the development of urban centres where the polite could congregate – assembly rooms, commercial pleasure gardens – and even the emergence of entire leisure towns like Bath which, under the direction of Beau Nash, 'Master of Ceremonies', became a major centre of this fashionable world. Here, in particular, social mores and behaviour were transformed. Goldsmith later described how at the start of the century 'general society among people of rank and fortune was by no means established. The nobility still preserved a tincture of gothic haughtiness, and refused to keep company with the gentry at any of the public entertainments of the place.'[55] But under Nash's direction, through the 1720s and '30s, such barriers were steadily broken down.

Membership of the polite was defined by 'taste', something which embraced a knowledge of etiquette, a familiarity with classical languages and myth, an appreciation of art, literature and music, and above all an understanding of – and an ability to participate in – the latest fashions. Taste was thus a driver of change, aspirational and at the same time castigatory. In much the same way as Madison Avenue advertising executives in the late 1950s used the fear of being unattractive and the desire to be admired as carrot and stick to sell products, so the eighteenth-century idea of 'taste' formed an important market mechanism. In the display of knowledge, accomplishments and wealth, gardens, like houses, played a crucial role. The expression of taste in major works of construction and landscaping, moreover, might in itself be thought to fulfil a public good, in terms of the ideas promulgated by men like Adam Smith:

The expense, besides, that is laid out in durable commodities gives maintenance, commonly, to a greater number of people than that which is employed in the most profuse hospitality. Of two or three hundred-weight of provisions, which may sometimes be served up at a great festival, one half, perhaps, is thrown to the dunghill, and there is always a great deal wasted and abused. But if the expense of this entertainment had been employed in setting to work masons, carpenters, upholsterers, mechanics, etc., a quantity of provisions, of equal value, would have been distributed among a still greater number of people who would have bought them in pennyworths and pound weights, and not have lost or thrown away a single ounce of them. In the one way, besides, this expense maintains productive, in the other unproductive hands. In the one way, there-fore, it increases, in the other, it does not increase, the exchangeable value of the annual produce of the land and labour of the country.[56]

The idea was widely expressed. Lady Sophia Shelburne of Bowood in Wiltshire thus com-mented favourably on the impact of Brown's improvements in 1767, describing how 'the number of Work People employed there makes Bowood have no appearance of the Scarcity so alarmingly conspicuous in most parts of the Country & so severely felt by the poor.'[57]

Not all members of the middling groups could be considered polite. Large gentleman farmers, major industrialists, bankers – these were men with whom a duke might now converse. But petty shopkeepers, small tenant farmers or the owners of minor industrial works were, where possible, excluded from their haunts. This said, because manners, knowledge and accomplishments were key attributes of membership, some individuals might be admitted to the inner circles of provin-cial society, at least, whose financial situation, observed objectively, might appear to have excluded. And for the same reasons the educated and the talented were able to converse freely with the highest in the land, especially when – as with Lancelot Brown – they were proffering advice on fashionable improvements. At the same time the emergence of polite society, the consolidation of the upper ranks of the propertied around a single shared culture, created new fault-lines in society, especially in rural areas. The real divisions were now between the propertied and the poor, and in particular the non-working poor.[58] Brown's career coincides with a period in which levels of poverty and unemployment began to rise steadily, increasing social tensions. Population growth stoked up inflation, decreasing the value of real wages, and reduced the possibilities of employment in the countryside, a development accentuated in some districts by a measure of rural de-industrialization as new modes of fac-tory production began to undermine traditional manufactures like textiles. Compared with other European countries, England in the middle and later decades of the eighteenth century was blessed with internal peace, with the dissolution of con-flicts within the upper classes through the devel-opment of a parliamentary system, and between the middle and upper classes through the emer-gence of polite society. But huge social tensions remained, and intensified, as the country indus-trialized and experienced rapid modernization of its agricultural system. The varied landscapes created by Brown and his contemporaries reflected these tensions, and they played an important role in defining, and articulating relations between, different social groups. They were an expression of the needs and aspirations of what Sir William Blackstone described in 1753 as a 'polite and commercial people'.[59]

A place in the country

In spite of the expansion of towns and, towards the end of the century, of industry, most of England would still have appeared, to our eyes, almost unbelievably rural. In 1750 few country towns covered more than a square kilometre. Even Norwich, probably still England's third largest city, was almost entirely confined within its medieval walls, embracing an area of just over two square kilometres, less than 5 per cent of the built-up area of the city and its suburbs today. Only London, with its satellite settlements, was truly urban in character. Home to over half a million people, its continuous built-up area covered less than five square kilometres, similar to that of a small country town today, but it was closely ringed by still separate but swelling villages like Paddington.[60] As we shall see, in some ways the districts around the larger towns and cities were gradually becoming suburbanized, in the sense that increasing numbers of individuals resided there who had little to do with the productive life of the countryside, either as producers or as landowners. But truly urban settlements covered a tiny area of the land surface, at least during Brown's lifetime. This was a rural world, much of it owned as landed estates.

Landed estates took a variety of forms but in general comprised continuous or near-continuous areas of land, owned as absolute private property (illus. 9). At their core was a mansion and its grounds, often accompanied by a park and 'home farm', which were kept 'in hand'. Beyond this lay an outer penumbra of farms and farmland which were leased, for defined periods of time, to tenants, together with a scatter of smaller areas which were again kept in hand by the owner, especially plantations and game covers.[61] There was a broad difference between the really large properties, covering 10,000 acres (c. 4,000 hectares) or more, and those of the local gentry, embracing a parish or two.[62] To some extent, but only to some extent, the owners of the largest properties were more likely to have a role on the national stage and the financial means to keep abreast of national if not international fashions in architecture and landscape design, while lesser landowners were more provincial in outlook. But there were many exceptions and – not least because of variations in land values – the size of an estate was no very good guide to its owner's wealth. A thousand acres in the Highlands of Scotland in the late eighteenth century, as today, compared poorly in financial terms with 10 acres in central London, and many spatially challenged properties grew wealthy on the income from coalfields or other mineral resources.

The first half of the eighteenth century was a period in which large estates tended to increase in size, mainly at the expense of small freeholders but also, to an extent, through the purchase of neighbouring lordships. Agricultural depression, combined with the Land Tax instituted in 1693, weighed more heavily on small farmers and the minor gentry than on the very rich, who often had access to other forms of income. In areas of poor soil, in particular – especially areas of light arable land such as the Lincolnshire and Yorkshire Wolds or the East Anglian Breckland – large estates often succeeded in gobbling up all neighbouring properties over vast tracts of land; but everywhere landed properties tended to grow in size, and also to become more continuous and consolidated, as owners sold off outlying possessions acquired through marriage or inheritance in order to purchase land nearer home. The ideal was to have absolute control over everything in view. As the steward of the Blickling estate in Norfolk, Robert Copeman, put it in a letter to the Earl of Buckinghamshire in 1773, 'If I hear of any uncultivated land or otherwise if adjoining part of your Lordships Estate to dispose of I will apply after it and acquaint your Lordship of it immediately.'[63] Lady Shelburne of Bowood in

Wiltshire described with evident pleasure in 1769 how 'if my Lord can purchase three fields from my Lord Bottetourt or from Mr Pitt the whole extent of the country between us & the Downs will be his & we shall have a Magnificent drive to them.'[64] Many large proprietors nevertheless continued to own outlying, subsidiary estates, and the wealthiest also usually possessed a town house in London which they occupied during the 'season'.

Estates were run on lines that became increasingly professional in the course of the seventeenth and eighteenth centuries and while owners made most of the strategic decisions, much was left to the steward or land agent who negotiated leases, supervised forestry operations and oversaw building campaigns. Such individuals also kept a close

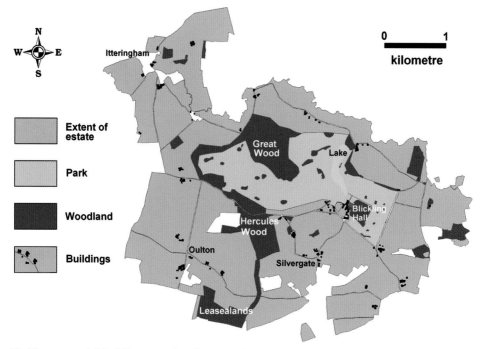

9 Blickling in north Norfolk, a typical medium-sized landed estate, *c.* 1840. Note the size of the park relative to the property as a whole, and the extent of woods and plantations. Great Wood is partly medieval in origin: the other areas of woodland were all planted in the eighteenth and nineteenth centuries. Some small, outlying portions of the property are omitted.

eye on the home farm.[65] Most estates retained some land 'in hand', farming it directly, partly because an interest in farming remained fashionable among the landed elite, even in the later eighteenth century. The stewards of men like the Earl of Buckinghamshire – who was ambassador to the Russian Court, among other things – took pains in their correspondence to acquaint their masters with the business of the home farm, describing such matters as the price of turnips and the sale of dairy cows. Copeman's letters regularly end with the assurance that 'the stock and every thing is well', sometimes qualified with such phrases as 'but so much rain that I am afraid to begin cutting the hay'.[66] We can assume that the Earl was interested in such news, and it is important to remember such mundane concerns when we admire the architecture of country houses or the design of their grounds. The belts and clumps of the landscape park, its expanses of grazed grass, formed part of the economic life of the estate, as well as expressing the owner's wealth and taste.

Yet at the same time we must be careful not to exaggerate the rural character of the landowning class, or its stability. Nor should we think of landscape design entirely in the context of large estates and long-established landed families. A rural property was as much an end in itself as a means to an end, and an elegant life in the country was something to which all successful members of society aspired. The countryside around large cities, especially London, was thus full of small 'villas', modish houses built on the sites of earlier farms by merchants, manufacturers or lawyers, often with only tiny estates attached, sometimes with no more than a small park. The more successful members of these groups,

moreover, strove to buy larger properties, and there was often a rapid turnover of landed estates in such districts. Cradock described in 1765 how 'negociators and attourneys are purchasing all the principal seats around London.'[67] Andrew Dury and John Andrews published a map of Hertfordshire in 1766 which, like other such maps made in the eighteenth century, includes the names of the principal landowners inscribed beside their seats. Well over 60 per cent of these properties appear to have been acquired by the families that owned them in the period since the Restoration of 1660; of these, most had derived their money from trade, finance or the law, and were thus recent recruits into the landowning class. Over a quarter of the named proprietors had either purchased their property themselves, or their spouse had done so.[68] The owners of eighteenth-century estates were not, therefore, necessarily occupiers of ancestral acres. In some districts, especially in the southeast, they were just as likely to be newcomers, and often parvenus. At least eleven of the individuals named on Dury and Andrews's Hertfordshire map were not in fact owners at all, but tenants, and as the century wore on renting a country seat became ever more common. In spite of the deeply held beliefs of provincial Tories, in parts of the country estates had indeed become just a species of property, not to be regarded in an overly sentimental fashion.

Whether they aspired to a true landed estate, or to a modern villa, possession of a fashionable house, with fashionable decor and furnishings, and with grounds laid out in the latest mode, was of particular importance to those whose principal wealth was derived from trade, for it demonstrated their creditworthiness in a society in which loss of confidence could lead to financial ruin. And ruin could certainly come to such people, as it could to more elevated and aristocratic investors, as the disastrous episode of the South Sea Bubble clearly illustrates.

By the middle decades of the eighteenth century, as already intimated, landed estates were actively involved in industrial and urban development in all parts of England. Even the local gentry often derived money from mills and brickworks. And as should by now be clear, the largest landowners gained much of their wealth from government office, or from investments in foreign trade, industry or financial speculation. These were the areas in which – as foreign trade expanded, and the scale of home production steadily grew – real fortunes were to be made. This said, as demand for agricultural produce escalated in the period after 1750, serious money could also be derived from agriculture, especially by making investments that could raise levels or production, or bring marginal land into cultivation. The 'improvement' of landed estates sometimes meant laying out a new park or gardens or planting trees and woods. But the term was also used, and perhaps more frequently, for the modernization of farming, especially through the enclosure of open fields and commons.

Enclosure has long attracted the attention of garden historians. Indeed, a number of writers – both in the past and among modern academics – have posited a close connection between the emergence of Brown's 'naturalistic' style and the replacement of open, irregular landscapes of open fields and commons in the middle and later decades of the eighteenth century by networks of hedged or walled fields.[69] The link was made as early as 1838 by the garden designer John Claudius Loudon:

As the lands devoted to agriculture in England were, sooner than in any other country in Europe, generally enclosed with hedges and hedgerow trees, so the face of the country in England, sooner than in any other part of Europe, produced an appearance which bore a closer resemblance to country seats laid out in the geometrical style; and, for this reason, an attempt to imitate the irregularity of nature in laying out pleasure grounds was made in England . . . sooner than in any other part of the world.[70]

In reality, as decades of scholarship have now made clear, most of England – and certainly the vast majority of lowland England – was already enclosed by the time Brown began his career as an independent designer in 1750. In some districts the countryside had always consisted mainly of walled or hedged fields; elsewhere vast tracts were enclosed, in a variety of ways, during the period between the fifteenth century and the start of the eighteenth (illus. 10, 11).[71] Of the approximately 30 per cent of the country that was enclosed, by parliamentary act or otherwise, after this, much comprised the great upland moors in the north and west of England, or other forms of common 'waste', the majority of which was mostly enclosed *after* the time of Brown's death – during the high-price years of the Napoleonic Wars. Most of the large-scale enclosures that occurred during Brown's lifetime were of large open fields in the Midlands and, while it is true that in many parishes this provided minor squires with the opportunity to create parks for the first time, most of the largest estates, even here, had enclosed the core of their properties by the start of the eighteenth century (illus. 12).[72] The idea

10 Typical old enclosed countryside, with farms scattered around greens, winding lanes and irregularly shaped fields, at Great Munden, Hertfordshire.

that enclosure as a process somehow inspired the 'naturalistic' landscapes of the time cannot be sustained.

This said, the wider consolidation of land-holding that was such a feature of the eighteenth century, to create extensive and continuous blocks of private ground – and which was effected not only by enclosure but, more importantly, through the systematic acquisition of neighbouring proper-ties – clearly provided the necessary canvas on which landscape parks could be created. Indeed, many of Brown's parks were laid out hard on the heels of major programmes of land acquisition. At Bowood, for example, much of the land for the new park established by Brown from 1763 had

been purchased by the Earls of Shelburne only a few years earlier; that section needed to create the lake and the rising ground beyond it, in the far west of the park, only appears to have been purchased in that same year.[73] And it is import-ant to remember, more generally, that in many other places the parks created by Brown were surrounded by countryside that was being trans-formed and modernized. The agricultural revo-lution did not only involve enclosures, and the adoption of new crops and rotations. It also saw the amalgamation of tenant farms to create more productive units; changes in soil character through large-scale field drainage and marling; alterations to the physical structure of the countryside through the amalgamation of fields and the reduction in hedgerow trees; and in many districts, especially towards the end of Brown's career, major changes in land use (with an expansion of arable cultivation in the east and south of the country, but a greater emphasis on pastoral pursuits on the heavy clay soils in the Midlands).[74] The urge to 'improve' farming was not simply the consequence of economic factors. It was deeply rooted in contemporary mentalities. The outcome of the Civil War had given a strong impetus to a Protestant ideology that emphasized the virtuous moral imperative to make things not only better but more profitable. There was in this period a noticeable renewal of interest in the classical literature of husbandry – in the writings of Varro and Columella, and above all in Virgil's *Georgics* – and this was accompanied by the publication of an increasing number of books on farming, forestry and estate management, such as John Evelyn's *Sylva* (1664). Such texts were enthusiastically read and digested by landowners at all levels. Brown's parks existed as islands within a wider matrix of a modernizing countryside, and their seemingly timeless landscape of close-cropped turf, placid waters, scattered trees and woodland was surrounded by activity and change.

11 Typical view in western Northamptonshire, showing countryside enclosed from open fields, by parliamentary acts, during Brown's lifetime.

12 Typical Midland landscape in the early eighteenth century: the area around Desborough and Braybrooke in north-central Northamptonshire. Note the complex mixture of unenclosed open fields (pink) and enclosed land (yellow).

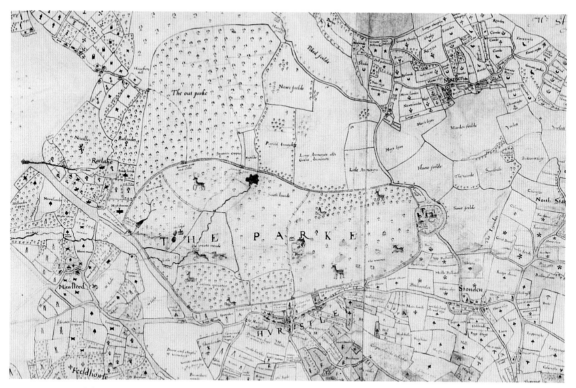

13 The medieval deer park at Hursley, Hampshire, as shown on a late sixteenth-century map.

TWO

Gardens and Society, 1700–1750

Although the landscape style which we today associate with Capability Brown was in many ways revolutionary, it developed out of earlier forms of design. Indeed, although Brown is still sometimes castigated as a man who 'swept away' gardens that were still formal, geometric and walled in character, at the highest social levels at least, such grounds had already been extensively modified along more serpentine, 'naturalistic' lines. To understand the character of landscape parks, as these emerged in the decades after 1750, and to understand better what they meant to contemporaries, it is necessary to review briefly how the design of gardens and parks changed over the five or so decades prior to the start of Brown's career. But we also need to understand this development within three wider contexts: that of the architecture and layout of the houses which such gardens accompanied; that of the ways in which gardens were used and enjoyed by their owners and guests; and that of the manner in which, during the first half of the eighteenth century, the business of gardening itself developed in this increasingly commercial world.

Landscape and architecture after the Restoration

Seventeenth-century gardens were, as readers will be aware, essentially 'geometric', 'formal' and 'unnatural' in character. But these simple terms obscure a complex sequence of change and development which we need only examine from the time of the Restoration in 1660. The design of late seventeenth-century gardens was based on a mixture of indigenous traditions and long-established Renaissance influences, but was in particular directly influenced by French and Dutch models, which had been directly experienced by the large numbers of English landowners who had been obliged to spend time in continental Europe during the Civil War. They featured topiary, neat gravel paths, plain grass lawns, bowling greens and – although often to a limited extent – parterres of cutwork or boxwork.[1] All these were placed within walled or hedged enclosures which, at the homes of the local gentry especially, also embraced farmyards, orchards, kitchen gardens and such things as dovecotes and fishponds. These features had important practical functions but they also served as signs of elite status and of the involvement of their owner in the productive life of the locality, and they might themselves be ornamented, or regarded aesthetically, to varying extents.[2] Canals or 'basons' often doubled as 'stews' or fishponds, while the deer parks and rabbit warrens attached to the larger residences were at once stores of elite food and signs of elite status. Even at the highest social levels, although there was generally a greater degree of segregation of the productive and ornamental aspects of the grounds than was the case among the local gentry, some of these superior resources were proudly displayed. Chatsworth House in Derbyshire was largely rebuilt, at enormous expense, by the 1st Duke of Devonshire between 1687 and 1707, yet the principal feature of the main view from the windows, to the west, long remained the extensive rabbit warren on the far side of the river Derwent.[3] Deer parks were particularly significant in this respect. Originating as wooded hunting grounds, often lying at a distance from the mansion, by the sixteenth century they had become a necessary adjunct to a great house (illus. 13, 14).[4] By the second half of the seventeenth century they were often crossed by one or more avenues – a sight familiar from the engravings published by Johannes Kip and Leonard Knyff in their *Britannia illustrata* of 1707 (illus. 15). Avenues themselves had been relatively rare features of the landscape before the Civil War. They were widely established thereafter, partly as a consequence of French influence but mainly, perhaps, in reflection of the confidence felt by landowners in the aftermath of the Civil War, and of the increasingly consolidated character of landed estates and enclosed character of the landscape. There was little point in planting them if you did not expect to see them reach maturity; and it was only possible to plant them over land you not only owned, but owned

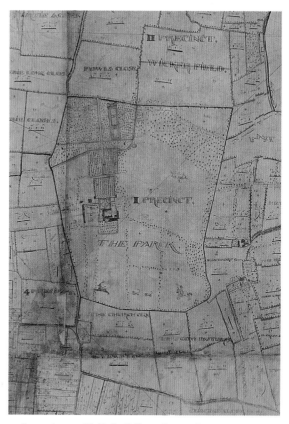

14 Somerleyton Hall, Suffolk, as depicted on an estate map of 1652. By the seventeenth century the majority of deer parks were closely associated with elite residences, often as here wrapped around the house and gardens. Note the lines of trees, indicating where hedgerows have been removed but timber retained. Already, the designers of parkland were consulting the 'genius of the place'.

as absolute private property, free of the rights of common grazing and access that existed over commons and open-field land.

In the first decades of the eighteenth century formal gardens underwent a number of key changes. They seem to have become simpler, as parterres were replaced by designs featuring wide lawns, gravel paths and simple topiary, and flowers were often relegated to discrete areas within them. In the words of Sir John Clerk of Penicuik, writing in 1727, 'The present method of

Gardening is a little alter'd vise into great pieces of open Green plots' (illus. 16).[5] These changes may reflect the influence of French trends in garden design, popularized by the writings of Antoine-Joseph Dézallier d'Argenville, whose book *La Théorie et la pratique du jardinage* (1709) was translated by John James as *The Theory and Practice of Gardening* in 1712.[6] This argued, among other things, that elaborate parterres should be replaced with simpler designs based on lawns, banks, steps, terraces of turf and simple clipped hedges. The change may also reflect the fact that gardens appear to have increased significantly in size during the first decades of the century,

raising maintenance costs, a matter noted by a number of contemporary writers. As Stephen Switzer put it in 1718, 'Gardens have gradually, insensibly, and at last even necessarily swell'd to a greater Extent than the Owner at first designed them, so great indeed as to sink under their own Weight, and to be a Burden too heavy for the greatest Estates.'[7]

Perhaps the most noticeable change was in the role of 'wildernesses' – ornamental woods/shrubberies, dissected by hedged paths. These had been a feature of gardens in the seventeenth century but they now came to occupy a larger proportion of their area, and were planted closer to the

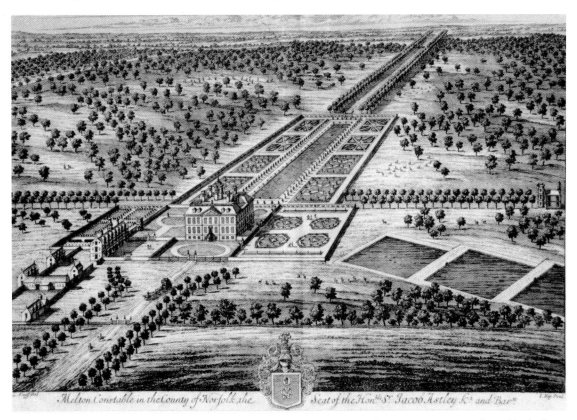

15 'Melton Constable in the County of Norfolk', as depicted in Kip and Knyff's *Britannia illustrata* of 1707. By the late seventeenth century parks were usually crossed by one or more avenues, but otherwise retained their irregular, naturalistic appearance. Note how the principal avenue continues the main axis of symmetry of both house and gardens. The features ranged at an angle to the rest of the design, to the right, are fishponds, probably of sixteenth-century or earlier date.

16 Raynham Hall in Norfolk, as drawn by Edmund Prideaux in *c.* 1725. By the 1720s the most fashionable gardens, while still essentially geometric in layout, were much simpler in appearance than those of the seventeenth century, comprising plain lawns, sparse topiary, clipped hedges and gravel paths. At some, external walls were already being removed, to open up views into the adjacent parkland.

mansion.[8] Such changes were most noticeable in gardens and landscapes created by the wealthiest individuals. But the same impetus, for a greater scale of design, could be enjoyed by smaller land-owners by availing themselves of the advice offered, in particular, by Switzer. His *Ichnographia rustica* of 1718 featured designs comprising an inner garden, laid out in the prevailing mode with plain grass parterres and gravel paths, and an outer landscape, comprising plantations and fields crossed by avenues and walks. Both were arranged around a central axis focused on the main facade of the house, which was to be continued 'as far as Liberty of Planting will allow'.[9]

The design of gardens in the late seventeenth century, and to a large extent in the early eighteenth, was closely tied to the architecture of the great house. Most of the garden could be seen from the house; the house could be viewed from most parts of the garden; and the garden walls of brick or stone formed a continuation of the structure of the house, just as the design of banqueting houses and other garden buildings often echoed its architectural style. Only in the wildernesses were separate spaces – hidden, private and meditative – to be found, although even in these it was customary for the principal *allées* to be aligned on the mansion's facades. The connections between architecture and garden design arguably went further than this, however, although charting the precise relationship between the two is rendered difficult by the fact that, on the whole, the design of gardens was changed more easily than the architecture of large houses. Moreover, scholars of country houses tend to concentrate on the greatest examples: the homes of the court aristocracy, designed by famous architects and often built from scratch. In reality, the houses of the broader ranks of the landed elite displayed much variety, in part because different kinds of owner made different demands on their homes, with those towards the top of the hierarchy designing houses more with the reception of numerous guests in mind; and in part because many country houses were an amalgam of different periods, with new ideas of domestic planning often squeezed uncomfortably into older frameworks. This said, it was at the highest social levels, and in houses newly built or extensively altered, that fashions were set, and here we can most clearly see how architectural practice affected the design of their grounds.

Since the early sixteenth century English architecture had been influenced by models derived, usually at second or third hand, from Renaissance Italy, each successive generation criticizing the attempts of their forebears to achieve close approximations to the correct forms of antiquity.[10] In the 1620s and '30s the architect Inigo Jones produced remarkable designs for country houses and public buildings that were based on the published works of the sixteenth-century Italian architect Andrea Palladio, but the financial difficulties of his principal patrons, the Crown and members of the court aristocracy, together with the impact of the Civil War and the Interregnum, stifled this stylistic development, and in the years following

the Restoration elite architecture adopted a different and broader range of classical forms, derived in particular from France and the Low Countries. More important than style, however, were the plans of such houses. Almost no residences of any size erected after the Restoration were, as most earlier ones had been, one room deep and ranged around two or three sides of a courtyard. They were instead compact double- or triple-pile structures. In most examples, the central body of the building comprised two large rooms, one behind the other – the hall and the saloon. From these, apartments – suites of rooms in linear sequence – led off, comprising withdrawing room, antechamber, bedchamber and cabinet or closet, each increasingly private in character – an arrangement often referred to as an *enfilade*. When large houses were used for parties or receptions there were only two main rooms where the majority of guests could gather, and they tended to do the same thing at the same time, such as dancing or dining. On these and other occasions access to the private apartments, and especially to their inner recesses, was restricted to the favoured few.[11]

Such a description rather ignores the various more private spaces available to the owner and his family, especially the common parlour; and it rather glosses over the fact that smaller manor houses lacked, and did not require, such an elaborate collection of rooms of parade – many for example having but a single withdrawing room, or truncated sequences of private rooms. But at the upper levels of society, in houses newly built, such 'formal' plans (to use Girouard's term) were the norm by the early eighteenth century, and these linear arrangements of spaces and features were expressed outwardly, in the elevations of the house and in the layout of its grounds. The main internal axis – of hall and saloon – was thus emphasized in the building's external elevation, being extended forward (or more rarely recessed), and often surmounted by a pediment which was sometimes placed above a free-standing portico. This axis was also extended outwards as the main alignment within the gardens and, beyond that, as the principal avenue, running out through the park or the adjacent estate land.[12] The minor axes of the house were not, it is true, so often emphasized by being continued as avenues and walks, but the general linearity in the plan of the house had strong echoes in the disposition of its surroundings. These forms of domestic planning and garden design were appropriate to a society in which hierarchy was still expressed in strict etiquette, parade and the formality of social encounters; while at the same time, the overall landscape reflected the position of the owner within his 'country', with the house sitting at the centre of a web of power.

'Formal' house plans took their most rigid and extreme forms in those great houses that were not just broadly classical in design but were thoroughgoing expressions of the Baroque – the grand, florid and dramatic style of classical architecture which had originally developed on the Continent as a physical expression of the ideas of the Counter-Reformation, and which had subsequently been widely adopted for the great palaces of absolutist monarchs. Houses designed in this manner in England were comparatively few in number – well-known examples include

17 Blenheim Palace in Oxfordshire, the most impressive Baroque mansion in England, was designed by John Vanbrugh and built between 1705 and 1722 for John Churchill, 1st Duke of Marlborough.

Chatsworth, Castle Howard and Blenheim Palace (illus. 17) – although perhaps more common than we usually assume, many, like William Talman's Kimberley Hall in Norfolk, having been given a fashionable 'makeover' later in the eighteenth century which removed their more flamboyant details.

The hierarchical, court-based character of society in the late seventeenth and early eighteenth centuries was also reflected in the way the business of architecture was organized. In the Restoration period the principal public buildings – the new churches erected after the Great Fire of London and additions to royal palaces, military and naval facilities – were still designed, as they had long been, 'in-house', by the King's Works or Office of Works. But the members of this body also worked on other commissions. In Summerson's words, throughout the period before the eighteenth century the Office acted as a 'nucleus of superior talent, its officers being employed by whichever patrons had the means to promote the most important buildings', including their own homes.[13] Inigo Jones was Surveyor of the King's Works – principal architect – from 1615 until the Civil War; Christopher Wren held the office between 1669 and 1718. The parallel office of Comptroller of the King's Works was also filled by some notable architects – Hugh May from 1668 until 1684, William Talman from 1684 until 1702 and Sir John Vanbrugh from the latter date until 1726.[14] Most of the principal professionals of note, such as Robert Hooke, served under these men. This is not to say that no other practitioners existed independently of this nexus; but many of these, like Roger Pratt or John Buxton, were 'gentleman' architects, wealthy men practising for amusement rather than profit.[15] In such

a situation, architectural taste was, as it had been for centuries, largely set by the royal court. The same was true of garden design, as we shall explain a little later. George London and Henry Wise established a major nursery business at Brompton Park in Kensington in 1688 and were responsible for the design of the gardens at Hampton Court and other royal residences under William and Mary, London becoming Royal Gardener under them, Wise going on to fill this post under both Queen Anne and George I. But at the same time the pair also designed the grounds of aristocratic clients, at Chatsworth, Longleat, Castle Howard and elsewhere. The design of gardens, even at the level of the aristocracy, was not monopolized by such men, but royal taste and patronage decisively shaped fashions in garden and landscape design, as they did those in architecture. Even in the middle decades of the century some vestiges of these systems remained. From 1735 until his death in 1748 William Kent was the Deputy Surveyor in the Office of Works under Richard Arundell; Brown himself benefited greatly from his appointment to the post of Royal Gardener at Hampton Court in 1764. But by this time the chief advantage of such a post probably came from its use as an advertisement, representing as it did a recognition of professional pre-eminence. The dominance of the court over taste in architecture and garden design was largely a thing of the past.

Palladianism and Rococo

In both architecture and landscape design, there were major shifts in style, patronage and organization following the accession of George I in 1714. When political power passed to the Whigs, so too did the lead in domestic design. Although seldom active in politics, Robert Boyle, 3rd Earl of Burlington, was part of the Whig group and a major patron of men like Colen Campbell, Henry Flitcroft and William Kent, as well as being a gifted architect in his own right; it was under these men that the Palladian style was now revived.[16] In its new manifestation – based in part on the writings of Palladio, and in part on the interpretations of his work by Inigo Jones – Palladianism involved adherence to strict rules of composition and design. Gone was the flamboyant, dramatic use of classical idiom that had characterized the Baroque. Rejected, too, was the loose and simple classicism of smaller manor houses – what we often refer to today as the 'Queen Anne' style. Instead decoration was reduced, stylistic devices were based on the precedents of Palladio's works and classical orders were correctly employed and never promiscuously combined in one facade, with (for example) a Corinthian entablature supported on Doric columns. Following Palladio, dimensions of rooms and elevations were determined by strict geometric ratios. As Robert Morris put it:

> In Musick are only seven distinct Notes, in Architecture likewise are only seven distinct Proportions, which produce all the different Buildings in the Universe, *viz* – the Cube, – the Cube and half, – the Double Cube, – the Duplicates [i.e. ratios] of 3, 2, and 1, – of 4, 3, and 2, – of 5, 4, and 3, – and of 6, 4, and 3, produce all the Harmonic Proportions of Rooms.[17]

The principal reception rooms of major houses were now raised up on a *piano nobile* a full storey above a basement or rustic, itself distinguished by an exterior of rough-hewn masonry. Palladianism, it was claimed, was a distillation of the true architecture of the ancients, transmitted by Palladio and Jones. In reality, of course, it represented yet another version of Renaissance architecture – of Italian interpretations of classical form – enthusiasm for which was now also fuelled by the growing popularity of the Grand Tour among the rich. Men who commissioned houses in this mode had often witnessed, at first hand, the elegance of Palladio's villas, for the first half of the eighteenth century saw a steady stream of English visitors to Italy and the development of a veritable love affair on the part of the country's elite with all things Italian – landscapes, antiquities, architecture – all combined in a warm, blurry haze of memory.

The new style of architecture was strongly promulgated in Colen Campbell's magnificent series of volumes *Vitruvius Britannicus*, published in the 1720s, and its adoption was encouraged by the success of a number of particularly famous buildings, including Burlington's own Chiswick House (closely modelled on Palladio's Villa Capra near Vicenza); Mereworth in Kent, designed by Campbell; and Robert Walpole's Houghton Hall, designed in part by Campbell, in part by Thomas Ripley and in part by James Gibbs. Through the 1730s and '40s the style was adopted for such houses as Houghton Hall in Norfolk and Wentworth Woodhouse in Yorkshire (illus. 18).[18] These were vast mansions, but other Palladian buildings were smaller structures, often referred to as 'villas' by contemporaries, usually the country residences of men with city interests, great financiers and merchants. The new style did not, it must be emphasized, develop directly under the patronage of the court, for the

Elevation of the South front of Houghton in Norfolk, the Seat of the Right Honourable Robert Walpole Esq.r Chancellor of Exq.r and first Lord Com.r of his Majesty's Treasury &c.

Erected Anno 1723. Designed by Colen Campbell Esq.r.

a Scale of 60 feet.

18 Proposed elevation for Houghton Hall, Norfolk, from Colen Campbell's *Vitruvius Britannicus* of 1725. When built, largely because of the input of James Gibbs, the corner towers were provided with domes, rather lessening its 'Palladian' appearance.

Baroque architect John Vanbrugh continued as Comptroller until 1726, and he was succeeded by Thomas Ripley, an individual who worked in but did not seriously adopt or develop the new architectural idiom. Not only was the monarchy's dominance of artistic patronage broken but the new style, many have argued, itself carried a political message – it was the badge of the new Whig elite.[19] Power now finally lay in the hands of enlightened aristocrats and their allies in the city, who could build Britain as the new Rome. British architecture in the thirty years leading up to the beginning of Brown's career was dominated by Palladianism, just as political life was dominated by the Whigs.

Unlike most of the labels that modern historians employ to describe the art and architecture of the eighteenth century, Palladianism was a term actually used by contemporaries, not coined in retrospect. But the style was not as new as proponents like Campbell often suggested. The writings of Palladio had continued to influence architectural design in England throughout the middle and later decades of the seventeenth century, albeit alongside other classical influences.[20] Many of Palladianism's characteristic elements – such as the use of low pavilions, flanking the main house and joined to it by colonnades – also featured prominently in houses designed by 'Baroque' architects like Talman. Even in the 1720s and '30s it was less distinct as a style than is sometimes implied, for many architects produced designs which were influenced both by Palladio's writings and by other broadly classical styles, including the Baroque, such as James Gibbs. We should also be wary – in spite of what has just been said – of seeing choice of architectural style as a sure sign of political affiliation, and of viewing Palladianism as a clear badge of Whig allegiance. Many avowed Tories were soon building houses in this mode, and Palladian architects in this new world of polite fashion and private patronage simply worked for whoever would pay them. Gibbs, for example, was commissioned, as we have noted, by Robert Walpole, but was also patronized by Tory grandees like the Earl of Oxford – whom Walpole was responsible for imprisoning. More importantly, like many of his contemporaries Gibbs made as much money from the newly rich as he did from the established elite, designing or improving many houses for men who had made their money in the South Sea or East India companies in the hinterland of London, such as Thomas Rolt at Sacombe in Hertfordshire or Jeremy Sambrooke at Gobions in the same county.[21]

Whatever the precise character of their architectural style – 'pure' Palladian, or some more complex mixture of influences – large houses erected in the 1720s, '30s and '40s, unless they were small 'villas' like Chiswick, continued to be laid out along the formal lines typical of earlier residence. The *piano nobile* comprised two large reception rooms in the centre of the building, one behind the other – the hall and the saloon – together with sequences of smaller rooms, making up private apartments, leading off from these.[22] Few separate spaces were thus provided on the 'floor of parade' for public entertaining. There were, it is true, some signs that this was beginning to change, even in the 1720s. At Houghton one of the four apartments was sacrificed, possibly as the building was being erected, to make way for a separate dining room and a picture

cabinet.[23] More radical was the design of Holkham Hall in the same county, the construction of which began in 1734. Here the private apartments were located in the flanking pavilions (of which there were four) and an elaborate sequence of public rooms was laid out, occupying the whole of the *piano nobile*, including a dining room, drawing room, picture gallery and library. In addition, and of great significance for the future, these were arranged not as a set of linear sequences, but on a circuit.[24]

Such developments reflected the emergence of new ways of entertaining, new customs of social engagement and new forms of social organization. We have already noted the development, from the beginning of the eighteenth century, but especially from the time of George's accession in 1714, of what is often termed 'polite society', in which all the members of the propertied classes, including upper-middle-class merchants, financiers and wealthy professionals, as well as gentry and aristocracy, associated in an easy and informal manner, without excessive displays of inherited rank and status. Urban centres like Bath and London played an important role in the development of the new culture, but private houses, both in town and in the country, continued to be the main arenas for fashionable entertaining. As Girouard and others have explained, it is within this context that we need to view the developments in domestic planning just outlined – the proliferation of entertaining and reception rooms, and their arrangement on a circuit. 'The formal house ceased to work. Instead of a hall and saloon, between the apartments which were the private territories of the people occupying them, what was now needed was a series of communal rooms for entertaining, exclusive of the hall and all running in to each other.'[25] But in fact there was a significant time lag between the two, in part because country houses took a significant amount of time to plan and build. Forms of social interaction, that is, developed more rapidly than the kinds of architectural spaces that they required. While there was a gradual proliferation of reception rooms, it was not until the 1750s that new houses began to be routinely planned to allow a circular pattern of circulation, and with numerous rooms for entertaining. For several decades, new social gatherings were thus often squeezed uncomfortably into old architectural spaces: by throwing open private apartments during public receptions, for example.

In many ways the overall style of great houses, as much as their internal layout, was also poorly suited to the needs of polite society. Baroque was a heavy, sombre yet showy architectural style, with (as we have noted) strong overtones of hierarchy, if not absolutism. The Palladian style, while subjectively perhaps lighter, was in its earlier manifestations at least also exclusive, or excluding, in the sense that only those who had a familiarity with the finer details of Palladio's writings could fully appreciate it. Both architectural styles also made for somewhat heavy, elaborate and intricate interiors in terms of painted (and gilded) decoration, luxurious textiles and sumptuous upholstery, all intended to display the wealth of the owner and by implication his superiority over visitors: grand interiors for grand houses.[26] It is not surprising, then, that in the 1730s and '40s rather different styles of internal decoration became popular, more suited to the times. If the overall structure and style of the house could not be changed, it could at least be softened with the appropriate decor.

'Rococo' is the term employed by art historians, although only since the 1830s, for the curving, playful and asymmetrical forms of decoration that were developed in France during the first decades of the eighteenth century, spreading to England from the late 1720s.[27] Unlike the Baroque and Palladian, the Rococo was not primarily an architectural style but a form of decoration, applied to furniture, ceramics, wall painting and plasterwork.[28] Flowing scrollwork, often in 'C' and 'S' forms and imitating leaves and flowers; elaborate carving, employing *rocaille* and acanthus leaves: all provided something more playful, less sombre and above all less intellectual than the architectural styles of the houses whose interiors they decorated (illus. 19). Some art historians, most notably Timothy Mowl and Brian Earnshaw, have emphasized the extent to which the new style was rather unsuccessfully imitated in Britain (as opposed to Ireland);[29] but new forms of naturalistic and asymmetrical ornament were widely employed in textiles and plasterwork through the 1730s, '40s and '50s, and increasingly on a new type of interior decoration, wallpaper, which became much more cheaply available at this time due to improvements in production. Heavy upholstery and wall hangings declined in importance, and light pieces of furniture produced by cabinetmakers began to replace older, heavier forms. Domestic interiors, in short, became less sombre, more playful and generally lighter.[30] Whatever the original significance of Rococo as a style had been in France, in England it fitted well into a world of less tightly structured social relations. Interior style reinforced the shift towards informality and comfort, and away from grandeur and parade.

Girendoles

Nº CLXXIII.

J. Chippendale invt et delin.   *Publish'd according to Act of Parliament 1760.*   *B: Clowes Sculp.*

19 The flamboyant Rococo curves of Thomas Chippendale's designs for girandoles, the mirrored brackets for holding candles, from the first edition of his *The Gentleman and Cabinet-maker's Director* (1754).

This more playful attitude to interior decoration was manifested in other ways. From the late seventeenth century there had been a growing interest in, and liking for, oriental styles and artefacts, stimulated in large part by the expansion of foreign trade. By the first two decades of the eighteenth century, at places like Burton Agnes, entire rooms were fitted up in oriental style – often an uneasy jumble of Chinese and Indian motifs.[31] 'Chinoiserie' was widely adopted for wall hangings, bed curtains and much else through the first decades of the century, and was even more widely employed in a whole range of materials and forms through the middle decades, especially wallpaper patterns.[32]

Country houses, planned and designed in a manner appropriate to older forms of social engagement, could thus be adapted to an extent to suit the easier spirit of the times. But some landowners – not many, although enough to be significant – completely rebuilt their homes in a manner that aped styles usually employed for internal decoration, styles very different from the Palladian. In 1735 William Kent himself designed new wings for an existing medieval tower house at Esher in Surrey, replicating – in playful, vaguely Rococo style – its medieval gothic appearance. 'Gothick', it should be noted, was not yet the asymmetrical, irregular style it was to become at the end of the century, under the influence of architects like James Wyatt. Gothick with a 'k' was a matter of applying medieval details – quatrefoil openings, turrets, battlements and the like – to buildings that were symmetrical in elevation, and with classical proportions. It is also worth noting in passing – again as a warning against seeing too neat an association of Whig ideology and Palladianism – that the house at Esher was the principal family home of Henry Pelham, major Whig politician and prime minister from 1743 until his death in 1754.[33] In 1741 Batty Langley popularized the Gothick style in his *Ancient Architecture Restored and Improved*, and later in the decade houses built or redesigned in Gothick mode were erected at Alscot in Warwickshire (designed largely by the owner, James West), Woodside in Buckinghamshire, Arbury in Gloucestershire and elsewhere.[34]

One aspect of polite society perhaps deserves particular emphasis at this point: what might be described as its essentially feminized character. The famous refusal of Beau Nash to allow the wearing of swords at the Bath assembly rooms was part of a wider development: public brawling and duelling were increasingly frowned upon as the century progressed.[35] By the 1760s the

'sentimental revolution' was under way, in which it became acceptable for men to give rein to their feelings and emotions – in extreme cases, to weep publicly – so that behaviour once reserved to women came to some extent to be shared by men. There were also changes in attitudes towards women, and in the character of the relationship between the sexes, although their extent remains contested. Lawrence Stone and Randolph Trumbach have both argued that the first half of the eighteenth century saw the rise of the 'companionate marriage', in which the importance of friendship, affection and respect between husband and wife were emphasized, shaping the choice of marriage partners.[36] Both historians have arguably exaggerated the extent to which the new mores represented a change from earlier behaviour, and as Fletcher has emphasized, the new forms of relationship 'did not mean that women gained greater equality in practice or that any kind of emancipated notion of femininity was promulgated ... the very essence of companionate marriage, it can be suggested, was the

20 'A Perspective View of the Bowling Green at Gubbins' [*sic*; now, and formerly, Gobions] as depicted by Jean-Baptiste Chatelain in 1748. Illustrations of gardens from the 1730s and '40s show clearly how spaces like these were used for informal, convivial recreation.

45

subordination of women'.[37] Nevertheless, women were now treated in a more equal way among the polite, even if real power remained with men. Illustrations of fashionable gardens in the early and middle decades of the century almost invariably depict men and women walking and conversing together on easy terms (illus. 20). The new fashion for light, playful decoration – for Rococo, chinoiserie – should in part be read in this light: the latter style especially was closely associated with women and women's spaces.[38] The popularity of Chinese porcelains and Japanese lacquerware, of tea drinking and the etiquette attached to it, reflected the development of a world economy, but also the arrival of a more feminized domestic environment.

Palladian and Rococo gardening

The major developments in the architecture of country houses and in the design of their interiors, which we have just described, were accompanied, as we might expect, by significant changes in garden design, changes which in many ways prepared the ground for the emergence of the style we associate with Lancelot Brown. But there was no steady, unilinear development from 'geometry' to 'nature', and we must be careful not to hasten the demise of the former. Well into the 1760s most country houses were set within landscapes that were dominated by avenues and other forms of geometric planting. Given the obsession of Neo-Palladians with geometry, regularity and mathematical ratios, a continued enthusiasm for landscape geometry in the first three or four decades of the century is unsurprising. The forecourt at Burlington's Chiswick villa thus had cedar trees planted in the 1:3:9:27 module

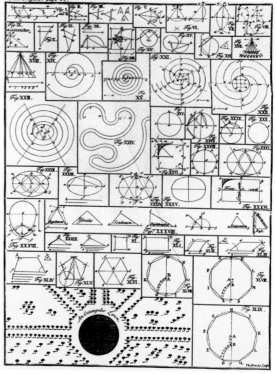

21 An illustration from Batty Langley's *Practical Geometry* of 1729, showing the mathematics underlying the layout of paths and planting. Geometric gardening was still flourishing in the first third of the eighteenth century.

recommended by the Italian architectural writer Leon Battista Alberti, whose book *De re aedificatoria*, an influential text among the Palladian clique, had been translated into English by Burlington's client Giacomo Leoni in 1726.[39] Right through the 1720s and '30s writers on garden design appear obsessed with geometry. Peter Aram's unpublished treatise 'The Practical Making and Management of Gardens', written shortly before 1730, described such features as the 'Tetrahedronic Grove', the layout of which was based on a triangle in which 'walks may be made which disposes the whole Figure into 4 Equilateral Triangles ye Centres of which are Statues within a circle'.[40] Batty Langley, whose

New Principles of Gardening of 1728 is often quoted as part of a shift towards more 'naturalistic' gardening, was also the author of *Practical Geometry*, published in 1729 (illus. 21).[41] In the former work Langley criticized 'gardens stuffed too thick with box', but he himself was no enemy of the shears, Horace Walpole asserting that 'All that his books achieved, has been to teach carpenters to massacre that venerable species.'[42] The key landscape designer of the 1720s and '30s, Charles Bridgeman, is often seen as a precursor to Kent and Brown. But in reality his landscapes were still for the most part highly geometric in character, featuring formal wildernesses, basons, linear vistas and avenues. They represented, in essence, large-scale versions of the more simplified geometric style that had been widely adopted in the gardens of elite residences since the 1710s, and they were usually strongly axial in character, based on a main avenue focused on the principal facades of the mansion, which continued the internal 'axis of honour', of hall and saloon.[43] In a world of formal houses, the formal landscape remained king.

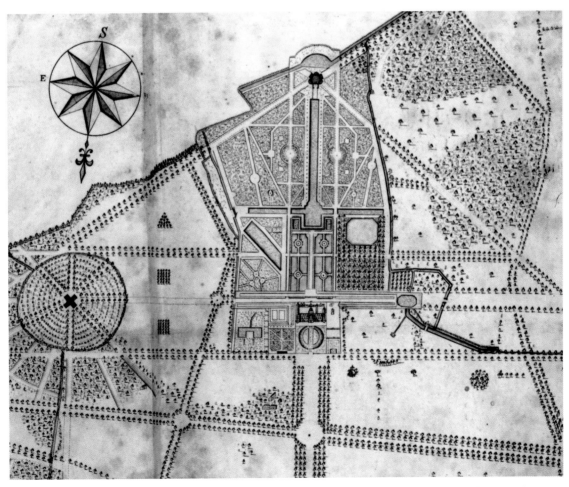

22 The gardens at Wrest Park, Bedfordshire, as shown on an estate map of *c.* 1730. The extensive wilderness is the most prominent feature of the gardens, taking up most of their area.

Nevertheless, while gardens remained essentially geometric in overall design, there were already, by the 1720s, noticeable shifts in their character. One of the most important, as we have already noted, was the proliferation and expansion of wildernesses. This development began in the first decades of the century but is particularly noticeable in the landscapes created by Bridgeman, and in the designs published by Langley, through the later 1710s and '20s. By the 1730s, at places like Wrest in Bedfordshire, wildernesses took up most of the area of the garden (illus. 22). This development was almost certainly the consequence of new ways in which gardens were used. The wide parterres and lawns that had characterized the greatest gardens in the late seventeenth and early eighteenth century were designed for public display and parade. Everything in the garden, and everyone, could be taken in at a glance – and their relative status assessed. Wildernesses, in contrast, were appropriate for use by smaller groups, for intimate encounters, exploration and discovery: so it is hardly surprising that they now became more prominent, at a time when patterns of social behaviour among the propertied classes were changing. Their clearings and cabinets, moreover, contained sculptures and buildings designed to display the taste, education and knowledge (especially of classical civilization, and the works of the great Renaissance sculptors and architects) of the owner. Both Langley and Stephen Switzer gave advice on which classical gods and heroes were suitable for which areas: Jupiter or Mars for the 'largest Open Centres', Neptune for spaces near basins and canals, fauns for the recesses of the wilderness.[44] Such features also served as subjects for discussion among visitors,

as well as evoking reminiscences of Italian groves or echoes of the 'Druidic groves' of indigenous antiquity. These effects were perhaps accentuated, from the late 1720s, by the tendency to remove hedges from the paths and *allées*, so that the wilderness was gradually transformed into a 'grove'. Thomas Hamilton, writing about wildernesses in 1733, thus commented: 'now I Hear they are weary of the Hedges.'[45] The gradual adoption, through the 1720s and '30s, of serpentine as well as straight walks within wildernesses, encouraged in part by the fashion for asymmetrical scrollwork on Rococo plasterwork and ornament, added to the sense of discovery and diversity (illus. 23). The proliferation and expansion of wildernesses also encouraged a different approach to the overall layout of the grounds around a house, one again with French roots, in the work of André Le Nôtre and Dézallier d'Argenville. While the central axis remained strong, the disposition of the parts to either side no longer needed be symmetrical where wildernesses formed a substantial portion of the grounds because, as Miller explained in his *Gardener's Dictionary* of 1731 – in what was almost a direct quotation from d'Argenville – the repetition of the same features on either side of a vista was neither desirable or necessary 'except in open places where the eye, by comparing them together, may judge their conformity'.[46]

Sometimes, however, wooded gardens were now established away from the mansion, for the 1720s and '30s saw a gradual but significant loosening of the relationship between the house and the garden. The great gardens at Gobions in Hertfordshire, designed by Charles Bridgeman in the late 1720s and added to over the following decade and a half, are largely forgotten today

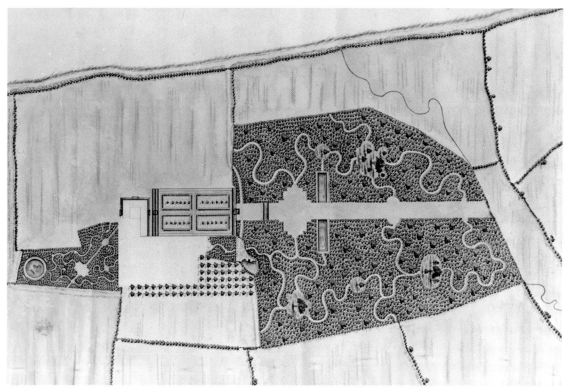

23 Kendals, Aldenham, Hertfordshire: an unfinished plan, probably from the early 1740s. Most of the garden takes the form of an extensive wilderness, largely created out of an existing area of ancient, semi-natural woodland: the walks within it are now serpentine rather than straight.

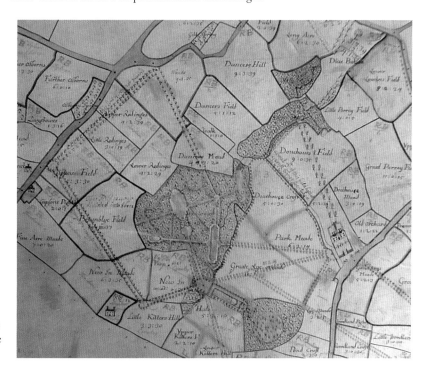

24 Undated map of Gobions in Hertfordshire, showing how the famous gardens were quite detached from Gobions House itself.

– Gobions House was demolished in the 1840s and, with the exception of a gothic gatehouse tower, the gardens survive only as earthworks. But George Bickham, author of the guidebook to Stowe published in 1750, thought them the second most important in England, and they were lauded by Horace Walpole in 1780 as a seminal landscape in which 'many detached thoughts, that strongly indicate the dawn of modern taste' could be observed, in part because of their 'pleasing Variety of Prospects'.[47] The gardens were laid out within an area of pre-existing ancient woodland some 200 metres to the south of Gobions House, on either side of the deeply incised valley of a stream, and comprised a network of paths

26 Detail from Charles Bridgeman's plan of the gardens at Gobions, showing Gibbs's Gothic gatehouse tower on the hill beyond the wood.

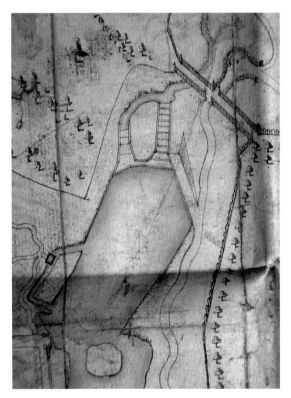

25 Detail from Charles Bridgeman's plan of the gardens at Gobions, probably drawn up in the early 1730s, showing the diminutive lake, cascade and paths cut through the woodland.

– some straight, some serpentine – that connected several distinct clearings (illus. 24).[48] These contained a bowling green, an ornamental canal, a grotto, a small lake with a cascade and a number of statues and buildings (illus. 25).[49] Bridgeman exploited the undulating local topography with considerable skill, ensuring that the garden's various elements were visually linked in a tantalizing fashion, inviting exploration. Much of the surrounding estate land, moreover, was crossed by linear avenues or walks, extending the line of the *allées* within the wood, and was incorporated into carefully composed views. On the low hill to the south a prominent eye-catcher terminated one of the main vistas within the gardens, a gothic gate tower designed by James Gibbs which still survives (it may pre-date his Gothic Temple at Stowe, often posited as the earliest garden building in this style; illus. 26).[50] The original plan also included, again on the low hill just outside the gardens, a romantic ruin, but this was probably never built. The most striking feature of the design, however – and perhaps the thing which made it so appealing to Walpole and Bickham – was the way in which the gardens lay far from, and could hardly be seen from, Gobions House itself. There was an axial avenue, focused on

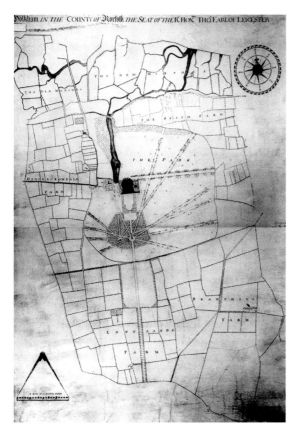

27 Map of the park at 'Holkham in the County of Norfolk', undated, c. 1745, showing 'Obelisk Wood', the detached wilderness occupying rising ground to the south of the house, with its temple and obelisk. The wood is dissected by straight rides, framing views which are described on the map: 'to Stiffkey Hills', 'To Wells Harbour'.

the main facade of the mansion, which connected the two but this was unquestionably an older feature and did not form a major articulating axis within the design. The gardens, in consequence, were something to be experienced in their own right, rather than functioning primarily as a setting for, or view from, the house. It is noticeable how the latter appears almost as an incidental afterthought in contemporary descriptions of Gobions, like that penned by William Toldervy in 1762.[51]

The framed views out from the gardens that were a key aspect of Gobions were a feature of other detached wildernesses or woodland gardens in the 1720s and '30s. Obelisk Wood at Holkham in Norfolk was planted soon after 1720 on the summit of a low hill some 600 metres to the south of the new hall, and was dissected by a network of straight *allées* focused on two classical structures, designed by William Kent – a temple and an obelisk. Looking outward, they framed distant vistas, and the 'target' of each is named on an undated map of c. 1750: 'to Wells Town', 'to Stiffkey Hills' and so on (illus. 27).[52] Around the same time Bridgeman laid out a similar wooded garden on the steep escarpment overlooking the park at Tring in Hertfordshire, 600 metres away from the house on the far side of the park. This likewise contained a temple and an obelisk, and gave access to a long terraced ride that commanded the immense prospect from the top of the Chiltern ridge, across the lowlands of north Buckinghamshire (illus. 28).[53] By the 1730s an interest in extended prospects, and on the provision of gardens and facilities from which these could be enjoyed, was widespread. A memorandum for gardening work to be carried out in association with the construction of a new

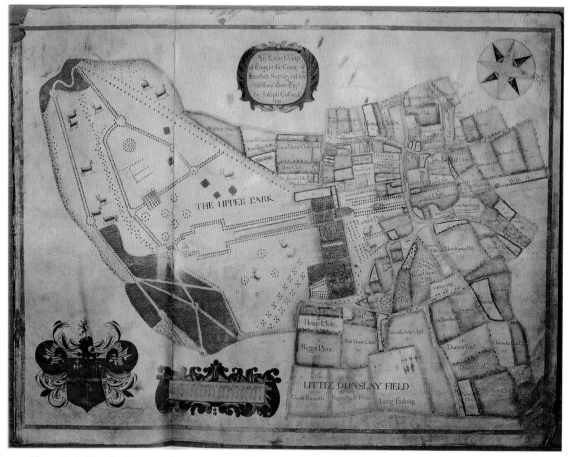

28 Tring Park, Hertfordshire, as shown on a map dated 1719, but added to and revised on subsequent occasions. The woodland garden or detached wilderness created by Charles Bridgeman can be seen bottom left, with obelisk and temple designed by James Gibbs. It occupied steeply rising ground on the Chiltern escarpment.

house at Kelmarsh in Northamptonshire around 1730 includes the note:

> In the first place tomorrow morning go [to] the oak at sun rise with the telescope and take your view and give Ringrove directions how to make the seat there. Get up the tall ash and take a view round, then go to Mount Sion and shew the hedges to be cut to open a view to Desborough steeple, this may be done by cutting one of Mr Rokeby's hedges.[54]

Garden historians sometimes write as if nobody much enjoyed commanding prospects, or created places from which these could be enjoyed, before the eighteenth century, but this is untrue. To take one example of many, the elaborate castellated 'lodge' of Bolsover Castle, erected in pseudo-medieval style by Charles Cavendish in the early seventeenth century to serve as a retreat from nearby Welbeck Abbey, was clearly built where it was so that he and his guests could enjoy the panoramic views to the north and west, across the Vale of Scarsdale: the arrangement of windows in this picturesque tower, with the largest facing north and west to command the prospect, leaves little doubt about this (illus. 29).[55] Nevertheless, an interest in distant views was unquestionably manifested more strongly in the elite landscapes of the 1720s and '30s than it had ever been before. To some extent, this desire to 'command the prospect' was connected with the increasing control the elite exercised over the local landscape as a consequence of engrossment and enclosure. To view was to command, and by the 1720s many estates formed unified, uninterrupted blocks extending over several square kilometres. A growing

interest in the improvement of landed estates perhaps also encouraged an interest in extensive views across them. But we should also note that at Tring, as in some other places, the view stretched for more than 40 kilometres, across land which lay far beyond the owner's possessions. Distant views were also intended to provide points of interest, discussion, diversion; subjects of easy conversation among the polite, to be enjoyed at a distance from the formality of the mansion.

The proliferation of wildernesses and wooded gardens, detached or otherwise; the loosening of the connection between house and gardens;

29 Bolsover Castle, Derbyshire. The 'Little Castle', erected within the medieval ruins in the 1620s, was an elaborate 'lodge' commanding magnificent views across the Vale of Scarsdale. Neither a liking for Gothick, nor an enjoyment of extensive prospects, were entirely new in the eighteenth century.

the increasing importance of extensive views across the landscape: all were thus major themes in the development of landscape design through the 1720s and '30s, and were all closely related to the emergence of new forms of social engagement. But from *c.* 1730 there was a more radical development. Whole sections of gardens began to be laid out on informal, serpentine lines within what still overall remained a geometric framework. Such gardens took many forms and passed through many changes in fashion, but formed in effect large 'outdoor rooms' that were ornamented in ways that echoed the objects or styles of decoration found within the mansion itself. Initially their inspiration was thus Palladian, or at least Italianate. William Kent, who emerged as the leading garden designer in England in the 1730s – having previously, and significantly, worked largely as a designer of interiors and of theatre sets – played a major role in this development.[56] His gardens were arranged as idealized versions of Italian landscapes. They were planted with clumps of pines and scattered ilex oaks and other trees, threaded with serpentine paths and

ornamented with obelisks, temples and the like, all strictly Palladian in design and casually distributed. At Holkham, for example, the geometric 'bason' only recently created immediately below what was to be the south front of the house (still under construction at the time) was, under Kent's direction, made less regular in outline in 1737, and connected to the newly made lake in the park by a 'serpentine river'. To one side – the west – a low hillock was raised, topped by the 'Seat on the Mount'. Other classical features, the two 'porches', stood at each end of the bason (illus. 30).[57] The planting was irregular and the whole area surrounded by a serpentine path. Kent's design is strongly reminiscent of the paintings of classical scenes by Claude Lorrain and Nicolas Poussin (and the popular engravings derived from these), romantic versions of the Italian landscape, which were widely hung on the walls of fashionable houses. Indeed, when the rooms on the south front of Holkham Hall were eventually completed over a decade later, Lord Leicester's famous collection of paintings by these very artists was hung in one of the rooms here.[58] Visitors could enjoy

30 William Kent's design for the South Lawn and 'Seat on the Mount' at Holkham Hall in Norfolk, *c.* 1740.

31 A detail of the 'General Plan of the Woods, Park and Gardens' at Stowe, Buckinghamshire, in 1739, showing how the serpentine and irregular 'Elysian Fields' were made within a wider landscape of geometric grandeur designed by Charles Bridgeman.

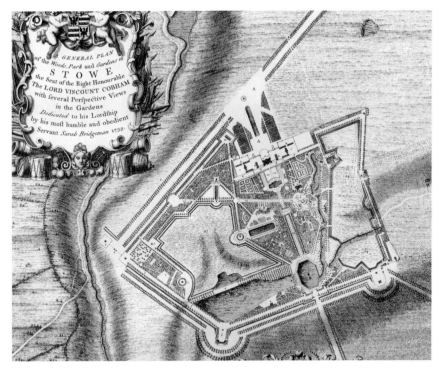

32 The Elysian Fields at Stowe, as it survives today, still cluttered with ornamental buildings.

the paintings, but also the view across – and shortly afterwards, a walk through – Kent's contrived three-dimensional version of the same kinds of scene. The structure of the wider landscape, in contrast, typically remained much more geometric. To the south a wide expanse of grass was flanked by parallel lines of pleached trees running up the hill to Obelisk Wood, the detached wilderness already described (see illus. 27). The entire design was organized around a single linear axis that was extended to the south for over four kilometres, terminating at an entrance lodge designed by Kent, again on strict Palladian lines. Other gardens designed by Kent similarly formed areas of serpentine irregularity within wider geometric frameworks, such as Stowe, where the famous Elysian Fields, with their winding paths and scattered buildings, existed within the wider, monumental landscape that had earlier been created by Charles Bridgeman (illus. 31, 32).

Yet while geometry continued to dominate the wider landscape of the park at such places, this too began to be infected by the burgeoning love affair with all things Italian. One important aspect of this was the widespread appearance of lakes, which seems to have begun shortly before 1710 but accelerated rapidly through the 1720s and '30s. Lakes do not form a part of the natural landscape of lowland England outside a few limited areas, and their inspiration clearly came from the inlets, estuaries and other water bodies, flanked by temples and other classical structures, found in the paintings of Claude and Poussin. Through the 1730s and '40s they tended to adopt more regularly serpentine forms, reflecting the wider popularity of curving, Rococo lines in garden design and in particular the influence

of the Serpentine or Serpentine River created in Hyde Park for Queen Caroline by Charles Bridgeman in 1730. Classical buildings also began to be erected in greater numbers beyond the gardens, not only in detached wildernesses but in the wider parkland. At Houghton in Norfolk, for example, the 'water tower' – a careful Palladian construction designed by Lord Pembroke, another amateur gentleman architect – was built at the end of the avenue running north from the pleasure grounds. The Palladian mansion, on the design of which so much attention and care was lavished, was itself a central object within the landscape, an idealized Italian villa to be viewed from detached garden or distant temple, or (as at Holkham) revealed suddenly on the approach. Such prospects of the house were enhanced by the removal of garden walls and their replacement by a fosse or haha, a fairly standard feature by the 1740s.

Although this 'Italianization' of gardens and parkland was closely related to the contemporary enthusiasm for Palladian architecture, the same penchant for large-scale landscape design occurred in other contexts. Sir John Vanbrugh designed the great house of Castle Howard in Yorkshire in an essentially Baroque mode and the surrounding landscape, unfinished at his death in 1726, displays a similar use of landforms to provide extensive views and dramatic settings for both the house and associated classical buildings, most notably the vast mausoleum (designed by Hawksmoor and built from 1729, although its location and character was based on Vanbrugh's ideas); here too a lake was created, to the southeast of the house. At Blenheim, similarly, Vanbrugh's landscape of monumental simplicity makes sophisticated use of landforms to display to best advantage the vast Baroque palace designed as a residence for the Duke of Marlborough, a lake again forming a key element in the design. All this said, the new modes of design were clearly connected very closely with the upsurge of enthusiasm for all things Italian that accompanied the Whig ascendancy in the period following the accession of George I.

The connections between landscape design, Palladian architecture and representations and experiences both of the Italian landscape and of classical antiquity were complex and multi-layered, as Hunt and others have discussed; many of the roots of the 'English' landscape garden evidently lay in Italian gardens and landscapes, or at least in English understandings and imaginings of these.[59] At the most basic level, idealized Italian landscapes served as three-dimensional mementos of the Grand Tours that many wealthy men had enjoyed in their youth, as did the paintings by Claude and Poussin that they avidly collected. These depicted imaginary but contemporary Italian landscapes, liberally stuffed with temples and other ruins from antiquity, as the settings for scenes from ancient myth. But there were many levels of meaning in all this, involving a fertile confusion between English garden, contemporary Italian landscape and the classical past; a confusion that is manifested with particular clarity in Robert Castell's *Villas of the Ancients Illustrated*, published in 1728, to which Burlington and Kent both subscribed, and on drafts of which both commented prior to publication.[60] The work was a translation of Pliny's letters describing his villas at Laurentinium and Tusculum, with Castell's added commentary, and it included supposed reconstructions of Roman gardens, some featuring circulatory paths around central green atria containing scattered trees and small naturalistic streams and lakes very similar to the gardens designed by Kent: one for a Tuscan park bears an uncanny resemblance to the kinds of design created by Brown and his contemporaries two decades later. Of particular importance is the fact that the paintings of Claude and Poussin – paintings widely disseminated in the form of engravings from the late 1730s – were categorized by contemporaries as 'history painting', highest in the hierarchy of genres. Their subject-matter was classical myths or biblical stories but, set within idealized *contemporary* Italian landscapes, they are given particular and local contexts. When Kent modelled the grounds of English country houses along similar lines, to resemble Italian landscapes, he affected a further translation, just as he and others did when they designed a country house as a Palladian villa, relocating fragments of Italy to England. Such landscapes could then serve as settings for specifically British historical themes – sometimes morally improving or politically inspired, as above all at Stowe.

As is well known, the gardens at Stowe – and especially the Elysian Fields – were laid out by Lord Cobham, now in political exile, to express his belief in true Whig principles, and his concerns about the way in which these were being betrayed by Walpole's administration.[61] Political meanings were embedded both in the structures and buildings, and in the visual relationships between them. The Temple of British Worthies contained the busts of Hampden, Newton, William of Orange and other figures appropriated to Whig mythology; the Temple of Ancient Virtue, with its busts of famous figures from Greek antiquity, was placed near the Temple of Modern Virtue, containing the statue of a headless figure, generally taken to represent Walpole himself. The Gothic Temple symbolized the supposed freedom of the ancient barbarian tribes (an association arising in part from a mistaken confusion of Gothic architecture and the Goths): across its entrance were written the words 'I thank the Gods I am not a Roman.' Stowe was a personal statement of Whig ideas, and the gardens at Chiswick created by Lord Burlington likewise contained an imposing exhedra with statues of Pompey and Caesar, despots responsible for the fall of the Roman Republic, confronted by Cicero, its defender. But other landscape gardens expressed rather different ideologies. Earl Bathurst thus laid out a vast woodland garden at Cirencester in Gloucestershire featuring a statue of Queen Anne on a tall pillar and other structures proclaiming his allegiance to Tory principles and the established Church. Others expressed broader philosophical concepts, like that designed by Kent for Queen Caroline in Richmond Gardens, with its Hermitage containing busts of Newton, Locke, Boyle and others proclaiming her ideas about science and 'natural' religion; or the macabre garden created by Jonathan Tyers at Denbies near Dorking, with its theme of death and mortality.[62]

Indeed, in the 1730s and '40s gardens became 'a realm in which aesthetic theories, philosophical ideals, poetic trends and even political ideologies could be illustrated to dramatic and innovative effect'.[63] Freed from the obligation of following fashions set by the royal court within a strongly hierarchical society, landowners could use the spaces they controlled in a host of new ways. But most of these evocative gardens contained no philosophical or political message at all, and from the late 1730s, mirroring to a large

extent the developments in interior decoration already discussed, they came to feature built structures in a wider range of architectural styles. Chinese buildings began to appear – the first probably the Chinese House at Stowe in 1738 (containing 'the figure of a sleeping Chinese lady');[64] and, following the publication of Batty Langley's *Ancient Architecture* in 1741–2, these were joined by fanciful 'Gothick' buildings – one of the earliest again at Stowe, Gibbs's 'Gothic Temple' of 1741. Soon all manner of weird and wonderful features were making an appearance in the gardens of the rich: hermitages, sometimes with a resident hermit, cottages, 'root houses', cascades, ruins, Turkish tents. In 1752 the Earl of Shaftesbury's gardens at Wimborne St Giles in Dorset featured a cascade, a 'thatch'd house', a 'round pavilion' on a mount, 'Shake Spear's House, in which there is a small statue of him', a pavilion and both a stone bridge and a 'Chinese Bridge'.[65] The extent to which such gardens proliferated through the 1740s is clear from the paintings produced by Thomas Robins in the 1750s, and from the descriptions penned by Richard Pococke of his travels through the west of England in 1750–51 (illus. 33).[66] In 1751 John Halfpenny published his *New Designs for Chinese Bridges, Temples, Triumphal Arches, Garden Seats, Palings, Obelisks, termini etc*, his Chinese take on a triumphal arch a particularly odd example of cultural crossover.[67] By 1756 John Shebbeare was able to assert that 'The simple and the sublime have lost all influence almost everywhere, almost all is Chinese or Gothic.'[68]

Whatever their precise character, gardens like these – often referred to by historians as Rococo gardens – were generally cluttered with buildings, structures and objects, as well as boasting exotic planting, using the latest shrubs acquired from remote lands, all intended to evoke emotional or intellectual reactions on the part of the visitor: to encourage political or philosophical musing, as at Stowe; thoughts of distant countries; reactions of surprise, melancholy or delight. They promoted discussion and conversation for, with their winding paths and irregular planting, they provided – as Timothy Mowl has pointed out – arenas for informal interaction away from the still formal straitjacket of the mansion itself, from the 'social disfunctionalism' of the great house.[69] The buildings in such gardens frequently contained provision for al fresco dining. Such gardens also created 'a frisson of excitement in visitors, to transport them pleasantly into a fantasy realm for an hour

or two' and, with their whimsical buildings set in increasingly colourful and informal planting, reflect to an extent the increasingly feminized character of country house interiors.[70] But they continued to co-exist with landscapes of a geometric character, forming one 'room' within a wider landscape of formal grandeur. Just as 'the Rococo, diversified by playful Chinoiserie elements and Gothic fantasy . . . flourished within the orderly framework of Palladian interiors',[71] so serpentine and irregular gardens usually existed within a wider geometric framework. In some cases, however, continuing the fashion for isolated gardens already described, they were placed at a distance from the mansion and its formal, geometric grounds, forming detached islands of playfulness.

33 Thomas Robins's view of the gardens at Honington Hall in Warwickshire in 1759, with gothic summerhouse.

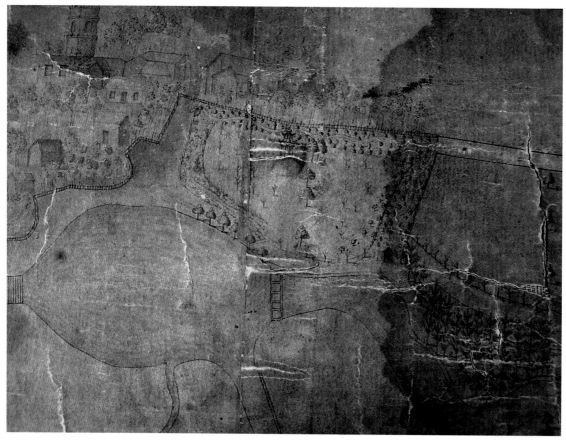

34 A rather faded map of Alscot in Warwickshire, undated but *c.* 1749, showing the Rococo gardens beside the river Stour, with the Chinese Temple on its mount, circuit path, exotic planting, 'alcove', cascade and diminutive lake. This ensemble lay quite detached from Alscot House itself, which stood some 600 metres away across the park, still set in walled geometric gardens.

Alscot in Warwickshire is a classic example. The estate was purchased in 1747 by James West, MP for St Albans in Hertfordshire and secretary to Henry Pelham, then Lord Chancellor, who in 1746 became Joint Secretary to the Exchequer. West was a Fellow of the Society of Antiquaries and a noted collector of books and antiquities, and immediately began to transform the landscape around the mansion.[72] He extended the existing deer park and, between 1747 and 1758, laid out an elaborate Rococo garden, featuring much ornamental planning, a serpentine circuit path and a range of buildings including a Chinese temple, a 'rotunda' on a mound, a root house, a Chinese seat, an alcove (the only feature still remaining) and 'a cell built for Shakespeare' (illus. 34, 35).[73] The river nearby was widened into an oval 'bason' and a cascade constructed.[74] Yet none of this formed the setting for the mansion itself, but instead lay nearly 500 metres away, on the far side of the park and on the far bank of the river Stour.[75] Until the 1760s the immediate surroundings of Alscot House continued to comprise walled geometric gardens, with straight walks, a bowling green and a wilderness. These, together with such features as the dovecote and an elaborate series of fishponds, were all carefully maintained. The only connection between the two areas of garden was provided by an avenue, one of several that ran across the parkland and into the surrounding countryside. At Davenport in Shropshire, similarly, the house was flanked by a geometric *patte d'oie* cut through woodland; the main Rococo features in the landscape – a hermit's grotto, cascade and Gothick octagon – were invisible from it.[76] We might note in passing that another detached garden area also existed at Alscot, on the crest of the hill a kilometre to the west. Here in the early 1750s James West raised a mount or 'terrace' and noted in his memoranda

book the many places which could be seen from it, some as much as fifty kilometres away.[77]

Isolated Rococo gardens formed an extreme expression of a wider theme. Geometric structures were focused on the architecture of the great house and provided a complement to its symmetrical architecture; they were associated still with state and parade. Serpentine and Rococo gardens, in contrast, provided spaces for more intimate and informal encounters. House and garden were thus often separated or even invisible from each other. This was true even in the case of the Elysian Fields at Stowe, and when Arthur Young visited in the 1760s his only criticisms concerned ways in which this isolation was breached. The view from the Temple of Friendship would, he

35 Alscot House, rebuilt by James West in Gothick style in the 1750s and '60s, viewed from the site of the detached Rococo garden.

thought, be improved 'when the wood is enough grown to hide the house', while to his description of the prospect to be enjoyed from the Gothic Temple he appended the note: 'Query, should the spires &c of the house be seen here?'[78]

Far from following a single path of development, moving under its own internal impetus from formal geometry to the irregularity of nature, the design of gardens and landscapes in the first three or four decades of the eighteenth century appears complex and confused. Italian and exotic influences, the use of gardens to express philosophical ideas or evoke emotions, the importance of expansive prospects and the manipulation of the landscape on an ever-greater scale were all prominent features. But these represented a number of parallel rather than convergent themes. Geometry thus happily

coexisted with 'informality' and while at some places gardens were hidden or divorced from the mansion, elsewhere the landscape seems to have been conceived primarily as its setting. Underlying this rich complexity, however, we can identify the impact of major social and political developments: the rise of polite society and the associated need for appropriate recreational spaces which, as yet, were not fully supplied by the architecture of the house itself; together with a freedom from the dominance of a single fashion, set by the royal court, which stimulated landowners to use landscapes in novel ways, entertaining or moral or both.

By the 1740s, at the highest social levels, as a result of these varied developments, many of the characteristic elements of Brown's landscapes were already widely deployed. At great residences

36 William Kent's design for the park and banqueting house at Euston Hall in Suffolk, *c.* 1738.

37 William Kent, ink and wash, unexecuted proposal for a Palladian villa overlooking the old house, Waynflete's Tower, at Esher Place, Surrey, c. 1730. The design envisages an open parkland setting for the new house while retaining the Tower as a folly; it is remarkably close to the type of landscape later created by Brown and his contemporaries.

like Chatsworth or Holkham clumps were planted on high ground several kilometres from the mansion; ornamental buildings and waterbodies proliferated in the wider landscape; and extensive prospects, to and from the mansion, were now of considerable importance. The necessary corollary of this was a decline in the number of avenues in the landscape around the house. The complex webs, focused on the mansion, that appear in so many of the illustrations in Johannes Kip and Leonard Knyff's *Britannia illustrata* were removed, for as viewpoints proliferated, prospects were disrupted by oblique alignments, by serried rows of trees running at an uncomfortable angle. Some of Kent's later designs, such as Euston in Suffolk (*c.* 1738), show open parkland, devoid of straight lines and avenues and with any residual geometry only subtly implied (illus. 36); in his designs for the deer park at Esher, drawn up a little earlier, the house forms the focus of the prospect within an open, apparently naturalistic landscape, just as mansions were later to form the key feature in Brown's landscape parks (illus. 37). By 1739, even as Brown was leaving his native Northumberland and heading south to Stowe, one contributor to *The World* was able to mock the current trend for 'moving earth', and the way that 'a Serpentine River and a Wood are become the absolute Necessities of Life, without which a gentleman of the smallest fortune thinks he makes no Figure in the country.'[79]

The business of gardening

When examining the evolution of garden design in the first half of the eighteenth century it is important to consider not only changing modes of design and their possible significance but the organization of gardening and landscaping as a *business*, not least because this can throw light on the character of the personal contacts and relationships between prominent practitioners, and thus on patterns of influence and the transmission of ideas. By the time of the Glorious Revolution in 1688 a number of significant nurseries had been established in London: as early as 1672 Captain Leonard Gurle's Whitechapel Nursery was supplying plants such as Dutch limes, laurustinus, 'Spruce Firs' and various other ornamental shrubs to places as far away as Ryston Hall near Downham Market in Norfolk.[80] But by far the most influential, in terms of the development of a landscape 'industry', was that based at Brompton Park in Kensington, which was founded in 1681 by Roger Looker, Moses Cook, John Field and George London. Looker, the Queen's Gardener, was the senior partner.[81] Moses Cook was the head gardener to the Earl of Essex at Cassiobury near Watford: John Evelyn recorded a visit there on 18 April 1680, describing how 'on the earnest invitation of the Earle of Essex I went with him to his house at Cashioberie . . . the gardens are very rare, and cannot be otherwise, having so skillful an artist to govern them as Mr Cooke, who is, as to the mechanic part, not ignorant in Mathematics, and pretends to Astrologie'.[82] John Field was the Earl of Bedford's gardener at Woburn Abbey, while George London was Bishop Compton's gardener at Fulham Palace, and a former apprentice under John Rose in the royal gardens. London seems to have taken the lead in the design arm of the business. According to Stephen Switzer, himself an apprentice of the nursery from 1698, it was

> common for him to ride 50 or 60 miles in a day. He made his Northern Circuit in five or six weeks, and sometimes less, and his Western in as little time. As for the South and East, they were but three or four days work for him; most times twice a year visiting all the country Seats, conversing with Gentlemen, and forwarding the business of Gard'ning in such a degree as is almost impossible to describe.[83]

This pattern of activity, vigorously pursuing commissions through extensive travel, is remarkably similar to that adopted by Lancelot Brown some seventy years later. London designed gardens for the Duke of Devonshire at Chatsworth in Derbyshire in 1688 and for Hugh, 1st Viscount Cholmondeley, at Cholmondeley Castle, Cheshire, in 1694; but it was for his work with Henry Wise, who became his partner at Brompton Park in 1688 (the older partners having by then died), that he is best known. Wise had himself been an apprentice at the nursery, and the two men worked together at a great many places. Their collaborations read like a list of the most important gardens in the land. Together they were responsible for major modifications to the royal gardens at Hampton Court, and those at Chelsea Hospital in London; and they worked at Longleat in Wiltshire (from 1682, for Thomas Thynne, created 1st Viscount Weymouth in that year); at Chatsworth; at Melbourne Hall in Derbyshire (between 1693 and 1706, for Thomas Coke); at Wimpole in Cambridgeshire (between 1693 and 1705, for the 2nd Earl of Radnor); at Bramham Park in Yorkshire (for Robert Benson, 1st Lord Bingley); at Badminton in Gloucestershire (for Henry Somerset, 1st Duke of Beaufort); and at Castle Howard in Yorkshire (for Charles Howard, 3rd Earl of Carlisle).[84] All these commissions, it is important to emphasize, were obtained via royal patronage. All the clients were Privy Counsellors at the time the work was carried out (William Blathwayt, for whom London worked at Dyrham Park near Bristol, was clerk of the Privy Council). Only a handful of London's clients, such as the London lawyer Thomas Vernon – by whom he was employed at Hanbury Hall in Worcestershire – were men outside this inner circle of court patronage; and it will be noted, from the dates of the commissions just listed, that the London/Wise partnership continued to draw on this court-based network right through the changes in monarch, and the associated changes in ideology and political personnel, which occurred in the later seventeenth and early eighteenth century. The Glorious Revolution and the accession of William and Mary to the throne in 1688, and the succession of Queen Anne in 1702, brought both winners and losers on the political stage, but the improvement business continued briskly.

We noted earlier the broad stylistic connections between the kinds of extensive formal gardens created by London and Wise, and the Baroque style of architecture employed for some of the greatest houses built in England in the late seventeenth and early eighteenth centuries. What also needs to be emphasized is that the building of such houses, and the laying out of their grounds, usually occurred – not surprisingly – at the same time, and were closely coordinated. Chatsworth is an important example. William Cavendish, 4th Earl of Devonshire, was a key beneficiary of the Glorious Revolution, becoming the 1st Duke of Devonshire in 1694, and from 1687 to 1696 major new work was undertaken at Chatsworth House, with the construction of new south and east fronts to designs by William

Talman. This was followed between 1700 and 1702 by the rebuilding of the west front, and from 1705 the north front, a project still uncompleted at the time of the first Duke's death in 1707. The former was designed by the Duke himself, assisted by the architect Thomas Archer, the latter by Archer alone.[85] The gardens were transformed during this same period, in part using foreign craftsmen but, inevitably, with the aid of London and Wise. The first contract for work here, drawn up in 1688, was with London alone, for the design of a parterre to the southeast of the house, for which he was paid £120.[86] Between August 1690 and March 1691 a large number of plants was 'sent out of Brompton parke': 5,000 'slips' of green lavender, 5,000 of white lavender, 3,000 'spike' lavenders, 1,000 Roman lavenders, 2,000 'common lavender[s]', ten striped (that is, variegated) hollies, six striped phyllerias, six striped box, ten scorpion senas, ten standard scorpion senas, forty standard white lavenders, forty standard green lavenders, twenty standard Roman lavenders, unspecified quantities of 'firs', 'three sortes of time' and one scarlet honeysuckle.[87] In 1694 a second contract was drawn up – this time with both London and Wise, now partners – for the design of a second parterre, this to be laid out in the area immediately below the new south front, which by this time was nearing completion, the design of the two clearly integrated and coordinated.[88]

Castle Howard was the next great mansion to be erected in the Baroque style. Here Talman failed to obtain the commission, which in 1699 was awarded instead to Sir John Vanbrugh, dramatist turned architect, but also, as we have seen, a designer of landscapes, a combination that was to become increasingly common as the century progressed. His knowledge of European architecture was extensive, in part because he had had the opportunity to study Louis Le Vau's work at Château de Vincennes from close quarters during his imprisonment there in 1691 (he had taken a leading role in negotiating the accession of William of Orange to the throne and had been arrested at Calais, returning from William at The Hague, and charged with spying).[89] The dramatic landscape that accompanied the house at Castle Howard was largely designed by Vanbrugh himself, although George London also contributed, originally suggesting in 1699 that nearby Wray Wood should be clear-felled, a proposal rejected by the Earl of Carlisle.[90] By 1705 Wise and Stephen Switzer were working on turning the wood into one of the very first of the detached woodland gardens, which was designed as what Switzer later described as 'a Labrynth diverting Model', that is to say, with meandering serpentine paths, rather than a network of straight *allées*.[91]

When London died in 1714, Wise promptly sold his interest in the nursery to two other assistants, Joseph Carpenter and William Smith, although he retained Brompton Park House while he continued in his post as Royal Gardener, from which he retired only in 1728.[92] Both London and Wise did well out of their business. By the time of his death London was the owner of a substantial freehold estate and held financial interests in mines in Wales (in addition to his co-ownership of the Brompton Park nursery itself). Wise had acquired a substantial property at Priory House in Warwick, and while his first wife was the daughter of Matthew Banckes, a master carpenter in the office of works and active at Blenheim, his second wife, Jane Bramston of Skreens, Roxwell, Essex, came from one of the principal landed families of the county.[93] He was said to have been worth no less than £200,000 at his death in 1738.[94]

The Brompton Park nursery dominated, perhaps monopolized, the design of the greatest gardens in the land under London and Wise, and to some extent that position was maintained under Carpenter and Smith until their deaths in the late 1720s. The centrality of the nursery in the development of gardening styles is evident from the fact that the key 'names' in garden history were all closely associated with the business. Stephen Switzer, in his own words, 'tasted . . . the meanest labours of the Scythe, Spade, and Wheel-barrow' as an apprentice at Brompton Park.[95] Like Brown, Switzer was the younger son of a family of yeoman farmers, with some 50 acres of copyhold land at East Stratton in Hampshire; his apprenticeship was paid for by a bequest in his father's will, proved in 1697, and he was on the nursery payroll by 1705, working at Blenheim in Oxfordshire, where Vanbrugh was now employed on the construction of the vast Baroque palace built for John Churchill, Duke of Marlborough, as well as on the layout of its grounds.[96] A letter of 1 April 1704 from Vanbrugh to William Boulter, joint comptroller of works at Blenheim with Henry Joiner, suggests that Switzer's employment here did not run smoothly:

> My Lady Dutchesses servant Ben was with me this morning, to desire I wou'd put him into some employ at Blenheim, telling me that there was some changes towards upon Mr. Wise's turning out Steven. I told him I believ'd he must be misinform'd, since I rec'd no letter relating to any such thing, which I should certainly have done, if there

was occasion to displace or take in any new clerks . . .[97]

But Switzer's dismissal from the garden work may have been to his advantage. By the following year he was back on the payroll at Blenheim working on the 'Business of the Bridge' with Vanbrugh and Nicholas Hawksmoor: the construction of the huge bridge taking the main axial avenue of this great formal landscape across the river Glyme, work on which continued until 1710.[98] After this, Switzer moved to Lincolnshire, where he was employed at Grimsthorpe by Robert Bertie, Marquess of Lindsey and Duke of Ancaster, to modernize and extend the gardens there: this was in 1715, the same year in which Vanbrugh was commissioned to design a new front for the house.[99] The fact that the two men were again working together illustrates clearly the kinds of personal relationships and professional networks that were central to the career progression of these rising stars of the gardening world. In 1715 Switzer published *The Nobleman, Gentleman and Gardener's Recreation*, which in 1718 would become the first volume of his three-volume work, *Ichnographia rustica*. By this time he was 'Stephen Switzer of Newbury, gardener', according to articles of agreement for works at Caversham in Berkshire drawn up with William, Earl Cadogan, MP for Woodstock and formerly Quartermaster-General for the Duke of Marlborough.[100] Switzer went on to have a long and successful career designing gardens and parks at numerous country seats including Audley End in Essex, Nostell Priory in Yorkshire, Stourhead in Wiltshire and Beaumanor in Leicestershire.

A more important figure in the Brompton Park nexus, and like Switzer originally an apprentice at the nursery, was Charles Bridgeman. He was probably the son of the gardener at Wimpole in Cambridgeshire, where London and Wise prepared and implemented designs for the gardens between 1693 and 1705 for Charles Robartes, 2nd Earl of Radnor. It seems likely that Bridgeman's apprenticeship arose from this connection.[101] A signed plan by Bridgeman for Blenheim, dated 1709, suggests that his apprenticeship had by then been completed.[102] Bridgeman appears to have been Wise's favoured protégé and he succeeded him in the role of Royal Gardener in 1728. But as well as his work with Wise at Kensington Palace and at Blenheim, Bridgeman built up a successful business of his own, designing parks and gardens on an impressive scale through the 1720s and '30s. Crucial to his career was the fact that, as we have seen, the central position of the royal court in both setting fashions and in dispensing patronage in gardening was now beginning to fade. In this increasingly complex economy, a new market for landscape designers was opening up. While Bridgeman continued to enjoy royal patronage, and his clients boasted many aristocrats and nobles – and Robert Walpole himself, for whom he designed the grounds at Houghton – he was more involved with the smaller estates of those whose wealth came primarily from business, rather than from land: upwardly mobile urban merchants, investors and businessmen looking for a place in the country within easy reach of the capital.[103] Of particular importance were individuals connected with the South Sea Company, until the expanding bubble – generating new wealth in a seemingly never-ending rise – burst dramatically in 1720. But Bridgeman's clients also featured several of the 'Nabobs' of the East India Company, many of whom built houses, and laid out gardens, in the hinterland of London. He often worked closely with the architect James Gibbs, the two apparently acting as informal partners, the one designing the gardens, the other making modifications to the house and designing garden buildings. One of Bridgeman's earliest commissions was Sacombe Park in Hertfordshire, where he prepared a plan for the gardens in 1715. His client was Thomas Rolt, who had bought the estate in 1682 having made a fortune with the East India Company (he was later accused of shady dealings with 'fictitious stock' in the South Sea Company).[104] Bridgeman designed the ornamental gardens, which only survive in archaeological form, as great earth terraces; John Vanbrugh designed the walled kitchen garden, with its massive buttressed walls; while Gibbs provided designs for a new house, although these were not in the event executed.[105] Other clients of a similar business background included Sir John Fellowes, a tobacco merchant who became sub-governor and a director of the South Sea Company (created a baronet in January 1719, his success was short-lived and the property was confiscated in 1721); Jeremy Sambrooke, whose gardens at Gobions, also in Hertfordshire, we have already described in some detail, and for whom Gibbs both designed garden buildings (including the surviving 'Gothick arch') and made modifications to Gobions House; and Benjamin Styles, another South Sea Company man, whose grounds at Moor Park, again in Hertfordshire, were transformed by Bridgeman between 1720 and 1728.[106]

Not only does Bridgeman appear to have tapped into a wider base of clients than earlier designers working on a national level. His mode

of working also represented a break from established tradition. While Switzer, with his small nursery at Millbank, and others continued to work as 'nurserymen designers', combining the formulation of proposals with the supply of plants, and thus the provision of contract works and the actual ownership of a nursery business, Bridgeman opted for a clear separation of design and implementation, the latter being carried out by contractors, including his former colleagues at Brompton Park. Such a procedure did not always run smoothly (in 1731 Joseph Carpenter's widow and John Smith's executor, Joseph Stanwix, were jointly suing Bridgeman in Chancery for unpaid bills) but it allowed him to take on a much greater volume of work in the rapidly expanding marketplace of polite park-makers.[107] This new separation of design from construction and planting foreshadowed the way in which Brown himself was to organize his business as this developed through the 1750s and '60s. And there were other broad similarities. Brown, as we shall see, was involved in a wide range of activities relating to the improvement of estates, and to an extent this was also true of Bridgeman, who for example was paid by the Earl of Lincoln to prepare a report on improving the main watercourse to the town of King's Lynn in Norfolk, in reply to an earlier report that had been made by the prominent cartographer Thomas Badeslade – for Robert Walpole, the town's MP.[108] Bridgeman is described in this as a 'surveyor', a term which, in this busy world, could mean anything from architect to engineer, from property agent to gardener, or a combination of several of these things. New kinds of employment were emerging as England's economy expanded and diversified, and the meaning of old labels became fluid with the decay of the old guild system. Skills learnt in one sphere of activity, moreover, might well be required in another, and men whom we think of simply as 'garden designers' in this period often had several other strings to their bow. The management of water, hydraulics, had many applications, aesthetic and practical, and was a matter of growing interest through the middle decades of the century, as water-powered factories proliferated and river navigation was progressively improved. Stephen Switzer himself wrote *An Introduction to a General System of Hydrostaticks and Hydraulicks, Philosophical and Practical* in 1729.

Not all of those involved in the design of gardens in the first half of the century were professionals. We have already noted how evocative, serpentine gardens like Stowe or Denbies were largely the vision of their owners, and from the late 1730s – and extending, as we shall see, into the time of Brown's career – similar, highly personal landscapes were created by men like Charles Hamilton at Painshill, the Lyttletons at Hagley in Warwickshire, and Philip Southcote at Woburn Farm, near Chertsey in Surrey. Sanderson Miller, a landowner from Warwickshire, was a particularly important figure: the architect of several country houses and garden buildings, he also prepared designs for gardens and landscapes, and was an important early influence on Brown, whom he probably first met at Stowe. According to his obituary in the *Gentleman's Magazine*, Miller was 'very intimate with the lords Temple, Lyttleton and Mr Shenstone, for whom he planned several buildings, which they erected, having had an exquisite taste in architecture', but this rather understates the extent, scope and significance of his work in designing houses and garden buildings, Thomas Lennard Barrett

complimenting Miller in 1746 that 'Your fame in architecture grows greater & greater ev'ry day & I hear of nothing else, if you have a mind to set up you'll soon Eclipse Mr Kent, especially in the Gothick way, in which to my mind he succeeds very Ill.'[109] By contrast, Miller's houses at Hagley and Croome are frequently held up as fine examples of English Neo-Palladian architecture.

William Kent, possibly the greatest influence on Brown, perhaps falls into an intermediate category. A man from a relatively lowly background, his artistic talents were recognized while still living in Bridlington, Yorkshire, when a group of local patrons financed a trip to London, armed with introductory letters to potential patrons there. With John Talman, a wealthy art collector, he then travelled to Italy, where he stayed from 1709 until 1719. He gained the patronage of Richard Boyle, Lord Burlington, whom he met in Genoa on his way home in 1719 – a fortunate meeting for both men – and on his return to England stayed at the latter's London house and then, from 1726 to 1729, worked on the design of Chiswick House.[110] Kent at this stage was employed principally as an interior designer, a role he continued to undertake – together with the design of furniture – throughout his career. But by the early 1730s he was also practising as an architect, especially of garden buildings, and soon after was involved in the design of the gardens we have already described, most notably at Stowe and Holkham. Kent was the greatest influence on Brown, as contemporaries recognized. He occupies a slightly different place in the development of the business of landscape design to most of the individuals we have been discussing. He did not run a business; his artistic projects were relatively few and often of long duration. He worked very much as the client of private patrons, men like Burlington and Coke, and moved easily in their elevated social world. Yet in these respects he was not entirely unique, and it is important not to exaggerate the commercial character of the world in which other designers, such as Bridgeman, operated. The court-centred patronage network of the seventeenth century was fading, but commissions were still largely obtained through the recommendation of one wealthy man to another.

IT IS DIFFICULT to understand the design of gardens simply in terms of the history of garden design. Instead, the creation of landscapes in the first four decades of the eighteenth century, as in other periods, is most usefully considered within the context of other activities and practices, especially architecture, domestic planning and interior design, all of which were in turn related to changing forms of social interaction and social organization. As Britain became less dominated by the culture of the royal court, and as its economy expanded and its inhabitants emerged as a 'polite and commercial people', new forms of landscape architecture of necessity developed. And at the same time, as we have seen, these very same social and economic currents were changing the business of gardening itself. All these complex trends intensified in the second half of the eighteenth century, the age of Lancelot Brown.

Often examined as a simple linear development, from 'geometry' to 'nature', on closer inspection garden design in the first three or four decades of the eighteenth century appears more complex and confusing. Not only did 'geometry' and 'nature' usually coexist in the same landscapes, but trends in design took forms that were to

some extent in opposition. On the one hand, serpentine gardens developed that were visually divorced from the mansion and its geometric setting, forming separate and discrete areas for informal intercourse, and for the expression of diverse personal views and tastes in a society no longer dominated by the fashions set by the court. On the other, landscapes were increasingly designed to provide extensive prospects, especially of the mansion itself. To some extent, the landscapes we now associate with Capability Brown were indeed a further development of these two opposed tendencies. But they also represented a resolution of the essential contradictions and conflicts between them.

The story we have outlined briefly above rests more on the evidence provided by the landscapes themselves than on the poetic and philosophical writings of men like Pope, Addison or Shaftesbury, the meanings of which are endlessly contested. It also considers landscapes primarily in terms of the way they were used and consumed, rather than as expressions of the particular 'genius' of individual designers or the philosophical or political ideas of their owners. For most of the gardens created in the 1720s, '30s and '40s were clearly intended to amuse, entertain, surprise and on occasion shock, rather than to educate or indoctrinate. They appealed to the emotions more than the intellect. Nobody kept a hermit in his garden to provide religious instruction: the one employed at Hawkstone in Shropshire approached visitors waving bloody stumps instead of hands, and shouting the words 'memento mori'.[111] Even where complex iconographic schemes, dependent on allusions to the classics, were an intended feature, this did not mean that they were of interest to most visitors, or understood by them. The fact that from an early date visitors could purchase a guidebook at Stowe, explaining what they were looking at, is a clear sign of that. Visitors – and most of the more famous gardens were open for some at least of the year for the entertainment of strangers – often amused themselves in unintended ways. Famously, Philip Southcote was forced to close his gardens at Woburn Farm after 'savages, who came as connoisseurs, scribbled a thousand brutalities in the buildings.'[112] Those excluded from the ranks of the polite often took matters a stage further, the delicate and often poorly built constructions of the Rococo garden an almost irresistible target for vandalism. In 1749 James West's steward, William Coombs, described with horror how unknown individuals had broken into the gardens at Alscot, 'gone into the root house and thrown what was there into the river; and pull'd up and torn all to pieces my Lady's root seat . . . on the hill in the Long Vistoe next the fir grove'.[113]

38 Wakefield Lodge, Northamptonshire, as painted by Paul Sandby in 1767, showing the house and landscape initiated by William Kent and completed by Brown in the late 1740s.

THREE

The 'Brownian' Landscape

IT MIGHT BE thought that an entire chapter devoted to dissecting the landscape style popularized by Lancelot Brown from *c.* 1750 is unnecessary because most readers will already have a pretty clear idea of what it was like. He and his contemporaries removed 'avenues, parterres, terrace, basins and canals – everything partaking of the old art and geometry' from the environs of great houses.[1] In their place they laid out what we now describe as 'landscape parks', informal and 'natural' in character, eschewing straight lines and formal geometry. They consisted of wide prospects of uninterrupted turf, scattered in an irregular and fairly sparse manner with both individual trees and clumps of woodland, mainly comprising indigenous species like oak, elm and beech. These were surrounded in whole or part by a perimeter woodland belt, similarly constituted. Where circumstances allowed, these designs were ornamented with serpentine or irregular bodies of water, and they usually contained a number of ornamental buildings – temples and the like – to vary the view. Walled enclosures close to the house were demolished, and the boundary between the grazed ground of the park and the lawns around the mansion was now marked in its entirety by a sunken fence or haha. Straight lines were everywhere replaced by curves and sinuosity: serpentine drives and rides thus ran across the parkland and, in many cases, down the centre of the perimeter belt; the haha between park and pleasure ground usually followed a smooth, geometric curve. Brown's landscapes were supposedly so 'natural' in appearance, and so English in character, that Horace Walpole believed that 'he will be least remembered: so closely did he copy nature that his works will be mistaken for it.'[2] Brown himself probably landscaped, during his long career, no more than 250 properties, as we have seen, but his style was immensely influential and was widely copied, so that many hundreds of landscape parks had appeared in England by the time of his death in 1783. And, because a successful style is one which is in no need of change, it is hardly surprising that many writers have suggested that once devised, Brown's essential formula remained unaltered. Tom Turner for example has argued that 'during the thirty-two years of his career as an independent designer Brown's style hardly changed and is easily represented by a single diagram.'[3]

There are however a number of good reasons for looking in more detail at the landscapes Brown created. The first is that their appearance now is not necessarily a reliable guide to how they would have looked when first made or, more importantly, how Brown and his clients believed they would look when mature. Age has changed them, and also changed their essential meaning. The second is that, while in very general terms the brief description presented above may be correct, much more needs to be said about, and can be learnt from, the details of Brown's designs, many of which, as we shall see, have been matters of keen debate among garden historians and others over recent years. The third reason is that, in spite of what is often argued or implied, Brown's style did in fact change in important ways during the course of his career, and these changes can tell us much about its significance. By examining Brown's stylistic development over time, moreover, we are able to throw some light on the question of how original his style really was at any stage of his career.

Brown's early years

Some books posit a sharp contrast between Brown's landscapes and the geometric gardens they replaced, but as we have seen, serpentine lines and irregular planting had become common features of gardens during the two decades before he began his career as an independent designer, especially at the highest social levels, even if they usually coexisted with geometric forms. In many ways Brown's landscapes were like those of William Kent, but writ larger across the landscape – both, as we have seen, worked together at Stowe – and in some ways the contrast between the two men appears less when we compare Brown's works with the designs produced by

Kent for landscapes at the scale of the park, rather than for pleasure grounds (p. 63). We should also perhaps emphasize that many of the key features of Brown's designs had an even longer history. Hahas had been used to define the boundary between the garden and park at some places, such as Houghton in Norfolk, as early as *c.* 1720; clumps had been widely planted before Kent used them, Philip Miller describing in 1731 how oak trees were 'very proper for a Wilderness in large gardens, or to plant in Clumps in parks'.[4] Brown combined an existing repertoire of features, developing ideas originally formulated by Kent and others, but in new ways.

Brown began to work on private commissions – 'on loan' as it were, from Lord Cobham – from the early 1740s, with activity of some kind recorded, usually imperfectly, at Wotton in Buckinghamshire, Finmere Rectory in the same county, Newnham Paddox in Warwickshire and Wakefield Lodge in Northamptonshire (illus. 38). More is known of his commissions in the 1750s, after he became an independent designer: at Packington and Longleat in Wiltshire, Warwick Castle and Charlecote in Warwickshire, Croome in Worcestershire, Petworth in Sussex, Kirtlington in Oxfordshire, Moor Park, Cole Green and Beechwood in Hertfordshire, Belhus and Short-grove in Essex, Burghley in Northamptonshire, Madingley in Cambridgeshire and Wrest in Bedfordshire. Often the precise character of his early work at a particular place is uncertain because he continued to add and alter the landscape in question beyond this phase of his career, and a lack of documentation prevents us from distinguishing 'older' from 'younger' work – as at Shortgrove in Essex, where a receipt in the Petworth archives for making a 'pool' in 1758 was the first stage in an engagement that continued, on and off, until at least 1770.[5] This said – and acknowledging that there are certainly other places where Brown worked in the 1740s and '50s, of which we know little or nothing – there are enough reasonably well-documented sites to provide some guide to the kind of work he was doing in the early years of his career.

Most of his early commissions appear to have been focused on transforming the immediate setting of the house, where walls were removed and fashionable pleasure grounds were laid out; and on creating lakes, usually at no great distance from the house, and separated from them by an expanse of smooth and levelled turf. Other interventions in the wider landscape usually seem to have been on a limited scale, and largely restricted to the planting of the lawn between

house and lake, or around the lake itself. The contracts drawn up for the work at Longleat in 1757 and 1758 were typical. They describe how terraces were to be levelled, land drained and walls removed, various basins and canals filled in or deformalized, and trees and shrubs planted and gravel walks laid out, all apparently in the area around the house. A haha was to be constructed, and modifications made to the existing 'serpentine water', so that its 'sharp turns' were removed.[6] At Petworth, where Brown had four separate contracts (1753, 1754, 1755 and 1756), most of the work undertaken again concerned the immediate surroundings of the house: levelling and turfing, taking down walls and a pigeon house, making a haha and planting trees and shrubs.[7] At Warwick around 1750, similarly, comparison of paintings made before and after his work in

39 Warwick Castle, Warwickshire, as painted by Canaletto in 1748, shows that the formal gardens had already been removed prior to Brown being commissioned to improve the grounds.

40 Francis Harding's painting of 1764 records the same view of Warwick Castle as the previous illustration, but *after* Brown's work there had been completed.

the castle grounds suggests alterations to the water, combined with levelling and planting in the vicinity of the castle itself (illus. 39, 40). The gardens and pleasure grounds he created in such contexts were elaborate and not obviously different from those being created by other designers in the 1740s and '50s. Surviving plans for Ingestre in Staffordshire (1756) or Badminton in Gloucestershire (*c.* 1752) show designs that are positively Rococo in feel (illus. 41, 42). At Petworth Brown was contracted to make and plant a gravel walk 'which is to lead from the Arcade, through the Old Nursery, the new Orangerie, and Terras, on through the laurels leading up to the Seat where the Duchess of Somerset used to drink here coffee'; and to 'finish the Parterre in front of the Green House'. A plan

(perhaps from 1752) details 'The Terrass reduced to a Fine Undulated hill adorned with groups of Cedars, Pines &c'.[8] What is particularly striking is the list of shrubs ordered for the pleasure grounds here in 1753, which included sweet briony, honeysuckle, altheas, spirea, oriental colluta, 'Cockgyreas', bird cherry, 'double cherry', candleberry trees, butcher's broom, ilex, sweet briar, double thorn, Persian jasmine, 'Virginian Schumachs', Virginia raspberry, tamarisks, American maples, sea buckthorn, 'trumpet flowers', roses, Portugal laurel, laburnums, lilacs, acacias and the roses 'Rosa Mundi', 'Maiden's Blush' and 'York and Lancaster'.[9] At Chatsworth, where Brown transformed the pleasure grounds in 1759–60, the estate vouchers record the purchase of thirty striped (that is, variegated)

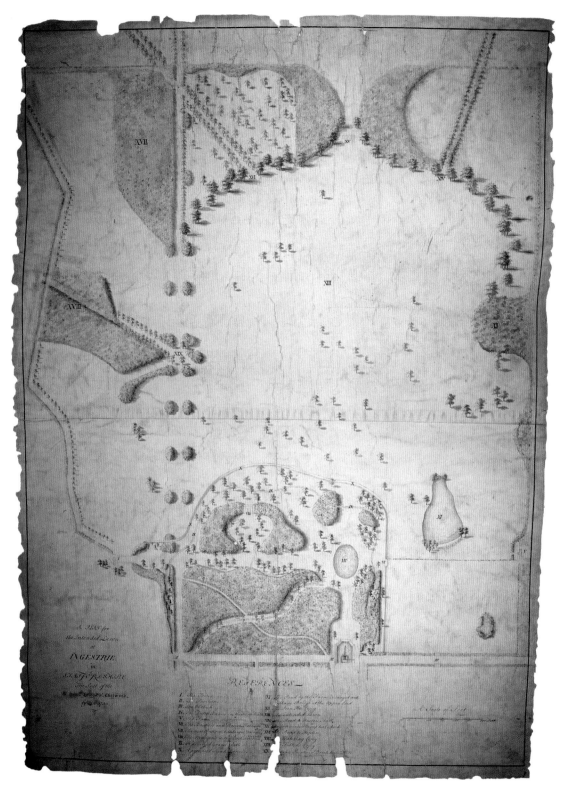

41 Lancelot Brown's 'Plan for the Intended Lawn' for Ingestre Hall in Staffordshire, 1756. Note the somewhat stiff, Rococo treatment of the shrubberies; the focus on the pleasure grounds in the vicinity of the house; and the survival of geometric features within the wider landscape.

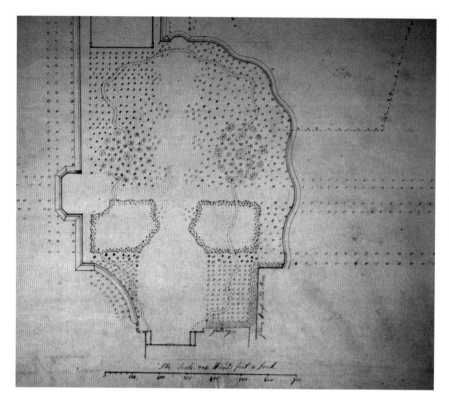

42 Brown's design for the pleasure ground at Badminton House, Gloucestershire, *c.* 1752. Of particular interest is the Rococo sinuosity of his proposed sunk fence, and the survival of geometric planting in the wider landscape. The layout of the shrubberies is closely comparable to the contemporary work of Robert Greening and others.

hollies and a 'parcel of flowering shrubs', while in 1761 payments were made to one John Naylor for travelling to Londesborough 'for shrubs'.[10] In 1759 a phenomenal range of trees and shrubs was sent from Philadelphia by James Alexander – over eighty varieties in all, including tulip tree, hickory, swamp viburnum, 'blue beryd Cornus' and honey locust: 'these ar what I hav collected but would hav contained sum more varietys only for the nesesity I was of putting them up in such a hurry becaus of a vessel sudently and unexpectedly sailing.'[11] The contract for Longleat describes how the walk from High Wood to the kitchen garden was to have verges adorned with 'shrubs, trees of curious sorts, and turf'.[12]

Moreover, like the gardens created by William Kent or the Rococo gardens of the 1730s and

'40s, Brown's early designs usually constituted serpentine sections within more structured and geometric landscapes; or, at the very least, avenues, formal walks and other geometric features often survived within or beyond the main areas of his activities. At Ingestre Hall, for example, the surviving plan, of 1756, shows a number of avenues and clumped avenues in the area beyond the gardens; that for Packington shows that the main avenues focused on the house were retained, as they evidently were at Longleat;[13] while at Belhus in Essex fragments of avenues, and the straight walks within an early eighteenth-century wilderness, survived until the Ordnance Survey six-inch maps were surveyed in the late nineteenth century. A more striking example, perhaps, is Moor Park in southwest Hertfordshire. The house here – originally erected in the 1720s for

Sir Benjamin Styles, partly by converting an earlier house, to designs by Sir James Thornhill – was built with the proceeds of trading in South Sea Company shares and was originally accompanied by extensive gardens designed by Charles Bridgeman, which were laid out mainly to the east of the mansion. Brown was called in by a new owner, Lord Anson, in 1754. Anson was a national hero who had commanded attacks on Spanish colonies in the Americas, sailed around the world and returned with booty worth the immense sum of £500,000. Brown's work, which appears to have been supervised by his associate Nathaniel Richmond, was largely targeted at Bridgeman's gardens, with their geometric basins and regular terraces.[14] Walpole visited the place in 1760 when the new works were approaching completion but was unimpressed:

> We went to see More-park, but I was not much struck with it, after all the miracles I had heard that Brown had performed there. He has undulated the horizon in so many artificial molehills, that it is full as unnatural as if it was drawn with a rule and compass.[15]

The clumps and mounds, which were intended to soften the hard edges of Bridgeman's level terrace, may have been positioned in part to obscure the shaped 'bastions' that projected out from it. Either way, Walpole perhaps judged the overall effect too early, for Thomas Whately, visiting the site ten years later, was more favourably disposed to what he described as the 'several hillocks, not diminutive in size and [made] considerable by the fine clumps which distinguish them', which he thought 'do more than conceal the sharpness of the edge; they convert a deformity into a beauty and greatly contribute to the embellishment of this most lovely scene'.[16] It is certainly clear that the diminutive and evidently artificial 'hillocks', which still survive (although now within a golf course), and the pleasure ground more generally, had more in common with the landscapes designed by Kent and others in the

43 Brown's unexecuted design for a temple, to be erected on an earlier viewing mount at Badminton House, for which he was paid in 1752.

1730s and '40s than with the kinds of sweeping, simple, almost minimalist landscapes that Brown was to produce in the 1760s and '70s (illus. 44). Planting mounds were a common feature of the former, with examples surviving at Houghton in Norfolk, and (for instance) shown on an undated plan of the grounds of another place where Brown was employed in Hertfordshire, Cole Green – unless this shows an early stage in Brown's own involvement at the place, which lasted from perhaps 1752 until 1761 (illus. 45).[17] More important, perhaps, is the fact that Brown appears to have been employed only here, in the immediate vicinity of the mansion at Moor Park, even though Anson reputedly paid

£6,000 for the improvements.[18] The wider landscape, dating in part from the seventeenth century and in part from the time of Bridgeman's activities in the 1720s, remained little altered. Dury and Andrews's county map of Hertfordshire, published in 1766 and apparently surveyed around two years earlier, thus shows the parkland occupied by a dense mesh of avenues, many of which survived into the nineteenth century (illus. 46). It is noteworthy that the paintings of the hall commissioned by a subsequent owner, Sir Laurence Dundas, from Richard Wilson, and executed between 1765 and 1767, show it as viewed from Brown's extensive pleasure ground and not from the wider, more geometric landscape of

44 Brown's 'hillocks' at Moor Park in Hertfordshire, constructed in the 1750s and criticized by Walpole in 1760, still survive within the golf course.

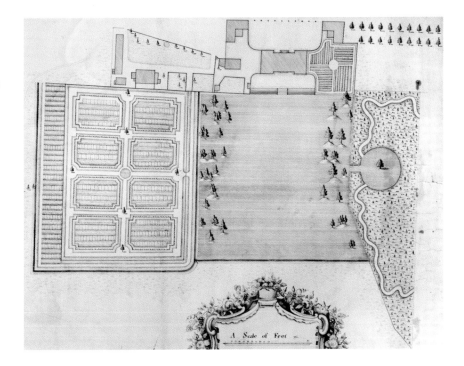

45 Cole Green, Hertfordshire: an undated map from the 1750s, showing planting mounds similar to those at Moor Park.

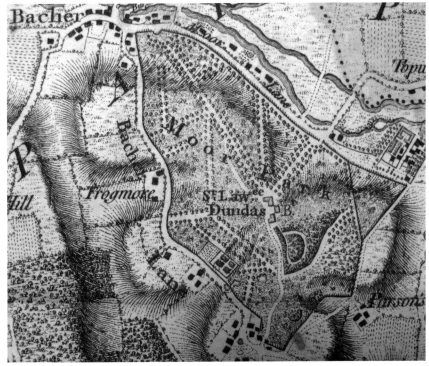

46 Detail from Dury and Andrews's map of 'Hart-fordshire', published in 1766, showing how Brown's pleasure ground at Moor Park coexisted with a landscape of geometric formality.

47 Richard Wilson,
Moor Park, Hertfordshire,
1765–7, oil on canvas.

the park, which must by now have appeared somewhat old-fashioned (illus. 47). It is also noteworthy that at Cole Green near Hertford, where Brown was paid at least £718 by William Cowper between 1755 and 1764,[19] Dury and Andrews likewise show a park crossed by numerous avenues, and containing other geometric planting; while at Ashridge in the same county, where Brown worked in 1759–60, an estate map of 1762 shows the main layout of avenues and linear vistas still in place, beyond the clumps and more serpentine planting in the vicinity of the house, itself designed by Henry Holland.[20]

Wrest Park in Bedfordshire, where Brown was commissioned by Philip Yorke in 1758, is another instructive case. The house already had extensive gardens laid out in a simplified geometric style in the early seventeenth century, with canals, extensive wildernesses and buildings including an imposing pavilion (which still survives) by Thomas Archer (illus. 48, and see illus. 22).[21] Although Brown embellished the planting and linked a number of drainage ditches and water bodies to create a 'serpentine river', running around three sides of the garden's perimeter (illus. 49), the essentials of the design remained, and to a large extent still remain, unaltered – so that Wrest is today one of the best places in the country to see a 'late geometric' garden, rather than a Brownian landscape. When Walpole visited in 1762 he described the 'wretched low bad house' with its gardens, 'very ugly in the old fashioned manner with high hedges and canals, at the end of the principal one of which is a frightful Temple designed by Mr Archer'.[22]

Brown's work as a designer of buildings, rather than just of gardens and landscapes, stands out at many of these places (illus. 50). At Wotton he prepared plans for an 'octagon', a Chinese tea house and an 'elegant bridge with colonnade' – presumably a Palladian bridge of some kind.[23] At Croome in the early 1750s he designed a rotunda, a grotto, a Corinthian temple on an island and – a little later, but effectively another garden building – a remodelled parish church, close to the hall.[24] At Petworth in 1753 he proposed a sham bridge, grotto and menagerie; at Ingestre in 1756 a sham bridge, rotunda, tower and menagerie; while at Wrest Walpole's criticisms of the gardens were tempered by his comments that 'Mr Brown has much corrected this garden and built a hermitage and cold bath in a bold good taste', in addition to the buildings

(most notably Archer's 'frightful temple') already in place.[25] At Temple Newsam in the early 1760s Brown designed and built sham bridges, a rotunda, a menagerie, a cottage, a dairy and a grotto.[26] But his work as an architect was not limited to garden buildings. Like Kent before him he also turned his hand to the design of houses. As early as 1747 or 1748, at Wakefield Lodge in Northamptonshire, he appears to have completed the construction of a house already designed by Kent; at Croome he may have acted primarily as executive architect to Sanderson Miller (illus. 51); but at Newnham Paddox he was largely responsible for the design

48 Wrest Park in Bedfordshire. Brown worked here in the late 1750s but the geometric gardens – including the great canal, terminated by Thomas Archer's Pavilion – still survive, beautifully maintained by English Heritage.

49 Brown's activities at Wrest Park, Bedfordshire, were largely restricted to the creation of a serpentine water running around three sides of the garden's perimeter, formed from a network of earlier canals and drainage ditches. The Chinese Temple is a modern recreation of a feature placed here in the late 1750s, about the time that Brown was working on the grounds.

of the building. Both the latter houses were in a broadly Palladian style, with corner turrets and central pediment, although rather plain and with principal reception rooms at, or near, ground level, rather than raised up on a *piano nobile*. Both houses took several years to build and at Croome the interiors – and especially the Long Gallery, constructed between 1761 and 1765 – were in a revolutionary new style, the 'Neoclassical', and were the work of Robert Adam, to whom we shall return at a later stage.

These were houses built largely or entirely from scratch. Elsewhere, in his early years, Brown adapted existed buildings, providing modern suites of rooms or other additions in appropriate architectural styles. At Warwick Castle he was initially employed – about 1749 – to modernize the grounds, removing terrace and parterres and replacing them with a smooth slope of grass leading down to the river. But in 1753 a second agreement was made with Lord Brooke, now for altering the castle itself. The porch and stairs of the Great Hall were remodelled, various changes were made to entrances and passages, the courtyard was levelled and a suite of family rooms was enlarged.[27] In Viscount Grimston's words, visiting a decade or so later, the Earl had 'made many that were small closets, comfortable rooms'.[28] Burghley is in some ways more interesting. This was, and is, a great Renaissance 'prodigy' house

50 The Gothick bath house at Corsham Court in Wiltshire, designed by Brown *c.* 1760
but modified by John Nash in the early nineteenth century.

from the sixteenth century, which Brown was asked in 1755 to modernize. He demolished the west wing, altered the principal elevations, made various changes to the interior and added a new greenhouse.[29] As at Warwick, but more clearly, Brown made no attempt to impose on the building elements of contemporary Palladian design. In a letter to Sanderson Miller, Lord Dacre described how 'Brown tells me that he has the alteration of Burleigh, and that not only of the Park but of the House which wherever it is Gothick he intends to preserve in that stile; and whatever new ornaments he adds are to be so'

– although, as Walpole noted, the original house was not, strictly speaking, in Gothick style at all.[30] Brown's greenhouse, which still survives on the northeastern side of the house, is especially striking, its windows with pointed arches, its parapets crenellated (illus. 52).

Brown's designs of the 1740s and '50s are not, therefore, entirely like those of his middle and later career. They were often fairly cluttered with buildings, geometric elements often remained in the surrounding landscape and the main focus was on the area around the house, where elaborate pleasure grounds were laid out. From the

51 Richard Wilson's 1763 oil of *Croome Court, Worcestershire*, was made at the conclusion of Brown's first phase of work there, and beautifully records the appearance of one of Brown's first large-scale commissions.

52 The greenhouse, Burghley House, Northamptonshire, designed by Brown in Gothick mode.

beginning, a key and recurrent feature was a smooth lawn stretching from the house down to a lake or other serpentine water body (illus. 53, 54, 55). But his designs do not otherwise seem to have engaged much with the park as a whole. Indeed, even where wider interventions were being made in the landscape, it is not always clear that these were necessarily directed by Brown himself. Chatsworth is an intriguing case. In 1758 work began on laying out a new park to the west of the house. The existing deer park lay in part on the sloping ground to the east, and partly on the level plateau above this, out of sight of the mansion. Roads were closed, vast plantations were established on the margins of the new park and much new planting was made within it.[31] Closer to the house, the river was widened and the area between it and the house was levelled and graded; fishponds and basins were filled in; and the gardens, already much simplified during previous decades, were further deformalized (illus. 56). Two new bridges, designed by the architect James Paine, were built across the river Derwent, one for a public road at the far south of the park and one to carry the main drive to the hall. Beside the river, some way to the south of the house, an ornamental mill in simple classical style was built (illus. 57). Horace Walpole

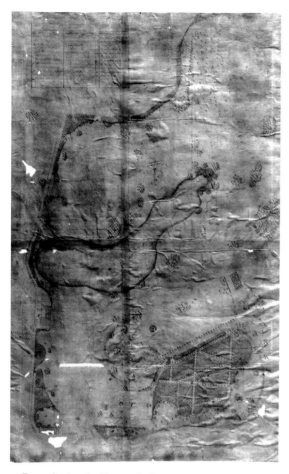

53 Brown's plan for Petworth, Sussex, 1753.

therefore, slightly ambiguous, and could be read to mean that Brown's activities were restricted to directing the changes to the contours. James Paine himself commented in 1767 that Brown was 'employed by His Grace in laying out the improvements near the house . . .'.[35]

This said, there can be little doubt that the main approach to Chatsworth House – crossing the Derwent on Paine's fine bridge, angled in such a way as to provide a perfect view of the mansion – was by Brown. Indeed, as his style matured through the late 1750s and early '60s more and more attention appears to have been given to the main entrance drive, laid out so as to provide the best possible view of the house and its setting and often crossing water at some stage – as at Shortgrove in Essex, although here the narrow lake has gone, leaving a bridge (probably designed by Matthew Brettingham) impossibly large for the infant river Cam it now spans (illus. 58). The line of the drive was designed to reveal the house, suddenly or dramatically, to the visitor; or to provide tantalizing glimpses, followed by a sudden reveal; or was otherwise manipulated for dramatic effect. At Bowood (1763) the main approach from the south crossed one arm of the lake, before being taken along a route that hides the rest; after a short interval the main part of the lake came into view, and then the house, revealed in its commanding position, looking down across the water. This concern, not just with the immediate setting of the house but with the way it was approached, was to intensify through the 1760s and '70s. The main drive to Burghley, which Brown appears to have designed and laid out in the mid-1770s (his engagement here, typically, was an extended one), crosses the lake by a fine bridge that he designed himself,

visited while the work was continuing in 1761 and recorded that the Duke was 'making vast plantations, widening and raising the river, & carrying the park on to the side of it, & levelling a great deal of ground to show the river, under the direction of Brown'.[32] The estate accounts record regular payments to Michael Milliken, Brown's associate, for 'moving earth', presumably in the area around the house and between it and the Derwent.[33] They make it clear, in contrast, that the wider planting in the landscape, within and around the new park, was carried out by the estate itself.[34] Walpole's quotation is,

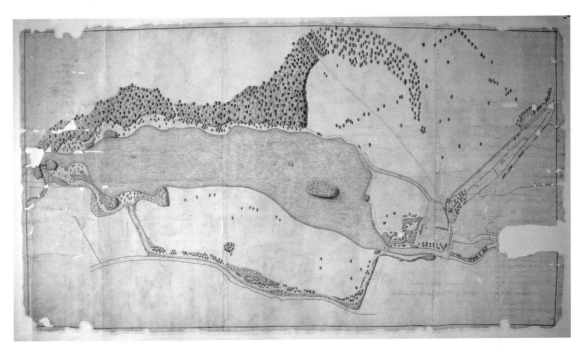

54 Brown's plan for 'The Intended Alterations at Trentham in Staffordshire', 1758.

55 J.M.W. Turner, *Petworth Park: Tillington Church in the Distance*, 1828, oil on canvas.

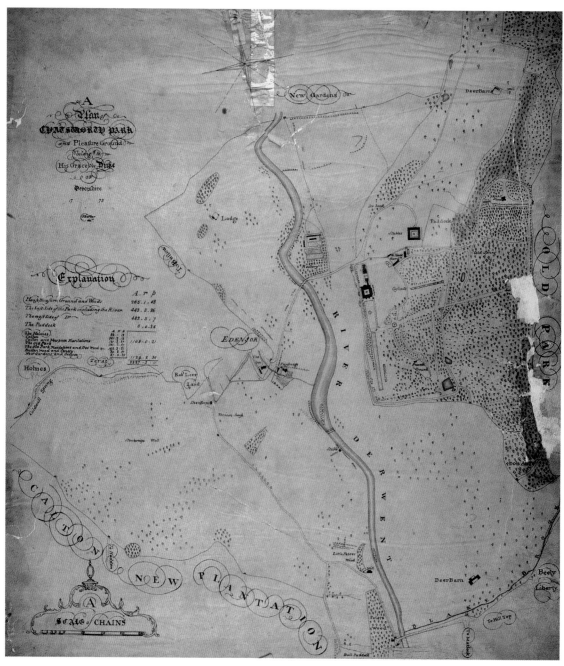

56 A 1773 plan by George Barker of 'Chatsworth Park and Pleasure Ground', Derbyshire, probably surveyed to show the recently completed 'improvements', begun in 1758.

57 Chatsworth Park, Derbyshire: the main approach, crossing the river Derwent on James Paine's elegant bridge.

58 Shortgrove in Essex: the bridge, probably designed by Matthew Brettingham, which carried Brown's main drive across a narrow lake, now dry.

providing a magnificent oblique view of the house, a composition remarkably similar to that at Chatsworth (see illus. 110). When Watts in 1779 described Burghley he noted the great alterations made 'under the Direction of Lancelot Brown' in the 'disposition of the Grounds and Water, *particularly in the Approach to the House*'.[36]

Brown's developed style

Through the 1760s and into the 1770s there were further decisive shifts in Brown's style. One important change was the decreasing significance of garden buildings in his designs. These did not disappear, but through the 1760s and '70s they became fewer in number. It is difficult to chart this development with any accuracy, in part because in some cases a failure to add garden buildings simply reflected the abundance of those already present in a landscape, but the pattern of change is clear enough. Whereas many of Brown's designs from the 1750s and early '60s included three, four or more built structures, by the late 1770s there were few, or even none at all. Although features like temples were still erected, moreover, as at Nuneham Courtenay in 1778, most of his designs were for less fanciful constructions: bridges or 'sham bridges', hiding the retaining dams to lakes; lodges; greenhouses; or parish churches, sometimes left marooned in a park by the banishment of an associated village (very occasionally, some 'vernacular' building from the earlier landscape might also be retained as an element in the view, such as the single cottage on the edge of the lake from the hamlet cleared at Bowood, or the watermill at the lake head at Benham Park). Brown's buildings were, in addition, more likely to be erected out in the parkland, at a distance from the mansion, rather than close to it, in the pleasure grounds. Typical was Fisherwick, where the design prepared in 1769 included only a Chinese pavilion, placed on the far side of the lake, in addition to bridges and a sham bridge, the latter forming the dam to the lake.[37] Brown's landscapes, in other words, became over time less like the cluttered Rococo gardens of the 1740s, or Kent's pleasure grounds of the 1730s. Such buildings as he erected, moreover, seem to have fulfilled a different role to those

that featured in these earlier gardens. Rather than acting individually to stimulate the imagination or the intellect, they were increasingly subservient to the wider design of the landscape. They might have particular functions, as places to visit, enjoy the prospect or take tea, but their main purpose was to focus a view or otherwise contribute to the prospects. They were being used in the manner that Thomas Whately advised in his *Observations on Modern Gardening* of 1770: 'either to distinguish, or to break, or to adorn, the scenes to which they are applied'.[38]

Another important tendency from the early 1760s was to surround the park with a continuous or near-continuous belt of trees, clearly separating it off from the surrounding countryside (illus. 59). And from around the same time, Brown's tolerance of residual geometric elements in the landscape, or perhaps that of his clients, appears to have declined steadily. Such features still appear in designs drawn up in the early 1760s, as

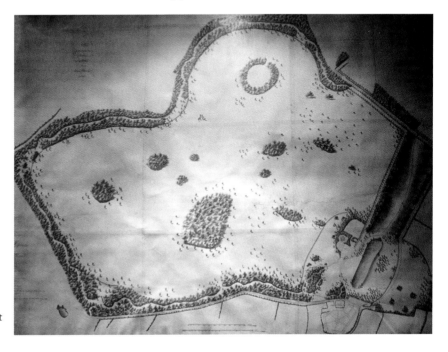

59 Brown's plan for Brocklesby in Lincolnshire, 1771, showing his developed style, with perimeter belt, circuit ride and clumps.

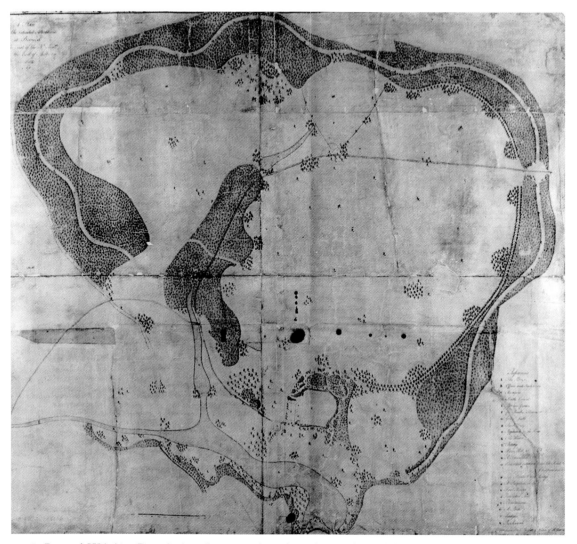

60 Bowood, Wiltshire: Brown's plan of 1763 is perhaps the earliest to show all the features of his fully developed style. Note the complex lake; the approach from the south (right), across two bridges; circuit ride; perimeter belt; and extensive pleasure ground.

at Temple Newsam (1762), but by the 1770s his plans rarely show stretches of avenue or straight vistas cut through woodland. Perhaps more importantly, alongside a growing interest in the approach to the house, the early 1760s seem to have seen a proliferation of drives and rides more generally. These ran in serpentine fashion through the park, and often through the perimeter belts.

Contemporary accounts, and sometimes the details on Brown's own plans, as at Lowther or Bowood (illus. 60), suggest a distinction between gravel drives, mainly but by no means exclusively forming the approaches to the house; and a wider network of grass rides, the latter usually including any perimeter circuit.[39] The French visitor François de La Rochefoucauld described how, on his visit to Heveningham in Suffolk in 1784 (where Brown's grand design was just being completed), he and his companion were lent horses by the owner and rode around the park 'always on paths of either turf or earth carefully sanded'.[40] Such was the importance of rides and drives in Brown's designs by the mid-1760s that some of his commissions, as at Weston in Staffordshire in 1765, seem largely to have involved their creation (illus. 61).[41] Close examination of the remains of Brown's drives suggest that they were often carefully engineered, slightly raised above or sunk into the natural surface to reduce gradients (illus. 62), and that they were sometimes provided with a small raised turf bank along their margins, presumably to ensure that the line of white gravel did not visually intrude on the prospects of open turf when viewed from a distance. The character of his turf rides is less clear. In some of Brown's designs they are lined with trees, almost like serpentine avenues, but whether they were otherwise defined and maintained simply by use, or with a measure of deliberate mowing, is uncertain – although the

latter would have been a major task, given their length, at places like Bowood. They were nevertheless in some sense 'constructed' by Brown, as their formation is stipulated in some contracts, while at places like Lowther their permanence and significance is signalled by the fact that they are taken across rivers on substantial bridges. Most could probably have been negotiated by wheeled vehicles with little difficulty, at least if the ground was dry.

All this was part of a wider development. Although Brown did not neglect pleasure grounds, his designs were now envisaged on a larger scale, embracing entire landscapes and dealing in detail with planting a mile or more from the house. Even where, as at Wimpole (see p. 134), he only dealt with a part of a park, this was often located away from the house, rather than comprising the area beside it. And as his emphasis on ornamental buildings declined, that on the basic building blocks of landscape increased: 'Brown in the course of his career gradually learned to think out his landscapes more in terms of ground, wood and water.'[42] In an oft-quoted passage – one of

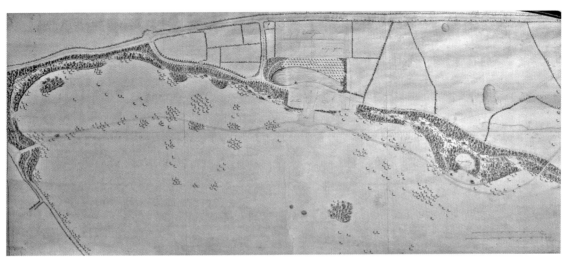

61 Brown's plan for Weston in Staffordshire, 1765, showing the prominent circuit ride.

62 The line of Brown's approach to Youngsbury House in Hertfordshire still survives. Note the gentle curve, and the way in which it is carried on a slight embankment across the lower ground.

the few in which he described his art – Brown explained how there was 'so much Beauty depending on the size of the trees and the colour of their leaves to produce the effect of light and shade so very essential to the perfecting of a good plan'.[43]

For reasons already explained – the extended character of Brown's association with many places and the difficulties of establishing the precise chronology, nature and extent of his activities there – the chronology with which Brown's mature style emerged is unclear. The first true circuit rides, running around the perimeters of the park (and initially resembling tree-lined serpentine avenues), are shown on plans from the start of the 1760s, for places like Corsham Court in Wiltshire (1761).[44] But it was only really with designs like Bowood (1763) that his fully developed style – circuit rides, perimeter belts, extensive planting – seems to have emerged.[45] While the precise chronology of Brown's stylistic journey may at present elude us, its scale is undeniable and is neatly summarized by comparing – as Fiona Cowell has noted – his plan for Ingestre in Staffordshire (see illus. 41), drawn up in 1756, with its emphasis on shrubberies, its residual geometric elements and its Rococo forms, with those for Heveningham in Suffolk of 1782, which exhibit 'a very different treatment of long, wide stretches of land' (illus. 63).[46]

The park was now being experienced in a different way, or perhaps more accurately, certain ways of experiencing the park were now being given particular emphasis. The attention paid to approaches, and the proliferation of rides and drives, indicate that the landscape was now considered not simply as a collection of static views, but as something to be experienced in its entirety, and experienced through movement, especially on horseback or in a carriage. Thomas Whately provided in 1770 an extraordinary description of the approach to Caversham House in Berkshire, the grounds of which had been landscaped by Brown in the mid-1760s. Progress is described in great detail and at great length, almost like a moving film, the passage continuing for nearly a thousand words:

the road passes between the groups [of trees], under a light and lofty arch of ash; and then opens upon a glade, broken on the left only by a single tree; and on the right by several beeches standing so close together as to be but one in appearance; this glade is bounded by a beautiful grove, which in one part spreads a perfect gloom, but in others divides into different clusters, which leave openings for the gleams of light to pour in . . .[47]

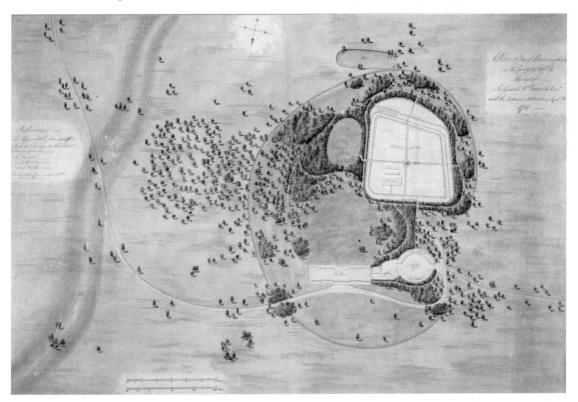

63 Brown's plan of the 'Intended Alterations' at Heveningham Hall in Suffolk, 1781, showing his fully mature style towards the end of his career. The tightly defined clumps of his earlier work have given way to a looser arrangement, with a penumbra of individual trees around the clumps to soften the visual effect. The simple C-form of the sunk fence is a strong organizing element.

The landscape was designed – its various elements combined and recombined – less like a series of static pictures than the words and punctuation in a sentence. In one of the few passages in which Brown described the principles underlying his art, in a conversation with Hannah More in 1782, this approach is neatly encapsulated:

> I passed two hours in the garden the other day . . . with my friend Mr Brown. I took a very agreeable lecture from him in his art, and he promised to give me taste by inoculation. He illustrates everything he says about gardening by some literary or grammatical allusion. He told me he compared his art to literary composition. 'Now *there*', said he, pointing his finger, 'I make a comma, and there,' pointing to another spot, 'where a more decided turn is proper, I make a colon; at another part, where an interruption is desirable to break the view, a parenthesis; now a full stop, and then I begin another subject.'[48]

The passage also conveys the sense of a landscape as a continuous if varied whole, the meaning of which might be changed – again, as with the punctuation of a sentence – by the alteration of a single element. Hannah More may have been reporting something often repeated by Brown, for an article in the *Gazetteer and New Daily Advertiser* for 1780, describing how the planting of a single willow had been Brown's sole contribution to the grounds of Garrick's villa in Hampton, noted: 'This single addition Brown compared to punctuation, and not without some felicity of phrase, called it a dot, the presence and operation of which, as it were, made

sense of the rest.'[49] This crucial importance of movement – and thus of the continuous rather than fragmented character of the experience of landscape – was also directly related to the smoothness of landforms so favoured by Brown, who would doubtless have approved of Edmund Burke's definition of beauty, which appeared, significantly, in 1756:

> Most people must have observed the sort of sense they have had, on being swiftly drawn in an easy coach, on a smooth turf, with gradual ascents and declivities. This will give a better idea of the beautiful, and point out its probable cause better than almost any thing else.[50]

Yet while Brown's landscapes may have now worked more as a continuum than as a series of set-piece views, this does not mean that particular prospects were not given special prominence within them. Temples and the like provided not only a focus for a view, but points from which the best prospects across the landscape could be enjoyed. But the key 'garden building' was now, in effect, the mansion itself, experienced in particular from the approaches in a manner very different from the way earlier houses, set within geometric landscapes, had been. In Whately's view, 'An avenue being confined to one termination, and excluding every view on the sides, has a tedious sameness throughout; to be great, it must be dull: and the object to which it is appropriated, is after all seldom shown to advantage.' He emphasized how 'buildings, in general, do not appear so large, and are not so beautiful, when looked at in front, as they are when seen from an angular station, which commands two sides at

64 Redgrave Hall, Suffolk, designed by Brown and erected in the 1760s, now demolished.

once, and throws them both into perspective'.[51] When the house was primarily experienced as constricted views along linear vistas, moreover, its relationship with the wider landscape was best represented, as in the views published in Kip and Knyff's *Britannia illustrata* and innumerable other engravings and paintings, from the air, where it formed the focal point in an often complex web of avenues and vistas. By the middle decades of the eighteenth century artists no longer used aerial views to depict the country house. The mansion, striking and alone within its park, was now represented at ground level, usually at an angle so that two of its sides were in view.

In this context it is important to emphasize that any reduction in the number of buildings in Brown's landscapes was not reflected in any diminution in his activities as a country house architect. On the contrary: the design of houses became a more important feature of his work

through the 1760s and '70s, an activity which, from 1771, he usually undertook in collaboration with the architect Henry Holland (his son-in-law from 1773). Commissions for rebuilding, remodelling or extending houses included Lowther in Cumberland (1762), Redgrave in Suffolk (1763, illus. 64), Broadlands in Hampshire (1765), Peper Harow in Surrey (1765), Fisherwick in Staffordshire (*c.* 1768), Temple Newsam in Yorkshire (1767), Claremont in Surrey (1770), Benham Park in Berkshire (*c.* 1772), Trentham in Staffordshire (*c.*1773), Tixall in Staffordshire (*c.*1773), Brocklesby in Lincolnshire (1773), Cardiff Castle (1777), Cadland in Hampshire (1777), Berrington in Herefordshire (1778) and Nuneham Courtenay in Oxfordshire (1780).[52] This is in addition to the numerous designs for stables, service ranges and the like that the pair prepared, as at Heveningham in Suffolk in 1775. The scale of Brown's activities in this respect was so great that, towards the end of his life and in the immediate aftermath of his death, they came in for particular criticism, most notably from James Paine in the second edition of his *Plans, Elevations, and Sections of Noblemen's and Gentlemen's Houses* of 1783. Paine drew attention, in particular, to Brown's lack of formal training or wider education, referring to him obliquely as one 'who, after being from his youth confined against his nature, to the serpentine walks of horticulture, emerge, at once, a compleat architect, and produce such things, as none but those born with such amazing capability, could possibly have done'.[53] But several years later Humphry Repton, in the Red Book for Panshanger in Hertfordshire, commented that 'In the dispute betwixt him and Pain [sic] the architect, the latter seemed to have the advantage because Brown has left nothing in writing, but if we compare the houses built by each, we shall discover that Brown has left many good specimens of his skill while Paine never built a house that was comfortable without alteration.'[54] Modern scholars like Robert Williams have echoed such sentiments, noting that while Brown's architecture was 'competent and conventional', it might have been more favourably received by posterity had his activities in this respect not been so greatly overshadowed by his fame as a landscape designer.[55] In 1805 Repton not only further defended Brown's reputation in this respect, but explicitly associated the character of Brown's landscapes with his role as an architect, famously noting that

> It has been objected to my predecessor, Mr Brown, that he fancied himself an architect. The many good houses built under his direction, prove him to have been no mean proficient in an art, the practice of which

he found, from experience, to be inseparable from landscape gardening.[56]

It is not surprising that a man so involved in the design of houses should consider so carefully their place in the wider landscape. Indeed, in Brown's designs the architecture of the mansion was consciously emphasized by removing to a distance, or hiding through the careful planting of trees and shrubs, all its necessary and often extensive accessories – service buildings, yards, stables, kitchen gardens and the like. While we often think of hahas primarily as a way of providing uninterrupted views from the pleasure ground into the park, their role in enhancing the view the other way – of the house, set in a landscape of open simplicity – was perhaps more important. Brown's contract for Weston in Staffordshire, drawn up in 1765, stipulates that the example here should be of 'Sufficient depth to keep out the Deer and hide the appearance of the Wall *from the park in general*' (our italics).[57]

But Brown's emphasis on parkland – on landforms and planting, on entire landscapes and the position of the mansion within them – was not associated with any diminution of interest in gardens and pleasure grounds. He continued to provide clients with spaces for flowers, shrubs and ornamental trees. Lady Sophia Shelburne described how, on a visit to Blenheim in 1766, she 'walk'd about the Garden and saw the work of Mr Browne . . . just before the windows is a pretty clump of flowers call'd a French basket'.[58] His design for Lowther Hall in Cumbria, drawn up in 1771, typically included 'A Place for the Flower Garden' (illus. 65); while at Heveningham, one of his last commissions, a visitor in 1784 described a flower garden immediately to the

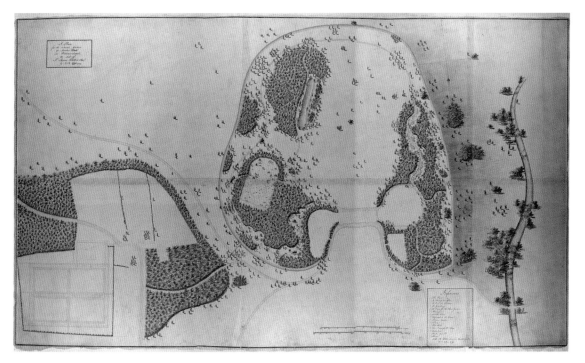

65 Brown produced two designs for Lowther Hall in Westmoreland, in 1763 and 1771. This, the latter, a 'Plan for the intended Gardens', is largely concerned with the area around the house and has a key which notes the position of, amongst other features, the sites for a flower garden and a menagerie.

east of the house.[59] Indeed, at places like Kimberley in Norfolk (1778) gardens and pleasure grounds were sometimes extended out, as linear shrubberies flanking serpentine paths, far into the surrounding park (illus. 66).[60] There was thus no simple shift, through Brown's career, from pleasure grounds to parkland. Both Lowther in Cumbria and Kimberley in Norfolk have two surviving plans, one from the mid-1760s and one from the 1770s, and at both places the first deals with the entire park, while the second is concerned mainly with pleasure grounds, kitchen gardens, hot walls and the like (illus. 67). It was with Brown's mature works in mind, rather than his earlier career, that Uvedale Price was later to comment: 'Mr Brown has been most successful in what may properly be called the garden, though not in that

part of it which is nearest the house', describing how the 'modern pleasure garden with its shrubs and exotics would form a very just and easy gradation from architectural ornaments, to the natural woods, thickets and pastures'.[61] Given that the 1760s and '70s was the golden age for the importation of flowering shrubs from America and elsewhere, as Laird and others have shown, it would indeed be strange if Brown's continued success had depended entirely on the composition of parkland scenes exclusively using native turf and indigenous hardwoods.[62] Writing about English gardens in 1784, the year after Brown's death, the French visitor Rochefoucauld commented how

Near the house, usually all round it, is what they call a garden. It is a small, well tended

66 Brown produced two plans for Kimberley Hall in Norfolk, in 1763 and 1778. The latter, shown here, was mainly concerned with the area around the house, and lying between the house and the lake. It featured a ribbon of pleasure ground which extended from the house, past the kitchen garden, to the lake edge. Here there was to be a bridge, providing access to the island, and beyond, to the woodland on the far shore.

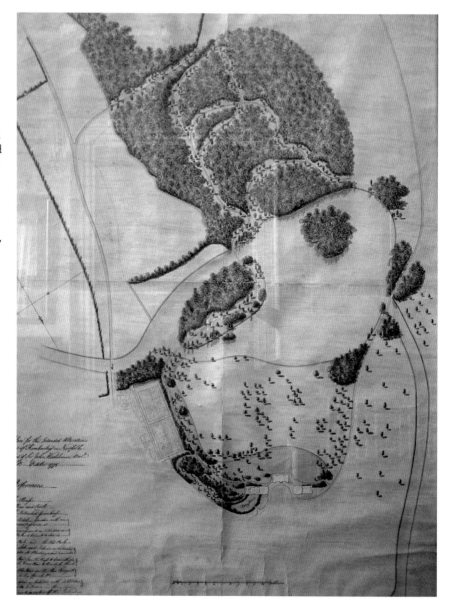

place for walking: there are little gravel paths, well-rolled, the grass is cut every week . . . Nor are flower beds forgotten, and always separated from the park by superb, well-made fencing.[63]

It is often said that the haha separated the grazed ground of the park from the mown ground of the pleasure grounds, but at larger residences, of the kind where Brown was usually employed, the sheer size of the latter suggests that this distinction may be too sharply drawn. Those at Moor Park, for example, seem to have extended over more than 15 hectares, while the area lying within the haha at Bowood covered nearly 40 hectares, and at Chatsworth more than 50.[64]

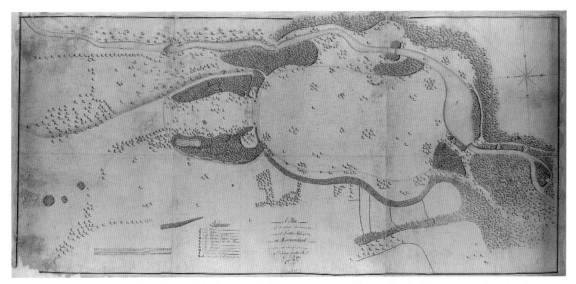

67 Brown's first plan for Lowther Hall, of 1763. The Rococo patterns of his earlier designs are gone but the shapes of shrubberies and plantations have an almost abstract character, reflecting in large part the configuration of the underlying land forms.

The amount of labour required to maintain such extensive lawns, in this pre-lawnmower age, would have been phenomenal, and it is not surprising to find evidence that this was in part achieved through carefully controlled grazing. The estate archives at Chatsworth, for example, record payments to 'Sam Furness and his boy for tending sheep in the Gardens'.[65] This said, the maintenance of shrubberies, flowerbeds and grass at places like these demanded large teams of labourers, Thomas Jefferson estimating that fifty men were employed in Brown's pleasure grounds at Blenheim in 1786.[66]

The capabilities of landscape

Brown's designs, unlike those of his successor Humphry Repton, were usually presented to the client, and to some extent presumably conceived, in plan form, rather than as perspective views. Only rarely, and mainly towards the start of his career, did he prepare pictures of his proposals, and these were generally elevations of buildings and structures. In part this preference for a plan view may have been due to the fact that, from the early 1760s, his landscapes were designed to work as a continuum, or at least as a whole series of experiences, and less as a few 'set piece' views. At the same time, the totality of the top-down plan perhaps expressed the mastery of the landscape that was necessary to bring out its latent 'capabilities', and also, perhaps, to inspire the confidence of customers. Drawing out the natural beauties latent in a scene involved, in addition to the construction of carefully placed buildings, the planting of trees – individually, or in clumps and belts; the manipulation of land forms; and, where possible, and usually associated with this, the creation of lakes or other water bodies.

It is sometimes suggested that Brown and other creators of landscape parks acted with remarkable prescience, planting trees and woods that they would never live to see reach maturity. To some extent this is true, and contemporaries often emphasized the intended rather than the actual impact of planting, Lady Shelburne thus describing Brown's plantations at Bowood in 1765 as 'very young but promising'.[67] Yet, leaving aside the fact that even oaks grow more rapidly than is often thought, easily achieving a height of 20 metres in twice as many years, we also need to remember that the 'improvers' frequently made good use of the trees already growing in the landscape. They were raw materials that constituted a major part of the 'genius of the place'. Sometimes woodland was judiciously thinned to leave a few parkland specimens; alternatively, vistas and prospects could be sculpted from continuous areas of woodland, as for example at Ashridge in Hertfordshire, where the 'Golden Valley' to the north of the house was created by removing trees at the base of a dry Chiltern valley and leaving the woodland, with carefully scalloped margins, on the upper valley sides. It is still a stunning sight (see illus. 108).[68] At Langley in Norfolk Brown's activities, in the mid-1760s, included the expansion of an existing deer park at the expense of Langley Wood, an area of ancient semi-natural woodland that lay immediately to the north. Brown's plan shows that the wood was to be thinned to leave an abundance of free-standing trees; sections were retained to form clumps.[69] More usually, existing woods, often of some antiquity, were connected by additional planting to form the perimeter belt, the shape and extent of the park thus emerging from the hints provided by the existing landscape. Pope had earlier described how the joining of 'willing woods' was one important aspect of consulting the 'genius of the place'.[70] At Bowood, for

example, much of the perimeter belt shown on Brown's plan of 1763 already existed, as discrete blocks of woodland interspersed in the fields, on an estate map made in that same year. As late as 1805 a survey of the park was still distinguishing between the 'old woods' and the 'plantations' made at the time of Brown.[71]

Much use was also made of free-standing farmland trees, principally hedgerow timber and pollards.[72] These were retained when the hedges were removed, although usually not in such numbers that they clearly stood in lines, and the active cutting of pollards – a practice which was generally regarded as barbarous by the upper classes by the 1760s and '70s – was usually brought to an abrupt halt.[73] One commentator described how Peper Harow House in Surrey 'stands in a Park formed of Inclosures laid together by Browne, the Hedge trees well clumped and the other plantations growing particularly well'.[74] Retaining old trees in this way gave a spurious air of antiquity to the newly created scene. As William Gilpin said of Cadland in Hampshire, the 'abundance of old timber gives the house, tho' lately built, so much of the air and dignity of an ancient mansion that Mr Brown, the ingenious improver of it, used to say "it was the oldest new place he knew in England"'.[75] In all this, Brown and other improvers worked to enhance the natural beauties of the site, to add, or subtract, judiciously so that its underlying essence was revealed. Almost all eighteenth-century parks contain trees older than the park itself, but in some cases these now dominate the landscape, as in Brown's Shortgrove in Essex. Short of bole and often hollow in the middle, old pollards from former hedgerows were of little interest to timber merchants when later generations of landowners fell on hard times and were obliged to harvest their parkland timber (illus. 68).

All this said, Brown's commissions (and those of other park-makers) often involved the planting of many hundreds, if not thousands, of new trees, sourced in a variety of ways: sometimes by Brown himself, using a network of local and national nurseries; often by the estate for which he was working. We usually think of Brown's parks – as opposed to his pleasure grounds – as being dominated by indigenous or naturalized hardwoods, and it is clear that oak, elm and beech, together with sweet chestnut and common lime,

were the most common specimen trees in his parks. But he also made much use of exotics such as London plane and evergreen oak, as well as planting a wide range of conifers, principally Scots pine, spruce and larch, as Kent had done before him. Indeed, the cedar of Lebanon has been described as Brown's 'signature tree'.[76] It is easy to assume that the conifers, at least, were used as 'nurses' or nursery crops in plantations of hardwoods, and to some extent they were, but close examination of Brown's plans often shows them scattered across the parkland turf, as at Kimberley in Norfolk, or grouped into clumps, as at Wimpole in Cambridgeshire (see illus. 84).

68 Corsham Court, Wiltshire. This oak, a former pollard, stands on a slight bank marking the line of a former hedgerow. It was already mature when the park was laid out. Most if not all of Brown's parks, like those of his fellow designers, made extensive use of pre-existing farmland trees.

The same approach was evidently adopted by other designers and Mason, writing in 1768, suggested that the 'greatest fault of modern planners is their injudicious application of *Fir-trees*. – A quick growth and perpetual verdure have been the temptations for introducing them; but these advantages are very insufficient to justify the prevailing mode, which gives them universal estimation.'[77] Conifers were also used to vary the margins of Brown's perimeter belts, as at Burton Constable in Yorkshire, where the minutes of meetings held between him and the estate's agent, Robert Raines, have survived.[78] Here the planting, almost certainly in the park rather than the pleasure grounds, included sugar maples and scarlet oaks, while other trees which – while indigenous – we would today perhaps associate more with gardens rather than parkland were widely established, most notably silver birch, which were purchased in their thousands.[79] Weeping willows are sometimes shown on Brown's plans, gracing the margins of his lakes or rivers, as are what may be balsam or Carolina poplars (illus. 69). The comments of visitors likewise suggest a more varied palette of planting than we generally assume. At Brown's Peper Harow it was noted by one that in the low ground by the lake – some way from the house – 'the plants in general grow remarkably well, especially the Americans which require bog earth.'[80] Most of the conifers and ornamentals used by Brown and his contemporaries not only grow fast, however: they also die young, and to some extent this has served to accentuate the indigenous, 'natural' character of eighteenth-century planting. The cedars which sometimes survive represent the long-lived tip of a rather larger iceberg that has vanished, leaving the longer lived oaks, sweet chestnuts, beeches and limes. The elms Brown so widely planted were, sadly, all lost to disease in the 1960s and '70s.

69 A detail from Brown's second design for Kimberley Hall in Norfolk, 1778, showing the planting by the lake. Weeping willows, conifers and what may be Carolina poplars are depicted. This is an extreme case, but many of Brown's plans show some exotic or coniferous planting.

Particular aspects of Brown's planting have been the subject of some debate among garden historians. The most important argument – because it affects to some extent how his designs were experienced on the ground – concerns the character of his perimeter belts. Most researchers have assumed that these were intended to provide a screen of vegetation, forming a clear boundary between the park and the wider landscape. Where drives wound through these belts, selective views out into the working countryside might be made at intervals, but overall the belt acted – as the alternative contemporary term suggests – as a 'screen'. Against this, John Phibbs has strongly argued that Brown's belts lacked any form of understorey and were intended to be visually permeable. The wider countryside was visible between the stems and beneath the canopy, the trees if necessary being pruned to achieve this.[81] This suggestion, which has implications for how we 'read' Brown's landscapes (as private and inward-looking, or as closely integrated with the surrounding countryside), should perhaps be treated with caution. Most if not all of Brown's belts unquestionably had some kind of planted understorey, coppiced or otherwise, to judge from surviving remains. At Burton Constable the minutes of the meetings between Brown and the agent, Robert Raines, leave little doubt as to the character of such planting, Hall concluding that

> Plantations, mainly the famed shelter belts forming enclosures on the boundary, were generally recommended to be 150–300 feet wide. For these Brown liked the underwood to be retained, thus creating a 'woodland' rather than the 'grove' that John Phibbs

suggests Brown typically designed for this feature.[82]

Mason, writing in 1768, argued against turning 'woods into groves' – that is, removing underwood to leave only timber trees – as a general principle. While agreeing that it gave 'an air of freedom' – that is, of movement – he argued that while a partial opening up, on the edges of a wood, could be beneficial, 'a total destruction of thicket is one of the greatest impediments to design.'[83] The fact that he makes this comment implies, of course, that it was sometimes practised, although the context of his writing may suggest that he was talking about clumps and woods within parks, rather than the belts on their periphery. All this said, many of the perimeter drives shown on the plans drawn up by Brown and his collaborators make little sense unless we assume that sections, at least, lacked a dense understorey, and allowed glimpses into and perhaps out of the park. For while some examples appear to weave in and out of the trees, others run for much of their length along the centre of the belt, suggesting a rather dull experience if both sides were, indeed, flanked by dense coppice or other underplanting, as for example at Brocklesby (1771; see illus. 59). Phibbs may, perhaps, have pushed his argument too far, but some sections at least of Brown's belts must have lacked an understorey.

This, however, does not mean that the boundaries of the park were anywhere visually permeable. It might be possible to see through the trees in places, into the park or out into the surrounding countryside, from a drive running within the belt. Yet at the same time, viewed from within the park – especially from the approaches, or the area around the house – the mass of trees, from a distance, would provide visual enclosure, obscuring views of the countryside beyond. The way that contemporaries discussed the difference between the scenery of the park, and that of the wider countryside, leaves no doubt that most believed they should not be visible at the same time, in the same view. Repton in 1792 condemned as peculiar the practice of some Norfolk landowners to 'unite Lawn with Corn Lands', which he deemed 'a false taste, as I hold them to be incompatible with each other'.[84] But this is not to suggest that landscape parks, whether designed by Brown or otherwise, were invariably enclosed and inward-looking spaces. Where, as at Luton Hoo in Bedfordshire or Castle Ashby in Northamptonshire, a house occupied a particularly commanding position, with views extending for many miles over lower ground, or across a wide valley, this was impossible. The working landscape was, nevertheless, experienced at a safe remove, and where ownership permitted might be embellished with plantations to provide a suitably sylvan backdrop, or to blot out unwanted views, especially of unimproved common 'waste'. A visitor described how the house at Peper Harow in Surrey, where Brown designed the landscape in the late 1750s, 'commands good views of the country in general, as well as its own home grounds', but the 'extensive heaths' in the distance had been 'sufficiently shut out' of the prospect.[85]

Just as Brown's planting schemes sometimes made use of pre-existing trees, so his water bodies were often created by joining or expanding earlier areas of water, such as canals or fishponds, as at Longleat in Wiltshire, Newnham Paddox in Warwickshire or Madingley in Cambridgeshire,

or mill ponds, as at Benham Park in Berkshire. Whether created like this, or made entirely from scratch, they were essentially formed by the simple method of erecting a dam across a watercourse so that water was ponded back behind it. This was a method which had long been understood, employed in the construction of mill ponds and large fishponds for centuries, and – since the 1710s – for ornamental lakes within parks.[86] Depending on topography, one, two or more separate bodies of water might be created, usually in such a manner that they appeared to be a single lake or 'serpentine river', the dams between them often hidden by bridges. At Fawsley in Northamptonshire, for example, the steep fall of the valley ensured that Brown was able only to make a string of lakes. Appearances were manipulated in other ways. The ends of the lakes were thus often concealed by planting, to provide an illusion of still greater size.[87]

For all their supposedly 'natural' appearance, Brown's lakes were alien impositions on the landscape, for outside parts of Cheshire and Shropshire, and the 'Broads' district of East Anglia, very few natural water bodies of any size actually existed in lowland England. Lakes were unnatural in other respects, often being highly engineered. Dams were complex features, usually incorporating some device to allow the lake to be emptied for maintenance as well as mechanisms to control the outward flow of water – it was imperative that the water levels remained relatively constant throughout the year – and to cater for spates after heavy rain. Brown's contract for Melton Constable in Norfolk in 1764 typically stipulated that he should supply the dam with 'a proper plug'; that for Petworth in 1756 bound him to 'make a proper plug and Trough to draw down the Water, as likewise a Grate for the discharge of waste water'; while that for Bowood noted that there should be 'Plugs, Grates and wastes for the discharge of floods'.[88] Many of Brown's dams had an ornamental cascade on the lower side, as at Charlecote; others, as at Fisherwick, were disguised as 'sham bridges'. Some, like those of his contemporary designers, had a thick layer of clay on the lake side, covered by a pitching of stones, but sometimes there was a thick central core of clay, especially where the lake had to support the heavy rockwork of a cascade.[89] Diagrams surviving in the archives at Bowood House, presumably for the dam retaining Brown's great lake there, show the typical asymmetrical profile of the structure, with a longer and gentler slope towards the lake and a sharper and shorter one away from it, and also the complicated 'plug' mechanism, consisting of a stout vertical timber housed in a brick-lined chamber that, when lifted, opened an outflow channel at the base of the dam.[90] Lakes were engineered in other ways. Even where the local geology was impermeable, a measure of 'puddling' with clay was sometimes required to ensure that the lake held water, usually comprising several layers of rammed clay. At Kimberley in Norfolk and elsewhere bypass channels were provided to reduce silting (contemporaries were as aware as modern owners of the problems caused by the inflow of sediment, one describing how the construction of Brown's lake at Peper Harow 'will be attended with some difficulty to secure it from choking by the sands that are continually washed down').[91] Some of the more complex lakes, as at Bowood, had small but separate water bodies at their upper ends, retained by small dams or slipways, which could act as silt traps.

Not all of Brown's designs included a lake. Some parks lay on dry uplands, like Beechwood in the Hertfordshire Chilterns, without streams or rivers running through them. In other cases bodies of water optimistically proposed by Brown remained unmade. They were either never begun, or were abandoned at an early stage as hopeless or prohibitively expensive, as perhaps at Langley in Norfolk. At some places rivers running through parks could not easily be dammed because their floodplains were too wide or for other reasons. At Chatsworth, the Derwent was prone to considerable variations in flow (often flooding the surrounding land in winter months) and had incised a deep channel in the floor of a much wider floodplain – all together posing insoluble problems of hydraulic engineering. Here, as elsewhere, the river was simply widened by constructing weirs to form a 'long water' (illus. 70).[92] Water features like this might be created for other reasons, as when a house occupied a low-lying site, so that it would have been flooded by the construction of a true lake, as probably at Audley End in Essex (illus. 71). In some cases, as at Corsham in Wiltshire, there was no watercourse that could be conveniently dammed, and Brown's proposed lake was to be fed from a number of small streams and springs. This was the situation at Cusworth near Doncaster, where memoranda and plans survive relating to construction of three lakes in the 1760s by Brown's contemporary and occasional rival Richard Woods.[93] A detailed survey was first made of the site and boreholes sunk to ascertain the disposition and depth of underlying clay deposits; undulations in contours, many the result of previous agricultural use of the site, were smoothed and other changes to the landforms

70 Aerial view of Chatsworth Park, Derbyshire, showing how the river Derwent was ponded back behind weirs to form a 'long water'.

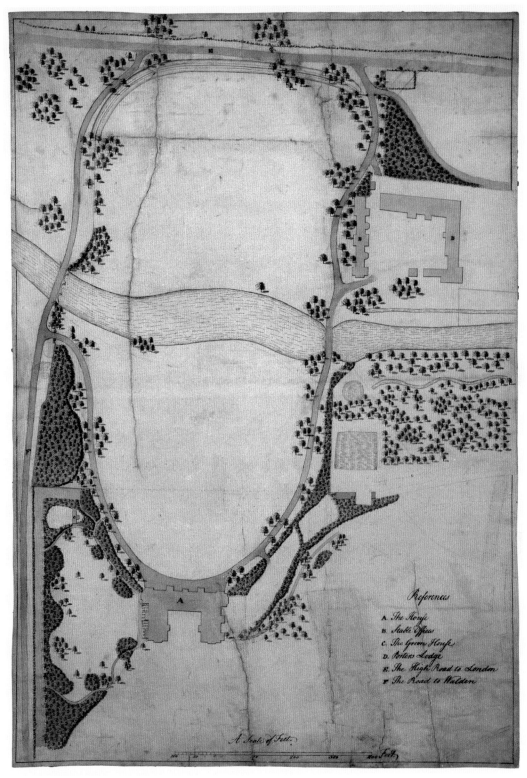

References

A. The House
B. Stable Offices
C. The Green House
D. Porters Lodge
E. The High Road to London
F. The Road to Walden

A Scale of Feet.

71 Brown's plan for Audley End, Essex, 1763, shows the river Cam widened into a narrow lake. At the top of the plan, the 'High Road to London' has not been screened by planting but is instead bounded by a sunk fence or haha. This would be one of the last plans prepared by William Donn for Brown before he left in that year (his watercolour of Audley End House would be engraved and published by Watts in 1779).

carried out before strenuous efforts were made to channel water from springs and field drains via an extensive system of channels and culverts. The various dams here were particularly complex structures, that between the upper and middle lakes incorporating a rock arch that formed the entrance to a boathouse; a cascade; and sluices for controlling water levels. It had deep foundations and stone walls supporting an inner core of clay, 'not too stiff or too soft'.[94] Some improvers went to particularly strenuous attempts to obtain a lake in unpropitious circumstances. One at Westwick in Norfolk in the 1770s employed 'two Archimedean Screws, to raise a sufficient Supply from a large Reservoir below to the Summit of the Hill'.[95]

Brown's ideal, and that of his contemporaries, appears to have been for the house to look down on water placed at a reasonable distance, with turf sloping uninterrupted from one to the other (illus. 72). But sometimes a mansion occupied a low-lying site – often an early house, of sixteenth- or seventeenth-century date, such as Burghley – so that lakes of necessity lay in uncomfortable proximity. The lake created by Brown's collaborator Nathaniel Richmond at Beeston St Lawrence in Norfolk in the mid-1770s lay so close to the mansion that within a few years it was demolished and rebuilt on higher ground.[96] Conversely, houses perched above particularly wide valleys – such as Luton Hoo in Bedfordshire or Shortgrove in Essex – might be positioned so far from the lake that it was hardly visible from them, especially if the house was located a little way back from the valley rim, although as at Luton Hoo, extensive grading of the contours might ameliorate this deficiency to some extent. Elsewhere the level character of the terrain, the absence of

any clearly defined valley, caused problems, as at Melton Constable in Norfolk, where Brown's lake, created in the mid-1760s, lies nearly a kilometre to the south of the house.

Whether (as was normally the case) formed by simply ponding the waters of a stream or river back behind a dam, or by the more complex method of channelling water from a variety of sources into an otherwise dry natural valley, the classic serpentine shapes of eighteenth-century lakes mirrored the natural contours. The lake emerged, as it were, from forms inherent in the landscape; Brown and his contemporaries simply brought them out. But nature often needed an extra helping hand: the contours were often graded and the lake sides slightly excavated, partly to give greater coherence and definition to the form and partly to ensure the visibility of the water from the house, or from approach drives. The shape of the lake was usually agreed with the client and then staked out on the ground prior to construction, and minor modifications were then made to the land surface to ensure that the water filled back to this line, or for other reasons. The contract drawn up for Trentham in 1759, for example, describes how Brown was to 'make the whole Water in Shape and Size according to the Stakes put in for that Purpose, forming its Edges quite round and making them correspond with the Ground on each side'; that for Bowood in Wiltshire stipulates that he was to 'make a good and sufficient head to cause the Water to flow in such a shape and manner as is agreed to by his Lordship'.[97] At Trentham it was also stipulated that the sections of the river Trent not being incorporated into the proposed lake were to be filled in and parts of the adjacent meadows raised and levelled.

72 Kimberley Hall, Norfolk, showing the classic Brown design feature of an expanse of smooth turf extending uninterrupted from house to water.

Comparison of the shapes of lakes shown on Brown's plans with their forms as executed indicates that Brown either surveyed the land very carefully prior to staking out or had an astonishingly good eye for contours. Sometimes, however, such a comparison indicates that modifications were made to the shape originally envisaged: at Cusworth, certainly, Woods informed his foreman that the shape of the upper lake, as staked out, was to be modified if it transpired that the water could not be seen from the upper floors of the mansion. Here, typically, the lawns leading down to the water's edge were shaped and smoothed, 'and to make it more beautiful some

soft swells may be left or formed where the stakes are placed'.[98]

Movement of earth and subsoil – to smooth ground, open up views, obliterate earlier field boundaries, fill fishponds and basins, level terraces and generally erase the scars left by formal gardening or earlier agricultural use – was an important part of Brown's designs, more so perhaps than in those of his many rivals, because he tended to work for the kind of wealthy client with the cash to pay for this most expensive of improvements. Brown's landscapes, to this extent, erased all signs of earlier history, as well as all aspects of local character. In some sense they were earth sculptures, expressions of smooth, abstract form. Levelling and earth-moving was followed, as both estate accounts and Brown's contracts make clear, by careful reseeding. The majority of such activity, even in Brown's later works, was directed towards the immediate vicinity of the mansion, which is today usually surrounded by an archaeological lacuna, devoid of earthwork traces of the pre-park landscape. The earthworks known as 'ridge and furrow', marking the plough-ridges in open fields, thus survive well across much of the park at Burghley, but are muted or obliterated altogether in the area around the house; they similarly cover most of Chatsworth's park, except in the area of Michael Milliken's earth-moving, near the house and between it and the widened river.[99] The smoothing of the ground surface between mansion and lake or 'broad water', as here, was a particularly important feature of Brown's activities. At Himley in Staffordshire, where Brown worked in the 1770s, there is a 'steady level gradient a quarter mile or more in length running from the house to the water'.[100] Often this is the main or even the only area where the sources suggest that earth was moved: Lady Shelburne, describing the works at Bowood in 1767 following the completion of the lake, noted: 'The work they are now upon is levelling the Lawn before the House to the Edge of the Water.'[101] Sometimes, as here, substantial alterations were made to the ground surface to ensure a clear view of the lake and the lake edge; sometimes the intention was simply to create a smooth, even surface. What is so striking about such endeavours is that, until we are told that this great effort has been made, we would often not know it. Vast amounts of money and labour were invested in activities that, because they served to bring out the inherent capabilities of a landscape – the hints for improvement, suggested by the topography – are often scarcely noticeable.

How original was Brown?

Although ostensibly focusing on the development of Brown's own style, the preceding paragraphs have begun to refer to the work of other contemporary designers, such as Richard Woods or Nathaniel Richmond. As we have already noted, Brown himself designed only a small proportion of the landscape parks created in England in the second half of the eighteenth century. It is customary to describe other landscape gardeners, even those with extensive practices, as Brown's 'imitators'. Yet it is hard to demonstrate that at any stage in his long career Brown was creating landscapes much different from those produced by his contemporaries. His style, as a number of writers have already argued, was not simply his own invention, but something more widely shared.[102]

Brown's early work – before the 1760s – was thus very similar to the Rococo garden designs which were being created around the same time by the three Greening brothers, Thomas (c. 1710–1757), John (1715–1770) and Robert (d. 1758). They were the children of Thomas Greening senior (1684–1757), who was the Duke of Newcastle's gardener at Claremont, and who worked with William Kent on the redesign of the grounds there in the 1730s, deformalizing parts of the landscape earlier created by Charles Bridgeman. Together with his son Robert, Greening took over the maintenance of Richmond Park following Bridgeman's death in 1738, and by 1743 was running a nursery at Brentford in Middlesex that was well enough known to be specifically labelled on John Rocque's map of the *Environs of Syon House* which was published in the same year.[103] From 1754 Thomas junior was given charge of both Kensington Gardens and St James's Park; Robert worked for a time as head gardener for Princess Augusta at Kew, and also prepared drawings for Philip Yorke for Wimpole in Cambridgeshire in 1752; while John became Master Gardener at Hampton Court, a post he retained until he retired in 1764, when he was succeeded by Brown himself.[104] The brothers' style, as exemplified by Thomas Greening's plan for Corsham Court in Wiltshire of 1747, or Robert Greening's design for Wimpole (see illus. 82), was informal and irregular, with serpentine gravel paths and shrubberies. It has been compared to the designs created by Batty Langley but is a world away from them, flowing and without significant geometric elements. Its remarkable similarity to Brown's own style is clear when Thomas's design for Wimpole is compared with Brown's for Ingestre in Staffordshire (1756) or Badminton in Gloucestershire (*c.* 1752) (see illus. 42, 43). It might be argued that the Greenings were largely concerned with pleasure grounds and shrubberies close to the mansion whereas Brown was already, by the 1750s, making changes to the wider parkland, creating lakes and levelling ground that separated them from the mansion. Yet design at this scale, as we have seen, was not in itself new, and here the obvious comparison to be made is with some of William Kent's designs from the 1740s, for places like Euston in Suffolk, or with his sketches for a proposed new house at Esher Place in Surrey, already discussed (see illus. 36, 37). Brown's use of highly defined circular

clumps in his early work is reminiscent of Kent's 'ten of spades' style of tree planting at places like Holkham.

Brown's work in the early stages of his career is also comparable with that of Sanderson Miller, the west Midlands 'gentleman architect', advocate of 'Gothick' and garden designer through the 1740s and '50s, as evidenced for example by Booth's plan for the gardens he designed at Wroxton Abbey in Oxfordshire, drawn up in *c.* 1750.[105] Brown was almost certainly influenced by him, and the two men were acquainted from at least 1740.[106] His treatment of the wider parkland is also closely similar to that seen in the work of Francis Richardson, who ran an extensive landscaping practice through the 1750s and '60s. Richardson was an east Midlands man – he was born at Duckmanton in south Derbyshire in 1698, married Mary Edoe in Cuckney, Nottinghamshire, in 1751, and was living in Worksop, where his son Francis was baptised, in 1758 (he died shortly afterwards but a second son, also Francis, was christened there in 1760). Much of his work was in the Nottinghamshire 'Dukeries', where he prepared designs for Worksop Manor and Welbeck in 1748 and for Thoresby in 1760 (illus. 73). But he also undertook commissions further afield across northern England: at Normanby Park in north Lincolnshire in 1756, at Kirklees Park in Yorkshire in 1757, at Blagdon near Newcastle in 1755, at Cannon Hall at Barnsley in 1760, as well as at Lowther in Cumbria and Atherton near Manchester.[107] It has been suggested that Richardson had a connection with Stephen Switzer, and this may well be correct, but his designs were more radical than Switzer's, clearly mirroring Brown's compositions in their flowing lines and irregularity. It is true that they still displayed a measure of stiff, residual geometry, but so too did Brown's own designs in the 1750s.

The way in which, by the late 1750s, Brown was making the house the central feature in a landscape largely emptied of geometric planting, with gardens relegated to a subsidiary position, was also at times anticipated by earlier designers. In the 1730s Charles Bridgeman produced a design for Brocket Hall in Hertfordshire featuring a landscape of elegant minimalism, completely

stripped of avenues, without any overall formal structure and with residual geometry subtly implied by block planting (illus. 74).[108] Here, as in other places by the 1730s, enclosures and courts were removed from one of the main facades of the mansion, so that it looked out directly over open parkland. Some landowners in the first half of the century, perhaps with particular architectural interests or particular pride in their houses, went further. Raynham in Norfolk was an

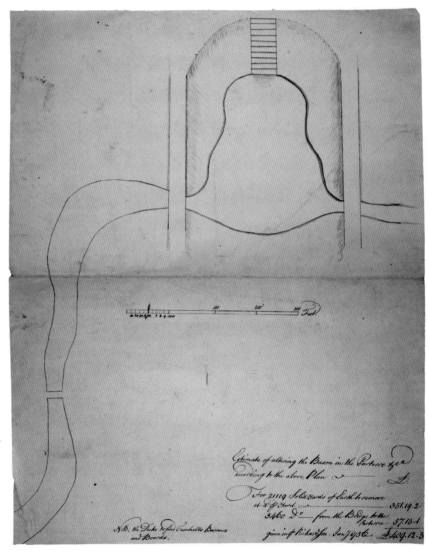

73 Francis Richardson's plan and estimate for 'altering the bason' at Thoresby, Nottinghamshire, 1756. The resultant serpentine lake is closely comparable to the kind of water body being created by Brown in the 1750s.

74 Charles Bridgeman's remarkably minimalist design for Brocket Hall's park in Hertfordshire, undated but probably *c.* 1735, seems to anticipate aspects of Brown's landscapes.

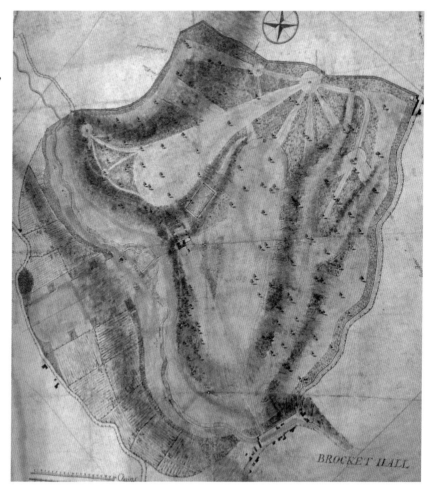

BROCKET HALL

innovative mid-seventeenth-century house, its design strongly influenced by the first wave of Palladianism, which was further transformed by William Kent in the late 1720s. One visitor in 1730 described how the house stood 'in an handsome Park, a River flowing by it', adding: 'there are no gardens here'.[109] Another, two years later, reported that the house stood 'free of all walls'.[110]

As we have suggested, it was only from around 1760 that the style we associate with Lancelot Brown fully emerged. By this time, however, other designers were producing very similar landscapes. Some, as we shall see, were former contractors and associates of Brown, most notably Robert Robinson, Thomas White, Adam Mickle and Nathaniel Richmond. The latter was perhaps the most successful in the south of England, while White dominated in Scotland and the north. Richmond worked with Brown at a number of places, including Moor Park in Hertfordshire, but as early as 1759 was receiving payments on his own account from Sir Kenrick Clayton of Marden Park in Surrey. He went on to establish a large business, his style continuing to develop in parallel with that of Brown, displaying only minor differences of emphasis, and these arguably in response to client briefs or site variables, rather than a consequence of real aesthetic differences. More important, perhaps, is the fact that similar designs were created by men with little or no connection with Brown's nexus. One was William Emes, who was born around 1730 but who first comes into the historical record in 1756, when he became gardener to Sir Nathaniel Curzon at Kedleston Hall, near Derby. Curzon was updating the landscape that had been created by Bridgeman in the mid-1720s and in 1758 a young Robert Adam, newly returned from his Grand Tour, 'got the intire management of his grounds put into my hands with full powers as to Temples Bridges Seats and Cascades'.[111] He produced a remarkable plan that seems to pre-empt Brown's mature style in terms of its complete rejection of geometry and its bold, flowing lines (see illus. 98). Adam subsequently took over from James Paine and Matthew Brettingham as architect for the new house here, and as designer of its interiors. Emes left Kedleston in 1760 but must have spent two

years working quite closely with this rising star of architecture, at a place that would set the style for the next decade in the way that Stowe had done for the previous one. Emes's parks – which he continued to create into the 1780s, mainly but not exclusively in the west Midlands – are again broadly similar to those of Brown: different in detail, perhaps, but no less 'naturalistic' in appearance (illus. 75).

Another independent designer of note was Richard Woods (1715–1793), who may have begun his career as a nurseryman at Chertsey in Surrey in the 1740s, subsequently working with Philip Southcote on the design or planting of the *ferme ornée*, or ornamental farm, at nearby Woburn Farm.[112] His earliest commission was at Buckland House in Oxfordshire in 1758, followed by Hartwell in Buckinghamshire in 1759. His career peaked in the late 1760s, and tailed off somewhat through the late 1770s and '80s, although he was still working – on a design for Stanway in Essex – when he died in 1793.[113] As we shall see, his designs often followed a rather different path to those of Brown, harking back

75 Design for Oakedge Park, Staffordshire, by William Emes.

in some ways to the Rococo gardens and *fermes ornées* of the period before *c.* 1750. But he was capable of producing very 'Brownian' landscapes, as for example at Wivenhoe in Essex (illus. 76), although as Fiona Cowell has suggested he was always more confident when dealing with smaller areas, with gardens and pleasure grounds, and was perhaps less bold in his use of large sheets of water than either Brown, Richmond or White. Of the various other surveyors and improvers who were apparently independent of the Brown nexus, but who were producing very similar work at around the same time, we should note in particular Samuel Driver and John Davenport. The former was a Kentish nurseryman whose design for Belhus in Essex of 1764 shows a remarkably assured and modern touch, and who prepared designs for places as far afield as Hillington in Norfolk in 1773 and Adlestrop in Gloucestershire in the early 1760s, at the latter

place perhaps working on the gardens at the same time as Sanderson Miller was working on the house.[114] Davenport, also a nurseryman but from Shropshire, had a large business which undertook not only the supply of plants to places as distant as Beechwood and Aspenden in Hertfordshire, but the design of a number of landscapes in fashionable 'Brownian' mode, especially in the West Midlands, from the 1760s into the '90s, including Croughton and Batsford in Gloucestershire.[115] Some of his commissions appear to have been on a similar scale to those of Brown himself. Between 1770 and 1783 he received no less than £4,000 from the Earl of Darlington for work at Raby Castle in Northumberland, and he was employed by Warren Hastings at Daylesford in Gloucestershire in 1790–91 to design a new pleasure ground, although he was apparently dismissed before his design was executed.[116] In short, rather than see Brown as an innovative pioneer, forging a

76 The lake and surrounding landscape at Wivenhoe Park, Essex, designed by Richard Woods, as depicted by John Constable in this oil of 1816. The site is now occupied by the University of Essex.

brand new style which other landscape gardeners, less able than he, copied and adapted, it is perhaps more useful to think of him as one of many talented designers who – building on the work of the previous generation – gradually developed a shared grammar of design through the middle and later decades of the eighteenth century. There may have been distinctive aspects of Brown's own landscapes, but many of these probably reflect the fact that his clients generally had more money to spare than those of other designers, especially to devote to such expensive improvements as earth-moving. His contemporaries also had particular stylistic idiosyncrasies regarding, for example, the termination of lakes and other water bodies. But it is the overall similarities, rather than the differences, which are most important, and most striking.

Consuming landscape parks

Brown's later landscapes, and those of his contemporaries, were experienced and consumed – as emphasized earlier – through movement along drives and rides as well as, perhaps more than as, a series of static views from the house and its immediate vicinity, or from other defined vantage points. But the buildings that were now more sparsely and widely scattered through the landscape, strung as incidents along the rides and drives, were also places of resort, where owner and visitors could take tea, converse and amuse themselves, as well as enjoy the prospect. When Caroline Lybbe Powys visited Chesterfield she 'drank tea in one of the buildings', and 'the family being very musical and charming voices, the young ladies sang', to the accompaniment of the gentlemen, on flutes.[117] Many such buildings,

like those in the gardens of the 1730s and '40s, contained facilities for making tea and preparing food. Other features on the circuit included menageries – collections of exotic animals – which had been a feature of some aristocratic parks (like Woodstock) since the Middle Ages. These were popularized in the late seventeenth century by the particularly elaborate example at Versailles, but increased greatly in numbers on English estates in the course of the eighteenth century.[118] Monkeys, zebras, wolves and big cats of various kinds were particularly popular as denizens. Brown designed examples at Petworth, Ingestre, Temple Newsam, Melton Constable, Cole Green, Lowther, Coombe Abbey and elsewhere, each comprising housing for the animals and, more importantly, buildings to accommodate the owner and his entourage of visitors when they came to inspect them.[119] That at Coombe was located far from the house and included an elaborate pavilion that still survives, probably designed by Henry Holland and inspired by that at Versailles. At Melton Constable, in contrast, the menagerie took the form of an oval brick enclosure attached to a seventeenth-century standing or hunting tower, now suitably Gothicized by Brown, which was located a short walk across the park from the mansion. At Lowther in 1771 the proposed example lay within the pleasure grounds, close to the mansion (see illus. 65).[120] At one level menageries were simply intended for amusement, as a hobby and as a display of status, for exotic animals were worth a lot of money. There was an active trade in them, which served travelling shows as much as aristocratic gardens. (Suppliers were not always reliable. In about 1730 Charles Lennox, Duke of Richmond, complained in a letter about a recent acquisition:

'I wish indeed it had been the sloath that had been sent me, for that is the most curious animal I know; but this is nothing but a comon young black bear, which I do not know what to do with, for I have five of them already'.)[121] But, like the collections of exotic plants in stoves and pleasure gardens, menageries also served to display aspects of new worlds revealed by European expansion. They represented in miniature the wider world, of far-flung trading contacts, from which the wealth to sustain landscaped grounds was now increasingly derived.[122]

Some of the larger eighteenth-century parks appear to have been de facto open to 'polite' members of the public. Caroline Lybbe Powys described in 1760 how, in the park at Edgcumbe in Cornwall, she arrived at a 'little temple', which had been 'fixed upon by a party of gentlemen and ladies, who came that day on a scheme of pleasure to Mount Edgecombe, as a place to enjoy in the most rural manner the cold collation they brought with them'. Others were open to the public on a more regulated basis, only on certain days. Holkham in Norfolk, where Brown or one of his team was responsible for remodelling the pleasure grounds, was open from at least 1760 on 'every Tuesday, but no other day. No persons will be admitted that do not tell their names.'[123] In 1788 a visitor described how he 'Went what they call the home circuit, with some of the ladies and gentlemen. This is a little tour to see the grounds, different vistas etc. Rode on horseback.'[124]

The lake at Holkham, originally created in the 1720s but altered by William Emes in the 1780s, had boats that, according to Repton in 1789, were 'properly rigg'd and dress'd in their colours on public days'.[125] Most if not all of the lakes designed by Brown and his fellows were used for sailing, and boats are frequently depicted on them, like those shown on Neale's engraving of Heveningham Hall in Suffolk (illus. 77), and on an early nineteenth-century map of Brown's park at Redgrave in the same county (illus. 78). As Kate Felus has emphasized, boats were a more familiar and more important feature of life in the eighteenth century than today, a major mode of internal as well as foreign travel, as well as being symbolic of England as a great trading nation and a military power. Sailing and rowing were obvious forms of recreation. 'On lakes and pools in designed landscapes, vessels came in a wide array of sizes, styles and colours; from the simple rowing skiff to scaled-down men-of-war and highly decorative yachts and galleys designed to complement the architecture of the garden or park.'[126] It is noticeable that areas of water were given irregular and serpentine forms much earlier than other aspects of designed landscapes, as Wendy Bishop has demonstrated, and it is possible that this may have been motivated by the increasing popularity of recreational sailing.[127] Kate Felus has described how, at Wrest in Bedfordshire, Brown's 'adapted lake, which encircled the gardens, would have been more conducive to easier, and probably more exciting, boating in larger vessels than the straight canal of the earlier gardens' (see illus. 48 above). Shortly after Brown worked here an elaborate rowing boat with chinoiserie decoration was commissioned, and launched on the water in 1766.[128] Such boats were a common feature of the middle decades of the century: examples include the 'Chinese Junk' that in the 1780s was sailed on the lake created by Richard Woods at Brocket Hall in Hertfordshire, but which had originally been constructed for the waters at Popes Hall, a few kilometres to the

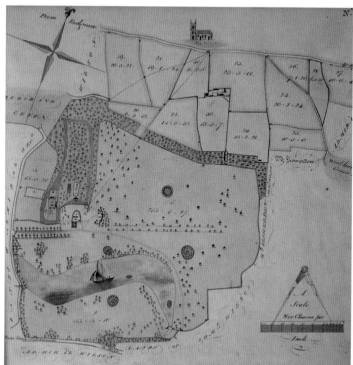

77 'Heveningham Hall in Suffolk', in William Watts's 1780 engraving from *Seats of the Nobility and Gentry* . . . (1779–86).

78 Redgrave in Suffolk, as shown in an estate map of 1804, with a large boat sailing on Brown's lake.

south.[129] Some lakes were used to stage *naumachia* – mock naval battles, in imitation of those held by the ancient Romans – for the amusement of visitors.

Whether the parks created by Brown or his imitators were much used for shooting in the eighteenth century is a more debated issue. A number of writers have suggested that landscape parks continued, like the deer parks from which they in part developed, to be major venues for recreational hunting. To Robert Williams, the landscape park was 'a private larder . . . a sylvan arena for blood sports'; to Timothy Mowl, 'the sporting element . . . had at least as much to do with Brown's minimalist tendencies as any conscious drive towards aesthetic elegance'; while Jane Brown has noted how the eighteenth-century park served 'the contented state of mind of the country sportsmen'.[130] But when Brown's distinctive style was emerging in the 1760s, shooting was still a relatively informal affair, rather different from the well-organized and competitive activity it was to become by the early nineteenth century.[131] The role of the park as a hunting ground has recently been challenged by John Phibbs, who has emphatically denied that Brown designed his landscapes with shooting in mind.[132] Yet game birds were certainly encouraged and protected in some at least of Brown's parks, as at Blenheim in Oxfordshire where, in 1787, John Byng saw 'in various parts of the park . . . clusters of faggots around a coop, where are hatched and reared such quantities of pheasants that I almost trod upon them in the grass'.[133] The various pieces of anti-poaching legislation passed in the first half of the eighteenth century, such as the Black Act of 1723, appear to assume not only that game was kept in parks, but that it

was principally to be found there. Shooting was already a central feature of country life and it is hard to believe that Brown transformed parks in ways that ensured that they could no longer function, in part, as game reserves for their owners. At a time when the sport remained a fairly casual affair, and when it was normal courtesy to allow polite neighbours to shoot over one's land, parks may also have provided a place where game could be reserved for the owner and his guests, and it is noteworthy that one foreign visitor noted in the year after Brown's death that

> General custom . . . has established a mutual understanding between all those entitled to shoot that a man leaving his own property can go right ahead and shoot anywhere without getting into trouble with the owner provided he doesn't enter the owner's parkland. The rules of polite behaviour prohibit this positively.[134]

When the park at Fisherwick, where Brown worked in the 1770s, was put up for sale in 1808 it was said to be 'abundantly stocked with deer and other game'. It is unlikely that this was a recent development.[135] Brownian parks made good places to rear and protect game, for clumps and narrow belts made excellent cover for the pheasant, a bird of the woodland edge;[136] while concentrating game in defined areas, protected by lodges, would have provided security against poaching, an activity that increased significantly in the second half of the century.[137] It is perhaps doubtful whether the form of the landscape park was critically shaped by such considerations. Yet given the importance of shooting in contemporary rural life, it is equally hard to believe that this important activity played no part in the emergence of the landscape style.

As well as being used for recreation, the landscapes created by Brown and other designers also had important economic roles, which doubtless encouraged their popularity among the lower ranks of the propertied class especially. Parks had to be grazed to be maintained, more usually now by sheep and cattle than by deer, and some sections were also mown as hay meadows. While in some circumstances more money could certainly have been made by ploughing them up and growing arable crops, the empty sweeps of turf were not entirely a waste of money.[138] The grazing of livestock had long been considered a more effortless, gentlemanly form of agricultural production than cultivation.[139] Although the rapid rise in population after *c.* 1750 placed a particular premium on cereal crops, the price of livestock products held up well, with demand coming especially from urban areas. For families like the Strutts in Essex, the production of meat was a profitable business that provided the capital to create Terling Place, with its fine park designed by Nathaniel Richmond. The fact that parks were often densely clustered in the vicinity of major towns and cities is worth remembering here. The largest population centres, such as London, required substantial quantities of hay to feed the vast number of draught horses kept there. Many examples were located in what was already becoming the 'hay belt' around London, where fodder production was a major activity.[140] Parks formed a major part of the 'home farm' and provided places where the gentry and aristocracy could indulge a fashionable interest in livestock improvement in this age of agricultural 'revolution'. Writing several decades after Brown's death,

the land agent John Lawrence commented that 'There cannot be more interesting objects of view, in a park, than well-chosen flocks and herds, nor more appropriate to the rural scene than their voices', later adding that the park, with the home farm, should be 'a theatre for the display of *all* the notable varieties of experimental husbandry'.[141] Indeed, the larger parks created by Brown, such as Langley or Melton Constable in Norfolk, had quite extensive areas under arable cultivation within the perimeter belt, although always at a distance from the mansion, and out of sight of it. As Repton was later to comment, 'we never see a park ploughed up, but we always attribute it to poverty'.[142]

Parkland plantations also had an economic role, forming part of the wider forestry activities on an estate. Landowners were obsessed with trees, and tree planting, in the eighteenth century. This enthusiasm is sometimes presented as something entirely new but in reality it represented an intensification of a much longer association, of ownership and forestry, extending back into the Middle Ages. Because only large landowners could afford to put tens or hundreds of acres out of cultivation by planting woods, sacrificing short-term returns for long-term profit, tree-planting was always considered a peculiarly elite activity, and thus symbolic of status. It is nevertheless true that interest in trees and woods increased markedly in the eighteenth century: partly as a consequence of the enclosure of marginal land, ripe for afforestation; partly because of the rising value of wood and timber; and partly because landowners were inspired by the writings of men like John Evelyn, whose book *Sylva, or a Discourse on Forest Trees* of 1664 was followed (and sometimes plagiarized) by a rash of similar texts, including Stephen Switzer's *Ichnographia rustica* of 1718. There was widespread concern that timber supplies were running dangerously low, Batty Langley in 1728 for example stating that 'our nation will be entirely exhausted of building timber before sixty years are ended'. Men like Philip Miller, James Wheeler, Edmund Wade and William Hanbury were also concerned, like the Whig government itself, about the implications of a timber shortage for Britain's naval power and commercial fleet.[143] Large-scale planting was thus a patriotic act, and in a wider sense planting trees demonstrated confidence in the future, and thus in the new political dispensation brought about by the Restoration and the Glorious Revolution. Only those who expected to pass on a property to their children and grandchildren would plant over it. Landowners planted woods to beautify their estates and to demonstrate their extent, and also to provide cover for game. But, important though these symbolic and recreational aspects undoubtedly were, tree-planting was also intended to make money.[144] While it is true that trees in the more visible areas of parkland would not have been managed primarily with economics in mind, money could nevertheless be made from the repeated thinnings of the nurse crop planted in clumps and belts, for trees were generally closely planted in eighteenth-century plantations – to suppress weed growth and because high rates of loss were expected – and they were thinned early and then repeatedly. The more remote areas of the larger parks were unquestionably managed primarily as forestry enterprises, as were the less visible portions of the perimeter belts, with much of the timber being felled (and then replanted) when it was eighty or ninety years old – in the case of Brown's plantings, in the middle decades of the nineteenth century.

Place-making

In the foregoing paragraphs we have fallen back into the old trap of discussing the work of Brown, and that of his fellow improvers, almost entirely in terms of the landscape park. It is therefore important to repeat once again that Brown in particular was as active in the garden and pleasure ground as he was in the park; that he designed many new country houses, and made numerous alterations to existing ones; and that he built new stables, greenhouses, cottages and occasionally farms. At places like Kimberley Brown's 'improvements' extended to the construction of a new drying yard, for the hall's washing; at Longleat in Wiltshire he constructed new fishponds within the kitchen garden; at Beechwood in Hertfordshire and Castle Ashby in Northamptonshire he constructed ice houses, the latter 'in a very Expensive manner and place'.[145] Indeed, he and his team could supply all the facilities required for a polite life in the countryside. Brown was, in his own words, a 'place-maker', not simply a designer of parks and gardens, and the same was true of most contemporary designers.[146]

One aspect of all this, often ignored, is Brown's involvement in land drainage, especially although not exclusively in those parts of the park lying in the vicinity of the mansion, between the mansion and the lake, or beside the principal drives.[147] In some cases, parallel sets of underground brick-built barrel drains were employed to this end; more usually he used so-called 'bush' drains, trenches cut a metre deep into the ground, backfilled with brushwood and covered over with soil, a cheap and surprisingly durable method. Drainage formed a part of many, perhaps most, of his commissions and was a concern from the earliest years of his career. The second agreement made with Viscount Weymouth at Longleat in Wiltshire in 1758 thus stipulated that Brown was to 'trench all the untrench'd Parts of the Ground on the outside of the Kitchen Garden and to drain it, wherever it wants it, with Stone Drains to convey the same into the above mention'd Stews' [fishponds]. He was also to 'drain all the ground between the ... sunk fence and the water and to Level the Same ... also to drain & level the Ground on the Lodge Side of the Water which his Lordship desired might be done this Season (Viz.) that Part which is visible from the Door'.[148] At Melton Constable in Norfolk – a park located on particularly damp and tenacious clay – drainage is mentioned in two of the seven clauses in the contract of 1764. The third clause stipulates that Brown was to 'make all the roads within the park ... and to drain all the wet parts where the roads are to go through'; the sixth, that he was to 'drain all the wet parts within the plantations on the sides of the drives and to make the walk or drive quite through the Plantation'.[149] Such concerns seem to have been shared by Brown's principal associates and competitors. Contemporaries, as we shall see, found damp, waterlogged or 'moory' ground, and lowlying, damp locations more generally, distasteful. In part because lakes, 'long waters' and cascades are more obvious features of the landscape – and more clearly related to 'garden design' – than drainage schemes, they have received more attention from garden historians, but the significance of the latter was not lost on contemporaries. At Croome, the monument put up by

Lord Coventry to celebrate Brown's achievements still bears the inscription:

> To the Memory of
> Lancelot Brown
> Who by the powers of
> His inimitable
> And creative genius
> Formed this garden scene
> Out of a moras.

Another striking and neglected aspect of Brown's work was an active involvement in the design of kitchen gardens. It is often stated that he was hostile to walled gardens and, insofar as any still remained in front of the main facades of the wealthy residences where he worked, this is true. As part of this antipathy it is said that he usually removed kitchen gardens far from the house. In reality, the situation is more complex. The fashion for moving these necessary features out of sight, to distant and inconvenient locations, was not initiated by Brown but had first emerged in the early decades of the eighteenth century. We noted earlier how one commentator described, as early as 1732, how Raynham Hall in Norfolk already stood 'free of walls'. He went on to describe how 'These my lord pulled down and made his kitchen ground and fruit garden, quite out of sight of the house upon the decline of the hill.'[150] Conversely, Brown himself often designed kitchen gardens. They formed part of the 'package' that he supplied at Castle Ashby, Charlton, Knowsley, Luton Hoo, Melton Constable, Newton Castle, Stansted Park, Tottenham Park and elsewhere. At Basildon in Essex the new kitchen garden was the only thing he appears to have provided.[151] Moreover, far from invariably placing them far from the house, Brown often constructed them close by, and provided them with direct access from the pleasure grounds. At Melton Constable in Norfolk the contract drawn up in 1764 with Sir Jacob Astley includes the clause:

> Article the 4th To make and plant all the intended kitchen and pleasure garden in all their parts, as also the sunken fence to enclose them, Sir Edward to be at all the expenses in walls and fence to the Pleasure Garden, the sinking of the ground excepted.[152]

The kitchen garden was built only a hundred metres to the east of the house, just beyond the stableyard, and the pleasure ground was wrapped round it and connected to it by a door. The wording of the agreement clearly implies that the two were, indeed, seen as part of a single 'package'

(illus. 79). Similar arrangements are clear at many of Brown's landscapes, such as Coombe Abbey in Warwickshire (illus. 80).[153] Other kitchen gardens designed by Brown, like that at Castle Ashby, were similarly placed; where an existing kitchen ground already lay close to the house, it was usually incorporated into the landscape design in this same manner, as at Heveningham in Suffolk. At Kimberley in Norfolk one of the two surviving Brown designs, that were drawn up in 1778, proposed a long, narrow pleasure ground which flanked a walk leading down to the lake, where a bridge provided access to further walks on an island (see illus. 66). Although this ribbon of shrubbery and ornamental planting could have been laid out to the north of the main vista leading from house to lake, it was instead made to the south, so that it ran straight past the kitchen garden, which had occupied a semi-isolated position – some 250 metres to the southeast of the hall – for several decades.[154] Brown provided

79 The kitchen garden at Melton Constable Hall, built in the mid-1760s, was one of many designed and built by Brown and his team.

it with a new subdividing wall, a 'hot' wall with internal flues and four stoke holes (see illus. 104). At Burton Constable in Yorkshire in 1773 Brown's plans seem to have included the creation of a gravel path 1.8 metres wide, leading to the kitchen garden; a similar walk seems to have been planned at Longleat in 1758.[155] Kitchen gardens could evidently form part of the polite landscape, even if their external walls were carefully screened by planting, especially of evergreens like yew, from view of park and pleasure grounds. Repton was later to praise the recreational role of the kitchen garden and to describe how 'there are many days when a warm, dry but secluded walk under the shelter of a north or east wall, would be preferred to the most beautiful and exposed landscape, and in the early spring . . . some early flowers and vegetables may cheer the sight'.[156] Kitchen gardens played an important economic role, supplying households with fresh fruit and vegetables throughout the year, but they were also objects of display, where owners delighted in the latest technologies – like the hot wall at Kimberley. Some also functioned, like the nearby pleasure grounds filled with exotic plants, as what Muckerji has decribed as 'living maps' of colonial relationships; they expressed, in Finch's words, the 'global reach of capitalistic trading systems and the role of particular families within them'.[157] The hothouse or 'stove' at Harewood was thus full of specimens of exotic plants brought from the Lascelles family's plantations in Barbados (see p. 18), including bananas, palms and the 'water lemon' *Passiflora laurifolia*.

Isolated kitchen gardens are indeed also found in Brown's parks, sometimes retained from earlier phases, sometimes (as at Chatsworth in Derbyshire or Charlton in Wiltshire) apparently

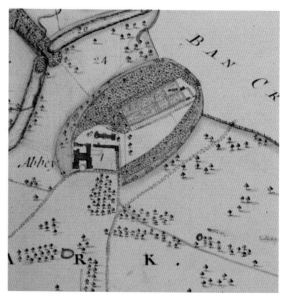

80 Coombe Abbey, Warwickshire: detail from an estate map of 1778, showing the typical way in which Brown wrapped his pleasure grounds around the kitchen garden.

constructed as part of the wider 'improvements' effected by Brown himself. But they were usually accessed directly from the main approach or (as at Charlton) from a circuit drive running around the park's perimeter. Even in these locations it is therefore unclear whether the kitchen garden was really being tucked away from the polite gaze. It is possible that just as Brown took the ornamental buildings which, in the early eighteenth century, had been densely clustered around the mansion, and scattered them more widely across the landscape, beside the gravelled drives, he similarly removed the walled garden from the vicinity of the house, yet made it a feature on a more extensive circuit.

Whether kitchen gardens were used as an extension of pleasure grounds, or regarded primarily as a productive space, is perhaps less important than the simple fact that Brown's activities frequently involved improving them, just as he was prepared to supply designs for greenhouses (as at Kimberley, Ashburnham or Burghley), stables, outbuildings and ice houses or to undertake large-scale drainage schemes. Brown could provide his clients not only with a fashionable home set in an elegant landscape, but with a range of well-designed facilities, suitable for a comfortable lifestyle in the countryside. In this as in other ways he was indeed a place-maker more than just a landscape architect or garden designer. And the same, to varying degrees, was true of his colleagues and rivals – of all the Capability Men.

THE STYLE OF landscape design we usually associate with Lancelot Brown did not emerge, fully formed, at the start of his career. It developed over time. To begin with his designs were focused on the pleasure ground, and the immediate vicinity of the mansion, more than on the wider parkland; they coexisted, to varying degrees, with older geometric features like avenues; and they contained numerous ornamental buildings and built structures. Most of his work in the wider landscape was focused on making lakes, and with the area lying between these and the house. By the late 1750s careful consideration was being given to approaches, but it was only in the course of the 1760s that his style matured. The whole landscape, especially experienced through movement, became more important than a limited number of points or views within it; buildings became sparser, and more subservient to the overall design; and the thoughts and emotions of visitors were stimulated not by the emblematic or associative power of particular prospects or features but by the overall topography, the raw

forms of which were embellished, following careful observation, by planting and the judicious alteration of the contours. The house became the principal garden building; the views towards it, from the proliferating rides or the main approaches, of key importance. Yet Brown and his associates and competitors were always more than creators of parkland and pleasure grounds. They provided designs for new houses and/or their interiors, or they worked closely with others who did so. They installed schemes of land drainage, constructed kitchen gardens, built stables and ice houses and provided, in Brown's own words, 'all the elegance and all the comforts that Mankind wants in the Country'.[158]

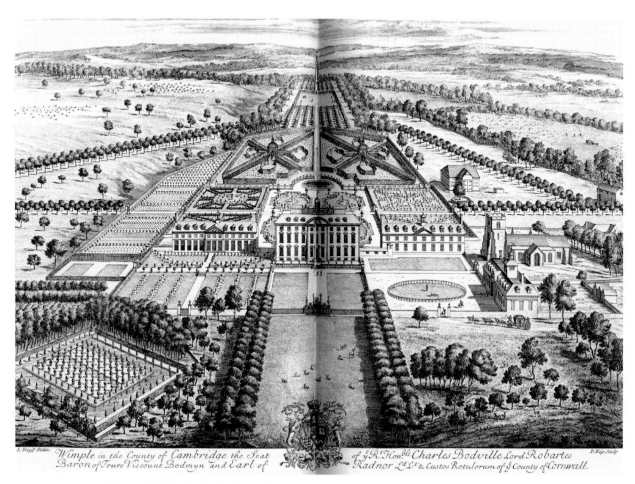

Wimple in the County of Cambridge the Seat *of ỹ Rt Honble Charles Bodville Lord Robartes*
Baron of Truro Viscount Bodmyn and Earl of *Radnor Ld Lt & Custos Rotulorum of ỹ County of Cornwall.*

81 Wimpole Hall, Cambridgeshire: the great geometric landscape, depicted by Kip and Knyff in
Britannia illustrata, 1707.

FOUR

The Brown Connection

IN ONE SENSE, whether Lancelot Brown did or did not invent the style of landscape design with which he is usually so closely identified is of little importance. For its popularity, like that of other styles of landscape and garden design, is best understood not as a reflection of the particular genius, but as the outcome of wider social, economic and ideological developments. It was the landowner who needed to be convinced that what was offered was worth buying, and he that pays the piper calls the tune. Styles of garden and landscape design must therefore reflect the shared lifestyle, attitudes and income of the class that commissioned them, more than the particular interests and concerns of the designers themselves, and a concentration on the former only provides at best half the story. These are matters to which we shall return at a later stage. A concentration on 'great names' in landscape history has, however, other problems. It is often assumed that Brown and his contemporaries were routinely responsible for the creation of entire parks as set pieces – that these were generated as works of art by single acts of genius. However, as we have already emphasized, neither Brown nor any 'improver' in the mid-eighteenth century usually created entire landscapes from scratch. All were

called upon to do so from time to time, but they were more often commissioned to expand, update or modify an existing park or garden, the scope of their work limited to a specific area or element of the landscape by the brief drawn up by the client. Frequently the design was then further interpreted by capable executive improvers or 'foremen' on site. The designer Nathaniel Richmond thus worked closely with John Hencher at Shardeloes in Buckinghamshire and at Saltram House in Devon, the former drawing up the broad plan but the latter providing the details.[1] The extent to which any eighteenth-century park can be described as the work of a single improver, in the sense that he personally was responsible for the entire design, in all its details, is thus limited. Most must, to varying extents, have been joint or team efforts. Most, moreover, are demonstrably palimpsests, multi-period artefacts where even the contributions of the great Capability Brown are underwritten, partly erased and overwritten, and sit alongside elements written in a range of hands: some surviving from earlier periods, some contemporary with his career, some made after his death.

Wimpole in Cambridgeshire, where Brown was active from 1767 through to 1772, provides a good example of this kind of complexity. An excellent estate plan of 1638 shows the countryside around the old manor house with roads, villages and both enclosed fields and extensive areas of open-field arable. The map was made shortly before a major transformation of the landscape took place: a substantial new house was built here by Sir Thomas Chicheley between 1640 and 1650, which was then extended between 1660 and 1710 by Sir John Cutler and by his son-in-law, Charles Robartes, 2nd Earl of Radnor.[2] During this period, in the 1690s, George London created the large geometric landscape recorded in Johannes Kip and Leonard Knyff's *Britannia illustrata* of 1707 (illus. 81). Much of the geometry of London's scheme remains today: the southern avenue (originally of elm, but comprehensively replanted with lime following its destruction by Dutch elm disease in the 1970s); the lines of the cross-axial avenues; and the main vista extending north from the house.

Charles Bridgeman, whose gardener father was associated with the improvements at Wimpole under George London and who himself served as an apprentice with London and Wise at Brompton Park, was the next improver to work at Wimpole, in the 1720s.[3] By this time the estate had been acquired by Edward Harley, son of Robert Harley, Queen Anne's Lord High Treasurer, whose wife Lady Henrietta Cavendish Holles had inherited it from her father, the Duke of Newcastle.[4] Bridgeman expanded London's basic geometry further into the countryside, creating the remarkably long southern avenue, and establishing new wildernesses, with fashionable winding walks, to the south of the Hall. As part of Harley's circle of friends, which included Matthew Prior, James Thornhill, James Gibbs and Alexander Pope, Bridgeman was a regular visitor to Wimpole until his death in 1738.

In 1740 the Wimpole estate was sold to Philip Yorke, who was Lord Chancellor from

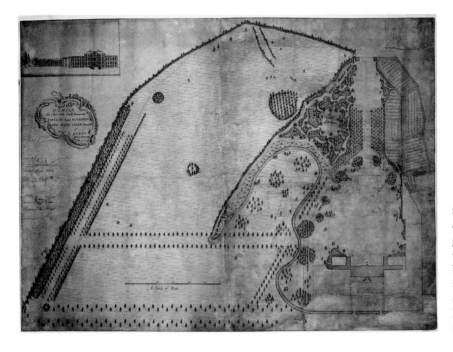

82 Robert Greening's design for the pleasure grounds at Wimpole Hall, Cambridgeshire, 1752, can be usefully compared with the roughly contemporary designs by Brown at Ingestre and Badminton (illus. 41 and 42).

1737 until 1756 and was created Earl of Hardwicke in 1754, and in 1752 the designer Robert Greening prepared plans for the removal of geometric parterres to the north of the Hall and their replacement with a fashionable Rococo garden. His design, as we noted earlier (and as Fiona Cowell has observed before us), is closely comparable to the plans being prepared by Brown at around the same time for places like Ingestre in Staffordshire or Badminton in Gloucestershire (illus. 82).[5] Greening also planned a new walled kitchen garden, to be placed in relative isolation to the north of the house, and proposed taking down the walls around the main gardens in order to open up views towards the north. Meanwhile, in the years between 1749 and 1752 Sanderson Miller – the 'gentleman' architect and garden designer whom we have already encountered on a number of occasions – made several visits to Wimpole and prepared drawings for a ruined castle, typical of his style and of his interests in indigenous antiquity. This was to occupy a site on

Johnson's Hill, over a kilometre to the north of the house, at the termination of Bridgeman's northern vista (illus. 83).[6] Its construction was not, however, immediately initiated, and from 1756 Miller himself suffered from increasing bouts of mental illness and did not really carry out any significant work after 1760.

When Brown was called to Wimpole by Lord Hardwicke in December 1767 he thus arrived at a place where the landscape had undergone a series of major changes over a relatively short period of time. Indeed, it is worth emphasizing that London and Wise's elaborate parterres had still formed the principal ornament of the grounds a mere four decades earlier, a space of time equal to that which separates us from the mid-1970s – the age of punk rock and Callaghan's government, well within living memory to those of us now in later middle age. More importantly, the grounds had even more recently undergone major alterations and modernization at the hands of Robert Greening – less than fifteen years before.

Hardwicke, in his initial approach to Brown, asked him to prepare 'the plan of operating for next year', and to estimate costs for what was considered to be the commencement of a three-year contract.[7] Although Hardwicke's agent wrote to Sanderson Miller on several occasions, there is no evidence to suggest that the latter was involved in the construction of the castle, which was now at last begun, and it was this that formed the focus of Brown's work in the north of the park, although he may also have been responsible for modifying Greening's garden to the north of the hall (illus. 84). The stream running through the north end of the park was dammed to form

a new lower lake, to the east of an existing complex of fishponds which were now amalgamated and serpentized. The resulting water body lay directly across the axis from the house to Miller's castle. The work was supervised on Brown's behalf by Thomas Biesley, to whom Brown made regular payments from 1756 until 1772, with a further payment to his wife, Susanna, of £7 in 1773.[8] The couple appear to have resided permanently at Wimpole during these years. Brown's involvement at Wimpole continued until the early 1770s, when his account book notes: 'Earl of Hardwicke, Wimpole, July 1772 Rec'd the Balance of all Accts. Excepting what is doing

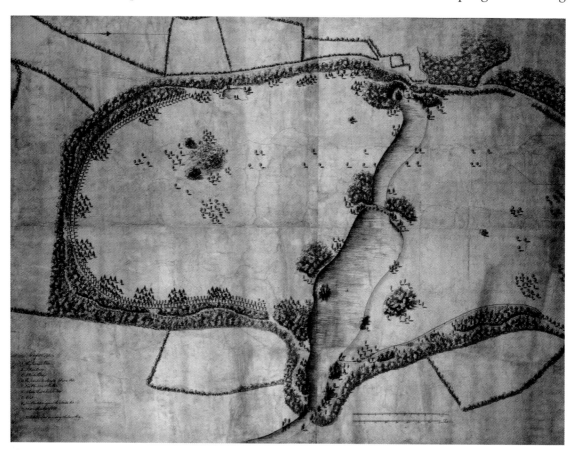

84 Brown's design for the North Park at Wimpole Hall, 1767. His activities were restricted to the area around Miller's 'castle'. Note, to the left, the clumps of conifers ranged on the inner edge of the perimeter ride.

at the tower & what has been done there by Beesley.'[9] Biesley's son was baptized in 1769 at Newport in Essex, although he and his wife were themselves described in the register as 'of Wimple in the County of Cambridge':[10] it is possible that Biesley had some connection with Audley End or Shortgrove, sites where Brown advised in the 1760s, both of which are within a mile of that town.

Within eighteen years of the completion of Brown's design, in 1790, further major works were underway at Wimpole, this time under the direction of William Emes, Brown's Midlands-based competitor (see p. 118). He demolished the kitchen garden that Greening had created to the north of the house and in its place made a new walled garden, together with new pleasure grounds and walks, in a position some way to the north-east, but linked to the north front of the hall by an ornamental walk. His proposal for a new serpentine lake to the south of the house was not, however, adopted. A few years later, in 1801, Repton produced a Red Book for Wimpole but most of his proposals appear to have been rejected. They included a recommendation that one of the double rows of trees framing the view to Miller's castle, which had probably been planted by Bridgeman, should be removed; a suggestion that the gardens to the north of the house should be enclosed by railings; and a plan to reintroduce there a geometric terrace, with formal flower beds.

Wimpole is in many ways a typical case. Although it features in most books as a 'Brown landscape', Brown's work was in fact largely limited to the north of the park and, although extensive, was essentially envisaged as a setting for a major ornamental building designed by somebody else. The landscape around the hall developed in a fairly piecemeal manner during the eighteenth century under a number of different improvers, each usually dealing with specific areas and often removing features only recently created by their predecessors, features which in many cases can scarcely have reached maturity. Of course there were many occasions where Brown had a freer hand, as we have seen. But Wimpole is a useful reminder that contemporaries did not necessarily regard him as a pre-eminent genius who should be given complete liberty to exercise his art. Nor did they necessarily believe that employing him precluded the acceptance of further contributions from other designers. At nearby Audley End in north Essex, similarly, Brown, Richmond and Woods were all employed within the space of thirty years, each carrying out different and defined programmes of work. Brown may have been the most sought-after landscape designer in the 1760s and '70s, and he could certainly choose which commissions to take up and which to reject. But he may not always have been the first choice of a wealthy landowner keen to implement 'improvements'.

The Brown business

Brown was a remarkably busy man, and potential clients might have to wait several years for him to visit their parks. He often held initial meetings with them in London, subsequently visiting them at their country seats, although sometimes the initial meeting took place at the seats themselves, Brown making a visit while undertaking work at some neighbouring estate.[11] He would then walk or ride around the land, pointing out potential improvements; further discussions would take place and the brief would be agreed, together with terms to proceed with survey and design work. Brown was a personable and knowledgeable individual and, by the time that his career was taking off in the 1750s, he knew the business of improving property from bottom to top. He was extremely well-connected, in terms of both trade contacts and client networks. And he was evidently well-endowed with the social skills necessary to converse with his elite clients on affable terms, many contemporaries emphasizing his charm and wit as much as his abilities as a designer. Chatham famously described how 'you cannot take any other advice so intelligent or more honest.'[12] The ability of an individual from a relatively lowly background to advise the aristocracy and, to an extent at least, lay down the parameters of correct taste is in itself a reflection of the degree to which social barriers, between the upper and middling ranks of society, had been lowered with the emergence of polite society. But not entirely: there are hints that Brown's easy manner did not always go down well with the more traditional members of landed society, especially in the early years of his career. In October 1756 Spencer Cowper advised his brother, who was employing him at Cole Green in Hertfordshire: 'As to Brown's Sauciness, I believe you have nothing to combat it with, but Patience.'[13] There are hints, too, in the sources that he may have intentionally kept clients waiting for his attentions, or for his advice, in order to further engage their interest. At Bowood he visited the 1st Earl of Shelburne in 1757 but carefully avoided giving detailed advice on the grounds, although he stayed for two days, presumably waiting to secure a full contract for the work.[14]

In an entrepreneurial age, Brown was an entrepreneur's entrepreneur. He was an astute businessman with a genius for organizing complex projects, and for making them profitable. But he always had a large number of commissions on the go at any one time, and when he did finally agree to undertake a project, contemporary correspondence makes it clear that he usually made no more than four visits each year to a particular site, often fewer. His progresses were arranged in regional circuits, with Brown spending a few days at each site, reviewing the works and giving instructions. Lady Shelburne of Bowood in Wiltshire typically recorded in her diary how, in August 1765, 'Mr Browne the Gardener came here to dinner . . . staid and spent the evening and giving directions to his Man.'[15] Brown's assistants carried out the survey work, drafted the plans that were presented to clients and actually executed the works. In the same way that a project architect today, working within a large international practice, might be responsible for much of what is presented in the name of the practice principal, so it was that Brown's very 'capable' associates were responsible for much of what was created in his name.

Brown, unlike his 'successor' Repton, did not therefore work as an isolated designer but was the head of an extensive and complex business organization. From the 1750s he was making large but intermittent and variable payments to a range of individuals, many of whom already had, or later developed, careers as architects or landscape designers in their own right (illus. 85). Some of these people worked continuously with Brown over several decades; others for a discrete period of years or, indeed, several such periods. Given the scale of the sums recorded it is clear that

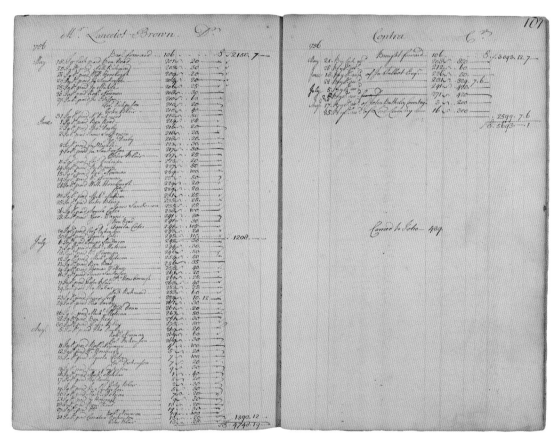

85 The ledgers containing Brown's bank account at Drummonds Bank survive and provide a fascinating insight into his business. This sample two-page spread from 1756 shows payments made to some of the first cohort of 'Capability Men' while the Contra side shows payments received from Lord Coventry and John Talbot.

these do not represent personal payments or salaries. They are better considered as subcontract payments covering the supply of supervision, contract labour and in some instances materials on a flexible, ad hoc basis, according to the needs of each project. Modern historians often refer to such men as his 'assistants' or 'foremen'. Contemporary accounts likewise describe them as foremen but also, significantly, as 'pupils', 'scholars', 'imitators' or 'followers'. The third and fourth of these terms were only really employed in a pejorative manner from the end of the century. In Brown's time 'imitation' did not necessarily

mean slavish copying, but was rather 'a method of translating looser than paraphrase, in which modern examples and illustrations are used for ancient, and domestick for foreign'.[16] Some garden designers in the eighteenth century thus imitated the history paintings of Gaspard Dughet, Claude Lorrain or Nicolas Poussin in another medium, the landscape itself, and in another environment, the English countryside, translating the original in a new way. These artists had themselves 'imitated' the Greek myths and Bible stories, translating them from their original time and setting into seventeenth-century Italy, the home country of neither painter; John Dryden had similarly 'taught Virgil to speak proper English' by translating his Georgics.

> By reading Homer, Virgil was taught to Imitate his invention: That is, to Imitate like him; which is no more, than if a Painter studied Raphael; that he might learn to design after his manner. And thus I might imitate Virgil, if I were capable of writing an Heroick Poem, and yet the invention be my own: but I should endeavour to avoid a servile Copying.[17]

It was in this sense that Brown was a 'follower' of Kent, in part because of his time at Stowe; he was an 'imitator', but certainly not a 'mere imitator', in the sense of an emulator or unoriginal copyist. As Horace Walpole observed in 1751, very early in Brown's career, of his work at Warwick Castle: 'It was well laid out by one Brown who has set up on a few ideas of Kent and Mr Southcote'; later describing him as 'the best imitator of Kent'.[18] Brown's able collaborators should, to an extent at least, be viewed in a similar light. His skilled draughtsmen, for instance, prepared presentation drawings, working up details under Brown's supervision, but nevertheless with their own input. His men on the ground adjusted the details of his planting, or the outlines of his lakes, as circumstances dictated, in a manner not dissimilar to that in which Sanderson Miller seems to have worked with Brown on the new house at Croome – or Zoffany and Richard Wilson worked together on the famous portraits of Garrick.[19] Collaborative work was very much the order of the day.

What largely differentiated Brown from his contemporary designers was not so much the originality of his style as the degree to which his name – his *brand* – became associated with the prevailing Whig elite, the extent of his economic success and the scale of his consequent social elevation. By the time Brown's career was taking off in the 1750s there were a host of other businesses catering to all the propertied levels of society, supplying advice, materials and execution for building and landscape projects large and small. Brown came to occupy the top end of this marketplace, gaining many of the best commissions from the wealthiest clients; but he was far from alone even there. Indeed, on occasions he lost out to rivals, as when Lord Arundel chose Richard Woods's design for the grounds of Wardour Castle in 1764 in preference to that prepared by Brown a few years earlier (although Woods was later replaced here by Brown, in 1771).[20]

Given what we have said about his mode of operation, an important facet of Brown's genius – and one explanation for his success – was evidently his ability to choose the right people to develop and execute his design outlines. Such men were recruited from varied backgrounds. Some came from the ever-expanding nursery business, for nurseries not only provided plants but often offered design advice and labour to customers, if only those dwelling in the locality. Samuel Lapidge and John Spyers, important colleagues in the later stages of Brown's career, both came from well-known nursery families. Others were apparently recruited from the staff of estates at which Brown worked, such as Adam Mickle. The leading improvers outside the Brown nexus had a similar range of origins, with Richard

Woods probably beginning his career as a nurseryman, for example, and William Emes as the head gardener at Kedleston.

Brown's collaborators, having worked with him for varying periods of time, might themselves then go on to develop independent careers, having benefited from the experience, contacts and reputation gained through their work with him – in much the same way that Brown himself had benefited from his association with William Kent. William Donn, one of Brown's first assistants, subsequently became a successful architect; Nathaniel Richmond, Robert Robinson and Thomas White became well-known landscape gardeners, the latter with a career rivalling Brown's own in terms of both the number of commissions undertaken and financial success. This pattern was again replicated with Brown's principal rivals, in a kind of cascade of expertise. Men like Emes and Woods likewise had associates, foremen and assistants, some of whom went on to have their own successful careers, if only on a local level. Samuel Gooch, for example, an individual about whom little is known, arrived in Norwich in February 1764 and announced in the *Norwich Mercury* that 'Any Gentleman that please to make Trial will find their Work faithfully executed in the neatest manner by . . . the above, many Years Foreman to the eminent Richard Woods, Land Surveyor and Designer of New Work.'[21] Emes's associate John Webb moved on to a successful independent practice, as did his foreman at Chirk Castle in 1764, Thomas Leggatt, and another foreman, Charles Sandys, who was advertising his services as a designer in London in 1794 as 'late foreman to Mr Emes'.[22] White and another of Brown's principal collaborators, Adam Mickle, both had sons of the same

name who continued their practices into the nineteenth century.[23]

Brown's network of contacts, and of co-workers, was built up gradually from the time he began working at Stowe. Whatever the character of his experiences in northeast England and Lincolnshire, it is quite clear that working closely with William Kent and Lord Cobham was not merely a formative aesthetic influence on the young gardener, but served as an introduction to a particular political set, 'Cobham's Cubs': disaffected Whigs but for the most part wealthy, and destined to be men of influence. They included the young Pitts, Grenvilles and Lytteltons, all of whom became members of the ruling political elite of the country during the period of Brown's career, beginning with the so-called 'Ministry of Cousins' of 1756. The contacts made among the tradesmen working at Stowe were equally important: the master joiner John Hobcraft, the scaffolder George Payne and William Davis and his company of plasterers all appear later as names in Brown's bank account. And it was at Stowe that Brown probably first learnt the skills of organization and management that underpinned his entire career. As clerk of works his role was to pay and manage the various tradesmen working on different aspects of the garden and its buildings. It was an invaluable training.

It was also at Stowe that Brown first met Sanderson Miller, with whom he was an almost exact contemporary (1716–1780). Miller, as we have already noted, was a minor Warwickshire landowner who inherited his father's estate at Radway in 1737, and who designed a number of gardens and landscapes in the west Midlands, as well as various garden buildings and two country houses, Croome and Hagley. George Lyttelton,

1st Baron Lyttelton, the owner of Hagley, was MP for Okehampton in Devon from 1735 to 1756 and formed part of the Whig opposition to Walpole's ministry. He was thus a close associate of Lord Cobham, and numbered among his friends Alexander Pope, Henry Fielding, James Thomson and Elizabeth Montagu: Miller's diary records, in November 1749, how he spent several days at Stowe in the company of Lord and Lady Cobham, Mr and Mrs Lyttelton and others: and also how, on the 7th of that month, he walked around the grounds with 'the company' and 'Mr Brown' for 'five hours'. In March 1750 he recorded that he had been 'drawing a Plan for Ld. Deerhurst', following the receipt of a letter from George William Coventry, Viscount Deerhurst, requesting a ground plan for a proposed new lodge at Croome. Lord Deerhurst clearly knew Miller well, having been an old student friend at Oxford, and had recommended him to Thomas Lennard Barrett for work at Belhus in Essex in 1745. In 1747 Deerhurst was urging Miller to visit Croome to discuss 'various projects to embellish that untoward place'.[24] Brown visited Miller at Radway in August 1750 and the latter probably recommended him for the post of executive architect for the new house Deerhurst decided to build at Croome after he had succeeded his father as 6th Earl of Coventry in 1751. Miller certainly recommended Brown to his friend Lord Brooke, to take over the work of improving the accommodation and grounds at Warwick Castle in 1749.

Brown's time at Stowe was thus vital in establishing connections, and further useful contacts were made soon after he set up as an independent designer. He prepared designs for Badminton in 1752 and it was there that he met Adam Mickle,

who was head gardener on the estate, and who had previously worked with William Kent on the construction of the Worcester Lodge there. Brown, always on the lookout for talented individuals, recognized Mickle's skill and by 1757 he had left Badminton, continuing to work with Brown until 1765. After a three-year pause the two men again worked together, Mickle now accompanied by his son, Adam junior – an arrangement which continued from 1768 until 1779. The Mickles were in Yorkshire by June 1775, when Adam Mickle junior's daughter was christened at the village of Maltby, close to where Brown was working at Sandbeck Park for Lord Scarborough.[25] Adam Mickle junior had perhaps been in the Yorkshire area for a year or so, working for Brown at Harewood.

Brown also made an important contact at his next major commission, at Warwick Castle. The payments made to Brown in Earl Brooke's account at Hoare's Bank run alongside ones made, from 1749 until 1760, to one Henry Holland. This was Henry Holland senior (1712–1785), a Fulham builder whose success is reflected in his nickname, 'bricklayer to the King'. He was the father of another Henry Holland, who would later marry Brown's daughter, work as Brown's partner and become an important architect in his own right (and employer of John Soane). It may have been as a consequence of working with Holland senior at Warwick, and then again at Croome, that Brown decided to move to Hammersmith, which was near Holland's place in Fulham. Holland was another very well-connected man and Brown, ever the entrepreneur, could always spot a good contact.

Brown constantly expanded his network of able collaborators, and of useful and powerful contacts, over the following years and it was his ability to establish connections and attract able workers, as much perhaps as any intrinsic skill as a designer, which underpinned the phenomenal expansion of his business. In 1753, the first year of his account at Drummonds Bank, his recorded receipts totalled £4,924; by 1768 this sum had risen to £32,279 (the latter figure equivalent to many millions of pounds today).

The Capability Men

Given the importance of Brown's collaborators in the development of the dominant landscape style of the later eighteenth century, and the extent to which past attention has focused almost exclusively on the achievements of Brown as an individual, it might be useful to discuss briefly the careers of some of these men – an exercise which also serves to throw more light on Brown himself. We may begin with two individuals who occupied key positions at the core of Brown's practice as this reached maturity in the 1760s, John Spyers (1730–1798) and Samuel Lapidge (1740–1806). The former undertook most of the draughtsmanship for Brown's survey and presentation plans from 1764.[26] He was the son of Christopher Spyers and the nephew of Joshua Spyers, of the Isleworth and Twickenham nursery dynasty. His father supplied plants to Carlton House in 1736; his uncle to Horace Walpole's garden at Strawberry Hill.[27] Spyers's first survey for Brown was made in April 1764, when he spent 24 days working at Tottenham Park in Wiltshire: he subsequently produced at least 31 further plans and maps for him.[28] After Brown's death he worked for a while with Samuel Lapidge and, in part because he had inherited his uncle's

property in Twickenham and his mother's in Isleworth, evidently died in 1798 a wealthy man.[29] In her will, drawn up in 1810, his wife Elizabeth left all his drawing equipment and his theodolite and stand to their son Joshua.[30]

Samuel Lapidge joined Brown in 1767 and continued his business after his death. He was born in 1741 at Old Windsor, where his father William was a gardener, and in 1759, at the age of eighteen, he was himself recommended by Richard Woods to Sir William Lee for Hartwell in Buckinghamshire as a 'very good gardener'.[31] In 1778 he married Sarah Lowe, daughter of George Lowe, a prominent nurseryman who was the King's Gardener at Hampton Court before John Greening took up the post. He died in 1758 leaving a copyhold estate at Hampton Court Green 'late in the occupation of Henry Wise Esq': the business was continued by his son Robert Lowe, Lapidge's brother-in-law, and his nephew, also George. They supplied plants to Brown on a number of occasions, and also to Richard Woods for his design at Cannon Hall in south Yorkshire in 1762.[32] As Brown worked with the younger Lowes at Hampton Court and was a friend of the family, it seems likely that he met Lapidge through them. Brown and Robert Lowe were the godfathers of Lapidge's son, Edward Lapidge, at his christening in 1779 (he went on to become an architect and a Fellow of the fledging Institute of British Architects).

Samuel Lapidge first appears in Brown's account at Drummonds Bank in 1767, and continued to work with him until Brown's death in 1783, when he was named in Brown's will as his successor in the business. Lapidge, 'who knows my accounts', was to complete any contracts currently in progress. He then worked at

Chalfont and Bulstrode in Buckinghamshire with William Ireland, another of Brown's collaborators, executing Brown's designs. He was also responsible for completing the works at Sandleford Priory in Berkshire, and perhaps at Buckenham Tofts in Norfolk. During his time with Brown he carried out surveys at Wrotham in Hertfordshire (1764), Putney Heath (1774), Berrington in Herefordshire (1781) and Fornham St Genevieve in Suffolk (1781) as well as at Sandleford Priory (1781).[33] He also seems to have undertaken some business on his own, advising the 5th Duke of Devonshire on improvements at Chiswick House in 1778 and opening his own account at Drummonds Bank the following year, receiving payments totalling £1,515 from Rowland Holt of Redgrave, Suffolk, Richard Hoare of Stourhead and others. Even Brown's key associates thus carried on some business on their own account while still in his employ.

We noted earlier the way in which many of Brown's associates had independent careers as gardeners, surveyors and the like before they worked with him; and how they sometimes went on to become significant designers afterwards. One of the most important examples is Nathaniel Richmond, whom Brown may first have met while working at Warwick Castle. Not much is known of Richmond's early life but he was probably born around 1720, as he was described as being 'in the 65th year of his age' when he died in February 1784.[34] Richmond was certainly living at Warwick in 1745, when he married Susannah Neale at Holy Trinity, Stratford-upon-Avon.[35] The removal and simplification of the geometric gardens at Warwick Castle was in progress by 1745, before Brown's involvement there, and it is possible that these works were

originally supervised and directed by Richmond, who had probably already completed his apprenticeship as a master surveyor by then.[36] By 1749 we find him supplying 'beech and larch trees' to Walter Gough of Perry Hall in Birmingham, and his eldest daughter Sophia was christened at Tardebigge parish church – immediately adjacent to the Hewell Grange estate, where both he and Brown were later to work.[37] William Shenstone was a frequent visitor to Hewell and it seems likely that Richmond would have known both him and Sanderson Miller as local architects and garden designers (Miller certainly knew Richmond's in-laws, the Neales, who were fellow landowners at Fenny Compton in Warwickshire).[38]

Richmond's name first appears in Brown's account at Drummonds Bank in April 1754 and in June of the same year his third daughter, Susanna, was baptised at Rickmansworth – the town next to Moor Park, where Brown began working in 1754.[39] It seems clear that Richmond was executing Brown's designs here (as he may already have done at Warwick). Richmond may also have worked with Brown at Syon Park for the Duke of Northumberland, and at Syon Hill for Lord Holdernesse, during the period from 1754 to 1759.[40] The association of the two men was, however, a relatively short one. In 1760 Richmond took out a lease from William Baker, an even more successful London builder than Henry Holland senior, for land and houses at Lisson Green, Marylebone.[41] Here he established a nursery (on what is now the site of Marylebone station) and a base from which to work as a designer. He employed Alexander Cunningham to deal with the nursery aspect of his business, and moved into the house at the nursery, Richmond moving out to live on nearby Bryanston Street on the Portman Estate in Marylebone.[42]

Richmond's first commission after working with Brown commenced in 1759. It was for Sir Kenrick Clayton at Marden Park, Surrey. An estate plan of 1761 shows a new hillside grove with cross walks to the rear of the house, which had probably been designed by him.[43] Clayton paid Richmond £500 between July 1759 and February 1761. The following year he was at Stoke Park, Stoke Poges, in Buckinghamshire where, according to John Penn in his *Historical Account of Stoke Park* (1813), he laid out a new park for his father, Thomas Penn. A design had been prepared by Brown for a previous owner of the property, Lady Cobham, in 1750 and it has been suggested that Richmond was simply executing and updating this.[44] But according to Britton and Brayley in their *The Beauties of England and Wales* of 1801 the lake there 'was originally formed by Richmond', and it seems more probable that Richmond was following his own design.[45] Like most of the Capability Men, Richmond knew how to handle bodies of water, and in 1763 he began two major projects which both involved the creation of large informal lakes: at Danson Park near Bexley in Kent and at Shardeloes near Amersham in Buckinghamshire.

At Danson Park he was employed by Sir John Boyd, the son of Augustus Boyd, originally from Northern Ireland and owner of several sugar plantations in the West Indies. Sir John, elevated to 1st Baronet Boyd in 1775, was Vice-Chairman of the East India Company and one of the 'associates' in the notorious Bunce Island slave trade (illus. 86).[46] The amateur garden designer Joseph Spence visited Danson in 1763 and made detailed

86 'A Plan for the Alterations Proposed at Danson in Kent', attributed to Nathaniel Richmond and referred to by Joseph Spence as 'Mr Richmond's plan' in 1763. Richmond's style is largely indistinguishable from Brown's, although with some idiosyncratic elements, such as his use of the complex curlicue shape for a lake head.

comments on Richmond's proposals that were generally favourable in character, although he thought there was a problem with the west view from the house, which might be 'too much blockt by the plantation in Mr Richmond's plan, from Wellsend Grove down to the little meadows'.[47] At Shardeloes, Richmond was commissioned to carry out a major re-working of a park that had reputedly been created out of a morass at the turn of the eighteenth century, and subsequently improved by Bridgeman around 1725.[48] The work continued for many years. An analysis of the account of William Drake, the owner, held at Hoare's Bank – and of William Drake's own copy of his account there

– shows that between April 1763 and February 1770 Richmond received over £1,087 for his services, while between May 1765 and February 1769 John Hencher, his deputy, received more than £1,257. The total cost of the improvements was therefore at least £2,343, and smaller payments continued to be made to Richmond until his death in 1784, and to Alexander Cunningham from 1780 until as late as 1788.[49] The central feature of the work was the extension of a formal canal into a large sinuous lake with a curious 'double curlicue' lakehead (a device of which Richmond seems to have been particularly fond, using it again at a series of lakes at Himley Hall in Staffordshire, where he worked for John Ward, Viscount Dudley, in 1770).[50] In 1776 Humphry Repton's friend the Revd Norton Nicholls, of Costessey in Norfolk, stayed at Shardeloes and described it to his wife:

The place itself is very fine – a magnificent white house with its lofty Portico in front crowns a green hill that falls by a steep but long descent to a fine piece of water; the valley that contains it admits on its opposite bank only a meadow & the turnpike road from London to Aylesbury & then a corresponding ascent rises in full view of the house skirted by endless woods of Beech – These too form the background of the house & accompany on each hand the continuation of the valley.

Richmond died of septicaemia in February 1784, his obituary in the *Morning Post* on 30 March of that year noting:

A few days ago, at his house in Bryanston-Street, Nathaniel Richmond, Esq. in the 65th year of his age; many years known among gentlemen of landed property, as an eminent improver of parks and gardens. As he was in the exercise of his profession about four months ago, his foot slipped through an iron grate over an area, which brought on a mortification in his leg, and was the cause of his death.[51]

By this time Richmond had worked on more than thirty sites, including Saltram House near Plymouth, Stanmer House in Sussex, Escot House and Eggesford in Devon, Eastbourne Place in Sussex, Hitchin Priory in Hertfordshire, Beeston St Lawrence in Norfolk and Badminton in Gloucestershire (illus. 87, 88, 89). It seems likely that more of his commissions will come to light as he becomes better known among researchers. In the course of his career he modernized at least six Bridgeman designs and a further six geometric landscapes of unknown authorship and expanded another dozen or so existing parks, but seems to have created only six new parks *de novo*, on 'greenfield' sites. According to Mrs Elizabeth Montagu (a good friend of the Lytteltons of Hagley Hall), Richmond was 'Mr Brown's best élève' [pupil].[52] Repton described, in the circular letter sent to friends and contacts at the start of his career in 1788, how landscape gardening had been neglected 'since the loss of Brown and Richmond', adding that 'the works of Kent, Brown and Richmond have been the places of my worship.'[53] Several years later, writing in his Red Book for Lamer in Hertfordshire, he asserted that he had 'always considered the late Mr Richmond as the only person since the immortal Brown whose ideas were at all correct on the subject [of landscape improvement]'. But in a characteristically Reptonish manner he went on to qualify this praise:

> He understood perfectly how to give the most natural shape to artificial ground, how to dress walks in a pleasure garden, and how to leave or plant picturesque groupes of trees, his lines were generally graceful and easy, but his knowledge of the Art was rather technical and executive, than theoretical.[54]

Although few of Brown's other associates achieved quite this level of fame as independent practitioners, many made a decent living for themselves after leaving his employ. William Donn was working with Brown as early as 1753, acting as 'surveyor' during the construction of Croome Court, and later referred to him as 'my old master', a phrase which may mean that he served as his apprentice, although there is no certain evidence for this. Donn prepared most of Brown's plans in the period between 1753 and 1764, when he left to pursue an independent career as an architect. In the latter year he opened a joint account at Drummonds Bank with another of Brown's first cohort of associates, James Sanderson (not to be confused with the architect *John* Sanderson). Together the pair designed and supervised improvements at Claydon House in Buckinghamshire for Ralph, 2nd Earl Verney (whose somewhat ambitious aim of eclipsing

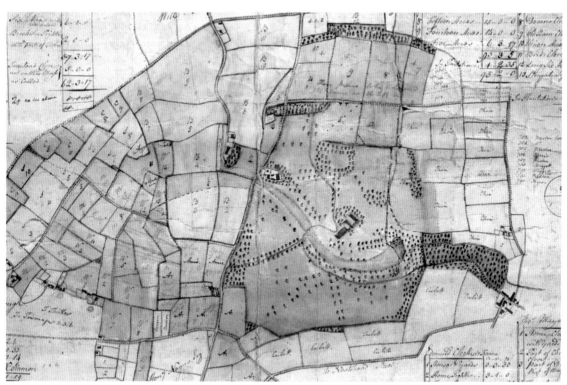

87 An undated estate map, *c.* 1785, showing the park and lake at Beeston St Lawrence in Norfolk, designed in the previous decade by Nathaniel Richmond.

88 The Orangery at Saltram House, Devon. The original design by Nathaniel Richmond was 'improved' by the estate gardener, Mr Stockman, as described in a letter of 1773.

Stowe was never realized). Sanderson, who by this time was operating a nursery business in Caversham, continued to work for Verney until his death in 1777: in his will he is described as a 'land surveyor'.[55] The partnership between the two men had ended in 1766, however, after which time Donn worked alone as an architect, with his own bank account at Drummonds. He achieved some success, executing Robert Adam's design for the 'Great Room' at Fife House in Whitehall for James Duff, 2nd Earl of Fife, who made payments, totalling £4,150, to Donn and Sanderson jointly in 1764 and to William Donn alone from 1765 until 1769; those made after 1767 were probably for work at Innes House, Elgin, which Duff bought in that year and for which Donn devised various architectural improvements.[56] Donn had other clients, and other commissions, at the same time. In 1764 the Duke of Grafton of Euston Hall, Suffolk, paid him seventy guineas, presumably for a survey: this was long before Brown worked

there in the 1770s. Donn also prepared designs for a new house at Abbey House, Cirencester, in 1774 and may have advised on its grounds.[57] He received payments from John Murray in 1768, before the latter was elevated to Duke of Atholl, possibly for work at The Hermitage, Dunkeld; designed and supervised the construction of Estcourt House in Gloucestershire in the 1770s; and worked with the Adam brothers on various projects from 1776 until 1783.[58] This was one of the many links, as we shall see, that connected the Adams with Brown. In 1777–8 Donn received £2,110 from Sir Richard Worsley of Appuldurcombe House, Isle of Wight, possibly for work with the architect James Wyatt. It is noteworthy that Brown was paid fifty guineas for a single visit to the same place, and for drawing up a plan, in 1779.

The individuals so far discussed all appear as recipients of payments recorded in Brown's account with Drummonds Bank. One person who does not so appear, yet who unquestionably

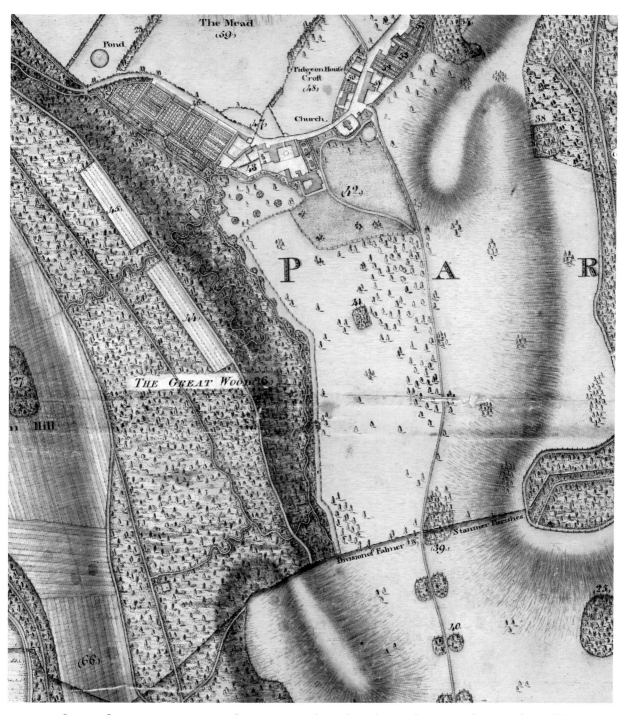

89 Stanmer, Sussex: an estate survey made in 1799–1800 shows the park some thirty years after it was designed by Nathaniel Richmond for Thomas Pelham in 1768–73.

worked with Brown in the early stages of his career, was Robert Robinson (1724–1794). Robinson arrived in Edinburgh in 1757, publicizing himself as a draughtsman and an '*executor of the Designs of Lancelot Brown*'.[59] According to the *Dictionary of Scottish Architects* he was the son of William Robinson, gardener, of Durham and born in 1734:[60] but this would make him remarkably young to be executing Brown's work in the early 1750s. He was more probably born in 1724, the son of the William Robinson of Whorlton, County Durham.[61] It is not clear why or when he moved south to work with Brown, or why he then moved north to Edinburgh, but once there he immediately attempted to open a school for the teaching of architecture and perspective, and three years later went into partnership with one William Boutcher, 'designing, drawing and executing all kinds of policy and gardening', advertising that he would 'continue to give designs, and carry on buildings, as formerly'.[62] He improved the grounds of Duddingston House, Edinburgh, during the 1760s for James Hamilton, 8th Earl of Abercorn; prepared designs for Careston, the seat of George Skene, in 1761; and laid out the grounds of Castle Grant for James Grant in 1764. A letter concerning his work at the last site describes him as an 'architect and layer out of pleasure grounds', the same combination of activities that Brown himself professed, but here carried out north of the border.[63] By 1764 he had established a nursery in Edinburgh but by the time he was made a burgess of Edinburgh 'for good services' in 1773 he was describing himself as an architect.[64] John Claudius Loudon, who in the following century became a prominent critic of Brown's style, was not surprisingly less than complimentary about Robinson's

own works, commenting in 1822 of the grounds at Duddingston House:

We know of no example in any country of so perfect a specimen of Brown's manner, nor of one in which the effect of the whole, and the details of every particular part, are so consistent, and co-operate so well together in producing a sort of tame, spiritless beauty, of which we cannot give a distinct idea. It does not resemble avowed art, nor yet natural scenery, it seems, indeed, as if nature had commenced the work and changed her plan, determining no longer to add to her productions those luxuriant and seemingly superfluous appendages which produce variety and grace. The trees here, all planted at the same time, and of the same age, all seem to grow by rule. The clumps remind us of regularly tufted perukes.

Robinson was not the only member of Brown's group who practised in Scotland, where Brown himself made only sporadic forays. Thomas White (1739–1811) worked with Brown from April 1759 until July 1765, and is known to have been involved at Chillington in Staffordshire, Glentworth in Lincolnshire, and Temple Newsam and Sandbeck in Yorkshire. His son, also Thomas, was baptised at Tickhill, near to Sandbeck, in 1764.[65] After parting with Brown in 1765 he immediately worked on his own at Harewood, Goldsborough and Newby, all in the West Riding of Yorkshire, although by 1770 he was living at Retford in Nottinghamshire.[66] He and his son went on to landscape more than 200 estates, almost all in Yorkshire and Scotland.[67] J. C.

Loudon was, once again, predictably critical of his work, describing him as

> an English professor, who was in the habit of making annual journeys in the north, taking orders for plans, which he got drawn on his return home, not one of which differed from the rest in any thing but magnitude. These plans were, in general, mounted on linen, which he regularly purchased in pieces of some hundred yards at a time, from a celebrated bleachfield adjoining Perth.[68]

Elsewhere he noted: 'White, senior, we believe, was a pupil of Brown, of much information on country matters, and generally respected in Scotland. Of his professional talents we have said enough, when we have mentioned their source.'[69]

White was immensely successful in financial terms, buying land near Consett in County Durham in 1773 which in time was expanded to an estate of nearly 800 acres, where he lived until 1800 (and for which he won a number of medals from the Society for the Encouragement of the Arts, Manufactures and Commerce for his large-scale tree planting).[70] He had almost certainly been an experienced gardener, surveyor and draughtsman *before* he was employed by Brown.

Of course, not all of Brown's collaborators went on to establish their own businesses in the way that White, Robinson, Richmond and Donn were to do. Some appear to have stayed with Brown for the duration of their careers. Jonathan Midgeley, for example, received payments from Brown from 1760 until 1778 and according to Dorothy Stroud worked at Charlecote in Warwickshire and at Castle Ashby in Northamptonshire.[71]

He was at Wynnstay in Denbigh in 1779, presumably executing Brown's design although paid directly by the owner, Sir Watkins Williams-Wynn.[72] Cornelius Dickinson similarly continued to work with Brown for most of his career, their association only coming to an end in 1782. He worked at Ditton Park near Slough between 1762 and 1774; at Sherborne in Dorset, where Brown was active in the 1750s and again between 1776 and 1779; and also at Harewood, where Brown worked between 1772 and 1777. He received relatively modest sums from Brown, usually less than £400 and often less than £200 in a year, suggesting perhaps specialized or consultancy work, possibly with a small team. In 1667 one Cornelius Dickinson endowed a charity to support the grammar school at Hatfield near Doncaster in Yorkshire (it still survives):[73] Hatfield Chase was one of the wetland areas where the Dutchman Cornelius Vermuyden had implemented major (and contentious) drainage and enclosure schemes in the early seventeenth century. Given that the Dickinson family owned land in this area in 1667, enough to give some away to endow the charity, and that they settled on Cornelius as a family name, it is possible that they were among the 'undertakers' or drainage engineers (many of Dutch origin) who were rewarded, in the customary fashion, with a portion of the drained land. Indeed, land drainage, and water management more generally, may have remained a family concern, perhaps explaining Cornelius's role in Brown's business. It is noticeable that the sites where he was employed posed particular problems in these respects. Sherborne in Dorset, where Brown prepared plans and commenced work on a large lake in 1753, largely occupied a floodplain; the house at Ditton Park in Buckinghamshire stood on a moated site on the levels of the Thames valley, and Brown's work there certainly included the implementation of an extensive drainage system (as well as the extension of the moat into a larger and more informal lake); while at Harewood Brown created a lake of 32 acres.

Some of the Capability Men not only worked for their entire careers with Brown, but continued after his death to collaborate with the inheritor of his unfinished commission, Samuel Lapidge. William Ireland came from a moderately prosperous background – his father was a maltster from Woburn in Bedfordshire, who on his death in 1754 left him copyhold estates in Lidlington and Ridgemont in Bedfordshire (his brother John receiving the family's freehold property in Woburn).[74] He may have trained as a gardener at Woburn Abbey, for his son was working there in 1820, supervising a team of ten men.[75] He received payments from Brown from 1768 but had probably worked for him before this, perhaps paid directly by clients, for he received a total of £652 14s. 7d. from Laurence Dundas of Moor Park in Hertfordshire in 1765.[76] By 1767 he was in charge of the work at Burghley and he later moved to Luton Hoo; Brown himself described him as 'sober, industrious and honest'.[77] He also worked at Stapleford in Leicestershire and at Trentham in Staffordshire.[78] Brown continued to make payments to him until his death in 1783, after which time he worked for Samuel Lapidge, to judge from the reminiscences of James Main, former gardener at Chalfont House in Buckinghamshire, in 1828.

In the summer of 1795 I entered as gardener into the service of the late Thomas Hibbert, Esq … At that time, there was groundwork going on at Bulstrode, then the seat of the late Duke of Portland, as well as at Chalfont House, under the direction of Mr Ireland, then foreman for Mr Lapidge, one of the successors to the business of the celebrated Brown … About this time, I think, Mr Lapidge gave up business, and works at both places were discontinued. Mr Ireland removed to the late Samuel Whitbread, Esq, or to Woburn Abbey in Bedfordshire, I am uncertain which; one or two of his sons, I believe, are still at Woburn.[79]

Others of Brown's collaborators eventually left, not to set up on business in their own right, but to take up employment as gardeners at specific places, usually with his help, or trading on his reputation. Benjamin Read received payments from Brown from 7 November 1755 until 1774: he was described as 'Mr Brown's Head servant' at Cole Green in Hertfordshire in 1756–7 and worked at Wootton in Buckinghamshire from 1758 until 1761, at Croome in the early 1760s, and at Blenheim in 1764.[80] He remained at the latter place in the employ of the Duke of Marlborough, his obituary in 1789 recording that he had 'for many years been employed by his Grace the Duke of Marlborough in forming ornamental plantations, and enriching the park and pleasure grounds at Blenheim; to which situation Mr Read had been recommended by the late Capability Browne'. Michael Milliken, also Millican, Mellican or Mellicent, was in some ways similar. He was born in New Luce, near Castle Kennedy in Stranraer in 1726, and first appears in Brown's bank account in 1755. Payments from Brown cease in 1760, after which time Milliken was paid directly by the

Duke of Devonshire for his work at Chatsworth; and in 1764 he married Mary Lees at Edensor, the Chatsworth estate village.[81] Brown sent for him in 1765 to become the gardener in charge of Richmond Gardens at Kew, first being paid through Brown and then, after 1783, directly, until his own death in 1800. George III evidently thought highly of him:

Amongst the many Loyal and Respectful Illuminations which took place on the 24th of this instant past some in the town of Richmond and on Richmond Green Mr Dundas' was Superb, Mrs Demainbray's Very Genteel, Mr Brown's looked well but Mr Milliken's Excelled all both in Taste and Elegance.[82]

Once again, this was a pattern repeated among Brown's collaborators and business rivals. John Sandys, for example, who became head gardener at Holkham in Norfolk and principal designer of the park in the 1780s and '90s, originally arrived as deputy to William Emes, who came to alter the northern end of the lake in 1782 (he was probably the brother of Charles Sandys, another of Emes's 'foremen': see above, p. 139).[83]

Brown's bank account and account books throw up a host of other names about whom relatively little is known. Many were apparently gardeners or nurserymen who were recruited locally, but who often then remained for many years in Brown's service. One was George Bowstreed, who was Brown's foreman at Southill in Bedfordshire in 1777–8, and who was the son of George Bowstreed of nearby Luton. The latter died in 1776, leaving his 'stock in Trade as a Gardener, of what nature or kind soever and all my implements and tools whatsoever and all my horses, carts and cattle . . . in my said Garden' to his wife. His son presumably continued the family business.[84] The family's association with Brown goes back to at least 1770, when one or other of the two Georges received payments from his account. Like William Ireland, Bowstreed continued to work for Brown until his death, and then for Lapidge after it. But like many of Brown's collaborators he also continued to engage in independent projects, receiving payments of £90 13s. in 1780 from Viscount Spencer for work at Wimbledon Park (where Brown had himself worked in 1765) 'in the Wood and Various Parts of the Park'.[85] Another example is Andrew Gardiner, who received payments from Brown in 1760 and 1761, between 1763 and 1769, and again in 1772 and 1773.[86] He was at North Stoneham, near Eastleigh in Hampshire, between 1775 and 1778, working with Alexander Knox, who also appears in Brown's account at Drummonds from 1761 to 1775.[87] Other collaborators who appear in Brown's accounts, or other sources, include the surveyor Cornelius Griffin, who worked at Copt Hall in Essex and Redgrave in Suffolk, and who was perhaps an East Anglian, although he died working for Brown at Alnwick in Northumberland in 1772; James and Thomas Hope, who worked for Brown at Rycote in Oxfordshire; and William Horsburgh, who was employed at Flambards in Middlesex.[88]

Commerce and landscape

This complex picture – of professional interdependence, intricate client networks and family connections – tells us much about the character of Brown's business and the reasons for its phenomenal success. One obvious feature was its flexibility: different contracts and different projects were organized in different ways. Sometimes, for example, estate labour was used to implement some or all of a design; sometimes local labour was directly recruited and directed by one of Brown's associates. Sometimes the risks of inflated costs were shared between client and contractor, as at Trentham in Staffordshire in 1759 where the contract included a final clause: 'should we be drove to the Necessity of giving a Shilling per Day to the Labourers, the advanced Expense of it is understood that the Earl shall have one half of it and Brown the other'.[89] In a similar way, clients agreed to supply very varying amounts of materials for the works. At Trentham, Earl Gower was to provide 'all the Bricks, Stone and Timber' that would be needed, together with wheelbarrows and 'Dutch carts'; at Melton Constable in Norfolk Sir Jacob Astley contracted to supply 'carts, wheelbarrows, six if it was but 4 able horses during the execution of the work as also trees and shrubs'.[90] What is particularly striking is that while money for particular projects often passed from clients, to contractors, through Brown's hands, it sometimes went directly. An example of the latter practice is provided by Chatsworth, where Milliken was paid directly by the Duke for 'earth moving'. His name first appears in the estate accounts in 1760, when he received £313 in twelve separate payments; in 1761 he received a further £637; from December 1761 to October 1762, £635; and from November 1762 to November 1763 no less than £710. The final payment – of £715, made for the period 1763–5 – is described as 'cash paid to Mr Millican on Mr Brown's account': this is the only direct reference to

Brown himself in the estate records.[91] It seems likely that some of the cases where Brown's collaborators repeatedly appear, and disappear, from his own account may be explained by variations over time in the method by which they were paid.

The scale and sophistication of Brown's business should be seen within the context of the wider economic and social changes of the eighteenth century. The expansion of the economy, the first steps towards globalization and the rapid growth in the production of goods and services were accompanied by major social and political changes that included, crucially in this context, a decisive shift from a small court-based group of 'taste-makers' to a wider group of wealthy individuals. Patronage by a largely aristocratic elite, comprising relatively few individuals, was replaced in the middle decades of the eighteenth century by a commercial marketplace for goods and services with clients and customers numbered in the thousands. The landscape industry – for by the time of Brown's death it was indisputably an *industry* – thus expanded hugely in scale, providing expert services for a far wider spectrum of society than had been served by the professional designers of the early eighteenth century.

As we also emphasized earlier, the economic expansion of the eighteenth century saw a significant improvement of the social and economic position of the 'middling sort'. One important effect of this was the steady expansion of grammar schools, which provided an education for those whose parents were insufficiently wealthy to have them attend the 'public schools' and universities, but affluent enough to have them stay on at school well into their teens: people like

Brown himself.[92] Such schools taught classics but also mathematics and a range of other useful subjects, including drawing, a subject that had been strongly advocated by John Locke in his *Some Thoughts Concerning Education* of 1693, on the grounds that it was

> Very useful to a gentleman on several occasions, but especially if he travel . . . How many Buildings may a Man see, how many Machines and Habits meet with, the Ideas where of would be easily retain'd and communicated, by a little skill in Drawing; which being committed to words, are in danger to be lost, or at best but ill retained in the most exact Descriptions? . . . But so much insight into perspective and skill in drawing as will enable him to represent tolerably on paper anything he sees, except faces, may I think be got in a little time, especially if he have a genius to it.[93]

This provision of an advanced and in many cases comprehensive education ensured that by the middle decades of the eighteenth century a new cohort of surveyors and draughtsmen was ready to service the expanding market for improvement. Many first served an apprenticeship as gardeners, surveyors, masons or joiners before becoming clerks of works, and finally businessmen and designers with their own projects and clients.

In addition to an expansion in middle-class education, the changing balance of social power, as well as the sheer scale of economic expansion and technological innovation in the course of the eighteenth century, also ensured that particular spheres of activity became increasingly professionalized. Academies, institutes and other professional associations aimed at controlling standards and membership developed apace. The Society for the Encouragement of the Arts, Manufactures and Commerce was founded in 1754 and the Society of Artists of Great Britain in 1761; Brown, Donn, Richmond and White, together with the architect Robert Adam and many others, were members of the former organization (disputes among members – notably William Chambers and James Paine – led to a schism that created the Royal Academy in 1768, with a membership limited to forty carefully selected artists). This rise of the concept of 'professions' helped to raise the status, and perhaps the artistic independence, of landscape designers. 'Gentleman architects' such as Lord Burlington or Sanderson Miller needed an executive architect or 'master builder' to develop their ideas into executable drawings and then to realize the actual building; but the credit for the structure remained with them. Burlington used his protégé Kent to this end; Sanderson Miller used John Sanderson and Brown himself. But, beginning with Charles Bridgeman in the 1720s, leading landscape designers and architects – men like Brown – gradually attained a social status, based on their professional activities, that allowed them to set the artistic pace. Henry Hulton, who had the dubious privilege of joining the newly formed American Board of Customs Commissioners in Boston in 1767, visited his brother-in-law Sir Jacob Preston at Beeston Hall, Norfolk, on his return to England in 1776 and described to his sister how 'Mr P had one of the Gentlemen Improvers here to modernise his grounds.'[94] He was referring to Nathaniel Richmond, and the phrase neatly captures, perhaps with a note of irony, the enhanced status of such men. All this said, professionalism had not yet set fixed limits on what an individual could do; nor was it assumed that any formal training was required to engage in a particular activity, as Brown's career demonstrates clearly enough. There was still considerable fluidity in the roles of surveyor, engineer, architect or indeed gardener. A person with training in one discipline might readily extend into others: thus Robert Adam, already an architect of some fame, was thought a perfectly acceptable choice as designer of a new pleasure ground at Kedleston in the early 1750s (see p. 118).

The emerging consumer society generated a marketplace for goods and services that, over time, delivered increasing amounts of economic power into the hands of the middling ranks of society – and increasingly to those members of that group who could not easily be incorporated into the ranks of the polite, as this was defined and conceived in Georgian England. Gradually, an emerging middle class not only pressed for wider political representation through voting reform and other changes. It also began to shape the character of 'taste' itself, most crucially in matters of garden design. These changes would not fully bear fruit until the nineteenth century, but by the time of Brown's death in 1783 they were already under way.

FIVE

Landscape and Modernity

L ANCELOT BROWN and the Capability Men thus transformed the landscape of England in the 1760s, '70s and '80s, employing business methods that to our eyes appear surprisingly modern. But what explains the character, and the popularity, of the specific style they promulgated – what explains the overwhelming success of the 'landscape park' (illus. 90 and 91)? This is a difficult question, and one which has been answered in a variety of ways by garden historians and others over the years. Some for example have interpreted Brown's style simply as the final stage in an inexorable linear development, from geometry to 'nature', which began with the simplification of geometric forms under Charles Bridgeman and continued through the irregular but somewhat cluttered gardens of William Kent, culminating in the sweeping simplicity of the landscape park itself. Indeed, such a view was already well established in the eighteenth century.[1] To others, the manicured naturalism of the new landscapes was an expression of philosophical or political principles – of the balanced and superior character of the British constitution, for example, poised between the autocracy of monarchy and the perceived anarchy of democracy, or of the rise of empiricism over Cartesian systematicism.[2] To a few, the style has no meaning: it was a fashion, as random in its character as any other, and as such requires no particular explanation. In the chapter that follows we suggest a range of social, intellectual and economic reasons for the popularity of the 'landscape' style, and argue that it was peculiarly suited to the times in which it was forged. Like the business practices of its creators it was intimately connected with the emergence of the modern world. Yet at the same time it drew on symbols and meanings of considerable antiquity, and it is these which we must first examine.

The park as landscape

One key feature of Brown's style is that it made the park, rather than the garden, the principal setting for the mansion, at least as this was viewed from a distance. Although gardens did not disappear, they were given a subsidiary role, in the sense that they were removed from the main facades and the distinction between them and the park was blurred with the adoption of the haha, a feature that appears in almost all plans, contracts and articles of agreement relating to Brown, the details of construction often carefully stipulated: that at Weston in Staffordshire in

90 Bowood in Wiltshire, showing the lake, house and expanse of carefully levelled turf between. This is one of the best preserved of Brown's landscapes, entirely designed by him, although with some later additions.

1765, for example, was to be retained by a stone wall 2.1 m (7 ft) high; that at Trentham in the same county in 1759 was to be 1.8 m (6 ft) deep, between 3 and 3.7 metres (10–12 ft) wide and retained with a wall of brick. Understanding the meaning of the park, therefore, can help us to understand the significance of Brown's designs.

Parks per se, as we have already noted, had existed for centuries. They had long been a form of landscape distinct from the garden or pleasure ground, and with a quite separate although related history.[3] Brown and his fellow designers, as contemporaries were clearly aware, were applying a particular design aesthetic to an existing landscape form, Thomas Whately famously declaring in 1770 that gardening was 'no longer confined to the spots from which it borrows its name, but regulates also the disposition and embellishments of a park, a farm, or a riding'.[4] The long history of parks begins in early medieval times, when they had been well-wooded venison farms and hunting grounds, often located some distance from elite residences. Many contained a lodge, which provided accommodation for the owner not merely while hunting but when wishing to withdraw from the daily ritualized social life of the mansion, to keep 'secret house' with a restricted group of companions.[5] Many parks also contained large

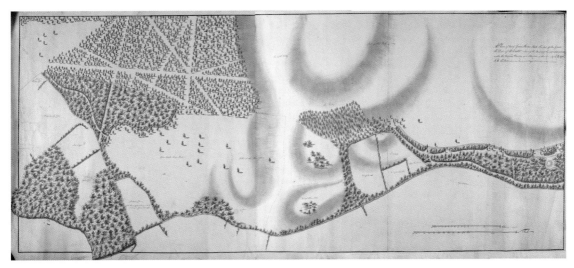

91 Brown's plan for 'Part of Grimsthorpe Park', Lincolnshire, 1772, is for a relatively small addition to the grounds.

fishponds – those described by Roger North in 1715 as 'great waters' – formed by erecting dams across the valleys of minor watercourses, so that the water was ponded back upstream, following the shape of the natural contours.[6] Their size in some cases approached that of Brown's lakes.

By the thirteenth century parks were the only really 'wild' landscapes left in England, areas in which the natural environment had been least modified by arable farming, or by the kind of intensive grazing which had created, and maintained, open commons, heaths and moors. And they had become – with the deer that lived in them – the exclusive province of, and therefore the symbol par excellence of, the feudal elite.

During the late Middle Ages the numbers of deer parks in England declined. The economic dislocations of the fourteenth century placed considerable strains on demesne incomes, while rising wages and the decline of customary services ensured that maintenance costs spiralled. Parks were increasingly restricted to the richest families. But more importantly,

they were now more closely associated with residences, for as they dwindled in numbers, the survivors were usually among the relatively few examples that had been located beside great houses. And as their numbers began to increase once again through the fifteenth and sixteenth centuries, these new creations were, almost without exception, similarly placed. There were changes, too, in the appearance of parks, with the emergence for the first time of true 'parkland'. Early medieval parks had, so far as the evidence goes, been densely treed wood-pastures, usually with relatively few open areas or 'laundes'. But as parks were brought into closer association with the residence they tended to become more open in appearance, and their layout and design came to be more carefully considered. The number of trees within them was reduced, for otherwise the house would have been hemmed in on one or more sides by woodland and it would not have been possible to demonstrate the wealth of an owner who was able to put vast acres out of cultivation in this manner. For while early medieval parks had been created at the expense of – had been formed out of – wood-pasture 'waste', most late medieval and early post-medieval parks were made out of cultivated land, because they were created close to long-established residences. Their makers accordingly retained existing hedgerow trees, woods and copses to provide the necessary sylvan prospects. Already designers of parkland were consulting, as their eighteenth-century successors were to do, the 'genius of the place' (see illus. 14). From the middle of the seventeenth century the park began to be wrapped around the mansion and its gardens, and in some places the boundary between it and the wider world was hardened with the planting, along the line of the perimeter fence or pale, of a thick belt of trees. And in the last decades of the century – for a few brief decades, lasting into the early eighteenth century – the geometric design of the garden was extended out into the park in the form of avenues, although these were an intrusion into the park's natural informality, rather than a radical displacement of it. Long before the arrival of Capability Brown the park was a distinct form of landscape, designed to varying degrees and with an immense pedigree loaded with significance and meaning. As Oliver Rackham has emphasized, Brown and his contemporaries were the 'heirs to a long tradition': the eighteenth century was simply the period in which 'their design became an art form'.[7] With their expanses of turf, irregularly scattered with trees, their blocks of enclosed woodland and their serpentine bodies of water, seventeenth-century deer parks would not have seemed entirely alien to those familiar with the landscapes of Brown and his contemporaries (illus. 92).

Parks were thus not a new type of landscape but a long-established one, transformed by the hand of taste, and Walpole famously noted the debt owed by eighteenth-century designers to these 'contracted forests, and extended gardens'.[8] But the Capability Men did more than apply a veneer of modish design to an old landscape. The style they forged also facilitated the spread of parks, which appear to have increased significantly in numbers in most parts of England in the middle and later decades of the eighteenth century. This was because one of their key achievements was to divorce the concept of the park from any necessary association with deer. There may have been examples of deerless 'parks' before the 1750s, but they were few and far between, and as late as 1755 Johnson's *Dictionary* simply defined a park as an 'enclosure for beasts of chase'. The various published county maps surveyed in the period up to and including the 1760s continued, in a similar manner, to depict all parks as ovals of deer-proof fencing. But by this stage very few new *deer* parks were being created, and in long-established parks deer were often beginning to give way to sheep and cattle. At some of the places where Brown worked his canvas was an existing deer park, and deer continued to be kept there by his clients, as at Petworth or Sledmere. But many of his commissions, such as Shortgrove, Broadlands or Croome, involved creating park landscapes that were grazed by domestic livestock alone. By the end of the century only a relatively small minority of parks in England contained deer.

The reasons for this severance of the long association of deer and park are complex. In part it mirrored a wider decline in interest on the part of the elite in traditional forms of livestock husbandry, involving the exploitation of semi-wild species, and yet at the same time the continuing value that they placed on the irregular, aristocratic landscapes in which these had been kept. It thus paralleled the disappearance of rabbit warrens, dovecotes and fishponds from the immediate vicinity of mansions, the significance of which we shall explore in a moment. The loss of deer from parks also probably reflects the fact that deer are voracious grazers, difficult to keep out of clumps and shrubberies, so that the more elaborately planted parks became, the less they

could be used for venison farming. But the separation of the two concepts – deer and parks – was also associated with the fact that, as parks proliferated, they descended the social scale. By the end of the eighteenth century even quite minor landowners could boast their own 'park'. But while such men could afford to create a private landscape of grass and trees, they were less able to go to the rather greater expense of encircling this with a deer-proof fence, and of maintaining a herd of deer within it.

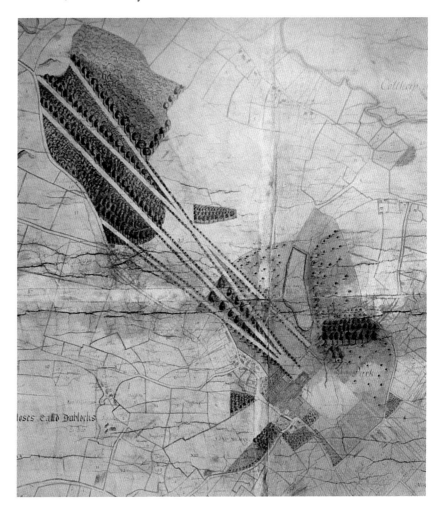

92 Blickling Hall and its park, Norfolk, as depicted on an estate map of 1729. The 'New Pond', a large fishpond within the park, already displays the kind of sinuous outline we associate with the lakes created by Brown and his contemporaries.

The social roles of the landscape park

There are good reasons why the numbers of parks should have increased in England in this manner. The population grew in the decades after 1750, rural unemployment rose and social inequality increased; the landscape park provided a measure of social isolation for the polite, a degree of privacy and seclusion from the wider communities around them. This development had in fact begun in the first half of the eighteenth century. Although many popular writers quote Goldsmith's poem *The Traveller* of 1764 – 'Have we not seen, at pleasure's lordly call/The smiling long-frequented village fall', so that the great house stood alone in the park, 'in barren solitary pomp' – most of the villages cleared to make way for parks had in fact disappeared before the start of Brown's career.[9] He was involved with the clearance and rebuilding of the village of Milton Abbas in Dorset and a substantial hamlet at Bowood in Wiltshire was removed when the park was laid out and partly drowned beneath the lake, the estate accounts recording rent remissions for cottages 'taken down to be overflowed by the Pond'.[10] But in general the great age of depopulation through emparking was over. Individual farms and cottages nevertheless continued to be displaced by parks, and the removal or diversion of roads and footpaths seems to have become more common in the second half of the eighteenth century. In 1773 an Act of Parliament established the mechanism of Road Closure Orders, by which only the agreement of two Quarter Sessions magistrates was required to close or divert a public right of way – a much easier and cheaper method than the writs of *ad quod damnum*, or the individual parliamentary acts, that had formerly

been required. Perimeter belts served to provide a measure of seclusion and privacy, as did the lodges which were erected at the gates of the larger parks. Parks removed the homes of local people, and the fields of their labour, from the polite gaze: contracts drawn up when parks were created are sometimes quite explicit in this, that which Brown made at Trentham including a clause about planting 'all the necessary Plantations to hide the village'.[11] Parks were thus private spaces, or at least spaces which were closed to particular social groups, a fact not lost on contemporaries. A local poet in Bedale in Yorkshire recounted, in the late eighteenth century, the changes wrought to the landscape in his lifetime, highlighting how the owner of the great house, The Rand, had removed neighbouring rights of way:

And now them roads are done away
And one made in their room
Quite to the east, of wide display,
Where you may go and come,
Quite unobserved from the Rand,
The trees do them seclude
If modern times, do call such grand
Its from a gloomy mood.[12]

The increasing importance of parks as insulating spaces in this period is also clear from the way in which existing examples were often expanded in order to ensure additional privacy. The fact that parks had economic functions, and were comparatively cheap to maintain for their size – principally requiring regular grazing by livestock, from which money could be made – may have made them particularly suitable as blankets of privacy, wrapped around the homes of the rich.

We must be careful, however, not to interpret all aspects of their design in terms of privacy and seclusion. The precise position of belts was decided, for example, by landforms: where possible the perimeter of the park – viewed from the main windows of the house – followed the line of rising ground, the woods serving to accentuate the height of the hills, as for example at Audley End or Chatsworth. In both these examples, moreover, a public road ran right through the centre of the park, midway between house and this terminating belt. At Chatsworth, while the main road leading along the Derwent valley was diverted away from the house when the new park was laid out around 1760, it was impossible to move it out of the valley (and therefore out of the park) altogether; while at Audley End, the north–south route running along the valley of the river Cam was an important turnpike road, which could only have been banished from sight at very considerable expense and at great inconvenience to the wider public.[13] In both these cases, as in others, the desire for privacy was not merely thwarted by practicalities and economics, but perhaps tempered by an equally strong wish to display the house, set in its modern landscape, to genteel travellers. At Chatsworth the views of the house from the road through the park were fleeting and tantalizing, but in the case of Audley End the main front of the mansion lay parallel to the road, and would have remained in full view of the passing traveller – set in Brown's simple yet stunning landscape – for several minutes, the road being flanked not by a hedge, but by a haha (illus. 93).

Indeed, parks were as much about articulating relationships between members of the social elite as they were about maintaining the barrier between that elite and the wider world. While the smaller parks attached to minor country houses were enjoyed recreationally – for riding, boating, driving and so on – only by invited guests, many of the larger landscapes were, as we have seen, more or less open to all members of the polite on a formal or informal basis. The landscape park served to exclude the poor, but it also provided a shared recreational arena, and a shared style, for the polite. It is true that not all who might be so accounted could afford to create a park, but a significant proportion could make a reasonable stab at making some version of the landscape of fashion. As Sarah Spooner in particular has shown, diminutive forms of park – complete with narrow belts, miniature tree clumps and small serpentine 'lakes' – appeared in some numbers, especially in the immediate vicinity of London, their size ensuring that extensive use was often made of 'borrowed' views. Some landowners even rented land at a distance on which to erect an eye-catcher.[14] In the mid-1770s Sir Benjamin Truman, a London brewer and owner of a house and small park at Popes near Hatfield in south Hertfordshire, was making annual payments to a neighbour, John Church, which the latter recorded in his field book, 'for leave to erect a temple in Pickbones Field – this is a view cut thro' Quails Wood from Popes Walk & like to be a standing Rent so long as any Gentleman lives there'.[15] In such districts, views into neighbouring parks were extensively exploited, to the extent that small landscape parks often developed as contiguous clusters, their stylistic development impossible to understand singly, rather than as a group (illus. 94). Contemporaries often called

93 Audley End, Essex, viewed from the old turnpike road to London. Compare with illus. 71.

such small landscapes 'paddocks' or 'lawns' rather than 'parks', but – carefully designed – they could boast an appearance broadly similar to that of the great landscapes created by Brown himself.

It is true that the association between Brown's style and *extensive* landscaping was a contemporary commonplace. The *Morning Post* for 30 July 1776 recorded what was probably already a well-worn anecdote about Brown:

He was sent for by a gentleman in Staffordshire who had more money than land – and upon being shown the ground – *That hill,* said Brown, *you must clump*. That I cannot do, said the gentleman, for it belongs to

Mr Jennings: *Well – we must pass over that; this valley must be cleared and floated.* Impossible, returned the other, for that also is Mr Jenning's. *Your most humble servant*, said Brown, taking an abrupt leave, *I think Mr Jennings should have sent for me, not you.*[16]

Gradations of wealth were thus signalled by the landscape park. But they were not signalled in a way that raised obvious barriers within the polite as a group. There was a contrast here with the great formal gardens laid out in the late seventeenth and early eighteenth centuries, which had very clearly displayed the social superiority of their owners. The largest mansions had vast gardens, the costs of maintaining which – clipping hedges, weeding gravel paths, rolling lawns – were obvious to any observer. Indeed, visitors often recorded, in diaries and tour journals, their principal dimensions, one in 1712 typically describing at Blenheim 'The Gardens of 80 acres, the middle gravel walk from ye House to ye End of ye Garden is 2220 feet long, ye many Hedges in ye Gardens are said to be in Content near 20 measured miles.'[17]

Huge sums could be, and often were, expended on the creation of the larger landscape parks, especially on the various schemes of earth-moving,

and much could be spent on the maintenance of gardens and pleasure grounds: Rochefoucauld commented in 1784 how English gardens cost 'prodigious sums to maintain'.[18] Yet at places like Chatsworth, the precise scale of the former certainly, and of the latter to a significant extent, were – by very nature of the 'natural' character of Brown's style – rather less evident than they had been in earlier forms of landscape design. Much money changed hands, much labour was expended, but the alteration effected was subtle, sometimes scarcely apparent, rather than obvious and naked. Visitors may well have been aware of the scale of the transformation which had taken

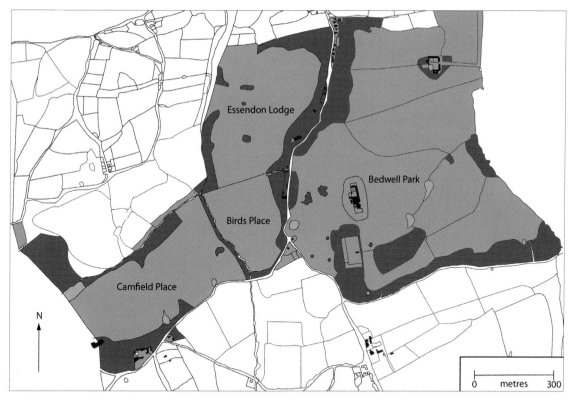

94 By the end of the eighteenth century, as Sarah Spooner has shown, the hinterlands of major towns and cities were often thickly studded with small landscape parks associated with diminutive 'villas', sometimes – as here, near Hatfield in south Hertfordshire – forming contiguous clusters, their design evolving in close relationship with each other. Based on late eighteenth-century estate maps and the early nineteenth-century draft drawings of the Ordnance Survey at the British Library, London.

place, and of the labour involved in subsequent maintenance, but their noses, so to speak, were not rubbed in it, and it was possible to create and maintain a broadly similar design without such expense, and on far fewer acres. None of this is to imply, of course, that the early adopters of the new style were drawn equally from all ranks of the polite: unquestionably, most were large landowners, wealthy merchants and financiers. Nevertheless, the new style helped forge a common taste, and a common world view, among the broad ranks of the propertied.

The urbanization of society

Landscape parks were related to deer parks, but they were not simply deer parks without deer. In spite of the fact that Walpole noted the debt owed by the eighteenth-century landscape park to the traditional deer park, in reality there were important stylistic differences between the two, differences which time has, to some extent, served to reduce. Not only were landscape parks often more open than their forerunners, with more extended prospects of uninterrupted turf. Deer parks had been characterized by indigenous trees, whereas the designs of Brown and his contemporaries also often featured a significant proportion of exotic species, especially fast-growing conifers. Landscape parks were more elegant, more overtly designed spaces, often partaking as much of the style of gardens and pleasure grounds as that of deer parks in the traditional sense. Deer parks, moreover, had been symbols par excellence of elite food production, and the primacy of the landscape park as a setting for the house necessitated not only the destruction of walled ornamental gardens,

but the removal of a range of other features and facilities devoted to the production of elite foodstuffs that had accompanied the mansion, including farmyards, nut grounds, fishponds and rabbit warrens. At Chatsworth in Derbyshire, for example, the removal of the great rabbit warren on the west bank of the Derwent, which had previously formed the main prospect from the house, was the very first change made when the new park was created, at least partly under Brown's supervision, from the late 1750s. A note in the estate accounts records that 'The Warren was destroyed 1758, sold all the rabbits', while the following year there are references to 'Pareing, burning and ploughing ye Warren'.[19] The destruction of such facilities – which had for centuries proudly proclaimed the active involvement of the owner in the productive life of the estate – and their replacement with the open, manicured landscape of the deer-less park, was arguably the most important feature of the eighteenth-century landscape revolution.

The landscape park may have been a symbol and sign of the polite, and of the emergence of a society that was horizontally stratified rather than vertically integrated, but we should not read it solely in terms of *rural* social relations, or rural life. Although the new landscapes were frequently described as both 'rural' and 'natural', many of their owners were, in an important sense, not really a rural class. Although many established landowners derived their income primarily from agricultural rents, and perhaps from their home farms, equally numerous – especially among the clients of Brown – were those whose wealth stemmed at least as much from active investment in colonial enterprises, industry and commerce. Moreover, many of those who acquired rural estates in this period were upwardly mobile individuals who had made their money entirely in such activities. Indeed, in cultural terms, the eighteenth-century elite was in many ways more urban than rural in character. Not only were Bath and London the centres of their social universe, with shops, public spaces, assemblies and other opportunities for fashionable consumption and display. Many provincial towns also fulfilled a similar role, if on a humbler scale. In the 1720s Daniel Defoe could already describe Bury St Edmunds – not a very large place – as 'the *Montpelier* of Suffolk . . . it being thronged with Gentry, People of Fashion, and the most polite conversation'.[20] From the later seventeenth century many large, elegant houses were erected in or on the edges of the bigger towns and cities, which began to exhibit a measure of social zoning, with areas suitable for the homes of the polite contrasting with areas of increasing poverty. Large town houses might resemble – more than we notice today, because of their settings – small country houses, and they were provided with often elaborate gardens and pleasure grounds. It is a sign of the times that when in 1788 a 'Genteel, large house' was advertised for sale in Norwich the particulars noted that it had 'every fashionable and domestic convenience – garden excepted'.[21] But improvements in communications with, in particular, the steady extension of the turnpike system ensured that most towns could be reached with relative ease from their rural hinterlands, and those hinterlands themselves began to change. As we have noted, most major towns and cities were, by the second half of the eighteenth century, usually surrounded by a penumbra of country houses and parks, mainly small or medium-sized, but

including larger examples. Such proximity not only provided owners with easy access to the attractions and facilities which urban centres had to offer, but allowed those with interests in town – commercial or industrial – to keep a ready eye on business.

This penumbra of parks and mansions was most marked, needless to say, in the case of the capital. Already, by the seventeenth century, it had become fashionable for wealthy people living in London to acquire a residence within an easy ride or drive of it. Not only fashion and society, and commercial activity, kept them so anchored. So too did politics – London was where all the important things happened, and where the main decisions affecting national life were made. Directors of city banks, wealthy merchants and retired army officers all moved en masse into counties like Hertfordshire, Buckinghamshire and Surrey in the course of the eighteenth century. Competition for properties forced up land prices and tended to preclude the development of very large estates, and Arthur Young commented in 1804 that 'Property in Hertfordshire is much divided: the vicinity of the capital; the goodness of the air and roads; and the beauty of the country' had led 'great numbers of wealthy persons to purchase land for villas'.[22] The distribution of Brown's known commissions follows this broad pattern, with a dense clustering around London, although the high density in the West Midlands, in the Black Country and the hinterland of Birmingham also indicates the economic vitality of this region in the middle decades of the eighteenth century (illus. 95). But most major provincial towns formed distinct foci for the social life of the polite, and were surrounded by elite residences set in fashionable grounds.

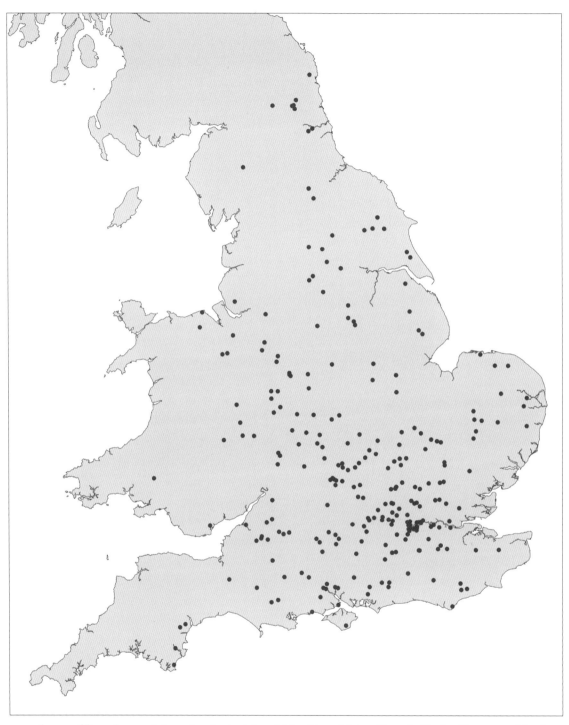

95 A map of Brown's commissions, showing both 'possible' and 'certain' sites. Compiled by Jon Gregory and Sarah Spooner for English Heritage in 2013. Note the strong concentration of sites in the area around London, and the thinner scatter through the West Midlands.

96 Detail from Dury and Andrews's 1766 map of Hertfordshire, digitally remastered by Andrew Macnair, showing the remarkable density of parks clustered around the county town of Hertford.

The county town of Hertford lay some way outside the orbit of London, and its attraction to the wealthy is clear from the dense packing of parks around it. In the 1760s, when Dury and Andrews surveyed their map of the county, around a quarter of the land lying within 5 kilometres of the town was already occupied by parkland (illus. 96). Horace Walpole in 1761 thought the route between Puckeridge and Hatfield 'the prettiest in the world, and sowed with at least one dozen substantial seats'.[23] In subsequent decades this clustering of designed landscapes was to increase still further, so that by 1799 Humphry Repton was able to comment with approval on the near-continuous belt of parkland owned by the various members of the Cowper family along the Mimram valley between Hertford and Welwyn – Panshanger, Cole Green (landscaped by Brown), Tewin Water and

Digswell (also by Brown) – and considered that their 'united woods and lawns will by extending thro' the whole valley enrich the general face of the country'.[24] Such clustering of parks and polite residences was particularly marked around the major provincial capitals. Norwich, for example, was by the 1780s surrounded by a dense packing of small and medium-sized parks, and villages like Catton (where Repton was to undertake his first paid commission in 1788) were becoming effectively suburbanized. Mostyn Armstrong in 1781 described the place as

A very pleasant village, and the residence of many manufacturers, who have retired from Norwich, and built elegant houses. The air is reckoned very healthful, and many invalids resort thither for the benefit of it. It is distant from the city a mile and half north . . . The late Robert Roger, esq. and Robert Harvey, esq., both Aldermen of Norwich, have erected handsome seats in this village; as also Jeremiah Ives Harvey, esq. and Mr Suffield.[25]

Proximity to Norwich allowed such men to keep an eye on their business interests, but also to enjoy the society and leisure facilities the city had to offer. Such facilities themselves also migrated outwards into the city's suburbanized hinterland. Mulbarton Hall, set in its 'beautiful fine Pleasure Garden', containing 'Evergreen and Flowering shrubs', was put on the market when its owner, the textile manufacturer Philip Stannard, went bankrupt in 1770.[26] Lying some six kilometres outside Norwich, it was purchased by Robert Parkerson, and re-opened 'for the reception of Gentlemen and Ladies, for Breakfasting, or Tea in the afternoon', the latter featuring 'fine Strawberries, and other Fruit as they come into season'. A coach operated several times a day, bringing customers from Norwich.[27]

The people who lived in these fashionable mansions played less and less part in the real, practical business of agriculture. The landscape they created around them reflected and expressed this fact. It was partly a desire to signal their difference from the farmers and other agricultural producers in the surrounding countryside – to affirm, very publicly, their membership of the polite – which encouraged landowners to clear away the barns, yards and orchards from the immediate vicinity of their homes, so important a feature of the 'landscape' style. But it was also because such things seemed offensive, uncouth, dirty. There remained some substantial landowners, living in more remote areas of the country,

who were happy to record in their diaries the produce of their orchards and the number of young pigs which had been born on their home farm that year; to retain walled gardens, fishponds and dovecotes in full view. But such individuals were, by the 1770s, becoming unusual. Great landowners might embrace a fashionable interest in estate management, agricultural improvement and enclosure: they expected to be kept informed of developments on their home farms. But farming was now something that took place at one remove, or more, from the mansion. In this sense, the landscape park – for all its homage to 'nature' – expressed a lifestyle increasingly divorced from real rural life. Indeed, the growth of interest in, and liking for, the 'natural' on the part of the wealthy in the course of the eighteenth century correlates pretty closely with their steady absorption into a mainly urban culture.

That culture was, above all, a culture of fashionable *consumption*, not of production: hence again the rejection of orchards, fishponds, vegetable gardens and nut grounds as a setting for the homes of the polite. Hence, too, the increasingly elaborate displays of flowers and flowering shrubs in the gardens and pleasure grounds, many derived, as we have seen, from America or the East. From the middle years of the eighteenth century the number of commercial nurseries expanded rapidly in provincial districts, away from London. This growth was partly fuelled by the demand for forest trees, for woods and plantations; partly by the escalating demand for hedging hawthorn, as the enclosure of the remaining commons and open fields proceeded apace; but partly by the demands for ornamental plants for pleasure grounds and gardens, both urban and rural.[28] Many of these enterprises sound, from contemporary descriptions, remarkably like modern 'garden centres'. Most supplied a phenomenal range of plants. When Parson Woodforde, the indefatigable diarist of Weston Longville in Norfolk, visited Aram and Mackie's nursery just outside Norwich in 1783 he bought twenty 'Turin poplars', ten plane trees, ten acacia, two vines, ten laurels, two 'double blossom thorns', two moss roses, ten evergreen cytisus, ten Weymouth pine and ten guilder rose.[29] This was the planting palette that shaped the gardens of the middle class, but also the pleasure grounds, and to some extent the landscape parks, of the wealthy, as a shared style of polite landscaping was forged.

The landscape style, domestic planning and the polite

At one level, the landscape park thus represents – as Whately's comments about gardening 'no longer confined to the spots from which it borrows its name', but informing the appearance of the wider estate landscape, should alert us – a kind of suburbanized, polite, tidied-up version of the traditional deer park, a particularly appropriate badge of distinction for an urbanized or suburbanized elite. But a number of other influences helped to shape its appearance. We noted earlier in this book the close connections that existed between architecture on the one hand and landscape design on the other; and we also emphasized the way in which Brown himself practised extensively as an architect. The architectural styles of mansions, and in particular their internal plans, were of necessity – and often in complex ways – connected with the layout and appearance of their grounds. London and Wise, and even Charles Bridgeman, thus

produced landscapes appropriate to the 'formal' plans, and Baroque styles, of late seventeenth- and early eighteenth-century houses, while Kent's idealized Italian scenes had served as a perfect complement to Palladian houses. In the middle of the century further changes in architecture occurred, with important implications for landscape design.

The first of these was the appearance of less architecturally 'accurate' Palladian houses: buildings which retained the general proportions of Palladio's designs, but which were less austere and were often smaller and more compact than those erected by the intellectual cognoscenti in the 1720s, '30s and '40s. They displayed more restrained classical detailing and often had no great portico – only a central pediment. The various 'villas' designed by men like Sir Robert Taylor, James Paine and Sir William Chambers from the early 1750s – such as Taylor's Harleyford Manor in Buckinghamshire – might even boast elevations which were different on every facade.[30] Harleyford also featured a prominent bow window running the full height of the house – an increasingly popular feature through the 1750s and '60s. Here, moreover, the principal floor was raised, not on a full-height rustic, but only on a low half-basement; and in the middle decades of the century many houses were built with their principal rooms at or near ground-floor level, including those designed by Brown at places like Newnham Paddox in Warwickshire or Redgrave in Suffolk. These stylistic changes were closely connected to significant developments in domestic planning. Somewhat belatedly, the more informal entertaining associated with polite society – which had arguably helped to inspire the more flowing and serpentine gardens of the

1730s and '40s – now found its full architectural expression. Following the lead taken by country houses like Holkham, and by urban houses in London especially, new country houses erected from the early 1750s no longer had plans based on the great formal axis of the hall and saloon, nor suites of private apartments arranged as *enfilades*. Instead the main floor of the house comprised a number of rooms for recreation and entertaining, arranged in a circuit and often placed around a central, top-lit staircase. When the house was used for entertaining, guests could drift easily between rooms in which diverse activities continued at the same time – card-playing, dining, dancing. It was this decline in the importance of linear axes that was reflected in the looser, more varied external elevations of many large houses.

The implications of these architectural developments for the design of the landscape were profound. Now that the formal plan of the house had declined in importance, its external expression in the form of axial avenues, symmetry and linear vistas became anomalous. The circular pattern of movement within the house could be replicated outside, not merely in the disposition of a 'serpentine' section of the gardens, but in the entire landscape – in the layout of the park itself. The connection operated on a number of levels. First, now that people were no longer accustomed to think of the house as a series of formal axes, they no longer expected to see these continued out into the grounds, and features like bow windows created a diversity of panoramas rather than prioritizing a limited range of framed prospects. Houses designed with a variety of facades were to be viewed not as a series of set elevations, but in a flowing, moving manner. Second, the way the surrounding landscape was used now mirrored

that of the rooms within the house – or to put it another way, the more informal patterns of intercourse that had moulded the design of the serpentine garden now shaped the wider parkland. In Girouard's words:

> The surroundings of . . . houses were reorganised in much the same way as the interiors, and for similar reasons . . . Guests or visitors, having done the circuit of the rooms, did the circuit of the grounds. Just as, at a big assembly, tea was served in one room and cards laid out in another, the exterior circuit could be varied by stopping at a temple to take tea, or at a rotunda to scan the view through a telescope.[31]

These developments also had implications for the changes in gender relations, and the development of a more 'feminized' society. Susan Groag Bell has argued that many women, throughout the eighteenth century, were keen gardeners and that while landscape gardens and parks – with their grand scale, implications of ownership and sometimes overtly political symbolism – were male spaces, gardens continued to be appropriated by women. 'Evidence abounds to indicate that eighteenth-century ladies gardened . . . Their flower gardens blossomed throughout the century even as the celebrated innovation of the landscape park was being shaped under male authority.'[32] This, moreover, may explain why flower gardens, shrubberies and the rest rather escaped the notice of contemporary commentators like Walpole or Mason, in spite of their ubiquity; and why modern scholars have sometimes assumed that Brown and his contemporaries set houses within open parkland, with no real gardens around them. It is certainly true that many aristocratic and gentry women were active gardeners. A visitor to St Paul's Walden Bury in Hertfordshire, for example, described how Mary Eleanor Bowes, Countess of Strathmore, 'pointed out to us the concern she had formerly taken in the shrubs, and flowerbeds, the lawns, the alcoves, and the walks, even the assistance her own hand had lent to individual articles'.[33] Lady Mary Coke described in 1767 gardening at her home in Notting Hill: 'The weather continues fine and pleasant. I planted many flowers and some plants but saw Nobody the whole day'; while in 1786 Hannah More remarked 'I work in my garden 2 or 3 hours every day ... I am rather proud of my pinks and Roses.'[34] William Shenstone's close friend and Viscount Bolingbroke of Dawley Farm's half-sister, Lady Luxborough, was a moving spirit in the polite gardening circle in Warwickshire. Estate maps and documents often identify particular areas of the immediate grounds of the mansion with the wife of the owner; the Duchess's Garden at Blenheim, for example, or Lady Buckinghamshire's Garden at Blickling in Norfolk. In this reading of the evidence, the eighteenth century saw, to some extent at least, a divergence of 'male' parks from 'female' gardens.

Such arguments should not, however, be pushed too far. Many gentlemen, as we shall see, were also enthusiastic gardeners in this period. In addition, where widows or single unmarried women controlled estates, they oversaw landscape improvements and park-making projects in much the same way as men. Elizabeth Montagu, the widow of the wealthy colliery owner and mathematician Edward Montagu, for example, commissioned Brown and Spyers to remodel the grounds at Sandleford Priory in the 1780s

and took a close interest in their activities.[35] The concentration of women's gardening activity within limited areas of the grounds of the country house reflects not so much particular interests, specific to gender, as the extent of control usually exercised by men in a patriarchal society over the landscape as a whole. But more importantly, whoever was in overall control of the design of the landscape park, some of its key features clearly indicate that it was laid out in a manner that ensured it could be enjoyed and consumed by both sexes.

The deer parks of the later seventeenth and early eighteenth centuries were certainly more an area of male than of female recreation. Hunting deer, while never exclusively an activity undertaken by men, was predominantly associated with them.[36] So, too, was the practice of fast riding across open parkland. Parks often provided one of the only places where gentlemen could ride fast, for long distances, unhindered by standing crops or fences – and at a time when the thoroughbred racehorse was the aristocratic status symbol par excellence. This association presumably explains the prominence of stables in parkland landscapes in the early and middle decades of the eighteenth century. At places like Chatsworth in Derbyshire or Houghton in Norfolk they were vast structures, designed by leading architects, and placed proudly in full view of house and park. But the horse was a particularly male symbol – its 'strength, speed and courage symbolised the superior status of its owner'.[37] Upper-class women did regularly ride, but modesty and mode of dress dictated that this was in a manner – usually side-saddle (with both legs on the same side of the horse) – which reduced the speed with which they could move. In the middle decades of the century improvements to riding dress, especially shortening of the skirt and riding coat, and a more masculine cut, made riding easier for women, but these innovations were widely criticized, Armstrong in 1763 for example commenting that 'This model of this Amazonian hunting-dress, for ladies, was first imported from France . . . but I cannot help thinking that it fits awkwardly on our English modesty.'[38] In short, while riding was emphatically not an exclusively male activity, it was one that was carried out with greater difficulty by women, at least when taking place over relatively rough ground; and in consequence deer parks were more likely to be ridden across by men than by women. The gravel drives and turf rides that featured so prominently in the parks of the Capability Men, however, do not only signal new recreational uses for the park, the sociable enjoyment of views and vistas, and of visits to temples and other ornamental buildings to take tea and the like. They also suggest that the park was being consumed in a more equal manner by both sexes, for they provided a ground surface better suited to the riding style of women, and allowed for the use of carriages of various kinds, generally deemed a more correct mode of transport for younger women especially. At the same time, while game shooting, as we have seen, often took place in parks, the rather more gruesome business of killing deer there declined rapidly after 1750. With their ornamental buildings in an often whimsical style, decorative planting and exotic trees, the parks created by Brown and his contemporaries were less masculine, more feminine spaces than true deer parks had been.

Changes in the design of country houses were thus closely related to the layout of the landscapes around them, and both together provided ideal arenas for polite interaction. But architectural changes in the 1760s arguably had another effect upon landscape design, crucial for the emergence of the style of Brown and the Capability Men: changes that constituted a challenge to Palladianism itself.

The rise of Neoclassicism

Palladianism, although a classical style, was essentially based on Renaissance interpretations of specifically Roman culture, understandings that were, in strict archaeological terms, often flawed. Palladio's designs for villas, for example – which became almost de rigueur for larger English country houses in the first half of the eighteenth century – had a rusticated ground floor and central projecting portico. These features were in fact derived, not from the *houses* of ancient Rome, but from Roman temples and public buildings, for these were larger structures which had generally survived in more intact if ruined form in the Italian landscape. As Allan Ramsay, the noted painter and antiquarian, observed in 1762:

> The present taste in architecture was formed, not upon the palaces and dwelling-houses of the ancient Greeks and Romans, of which there were no vestiges at the revival of the arts, but upon their temples and other buildings, from which the ornamental part has been borrowed and applied to domestic use, in a manner abundantly absurd, for the most part . . . which, nevertheless, custom has rendered agreeable to the sight.[39]

Ramsay's comments reflect the fact that in the middle decades of the eighteenth century a more accurate knowledge of classical art and architecture began to be disseminated across western Europe. Men such as the Abbé Winckelmann and the Comte de Caylus produced illustrated books on Roman antiquities, especially mosaics and sculpture, the result of close personal study of antiquities in Italy.[40] At the same time, dilettantes and intellectuals also began to explore the wider legacy of the classical world, turning their attention to Greek as well as Roman art and architecture, of which the Palladians had little enthusiasm and less knowledge. Particularly influential was Winckelmann's *Reflections on the Imitation of the Painting and Sculpture of the Greeks*, which appeared in 1755.[41] In the 1750s James 'Athenian' Stuart and Nicholas Revett, funded by the Society of Dilettanti, journeyed together to Athens, recorded the antiquities there, and published the first volume of their *Antiquities of Athens* in 1762.[42] By this time, the scale of archaeological excavations – initially to provide antiquities for the profitable foreign market – was increasing in southern Italy, and large numbers of Greek red-figure and black-figure vases reached England, many acquired by Sir William Hamilton (the British representative for a while at the Sicilian court in Naples) and eventually displayed at the collection he established as the British Museum. In Italy, Pompeii and Herculaneum were systematically excavated, the first beginning in 1738 and the second in 1748, and the finds from the latter were displayed to avid foreign visitors in museums near the site at Portici. All across Europe, this new knowledge helped fuel a reaction against the perceived errors of Palladianism as an architectural style, and also against the excesses of the Rococo as a form of internal decoration. For it became apparent, from excavations at Herculaneum especially, that Roman houses had been decorated with light, rather delicate painted schemes, featuring figures, foliage, birds and much else. They had not had the austere interiors envisaged by many Palladian designers, nor yet the flamboyant and flippant displays associated with the Rococo.

The impact of Neoclassicism on country house architecture in England is usually associated with the activities of Robert Adam. He was already an architect, trained in his father's Scottish practice, when in 1753 he travelled to Rome and embarked on a major project to measure the principal classical buildings there, in association with the great French draughtsman Charles-Louis Clérisseau, in an uncompleted attempt to update Desgodetz's book *Les Edifices antiques de Rome*. Clérisseau, and men such as Cardinal Albani and Piranesi, introduced him to the latest ideas not only about antiquity, but about the practice of architecture itself.[43] Adam came to join the ranks of those now questioning the God-like status of Palladio as an authority on the works of the ancients, finding him 'most faulty in many things and very unjust over his measurements'.[44] He became 'determined, in imitation of Scottish heroes, to attack Vitruvius, Palladio, and those blackguards of ancient and modern architecture, sword in hand'.[45] Perhaps more importantly, he also became convinced, from his study in particular of the public baths of Diocletian and Caracalla, that 'these Emperors have shown mankind that true Grandeur was only to be produced from simplicity and largeness of parts and that conveniency was not inconsistent with decoration'.[46] Returning to London in 1758, Adam began to put his ideas about 'The True, the Simple and the Grand

Architecture' into commercial practice, although it should be emphasized that he was no slavish copier of antiquity, but a designer of genius who also drew on other influences – the works of the English Palladians, and the buildings recently erected in France.

Although not denying the crucial significance of Adam in the rise of the new taste, stylistic change is always too complex to be ascribed to the genius of one man, or even to a wider group of artists, in this case including men like Revett and Stuart. The genesis of the new fashion was more gradual and complex than sometimes implied. As well as being part of a Europe-wide shift in the arts, Neoclassicism in Britain also had earlier indigenous roots – hardly surprising, in an age of educated antiquarians deeply imbued with a knowledge of classical civilization. Palladianism itself morphed easily into a quest for antique accuracy, perhaps especially in the context of the broader Scottish Enlightenment of which Adam formed a part. Sir John Clerk of Pennicuik, friend and patron to Robert Adam's father, had as early as the 1720s designed a new house at Mavisbank in Midlothian based, in part, on his understanding of Roman civilization derived from his knowledge as a practising archaeologist: 'To his empirical mind the excavation of Roman villas in Midlothian and the designing of a new house for Pennicuik were complementary activities.'[47] All this said, the impact of Adam as an individual is difficult to exaggerate.

Capitalizing in part on the contacts he had made with visiting English noblemen while staying in Italy, Adam's London practice flourished and he soon became known as a designer of buildings. By 1762, as we have seen, he was already in charge of the construction of a new house at Kedleston in Derbyshire for Sir Nathaniel Curzon, having previously worked on the design of temples for the grounds – preparing a plan for the grounds that is remarkably 'Brownian' in character (illus. 97, 98). Originally commissioned to oversee the execution of designs by James Paine and Matthew Brettingham, he began to make his own contributions to both the interior and exterior of the mansion. Other important commissions followed: Syon House in Middlesex in 1762, Luton Hoo in Bedfordshire in 1766, Harewood in Yorkshire in 1766 (again adapting earlier designs, this time by John Carr).[48] But while a successful architect Adam was, perhaps, more important in his role as what we would today call an interior designer. With his brother John he provided not only light, elegant and airy rooms based ultimately on the new understanding of classical styles, but in some cases the furniture to fill them (illus. 99, 100).[49] Indeed, the sophistication of his business echoed that of Brown itself – as did the somewhat repetitive character of its products.

> A large team of craftsmen was well controlled; quality of work and costs were assessed carefully, but much was created which was too similar. Adam's ceilings are colourful and well finished ... but comparing them is a weary business and differences are often minimal.[50]

Palladianism – especially the strict Palladianism of the 1720s and '30s – had, in general, made for sombre interiors. By the 1740s a Palladian exterior often hid rooms which were decorated and furnished, as we have seen, in a very different

97 The south front of Kedleston Hall, Derbyshire, designed by Robert Adam and built between 1760 and 1765.

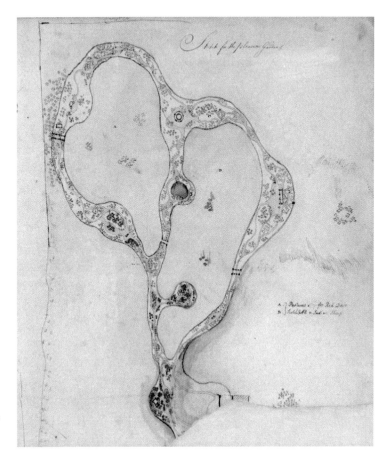

98 'Sketch for the Pleasure Garden, at Kedleston near Derby', c. 1758, attributed to Robert Adam.

99 The Library at Kenwood House is a fine example of Robert Adam's elegant and restrained Neoclassical style.

manner. The new style, in contrast, provided an overall coherence to houses, which could be classical both outside and in, with the latter sufficiently light and delicate to appeal to the new tastes of the polite. Adam's interiors thus fitted in well with Palladian houses, giving them an overall classical feel, but they unquestionably worked best in houses newly designed or extensively remodelled in Neoclassical mode.

As the Adam brothers began to provide fashionable new interiors for the wealthy through the 1760s, others – displaying the commercial acumen typical of the age – provided a range of consumer goods in a broadly Neoclassical style. Thomas Chippendale, a leading London cabinetmaker, produced an influential book of designs in 1754,

The Gentleman and Cabinet-maker's Director. Most of the pieces illustrated were in a broadly Rococo style but by the time a revised edition appeared in 1762 many of the designs were in a thoroughgoing Neoclassical mode, with simple lines and elegantly and rather sparsely decorated with carved swags, fruit, flowers and leaves, urns and other classical details.[51] But, in another striking parallel with Brown and his team, Chippendale not only provided individual pieces of furniture for wealthy clients, but advised on soft furnishings and worked with other professionals to provide entire schemes of interior decoration, at places like Nostell Priory and Normanton Hall in Rutland – often undertaking subcontracting when clients required specialist work outside the

100 Bowood House, Wiltshire: detail from the library doors, designed by Robert Adam.

professional skills of the firm itself.[52] Sometimes, not surprisingly, the business provided its services to houses where Adam was also working, as at Harewood in Yorkshire in 1767 – where Brown and his team were also busy transforming the grounds.[53] The popularity of the revised edition of Chippendale's *Director* ensured that Neoclassical styles of furniture were widely copied by provincial craftsmen: by the 1770s it was the dominant fashion in furniture design.

Equally important were the new ceramics produced, on a steadily increasing scale, by Josiah Wedgwood at his factories at Burslem in Staffordshire. Through the late 1750s he perfected a type of cream-glazed white earthenware, which came to be called Queensware, and which 'owed much of its success to the essentially neo-classical qualities of purity and simplicity of form'.[54] From 1767 he was marketing Black Basalte ware, a hard stoneware used to make urns, medallions, plaques and candlesticks with decoration inspired by antique originals, many taken from the Greek and Italian vases collected by men like Sir William Hamilton. Vases of the latter type were widely (if erroneously) known as 'Etruscan' and Wedgwood's new factory, opened in 1769, was christened 'Etruria'. From the start, Wedgwood and his partner, Thomas Bentley, seem to have been aware that they were addressing a gap in the market: Neoclassical interiors needed vases, urns, statuettes and ceramic tablets in an appropriate style.[55] By 1775 Wedgwood was producing Jasper ware, a fine-grained unglazed stoneware that was stained blue (more rarely green, black or yellow) and decorated with simple classical designs (bas-relief figures in classical dress, florets, urns and the like) that were made in separate moulds and then applied to the surface of the piece (illus.

101).[56] Tableware, vases and furniture moulds were all produced in this manner, together with medallions carrying portraits in the classical style. The 'antique manner' could be incorporated into every aspect of domestic design, from the overall form of a building to the decoration of its rooms, the style of its furniture and the character of its tableware. But what is also important is that, in Kelly's words, the new style's 'neatness of scale and proportion, in particular, made it very appropriate for small and medium sized houses'.[57] Mass-produced Neoclassical furniture and ceramics were cheap enough to be acquired by all who could aspire to membership of the polite.

The Neoclassical landscape

Capability Brown and his team were not isolated from this major shift in taste. Brown's direct connections with the Adam brothers were many. In the late 1760s Brown worked as architect on the houses at Croome and Ugbrooke for which they provided the interiors, while he and his team improved the grounds of a number of houses at precisely the same time as Adam was revamping them, to varying degrees, in the new fashion, including Alnwick in the early 1760s, Audley End in 1763, Luton Hoo and Compton Verney in the mid-1760s and Harewood at the end of the decade.[58] It is particularly noteworthy that one of the earliest fully developed Brown land-scapes – with belts, circuit drives and the rest – at Bowood, begun in 1763, was designed to complement a house which was being radically modified by Adam (with the actual work being supervised by Henry Holland), and as a setting for the fine mausoleum recently designed by Robert Adam for the 1st Earl Shelburne. In

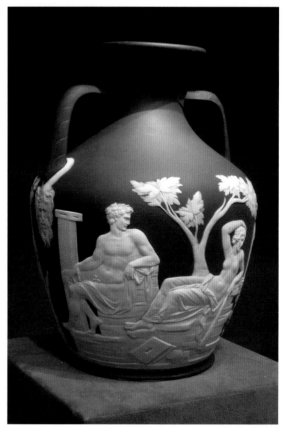

101 An example of Josiah Wedgwood's Jasper ware: the Portland Vase, *c.* 1790.

Stroud's words, 'Adam could hardly have hoped for a more advantageous setting for his fine classical essay, with its Doric portico guarding the entrance to a domed, top-lit cella containing Carlini's monument to the Earl, a simple sarco-phagus resting on a high plinth with an inscribed tablet.'[59] Brown's landscapes similarly comple-mented numerous houses where Chippendale coordinated the internal decoration or where Wedgwood supplied architectural details or decorative features. When Brown designed a new mansion for Lord Gower at Trentham in Staffordshire, a few kilometres from Wedgwood's factories, the library was provided with a tablet and two friezes in Jasper ware, Wedgwood later describing to his partner Thomas Bentley how

> He [Brown] express'd his strongest appro-bation and even admiration of what he had seen. He preferred them greatly to sculpture in marble, and would make use of them himself as an architect when he had an opportunity and recommend them everywhere. He assur'd me of his real attach-ment to our interest from the merit of our productions . . . Mr Brown said they were pretty colours and he should not object to those for the ground of a room, but they did not come up to his idea of the ground of a tablet, nor would any other colour, unless it was a copy of some natural and valuable stone . . . This gentleman, if there is any confidence to be placed in the greatest appar-ent sincerity and earnestness, means really to serve us, and he gives for his reason – because we deserve it.[60]

The men were evidently kindred spirits.

Brown's own architectural works reflect, in general terms, the gradual relaxation of Palladian forms and their subsequent replacement by Neo-classical ones. His early houses, such as Newnham Paddox with its corner turrets, were firmly in the Palladian tradition, although in keeping with the work of other designers they now eschewed such strict elements as the *piano nobile* raised a full storey above a rustic. By the late 1760s, at places like Claremont, Brown and Holland were together

102 Benham Park near Newbury, Berkshire, viewed from the south. Built in the late 1770s, this Neoclassical composition by Brown and Holland appears perfectly in harmony with its minimalist landscape. The upper floor is a nineteenth-century addition.

producing designs that were more Neoclassical than Palladian in inspiration. Benham Park (illus. 102), built in *c.* 1775, is a thoroughgoing Neoclassical house, as is Berrington in Hereford-shire (1778), although in both cases the design may have owed more to Henry Holland than to Brown.

Yet it is important to emphasize that Neo-classicism, as it gradually affected a range of arts in Europe, was not simply about a more faithful imitation of the culture of Greece and Rome. It also, just as importantly, involved a taste for the simple and the 'pure', and a reaction against 'superfluous ornament'. Imitation of antiquity was a way of returning to a 'true style', to the essence of things. But the true and the unchanging could only be discovered through the application of reason, and through observation.[61] In this age of science and industry, moreover, the idea was not merely to imitate, in a slavish manner, the styles of distant times. 'Wedgwood's method, in the approved manner of neo-classicism, was to improve upon rather than copy the antique.'[62]

The landscapes created by Brown and the Capability Men can be read as expressions of this same nexus of ideas. Their style mirrored the concerns of the Neoclassical architects, with its emphasis on planes, simplicity and distinct, con-tinuous outlines rather than on the complex, fussy forms of the Rococo, or the rugged and broken lines beloved of later 'Picturesque' designers. They contained allusions to antiquity, and usually to classical antiquity – now often executed in more archaeologically accurate mode (illus. 103). But they were also about antiquity improved, even about modernity. Kitchen gardens with ingen-ious hot walls and stoves were also strung along the circuit (illus. 104, 105, 106), and collections of exotic animals discovered through modern exploration. Above all they expressed the concept

103 The parish church of Ayot St Lawrence in Hertfordshire, which stands within the park of Ayot House, was designed in 1778–9 in the form of a Greek temple by Nicholas Revett for Sir Lionel Lyde, tobacco merchant and Director of the Bank of England.

104 The 'hot' wall added by Brown to the kitchen garden at Kimberley in Norfolk as part of his improvements in 1778. The stoke holes are visible on the left of the picture.

105 Brown's design for a greenhouse at Ashburnham in Sussex, c. 1767.

that the ideal landscape – certainly the ideal landscape for the man of wealth and taste – was that of nature's beauties judiciously revealed: an ideal distilled through observation and abstraction. Brown's very moniker reflects his insistence, widely shared, that the pure and essential character of place could be brought to the fore through the exercise of human agency. A landscape had 'capabilities' that could be highlighted and perfected once they had been identified. This was

106 Brown's plan for Hill Place, Horsham, Sussex, 1769. The key notes the position of the old and the new kitchen gardens, the approaches, the 'water as intended', as well as the gravel walks, the 'new road through the grounds', and the approach to the house. The kitchen garden is accessed directly from the main 'gravel walk' leading through the park.

different from the notion inherent in the gardens of the 1730s, '40s and early '50s that a landscape should be liberally stuffed with emblematic features, the associative power of which would transport the viewer to some distant place or time. It was the totality of the design that mattered, and the essential truth it revealed was timeless and eternal, and accessible by all with the required 'taste'. It was not, as earlier forms of landscape architecture had been, a matter of ephemeral fashion or whim. As Brown himself put it: 'Place-making, and a good English Garden, depend intirely upon Principle and have very little to do with Fashion, for it is a word that in my opinion disgraces Science wherever it is found.'[63]

The essential shapes of lakes and shrubberies on Brown's plans reflect this journey, moving from serpentine but highly structured Rococo forms to stylized flowing lines, abstract yet reflective of and shaped by the underlying topography. Earlier generations of garden designers had perhaps been moving in this direction. In some of Switzer's writings, for example, we can discern the notion that the study of concrete 'Nature' through observation of actual landscape, an essentially empirical approach, was preferable to a conception of ideal Nature based on logic and geometry – the old Neoplatonic concept of natural forms. 'The natural Gardener [will make] his Design submit to Nature, and not Nature to his Design.'[64] Some of the stripped-down parkland settings for houses produced by Kent, and even by Bridgeman, in the 1730s and '40s seem to express similar notions. But in general, when writers in the first half of the century talked about consulting the 'genius of the place', this was more to allow the particular characteristics of the local topography to generate variety in a design: the earlier phases of the 'landscape' movement,

the designs of William Kent and what are loosely described as Rococo gardens, were all about exploration and the diversity of experience. Brown's assessment of a place's 'capabilities' and his careful manipulation of land forms, water and planting were intended to achieve something different: to create an ideal landscape based on unchanging principles that to a significant extent transcended the particular character of an individual locality. The configuration of landforms was revealed and accentuated by the creation of lakes, for the edges of the water, backing up behind the dam, served to reveal with clarity the form of the contours, albeit with some additional, selective sculpting. It was for this reason that the margins of Brown's

107 Brown's magnificent lake at Castle Ashby, Northamptonshire.

water bodies were kept scrupulously free of reeds and other vegetation (illus. 107). In a similar manner, planting the upper slopes of valleys (as at places like Ashridge) or the summits of hills both displayed and accentuated the raw shapes of the ground surface (illus. 108). In the earlier chapters of this book we used, as many garden historians do, the term 'formal' to describe the geometric gardens of the seventeenth and early eighteenth centuries, in part to avoid an endless repetition of the word 'geometric'. And given that they served as arenas for structured, highly formalized social encounters, the use is perhaps justified. But the landscapes of Brown and the Capability Men are perhaps more aptly described

in this way, as they relied on pureness of form – of the natural form, of the land surface. In the words of Robert Williams, Brown sought to reveal the 'timeless, unchanging permanence of form hidden beneath [nature's] superficial and local variations'.[65]

In Brown's landscapes, largely cleared as they were of the clutter of temples, tents and fake ruins, the house became the principal and in some cases the only garden building, the main focus of the views from the approach and the circuit drives, stripped often of service ranges, yards and other distractions. The sparse simplicity of the landscape park – the sweeps of turf, the swelling, smooth landforms, the shimmering acres of

108 The 'Golden Valley', Ashridge, Hertfordshire.

109 Brown worked at Ickworth in Suffolk between 1769 and 1776 but on a landscape focused on a different house, on a different site, to that shown here. This section of parkland may include some of his planting; either way, the simple landscape provides an ideal setting for the 4th Earl of Bristol's unusual Neoclassical house, erected in the 1790s.

water – provided peculiarly suitable settings for houses with stripped-down classical lines, just as Wedgwood's Jasper ware was intended from the start to harmonize with Neoclassical interiors. Brown's own compositions in this mode, such as Benham Park, seem to sit perfectly in the landscapes he designed for them (see illus. 102), and the same is true of buildings and landscapes in these styles more generally, as at Ickworth in Suffolk (illus. 109).[66] But as we have seen, Brown, like Kent, was not averse to designing buildings in Gothick style, and his landscapes served equally well as a setting for ancient houses like Burghley, or Baroque mansions like Grimsthorpe, as for houses newly built in Neoclassical mode (illus. 110, 111). It was the relationship of mansion and landscape, direct and simple, and the primacy of the former in the latter, that was key.

The harmony of architecture and landscape design operated the other way, moreover, for the views across the simple parkland, and tasteful shrubberies, worked well from light and airy interiors designed in the style of Adam. It is important to emphasize once again how often the redesign of landscapes by Brown and his associates coincided with the building of a new mansion, or with the extensive remodelling of an existing one. When Brown began to work at Kimberley in Norfolk in 1762, for example, Thomas Prowse's remodelling of the Hall – originally built around 1712 – was still continuing. The work involved widening all the windows, 'in order to come all four foot wide which was but 3 foot 6 inches':[67] the improved views across Brown's parkland would have harmonized particularly well with the interior plasterwork, in Neoclassical mode,

110 Burghley House, Northamptonshire: the sixteenth-century house in its setting beside Brown's lake, viewed from the bridge he designed in the 1770s.

being added by John Sanderson, one of Sanderson Miller's associates. Lady Elizabeth Montagu of Sandleford Priory in Berkshire described in 1782 how Brown 'has made a plan to make my grounds, in prospect of the house and new rooms, very pleasing', adding, in a subsequent letter:

> Mr Brown . . . has much improved the view to the south and having at my request made a fair light over the east window so that the arch formed by the trees is now visible. These rooms are the most beautiful imaginable with the shelter the comfort the conveniences of walls and roofs you have beautiful passage of the green shade of a grove.[68]

Where Brown undertook more extensive architectural alterations, the relationships between house and landscape could be complex and sophisticated. At Corsham Court in Wiltshire in 1761 he made considerable modifications to the existing sixteenth-century mansion. He widened both the east and the west wings, much of the former being occupied by a magnificent gallery, designed to house Paul Methuen's fine collection of pictures, inherited from his godfather.[69] Both wings are designed in a style that, from the south (entrance) front, strongly echoes the house's sixteenth-century architecture. But the north front of the hall was rebuilt in 1742 in a vaguely Palladian style to designs by Nathaniel Ireson; the east front of the east wing, which adjoins it, was accordingly designed by Brown in a loosely classical mode. Brown also remodelled the park and pleasure grounds and the windows in the picture gallery – in the east front – would have looked out towards the lake, although this was not in fact constructed until Repton was called in in the early nineteenth century.[70] The view eastwards, across Brown's parkland, was enhanced by the fact that the gallery was raised up significantly above ground level. These views, through the large windows of the gallery, seem to fit perfectly the interior of the gallery, designed by Brown and with a ceiling – Rococo, but with Neoclassical elements – by Thomas Stocking. The room was equipped with mirrors by Adam and a set of furniture by Chippendale. Where Brown was responsible not only for the design

of both a house and its grounds, but for the siting of the former, landscape and architecture could be brought into even greater harmony. Watts described how Brown and Holland's new house at Claremont was 'Happily designed and situated, as to command fine views from the four fronts'.[71]

Such close integration of house and landscape was not in itself new. As we have seen, the formal gardens of the seventeenth century had in one sense functioned as outside 'rooms', an extension of the formal space of the house. But what was new, perhaps, was the sheer extent to which the designs of the house and its grounds were now integrated, and in a manner that reduced the relationship between the two to its bare, formal essentials; in part this was because the design of

111 Grimsthorpe Castle, Lincolnshire: Vanbrugh's Baroque house, overlooking the lake within Capability Brown's park.

both was often in the hands of a single individual, and most expertly in the hands of Brown. In the words of William Mason:

> Brown, I know, was ridiculed for turning architect, but I always thought he did it from a kind of necessity having found the great difficulty which must frequently have occurred to him in forming a picturesque whole, where the previous building had been ill-placed, or of improper dimensions.[72]

Indeed, it might be argued – adopting a broader perspective – that the more general rise of the 'landscape' style in the middle decades of the eighteenth century was associated with the blurring of the lines between architecture on the one hand, and garden design on the other. Leading seventeenth-century garden designers like London and Wise do not appear to have provided designs for houses, or even for garden buildings, and their concentration on the design of planting – and on that of basic hard landscaping – was continued by other members of the Brompton Park tradition, Stephen Switzer and Charles Bridgeman. But Sir John Vanbrugh was an architect turned landscape designer and William Kent designed interiors, and garden buildings, before turning his hands to garden layouts. Brown, followed by Repton, represents an intensification of this trajectory, one which, while perhaps independent of the new Neoclassical sensibilities, nevertheless accorded well with them.

Neoclassicism, modernity and improvement

The new Neoclassical taste was more than just an architectural fashion or a style of decoration. To varying degrees, to different bodies of consumers, it meant something, or perhaps more accurately a range of things. Like Palladianism, it embodied or was allied with certain broader philosophical attitudes. Neoclassicism originated in France as, in essence, a reaction against the Rococo, which its proponents dismissed as a frivolous mode of decoration, bereft of meaning and decadent; and also against the Baroque, still the dominant architectural style in most parts of the Continent, which was (and had long been) identified with the ancien régime of European court aristocracies, and thus with authoritarian power and religious 'superstition'. These two broad styles – one principally decorative, the other architectural – were thus together identified with the status quo, with the old order. Neoclassicism in contrast was broadly aligned, in France especially, with the philosophy of the Enlightenment, and appealed to those sections of society keen on reforming social and political institutions, replacing tradition and superstition with rationality. As Adrian Forty has emphasized, the study of the physical remains of the classical past was not an end in itself, nor was it simply undertaken to provide stylistic models. Instead it 'provided inspiration for how the present could be'.[73] In Hugh Honour's words, 'Neoclassicism, in its most vital expressions . . . sought to bring about – whether by patient scientific advance or by purgative return à la Rousseau to primitive simplicity and purity – a new and better world governed by the immutable laws of reason and equity.'[74] Yet at the same time the style offered a measure of reassurance in a rapidly changing world, for to contemporaries the classical past appeared not only rational but stable: Neoclassicism, in Hilary Young's words, was popular because it offered a 'fusion of modernity with Classicism, a combination that allowed the middle and upper classes to feel at ease with the march of progress'.[75]

Of course, there was never a simple connection between social philosophy and an enthusiasm for particular styles of art or architecture. It was Madame de Pompadour's cousin, the Marquis de Vandières, who was sent in 1749 to Italy and returning in 1751 commissioned sculptures, paintings and buildings in Paris in a more rigorously classical style.[76] Moreover, Neoclassicism carried rather different meanings in England from those in France and other European countries, because of different political histories and different social structures. England had undergone a revolution in the middle of the seventeenth century that had swept away the structures of the absolutist state and arbitrary royal power that had continued to survive in France and in many other parts of Europe. These political gains had been further consolidated by the Glorious Revolution of 1688 and the Hanoverian succession of 1714. The Palladian revolution, the triumph of a more 'accurate' classical form of architecture over the Baroque, reflected the ascendancy of an oligarchy of wealthy landowners, businessmen and financiers, and the triumph of Parliament over the untrammelled power of the Crown. This said, these groups, and also a wider constituency of consumers, were ready for a style that would take this revolution in taste much further, at a time when England was poised for economic take-off into industrial and agricultural revolution. There was a clear link between Neoclassicism on the one hand and the rage for 'improvement' in all its forms that was now sweeping through the country on the other.

'Improvement' is itself a slippery term, used in a wide range of contexts, as we have already seen.[77] In terms of landscape and land management, improvement might mean the creation of a fashionable parkland setting for a mansion, or the creation of an elaborate pleasure ground with exotic buildings. Sir John Parnell's description of Stourhead, made in 1768, opens with the comment that he came 'to view the improvements', goes on to note how he was 'charmed with a fine view in an improvement'; and asserts that he 'never beheld such a goodnatured improvement', which included 'the most elegant expensive building I ever saw in an improvement'.[78] In these contexts, the demonstration of personal wealth displayed through making aesthetic changes to the landscape was critical. As Sterling explained to Lord Ogleby in *The Clandestine Marriage* (1765), 'The chief pleasure of a country house is to make improvements, you know, my lord. I spare no expence, not I.'[79] But the term 'improvement' was also used, and perhaps more frequently, to describe practical changes, applied to the wider estate landscape. The enclosure of open fields and the reclamation of heaths, moors and other common land was frequently so described. So, too, were the schemes of afforestation that were, throughout the eighteenth century, so fashionable among landowners. And in an age of restless commercial expansion, the word could be applied to many other key transformations of the environment that were intended to increase production and profit, including the creation or upgrading of roads, canals or port facilities, the making of elegant new urban spaces for polite consumption and parade – even, in time, the provision of better prisons and workhouses.[80] 'Improvement', in short, could mean very different things in different contexts. But it always involved an assumption – foreign to the period before the Civil War, but firmly in the ascendant by the time of Brown – that nothing in the universe was God-given and immutable. Anything could be changed by human agency, by the application of knowledge, taste and capital, in ways appropriate to use and character. This was more than an expression of Whig ideology. It was the spirit of the times.

Making places

It is within these wider contexts of 'improvement' that we need to examine some of the details of Brown's work for, while often today thought of as a 'landscape designer', he was as we have seen a 'place-maker' who attempted to supply, in his own words, 'all the elegance and all the comforts which Mankind wants in the Country' – civilizing, as it were, the existing rural environment in a range of ways in order to make it suitable for a polite clientele with increasingly urban tastes.[81] Careful examination of his plans for places like Hill Place in Horsham, Sussex (see illus. 106), indicates the wide range of feature present in such landscapes, the key noting the position of the haha, the 'intended water', the 'Ride', menagerie and 'gothic building', as well as that of the ice house, the 'Melon Ground and Stoves', the orchard, kitchen garden and stables; he also supplied a design for a greenhouse. But what is equally striking is the fact that aspects of 'place-making' represented wider forms of 'improvement', here applied to the particular context of the residences of the wealthy.

The enthusiasm of Brown, or his clients, for water management and land drainage is a case in point. In medieval times, and well into the

seventeenth century, important houses had often been built in low-lying sites because moats, fishponds and ornamental or semi-ornamental water features had been key markers of status. As late as 1724 the writer Roger North could write in praise of moats, and of canals in close proximity to the house; sales particulars for East Harling in Norfolk, drawn up in 1707, typically describe the hall (an 'ancient building') as standing 'low for the convenience of fishponds, and water, but dry'.[82] In the course of the eighteenth century, however, sites close to water were increasingly regarded as unhealthy, and writers like John Armstrong urged the avoidance of 'mournful plains/Where osiers thrive and trees that love the lake' as places to build. If such locations could not be avoided, then the reader was enjoined to 'Correct the soil, and dry the forces up/of watry exhalation; wide and deep/Conduct your trenches thro' the spouting bog'.[83] The best solution, however, was to select a drier and preferably elevated site:

Chiefly for this I praise the man who builds
High on the breezy ridge, whose lofty sides
Th'etherial deep with endless billows laves,
His purer mansion nor contagious years
Shall reach, nor deadly putrid airs annoy.[84]

Where mansions were built or rebuilt on new sites in the course of the eighteenth century these were almost invariably in elevated locations, looking down on valleys where, whenever possible, rivers were ponded back to form lakes, distant yet visible from them. There was a growing distaste for damp, 'moory' ground even where it lay at a distance from the mansion, and much effort was directed towards improving the condition of low-lying grassland within parks. If it could not be so improved, it should be drowned if possible beneath the waters of a lake. Lord Dacre thus described in 1759, in a letter to Sanderson Miller, how Brown's proposed lake within the park at Belhus would be

> A very great ornament to that side of the Park and quite change the Face of it. By what I have said you will immediately conceive that all the rushy part of Bumstead Mead will be converted into water, and that the Black moory soil will be taken away till we come to the parts of the meadow that rise and where the soil is gravel.[85]

Nothing came of the proposal until the 1770s, but Dacre continued to worry about the damp and marshy condition of the spot, noting in 1761: 'The truth is that I never ride that way without longing to do something there; as I know that that coarse meadow and moory sided canal might be converted into a very pleasing scene: and Brown is of the same opinion.'[86]

What also needs to be emphasized is that control of water within pleasure ground and park, the creation of artificial water bodies and of expanses of dry turf through drainage were closely allied to other contemporary forms of improvement. The principles of agricultural land drainage using 'bush' drains, lined with twigs and branches, for example, had long been appreciated in England but had usually taken the form of laying single drains, or small groups of drains, to improve particularly damp areas of ground. The practice of 'thorough' drainage, in contrast – filling a field with a network of drains – seems only to have developed in the course of

the eighteenth century; in the period after 1750, as agricultural prices rose, it spread rapidly, becoming standard practice in arable districts.[87] By the time of Brown's death it was even being adopted – in the form of stone-lined 'soughs' – in upland districts, especially where damp, acid moorland was being reclaimed. Other forms of agricultural water management were also important in this period. The 'floating' or irrigating of watermeadows to force an early growth of grass, and to ensure a bumper hay crop in the summer month – a procedure that involved constructing a complex network of artificial channels and sluices, which also served to better drain the areas in question – had first been adopted on a large scale in the early seventeenth century, but seems to have expanded rapidly after the Restoration, and especially from around 1700, particularly on the chalklands of southern Britain.[88] Landowners keen to demonstrate their involvement in agricultural innovation often constructed examples within their parks, as at Woburn Abbey in Bedfordshire where the system of leats and 'carriers' was fed from the Temple Reservoir.[89] The second agreement made by Brown with Viscount Weymouth at Longleat in 1758 stipulated that a number of the ponds near the mansion should be thrown together and a substantial head of water thus created which could be used to supply the intended offices, to 'occasionally' clean the house, and 'to float the Meadows'.[90]

The most important 'improvement' involving large-scale water engineering was, however, the creation of the canal network, the expansion and development of which was broadly contemporary with Brown's career. Lake-making and canal construction employed similar methods and techniques. Improvements had been made to navigable rivers since the Middle Ages, and the first major canal in England was constructed as early as 1566 (the Exeter Canal in Devon). But the next (the Sankey Brook Navigation, connecting the coalfields of south Lancashire to the Mersey) came in 1757, soon followed by the Bridgewater Canal, connecting the Duke of Bridgewater's coal mines at Worsley with Manchester, which was constructed between 1759 and 1761 – precisely the same years in which the duke's grounds at Ashridge in Hertfordshire were being landscaped by Brown and his house was rebuilt by Henry Holland. Canals proliferated rapidly thereafter.[91]

Another key element of Brown's parks, the gravelled drives approaching the house, crossing the park and sometimes running through the circuit belt, were also a particular manifestation of a more general 'improvement'. In the early eighteenth century – at the time of London and Wise – road travel had been a slow and difficult business, for even the major routeways had, at best, only sporadic and rudimentary surfacing. Until the later seventeenth century the maintenance of all roads, even the most important, was the responsibility of the parishes through which they ran, and local people often had neither the resources nor the will to maintain to a proper standard major routes, heavily used by traffic. Daniel Defoe memorably described how the highway leading from Baldock to Stevenage in Hertfordshire was so bad that farmers set up tolls on the gates into adjacent fields, 'which travellers always chose to pay, rather than plunge into sloughs and holes, which no horse could wade through'.[92] Some roads were improved through acts of individual philanthropy but it was only from the late seventeenth century that bodies

called 'turnpike trusts' began to be established, by individual Acts of Parliament, to take on the care of the most important routes. Their trustees were empowered to erect toll gates, charge tolls and use the proceeds to pay for repairs and improvements, after a proportion had been taken as profit. A large number of trusts were established in the first half of the eighteenth century but it was the period from 1750 to 1780 – that is, the years of Brown's career – which saw the consolidation of a national system, with over 300 turnpike acts passed between 1750 and 1760 alone, affecting some 10,000 miles of road.[93] Construction techniques were improved markedly under the direction of men like John Metcalf, who perfected the construction of well-drained roads on firm foundations, with a smooth convex surface of stone or gravel on a foundation of heather or brushwood. The number of road bridges, in particular, increased massively during the period of Brown's career. 'In the mid-eighteenth century bridges were still the exceptional way of crossing large rivers, and many of those that did exist were too narrow for horse-drawn vehicles. Fords and ferries predominated'; but 'the rapid increase in road traffic brought about by turnpiking, and the demand for shorter routes' led to a spate of bridge construction thereafter.[94] By the time of Brown's death in 1783 the state of public roads was vastly better than it had been in the first half of the century.

During the same period there were, moreover, significant developments in the design of carriages. Until the early eighteenth century suspension had been rudimentary, in part because road conditions ensured that traffic usually moved at low speeds. The better opportunities for travel presented by improved roads saw the publication of a range of texts describing new designs for wheels, axles and suspension. Technical innovations, many of them the subject of patents, went in and out of fashion, but of particular significance was the widespread adoption in the first half of the century of C-spring suspension on coaches, the main form of both public and private travel.[95] The middle decades of the century saw the development of a new range of pleasure vehicles, smaller and lighter than anything seen before, a powerful indication that driving could now be an enjoyable leisure activity. By the 1740s the landau, a four-wheeled carriage with a two-part hood that could be thrown back so that passengers might enjoy the open air, was coming into widespread use. By the 1750s it had been joined by the curricle, a light two-wheeled carriage, and the phaeton, a light open-topped vehicle on which the seats were raised high above the ground, and which was known for its ability to negotiate sharp bends: the sports car of its time.

The networks of drives that made their appearance in the parks of Brown and other improvers through the 1760s represented, in an important sense, an extension of the new, improved road network. Of particular significance are the bridges that were a central feature of many park designs (illus. 112). Most were gratuitous, unnecessary adornments: Brown, and to an extent his contemporary designers, went out of their way to carry approaches across rivers or lakes, even where other routes would have been possible and easier. A passion for bridges cannot be seen in isolation from the sudden upsurge of bridge building that occurred in the wider countryside: they were symbols of modernity. And the very importance of drives and rides reflected new possibilities of, and a new attitude towards, travel in horse-drawn vehicles, and the new forms of such vehicles that were now becoming available. If these improvements had not occurred, it is hard to believe that Brown's serpentine rides and drives – and the way in which his landscapes

112 Brown's design for a bridge at Grimsthorpe Castle, Lincolnshire, 1771.

were designed around them – would have been so popular with his clients.

THE LANDSCAPES CREATED by the Capability Men cannot be understood simply in terms of the history of garden design, not least because parks and pleasure grounds often formed part of a wider package of improvements that might embrace anything from the rebuilding of the house and the drainage of its vicinity to the design of kitchen gardens or even drying yards. The work of Brown and his associates was the manifestation, in the context of the homes of the wealthy, of a more general spirit of 'improvement', and expressed at a domestic level many of the wider concerns, and wider achievements, of society in this age of economic and environmental transformation. But the social and ideological developments that were the preconditions for agricultural and industrial revolution themselves shaped the design of country houses and their grounds, providing spaces and facilities suitable for the lifestyles of the polite, and a way of separating this group from the rest of society. And at the same time, the essential aesthetic of the 'landscape' style constituted one manifestation of the new Neoclassical taste that now dominated architecture, interior design and much else, and which was, in Britain as in other European countries, so closely allied to the improving ethos which underpinned the ideology of the dominant groups in society.

SIX

Alternatives and Oppositions

THE FORMULA DEVELOPED and propagated by Lancelot Brown and the Capability Men through the 1760s and '70s was immensely popular and successful. By the 1780s the majority of important houses in England stood in some version of a landscape park (illus. 113). We should not, however, assume that their style was universally adopted, or universally admired. Historians, perhaps especially garden historians, sometimes exaggerate the extent to which particular fashions were embraced by society, underestimating the importance of alternative stylistic currents, including both parallel streams of ideas and the continued survival of earlier, supposedly moribund traditions. Yet because the dominant styles in any period generally developed from one or more of these earlier fashions, and particular gardens might thus at any one time embrace, to varying degrees, the old and the new, the identification and even definition of such alternatives can prove problematic. In the case of the 1760s and '70s, this difficulty is compounded by the fact that some of the most famous gardens in the land, widely admired and extensively visited, are often discussed as if they were simply versions of the kinds of landscapes created by Brown and his fellows, whereas in reality they followed different principles of design, and were to some extent used and experienced in different ways.

The Rococo survival

In 1751 Walpole expressed his delight in the 'Albano glut of buildings' at Stowe but, by adding the words 'let them be ever so much condemned', implied that such architectural clutter was no longer universally admired.[1] By 1768 other famous landscapes were being criticized on similar grounds, Sir John Parnell noting of Philip Southcote's *ferme ornée* at Woburn Farm:

> Where different nations are thus introduced into an improvement they should at least be hid from one another by an hill, wood or clump of trees . . . to exhibit a Greek Temple within an hundred yards of a Gothic which comes again as near a Chinese is as irreconcilable to Fancy as to Nature or Reason.[2]

But the evocative and emblematic gardens of the late 1730s and '40s, with their ornamental buildings, serpentine paths and exotic planting, and from which Brown's own designs steadily

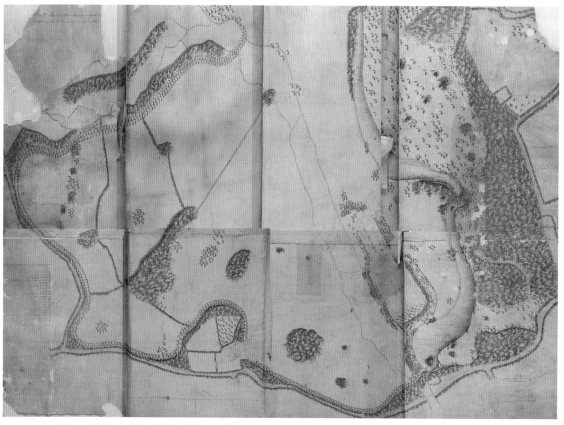

113 Brown's design for Ashburnham in Sussex, 1771, with lake, clumps, perimeter belt and circuit ride.

diverged, did not suddenly disappear in the second half of the century. On the contrary. While the increasingly professionalized gardening business produced large-scale landscapes in which land-forms, planting and water were the key elements, many wealthy and educated owners continued to create or develop gardens in a broadly Rococo tradition, essentially extended pleasure grounds liberally stuffed with exotic buildings and struc-tures. The decline in the dominance of the royal court in determining fashions in garden design, and the other changes in social organization which encouraged the rise of the Capability Men and their landscapes of Neoclassical simplicity, also set numerous talented amateurs free to design all

kinds of weird and wonderful landscapes; and the advent of Brown did not see a sudden cessa-tion of their activities.

Stourhead in Wiltshire is a classic example. Henry Hoare, a wealthy banker, began to lay out the gardens here following the death of his mother in 1741, creating a busy, eclectic compo-sition around a small lake in a steep-sided valley.[3] In typical fashion, the main area of the gardens lay away from, and was largely invisible from, the mansion itself, the immediate surroundings of which included an avenue of pines and other geometric features (illus. 114, 115). The gardens as we see them today, as is so often the case, provide a somewhat misleading impression of their

114, 115 Views made in the
1770s of the gardens at
Stourhead in Wiltshire,
by Coplestone Warre
Bampfylde.

original appearance, not so much because of the
overlay of Victorian planting but as a consequence of the loss of many of the less permanent
wooden buildings, leaving behind only Hoare's
more elegant stone-built classical temples beside
the lake: the Temple of Ceres or Flora, the Grotto
of the Nymph and the Pantheon or Temple of

Hercules, their disposition evidently intended to
mirror the elements in one of Claude Lorrain's
paintings. No trace remains of the other structures, many lining the zig-zag descent to the
lake: the Turkish Tent, Gothic Greenhouse,
Chinese Pavilion, Chinese Ombrello, Hermitage
or Venetian Seat (the mosque that was to occupy

one of the islands in the lake does not appear to have been built).[4] The precise order in which these buildings appeared is not entirely clear but the gardens evidently continued to develop along these superficially old-fashioned lines right through the 1760s, and even into the '70s: the hermit's cell was added in 1771 and the present form of the Grotto of the Nymph is the consequence of a rebuilding as late as 1776.[5]

Equally famous were the gardens at Hagley in Worcestershire, where Sir Thomas Lyttelton, and more importantly his son George Lyttelton (who succeeded to the estate in 1751), laid out a pictorial circuit walk in an extended garden of around 60 hectares, punctuated by ponds, cascades, seats, a mock castle designed by Sanderson Miller, 'Pope's Seat' (a Palladian temple-like building), a grotto, a rotunda, other Palladian buildings, the Temple of Theseus (designed by James 'Athenian' Stuart) and various urns and sculptures (including a much-admired statue of Venus).[6] Although much of this was laid out before Brown's new style really emerged – the castle was erected in 1747–8, as was the rotunda, and the Temple of Theseus in 1758 – the gardens continued to develop through the 1760s, with the Palladian bridge being built around 1764 and other features added up until the time of Lyttelton's death in 1773. The famous and much-visited gardens at Painshill in Surrey – with amphitheatre, ruined abbey, Turkish tent, 'Alpine valley' and much more – similarly continued to evolve well into the period of Brown's dominance, up until the death of their owner, Charles Hamilton, in 1773 (illus. 116). Even after this visitors still came, as they did to other famous

116 Gothick summerhouse (*c.* 1750) and the lake at Painshill, Surrey.

117 Shugborough in Staffordshire *c.* 1780, showing the Palladian bridge, triumphal arch, the 'Lanthorn of Demosthenes', the pagoda and the obelisk, all erected (with other features) between 1747 and 1771 by Thomas Anson, after he had cleared away the village of Shugborough from beside the Hall.

Rococo gardens. In 1777 Heeley published his *Description of Hagley Park*, evidently aimed at the tourist, full of energetic appreciation for the place:

> An elegant temple, rising in a circular bend ... will fasten your attention, and compel you to acknowledge, no building ever stood so powerfully conducive to the pleasure of landscape; as you walk along, your eye is for ever upon it, til you come to a green seat, which probably will detain you for a moment in pleasure, before you enter the environs of the Grotto.[7]

As late as 1791 one visitor recorded with approval how 'the walks are much enhanced by all kinds of exotic trees and lead sometimes through ruins or towards a hermitage, sometimes

towards a Greek temple from which one enjoys a very splendid view or towards the Temple of Bacchus in fine architectural style.'[8]

Such famous examples, widely visited by the educated public, could be augmented with a host of less well-known places laid out in similar style. The park at Shugborough in Staffordshire contained, by the 1770s, a Chinese pagoda, a 'Temple of the Winds', an arch based on the arch of Hadrian in Athens, the 'Lanthorne of Demosthenes', a Palladian bridge and numerous other features (illus. 117).[9] At Kew, the residence of Princess Augusta, the 1750s and '60s saw the erection of an 'Alhambra', a 'Chinese Menagerie', numerous classical temples, a Turkish mosque ('whose dome is crowned with a crescent and decorated with Arabic inscriptions taken from the Koran'), a 'Gothick cathedral', the tall pagoda which still survives, a ruined arch and much else, mostly designed by the architect William Chambers. In 1791 the gardens still contained 'an infinity of temples, kiosks, etc'.[10] Thomas Villiers, Earl of Clarendon, began laying out the grounds of The Grove, just to the north of Watford in Hertfordshire, around 1755, and continued to work on them until his death in the 1770s. By this time the landscape contained a Temple of Pan, the Praeneste or Temple of Fortune, a Mausoleum, a 'Scotch Hut', a Tuscan Seat, a ruined tower, a pyramid, an ornamental hoggery, several 'druidical seats' and a 'rustic seat'.[11] Other noted examples include Halswell in Somerset, begun by its owner, Charles Kemys Tynte, in 1740 but added to and altered until at least 1780: its ornaments included a diminutive lake, retained by a bridge-dam, a druid's temple, a rustic hut, a grotto and a rotunda known as 'Mrs Busby's Temple'.[12]

In some cases, gardens of this kind survived into the 1760s or '70s simply because the owners had not got round to upgrading to something simpler and more fashionable. The Rococo gardens laid out by James West at Alscot in Warwickshire in the 1750s (see pp. 60–62), for example, were still in existence in 1764, when Richard Jago, Sanderson Miller's friend and associate, described in his poem *Edge Hill*:

> Alscot's swelling lawns, and fretted spires,
> Of fairest model, Gothic or Chinese.[13]

But they had evidently ceased to exist by the time of West's death in 1772, an inventory drawn up at the time making no reference to them. They may well have been removed on the advice of Brown himself, who almost certainly visited Alscot while working at nearby Compton Verney

and Compton Wynyates in 1767.[14] Yet as the previous examples indicate, in many places emblematic, serpentine gardens were still being actively extended or created anew, even at the highest social levels, well beyond 1760. They were not simply replaced by the simpler style we associate with Brown, but continued alongside them.

There were a number of reasons for this. In some cases, these landscapes were long-term personal programmes that had been commenced before the style of the Capability Men became fashionable. Men who had begun a project in relative youth, on inheriting a property, were often unwilling to curtail their endeavours and create something more fashionable in middle age. Some of these designs, moreover, such as Kew, were associated with relatively small properties, often located in the immediate vicinity of the metropolis, where land prices often precluded the creation of extensive parks on the Brownian model. The Gunnersbury estate was purchased in 1763 by the 2nd Earl of Bessborough and John, Lord Berkeley, in trust for Princess Amelia, daughter of George II. It was conveniently located within reach of London, and not far from her father's former summer residence at Kew. Over the following quarter-century Princess Amelia made numerous changes to the grounds, allegedly spending £20,000 on the landscape.[15] On her death in 1786 Angus described how the gardens had been 'greatly improved by her Royal Highness, to which many Additions were made by Plantations, additional grounds *and elegant erections*'.[16] The latter included the Temple, a classical brick building again designed by Sir William Chambers which still survives to the north of the Round Pond; a Bath House, containing a fashionable cold plunge bath; an alcove seat; a 'gothic temple';

and a 'rotunda', together with a greenhouse, pinery and hothouse, all connected by winding paths in an extensive but garden-like landscape planted with cedars and other trees.[17]

People with much wealth and education, but with relatively few acres at their disposal, were understandably drawn to this style of design, not least because the abundance of buildings provided numerous opportunities for fashionable entertainment. Contemporary commentators make clear Princess Amelia's predilection for lavish social gatherings at Gunnersbury: one in 1768 was described as a 'huge party of 300 people' with 'supper, fireworks and a ball'.[18] Indeed, the association between gardens in serpentine style, containing a wealth of evocative features and eclectic buildings, and relatively small properties, was a recurrent theme of commentators right through the middle decades of the eighteenth century. As early as 1734 Thomas Robinson had described how the gardens at Carlton House in London's West End had been laid out 'after Mr Kent's notion of gardening': 'By this means I really think the twelve acres the Prince's gardens consist of, is more diversified and of greater variety than anything of the compass I ever saw.'[19]

The association could be interpreted in a different way when those with large estates commented on the gardening efforts of suburban parvenus, as in 1752 when Francis Coventry parodied 'Squire Mushroom', who turned a farmhouse into a villa and laid out a serpentine garden with a 'yellow river stagnating through a beautiful valley, which extends near twenty yards in length'. This was crossed by a bridge 'partly in the Chinese manner' that led to a grove containing a hermitage and a temple.[20] Such diminutive designs – and their ability to create an illusion of space – are

similarly parodied in Garrick and Colman's *The Clandestine Marriage* of 1765, when Lord Ogleby compliments the serpentine walks in Sterling's gardens: 'Admirably laid out indeed, Mr Sterling! One can hardly see an inch beyond one's nose any where in these walks. – You are a most excellent oeconomist of your land, and make a little go a long way'. Such criticisms of suburban Rococo were still being levelled by Whately in 1770, when the open parkland style of the Capability Men was well established as the dominant fashion:

From a general view of our present gardens in populous districts, a stranger might imagine they were calculated for a race of LILLIPUTIANS. Are their shade, their ponds or their islands proportionable to common mortals? Their winding walks – such as no human foot-step (except a reeling drunkard's) could have traced. Yet these, in the eyes of the proprietors, are perfect models of the CHINESE; though the only part that can be called so, is their ridiculous style of architecture in both rails and temples.[21]

Cowper, writing as late as 1785, described wildernesses that 'with curvature of slow and steady sweep/give ample space to narrow bounds'.[22]

Another reason for the continued vitality of the older style, however, was simply that it was popular with many people. As we have noted, the kinds of parks created by Brown were designed in part for informal entertaining – they were the secluded playgrounds of the wealthy. But none were consumed so avidly by the polite public as the great gardens of Painswick or Stourhead. In Timothy Mowl's words, these later Rococo gardens 'really gave pleasure. They were the Alton

Towers and the Disneylands of their time offering harmless, interactive, psychic thrills.'[23] Indeed, places like Painshill, Stourhead and Stowe were still on the tourist trail in the 1790s. The more famous examples, moreover, were the intensely *personal* creations of dedicated, sometimes obsessive owners, men who might commission architects like Chambers or Stuart to design particular buildings, but who retained overall control of projects that might evolve over a lifetime. It was this degree of personal involvement, as much as their sometimes crude appeal to the emotions and the imagination of visitors, that set these landscapes apart from the creations of Brown and his fellows, in which a package of naturalistic simplicity was, as it were, bought 'off the shelf', as a commercial product. This said, the two broad styles often merged, serving to confuse and muddy the neat definitions and categories employed by the historian.

The work of Richard Woods is particularly noteworthy in this respect. In contrast to Brown, whose career covered more or less the same span of time from the 1740s to the 1780s, Woods's style did not develop steadily along simpler, sparser lines. Indeed, as Fiona Cowell has emphasized, it remained remarkably static.[24] Although he did design parks in a vaguely Brownian style, his main emphasis was on pleasure grounds, which might take complex and cluttered forms, even towards the end of his career: 'Woods' plans for Hengrave (1777) and Wormsley (1781) include large areas round the house that are far closer in feeling to a Rococo design than to a truly naturalistic layout, full of winding paths, intricacy and incident.'[25] At Wardour Castle, where he was commissioned to improve the grounds between 1764 and 1767, following Lord

Arundell's rejection of plans submitted by Brown himself, Woods's plan featured no fewer than ten buildings and structures, although only a minority were ever actually built (illus. 118).[26] His garden buildings continued to be designed in Gothick and Chinese styles well into the 1770s. It is worth noting, perhaps, how Batty Langley's *Gothic Architecture Improved*, first published in 1741 and mainly intended to provide designs for garden buildings, was still being reprinted as late as 1790.

While the number of entirely new gardens created in a thoroughgoing Rococo style after the late 1750s was probably small, many designed landscapes in England thus continued to display some of their key characteristics, especially the use of large numbers of exotic buildings, and of inscriptions to alert visitors to the meaning of particular scenes or prospects. Some of the gardens that are widely interpreted by garden historians as representing a novel challenge to the dominant style of Brown and his collaborators might be better interpreted as part of this continuing, parallel tradition. Those at Nuneham Courtenay, laid out by William Mason in 1771, are often given as an example of a new taste for flower gardens, reacting against the bland and featureless parkland of Brown. But as we have seen, the Capability Men were no enemies of the flower garden; and between Mason's famous beds 'little paths wandered, leading either to a bust or an interesting inscription, or a grotto, a temple etc'.[27] The continued survival of these cluttered gardens might appear to be opposed to the avowed popular enthusiasm for 'natural' landscapes, but contemporaries in the 1760s and '70s found a variety of ways of resolving the contradiction, Sir John Parnell in 1768 justifying the

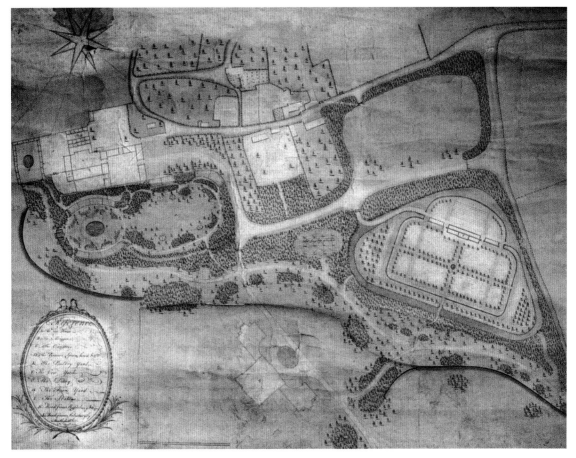

118 Richard Woods's design for the immediate surroundings of the new house at Wardour Castle, 1770, showing the ornate and rather old-fashioned pleasure ground (wrapped, typically, around the kitchen garden). This was one of three plans which Woods prepared for Lord Arundel.

exotic collection at Stourhead with the statement that 'all buildings being artificial, none can strike with impropriety as being unnatural'.[28]

The survival of geometry

More remarkable, perhaps, than the enduring vitality of the Rococo tradition into the age of Brown is the continued existence in many places of walled gardens and geometric landscaping. Once again we need to distinguish the survival of older forms into a new age from their active

creation, and with enclosed and formal gardens, more than with serpentine Rococo designs, the former was clearly more important than the latter. We should certainly not hurry the demise of formality. It was only in the course of the 1760s that geometric elements began to seriously go out of fashion even in the highest circles. Humphry Repton, looking back from 1806 to a time when he was 'about ten years old' – around 1763 or 1764 – recalled how his father, on seeing the new vogue for implying vistas with planting, had commented that 'perhaps, this will lead to the abolishing of avenues.'[29] Even in Hertfordshire, in the hinterland of fashionable London, the detailed county map surveyed by Dury and Andrews around 1764 and published two years later shows some mansions which appear to be set in essentially 'naturalistic' landscapes, with woods and drives entirely serpentine or irregular in layout, of the kind popularized by Brown. But they constitute a minority. The overwhelming majority of large houses are shown with grounds that are dominated by geometric blocks of woodland, formal water features and avenues, the latter often present in large numbers and sometimes extending out beyond the park into the surrounding countryside. Of course, in many if not most cases such geometric structures will have coexisted, in the manner already discussed, with areas of more serpentine layout, and with irregular planting. But geometry was a prominent feature, structuring the experience of the overall design. By this time, no doubt, much of this old-fashioned landscaping was in the process of being removed. Yet even in the 1770s large-scale geometric planting had its supporters. The mythical squire Mr Alington in Craddock's *Village Memoirs* of 1775 voiced what may have been a widespread belief: 'It is supposed by modern rules that all avenues of course must be cut down, but I am far from thinking that they may not frequently remain to great advantage.'[30] Even after Brown's death, in 1785 William Cowper could both bemoan the loss of avenues and suggest that a proportion still survived ('Ye fallen avenues once more mourn/Your fate unmerited, once more rejoice/That yet a remnant of your race remains').[31] Geometry was clearly alive and well in the 1760s, and even in the following decade died only a slow death.

Such an enthusiasm for older forms of landscaping well into the second half of the eighteenth century is perhaps less surprising than it first appears. Historians of gardens, as much as most contemporary enthusiasts, tend to emphasize the new, the novel, the cutting-edge. The men and women who planted the avenues, groves and *allées* around their homes in the 1710s or '20s when they first inherited or purchased their estates might be understandably reluctant to fell them in the 1760s when they were still barely mature. It is noticeable that on Dury and Andrews's map of Hertfordshire most of the landscapes which are entirely devoid of obvious geometric elements were new places, established on virgin sites, like The Grove to the north of Watford, which we described a little earlier. Not surprisingly, it is the long-established places where formal elements are still prominent. This, however, may also hint at other reasons why such features might be retained. Hertfordshire, as we have seen, was one of those districts, lying in the immediate hinterland of London, where large numbers of 'villas' were erected by retired army officers, successful merchants and bankers in the middle and later decades of the century. Established landed families may have wished to signal their longevity in the county by retaining some vestiges of the landscapes of their forefathers, against the tide of new gardens being created, in the most fashionable style, by 'new money'.[32]

There were, however, a number of other circumstances that might encourage the survival of older forms of garden. It is noticeable that while, in general, Brown's designs drawn up after *c.* 1760 tend to eschew avenues and similar linear, geometric elements, he appears to have made an exception in the case of houses built in the sixteenth or early seventeenth centuries. At Corsham Court in Wiltshire, a house of 1582, the east avenue was removed but those focused on the north and south fronts were allowed to remain; the great avenue running southwest from Castle Ashby in Northamptonshire was retained; many of the lime avenues aligned on Burghley House survived. Evidently, Brown – obsessively aware of the relationship between a house and its landscape – considered that some retention of geometric formality was appropriate for places like this. Indeed, we should note that in spite of the rage for Palladian, and subsequently Neoclassical, architecture, houses built in older styles were not always regarded with disdain by eighteenth-century commentators, especially if they had important historical associations. Blickling Hall in Norfolk, the home of the Earls of Buckinghamshire, was largely rebuilt at the start of the seventeenth century and by the middle decades of the eighteenth was thought old-fashioned and gloomy by some observers. But most, perhaps responding to its (largely mythical) connections with Anne Boleyn, were more complimentary. Sir John Clerk of Penicuik in 1733 described it as a 'fine old house'; Arthur Young in 1771 considered the house 'a large and good one'; while Horace Walpole's friend the poet Hannah More memorably suggested that 'You admire Houghton but you wish for Blickling; you look at Houghton with astonishment, at Blickling with desire.'[33] When the medieval north range, which had escaped the seventeenth-century rebuilding, was demolished in the 1760s its replacement – designed by the Ivory brothers, local architect/builders – copied very closely the appearance of the other parts of the building, even down to reusing much earlier brick in its construction. It is not surprising, then, that while

much of the old formal garden at Blickling was swept away and replaced with a more irregular 'Pleser Grownd' in the 1760s, the formal wilderness planted in the early part of the century was allowed to remain, the historian Mostyn John Armstrong describing in 1781 how the grounds were 'everywhere in this part preserved in the old style of gardening, with cut hedge etc'.[34] When old gardens, especially walled gardens, eventually came tumbling down, as most did by the 1780s or '90s, even at the level of the provincial gentry, the change was often regarded with mixed feelings. When, under the direction of Nathaniel Richmond, those at Beeston St Lawrence in Norfolk were finally demolished, the owner's brother-in-law lamented their loss in a letter to his sister. He described how Richmond was:

> Busy levelling his lawns, removing gardens, walls and trees and laying out a new kitchen garden more remote from the house. How it would grieve you if you were here but so it must be … Our ideas are more extensive than those of our ancestors. They were cribbed up in small apartments, and sat in little cane chairs admiring the pretty gardens edged with box and yew trees. We now indulge in elbow chairs, in apartments 20 feet by 30 feet by 15 feet high, and must extend our view over improved grounds as far as the eye can see without any disagreeable object intervening.[35]

Walled gardens had, in fact, an enduring appeal – as we have seen, Brown's kitchen gardens were frequently connected to the pleasure ground and were used recreationally to an extent – and many wealthy families must have been torn between the needs of fashion on the one hand and the dictates of convenience, recreation and familiarity on the other. Something of this tension is apparent in the comment made by Horace Walpole in 1780 that 'Whenever a family can purloin a warm and even an old-fashioned garden from the landscape designed for them by the undertaker of fashion, without interfering with the picture, they will find satisfactions on those days that they do not invite strangers to come and see their improvements.'[36] It is noticeable that at many of the places where walled gardens of sixteenth and seventeenth-century date have survived beside country houses, they occupy the area to the north, with fashionable parkland stretching to the south, where it could be viewed from the reception rooms on the warmer, south-facing side of the house.

The particular enthusiasms of individual owners might provide an added reason for the retention of walled enclosures. Many members of the local gentry, as much as their wives, had keen horticultural interests that were best catered for in the microclimate provided by garden walls. Sir Martin Browne ffolkes, who inherited the extensive Hillington estate in Norfolk in 1773, commissioned the designer Samuel Driver to draw up plans for a landscape park and paid him for laying out a shrubbery and supplying plants.[37] But his real interest was in the walled gardens that, although truncated, continued to survive in part beside the hall. Between 1774 and 1780 these were renovated, a new enclosure with a 'hott' wall constructed, much work carried out on the existing orangery, a new pinery and hothouse built, and large numbers of new plants acquired.[38] ffolkes was a fanatical gardener who kept up a lively correspondence with fellow enthusiasts,

one of whom commented: 'I am fearful, by your great success, you will be tempted to stay too long in the hot house to the injury of your health.'[39] He was not unusual in his direct involvement in gardening, and many gentlemen's libraries contained, alongside the works of Switzer, Whately or Mason, one of the many revisions of Henry Stevenson's *The Gentleman Gardener's Recreation* (the last in 1764), which provided very practical advice on the propagation, planting and care of a wide range of garden plants and vegetables. The poet William Cowper was thus not expressing some eccentric or unusual opinion, but rather a widespread if by now minority view, when he described in his poem *The Task*, published in 1785, the pride a gentleman might derive from walls espaliered with fruit trees, the pleasures of cultivating the 'prickly and green-coated gourd', even the satisfaction to be gained from the 'stercoraceous heap' of manure provided by the stables. The gentleman gardener not only produced fruits and vegetables, but raised flowers and planned their display:

He, therefore, who would see his flowers disposed
Sightly and in just order, ere he gives
The beds the trusted treasure of their seeds,
Forecasts the future whole; that when the scene
Shall break into its preconceived display,
Each for itself, and all as with one voice
Conspiring, may attest his bright design.[40]

Cowper himself, while he counted many members of the gentry (and even the minor aristocracy) among his friends, was essentially from a middle-class background, but the sentiments of the poem clearly embrace those of a more exalted station, assuming as it does that the gardener owns some expensive facilities:

> Who loves a garden loves a green-house
> too
> Unconscious of a less propitious clime,
> There blooms exotic beauty, warm and snug,
> While the winds whistle . . .[41]

The ideological implications of gardening as expressed by Cowper (in what Daniels has described as a 'popular antidote to aristocratic excess')[42] were also, perhaps, more widely recognized among members of the landed classes than we often assume, and may explain much about the resistance to the landscapes crafted by the Capability Men which we encounter in the 1760s and '70s. The sweeping parkland of Brown was indeed, Cowper believed, the style of the times; but the times were out of joint. Commerce, and the dominance of the metropolis, had destroyed a country that had once been 'plain, hospitable, kind'. It was in this context, in which 'improvement' was 'the idol of the age', that the new landscape style, so forcibly marginalizing useful production, found a ready market:

> The ominipotent magician, Brown, appears!
> Down falls the venerable pile, the abode
> Of our forefathers – a grave whisker'd race,
> But tasteless. Springs a palace in its stead,
> But in a distant spot . . .[43]

Ferme ornée and deer park

The idea of the ornamental farm or *ferme ornée* can be traced back at least to the 1710s. In 1712,

in a famous article in *The Spectator*, Joseph Addison asked:

> Why may not a Whole Estate be thrown into a kind of garden by frequent plantations, that may turn as much to the profit as the pleasure of the owner? . . . Fields of corn make a pleasant prospect; and if the walks were a little taken care of that lie between them, if the natural embroidery of the meadows were helped and improved by some small additions of art, and the several rows of hedges set off by trees and flowers that the soil was capable of receiving, a man might make a pretty landscape of his own possessions.[44]

Such concepts also appear in Stephen Switzer's large-scale landscape designs, discussed and illustrated in his *Ichnographia rustica* of 1718, which featured networks of formal avenues continuing the lines of the walks in the gardens beside the mansion, out through the surrounding farmland, so that the aesthetic areas were 'thereby vastly enlarged, and both Profit and Pleasure may be said to be agreeably mix'd together'.[45] Elsewhere Switzer suggested that 'a decent Walk carry'd thro' a Corn Field or Pasture thro' little natural Thickets and Hedge Rows, is as pleasing as the most finish'd Parterre that some Moderns have been so fond of'.[46] Switzer was probably the first to use the terms 'ornamental farm' (in his *Practical Husbandry* of 1733) and *ferme ornée* (in the 1742 edition of *Ichnographia rustica*). By this time, however, the serpentine lines and eclectic buildings of the Rococo garden (rather than an essentially geometric structure) formed the aesthetic that was being imposed upon, or intermingled with, the working countryside.

Between the late 1730s and the 1750s Philip Southcote developed an influential and much-visited *ferme ornée* extending over some 58 hectares at Woburn Farm near Chertsey in Surrey. It consisted of a sandy path running through the fields, flanked by a herbaceous border comprising hollyhocks, lilies, goldenrod and crown imperial, with an edging of pinks and backed by the existing hedgerows, suitably ornamented with shrubs like lilac and mock orange. The farm was as full of exotic buildings as any Rococo garden of more usual form, with Gothick, classical and Chinese structures all littering the circuit path.[47] Equally well known was the landscape created at the Leasowes near Halesowen in the West Midlands from the mid-1740s by William Shenstone, which again comprised a path through hedged fields, ornamented with the usual range of items including a root house, a Temple of Pan, a 'gothic alcove', cascades, seats, statues, urns and the genuine medieval ruins of a priory (illus. 119). Inscriptions gave particular meaning to carefully chosen views of distant objects.[48]

Rather simpler versions of landscapes like these, with fewer buildings but with the same kinds of paths flanked by ornamental planting, were probably more common than we suppose, largely because most of their features were highly ephemeral, and they are difficult to identify on maps. There must have been many places like Cole Green, in the Mimram valley to the west of Hertford, where in the 1730s the Cowper family had both a pleasure ground and a small park, and a *ferme ornée*, a memorandum drawn up when the landscape was created describing how:

If these things are compleated ye Park at Cole Green may be enlarged and a very

pretty farm made round it which if paled out any Game may be preserved and ye Farm laid out with Walks & planted & water may be found in ye meeds to make a pretty effect.[49]

A slightly later memorandum refers to maintenance work: 'The hedge in Old-Field on each side the seat trimmed and the weeds in the slips mowed or stabbed up'.[50] Paths laid out through the farmland could lead to important views or landscape features of particular note, as at Panshanger, a few kilometres to the east of Cole Green, where in 1757 the Revd George Harris recorded how he 'Walk't round the Dean's teritorie. The finest oak in all this country is in his woods – 5 yards & half round, & not the least decayed – he has made a grand Walk thro[ugh] the coppice to it. 'Tis of a great height.'[51] Such creations are usually discussed primarily as a feature of the period before the 1760s. But there are grounds for believing that this approach to landscape design – so different from the sweeping parklands of Brown and his collaborators, which actively worked to *exclude* signs of active agriculture – continued to flourish right through the time of Brown's career, as another popular alternative to the landscape park. Certainly, as we have already noted, Thomas Whately in 1770 argued that the activity of gardening was no longer confined to the area beside a mansion but now affected the disposition not only of the parks of the gentry, but of their farms: he defined an 'ornamented farm' as 'a walk, which, with its appendages, forms a broad belt round the grazing grounds and is continued, though on a more contracted scale, through the arable'.[52] Richard Woods, whose designs for pleasure grounds have already been noted, was responsible for a number of such landscapes, aptly described by Fiona Cowell as comprising 'a ribbon of garden, wide or narrow, through or encircling hedged fields'.[53] At Hatfield Priory in Essex, a new house built on a virgin site, Woods in the 1760s laid out a circuit walk around both arable fields and a diminutive 'park', comprising pasture closes separated by hahas. As Cowell notes, the design made 'no attempt to plant out the agricultural activity, which instead is brought into the designed landscape'.[54] At Wormsley in Buckinghamshire in 1779 there were likewise arable fields within the perimeter walk, while at Brizes in Essex in 1780 a circuit path, ornamented with shrubs and with a bench flanked by beds of flowers, gave views across pasture fields, divided by

hedges sunk in hahas (illus. 120). In this case, as Cowell notes, the hidden divisions between the fields would have provided a park-like view from the house, blurring the distinction between park and ornamented farm; but the difference from Brown's designs nevertheless remains.[55] It is noteworthy that all three of Woods's clients at these places were minor local gentry, and this particular form of design had an obvious appeal to those who either lacked the resources to create a Brownian landscape park, were particularly involved in practical agriculture, or both. In some cases, however, landowners possessed both a park (usually a small one) *and* a circuit walk running through farmland. Park and ornamented farm might fulfil different roles in the lifestyle of the rural landowner, as Whately explained:

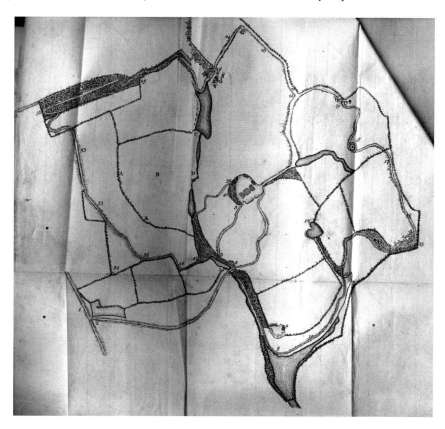

119 Plan of The Leasowes in the West Midlands, one of the most famous eighteenth-century *fermes ornées*, which was published in William Shenstone's *Works in Verse and Prose* (London, 1764), vol. II.

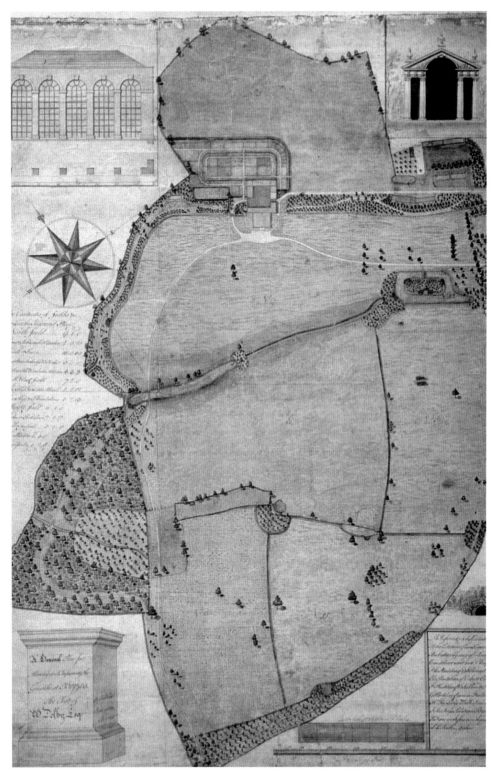

120 Richard Woods's 'General Plan for Altering and Improving Grounds at Brizes', Essex, 1788, shows what is essentially a simplified version of a *ferme ornée*.

A simple farm may undoubtedly be delightful; it will be particularly acceptable to the owner, if it be close to his park or his garden; the objects which constantly remind him of his rank, impose a kind of constraint; and he feels himself relieved, by retiring sometimes from the splendour of a seat into the simplicity of a farm; it is more than a variety of scene; it is a temporary change of situation in life, which has all the charms of novelty, ease, and tranquillity to recommend it.[56]

It is hard to know how common these various forms of ornamental farm may have been in the period after *c.* 1760, but one possible indication that minor landowners often planted up their home farms in an ornamental fashion is provided by the Lombardy poplar, a tree that was introduced from northern Italy as late as 1758 but which appears regularly in John Constable's paintings of the countryside around the Suffolk/Essex border. It evidently gained rapid popularity, presumably because of its associations with the Italian landscape and its speedy growth. It certainly had little else to recommend it, as it has no real use as timber, and makes but indifferent firewood.

Richard Woods's design for Brizes shows that the idea of the *ferme ornée* was still going strong as late as the 1780s, if now in more muted form – with fewer exotic buildings and the like. By this stage, the concept was perhaps blurring with that of the 'model farm', as the nineteenth century would describe it, as enthusiasm for agricultural improvement reached new heights. But even in the 1740s landscapes like Woburn had not merely been about the creation of Arcadian

scenes in an English landscape. They were more than ribbons of shrubbery, decorated with urns and root houses, scattered through the fields. As Chambers has pointed out, they drew on the notions of rural retirement so prominent in the writings of Pliny and Virgil, and were landscapes in which 'agricultural improvement, botanical experimentation, philosophic speculation, rural retirement, and arcadian landscape come together in the recreation of an Augustan ideal'.[57] Woburn, in Mowl's words, was 'not merely an eccentric garden strip, it was a real farm run to the latest advances of farming practice'.[58] The concept could thus develop relatively easily along lines more agricultural, and less emblematic, and in 1785 and 1786 Thomas Ruggles wrote a number of articles for the *Annals of Agriculture* which suggested ways in which the practical business of farming could be carried out in a manner that also accentuated the natural beauties of the landscape. Some of his ideas were bizarre and impractical but others were clearly a continuation of the established *ferme ornée* tradition, such as the planting up of field corners to obscure the rectangular shape of enclosures, mainly with conifers like Scots pine, larch, silver fir and Weymouth pine; the placing of inscriptions to explain the significance of particular views; the creation of grass paths around field margins; the planting of weeping willows beside field ponds; the cutting of paths in a serpentine or 'devious' manner through woods and groves close to the house; and the beautifying of hedgerows by planting roses and other native shrubs.[59] A decade later, in 1796, John Plaw published his *Ferme ornée; or, Rural Improvements*, which contains fanciful designs for fencing, ornamental cattle sheds and poultry houses, cottages and farmhouses.[60] And a few years after this, in 1803, Repton expressed his reservations about the 'ornamented farm' as a concept, but conceded that 'in the prevailing rage for agriculture, it is unpopular to assert, that a farm and a park may not be united'.[61]

We have so far discussed parks and *fermes ornées* as if they were discrete and separate forms, but the line between them was often made indistinct, in the case of many of the larger parks especially, by the presence of a home farm within the park belt. When Holkham in Norfolk was expanded to the south in the 1780s and '90s by Thomas William Coke, and enclosed by a continuous belt designed by John Sandys, the new section of the park was almost entirely divided into hedged fields under arable cultivation, albeit ornamented with a number of large clumps. The only 'garden building' within the new extension was the Great Barn, erected in 1791 to the designs of Samuel Wyatt, which formed the setting for Coke's 'sheep shearings', early agricultural shows.[62] Coke was a noted 'improver' but the arrangement was a common one, and many of Brown's parks – such as Melton Constable or Langley in the same county – likewise incorporated arable within the perimeter belt, although always out of sight of the mansion.[63] In the particular case of Holkham the combination of 'beauty and utility' was widely admired. A rather different complication is presented by landscapes further down the social sale, at the level of the small 'villa'. Where a diminutive park or 'paddock' was no larger than a small field, yet surrounded by a circuit walk, the line with a *ferme ornée*-type landscape was obviously blurred. Indeed, the line between a 'park-like paddock' and an ordinary pasture field might largely be in the eye of the beholder. Some of this terminological confusion is reflected in Whately's comment in 1770: 'Many gardens are nothing more than such a walk round a field; that field is often raised to the character of a lawn; and sometimes the enclosure is, in fact, a paddock.'[64]

As the presence of arable within the perimeter belt at places like Holkham indicates, 'park' was a somewhat poorly defined, elastic term in the middle decades of the eighteenth century; and in a further level of complexity we should note that while the necessary association of deer and parks had been decisively severed by the Capability Men, many true deer parks – densely timbered wood pastures – nevertheless remained. Often their survival was associated with the maintenance of old-fashioned walled gardens in the area around the house, and/or with the retention of a house in some archaic architectural style, as at Thornham in Suffolk where the hall, as shown on a map of 1765, was still flanked by walled enclosures and approached along a straight avenue running through a deer park of nearly 35 hectares which no attempt appears to have been made to 'landscape'.[65] It is probable that this arrangement remained in place until at least the late 1770s.[66] At Benacre in the same county a survey of 1778 shows the hall set within a compartmentalized deer park, subdivided into three paled enclosures, and still surrounded by walled gardens.[67] Even where more fashionable gardens were laid out, parks sometimes retained their rough, wood-pasture appearance, little affected by the smoothing lines of fashion.[68] At places like Walcot in Shropshire, purchased by Robert Clive ('Clive of India') in 1764, deer were actively maintained in the park well into the 1770s, the agent calculating, in 1771, the expense of maintaining the fences, feeding the deer, wages for the keeper and other costs at no less than £1,016 per annum, a sum that would be reduced to £150 if 'the Deer (were) destroy'd and the Park made a Ley'.[69] Even after William Emes added a lake, and fashionable pleasure grounds, in 1774 the park itself remained little altered. The number of parks in this county where deer were kept declined over time but, as Sandra Morris has shown, at a slower rate than might be expected: around 24 were recorded on Morden's map of Shropshire, published in 1695, and there were still sixteen when Greenwood's map appeared in 1827.[70] The deer park at Ludford in that county, created in the first half of the eighteenth century, was still functioning in 1805, when the owner, William Lechmere Charlton, bequeathed to his wife, in addition to Ludford House, 'all the provision for housekeeping in the house and such of the liquors as she may have occasion to use and his stock of deer in the park'.[71] Shropshire, along with the adjacent county of Hereford-shire, may be slightly atypical in this respect – fewer deer parks seem to have survived in the southeast of the country, or in the central and eastern Midlands – but in most regions some examples largely or entirely escaped the attention of the 'improvers'. Occasionally, even detached deer parks on the old, medieval pattern were still maintained, as at Boreatton Park in Shropshire; and, in another level of blurring and complexity, these were themselves occasionally 'landscaped'. At Cholmondeley Castle in Cheshire, for example, a deer park lay some two kilometres from the house, at the end of an avenue running through fields, and was still being actively managed as a venison farm well into the eighteenth century.[72] In 1777 William Emes prepared an estimate for planting and fencing 'in Chomondeley Park',

'as the plantations are now marked out & measured', with beech, oak, sweet chestnut, elm, sycamore and Scots pine, and a map of 1781 leaves no doubt that this activity does not signal the creation of a new park, beside the mansion, but rather the establishment of a large number of small, naturalistic clumps within the *old* park, which was itself now extensively cleared of existing trees (illus. 121).[73] As far as the evidence goes, deer ceased to be maintained around this time and the park now functioned as a place to visit, picnic and ride in. The tidying up and aestheticization of isolated parks and wood pastures in this way may, once again, have been more common in this period than we suppose: Brown himself may have done something broadly similar, although less radical, at Hatfield Forest in Essex.[74]

Although Caroline Lybbe Powys was in broad terms correct in her observation, made in 1776, that 'The rage for laying out grounds makes every nobleman and gentleman a copier of their neighbour, till every fine place throughout England is comparatively, at least, alike',[75] we should thus not underestimate the diversity of designed landscapes in England in the 1760s and '70s: with the survival of old forms like the walled garden and the wood-pasture deer park; the continued vitality of what might broadly be described as Rococo gardens; the fusion of the latter, to varying extents, with the dominant 'Brownian' fashion; as well as the continued enthusiasm for forms of 'ornamented farm'. And this is without discussing the various kinds of urban garden – commercial pleasure grounds in London and the main provincial cities, urban squares and the gardens of the private houses, many of which were the second homes of the

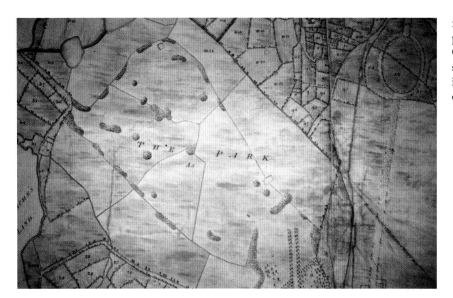

121 The detached deer park at Cholmondeley Castle in Cheshire, landscaped by William Emes in 1777, as shown on an estate map of 1781.

landowners – all of which continued to display, to varying degrees, relatively structured and geometric forms.[76]

Chambers and Gilpin

Most published books on garden history acknowledge that Brown was not universally admired, but – reflecting perhaps the dominance of literary approaches within the discipline – tend to substantiate this through an analysis of contemporary published texts on garden design, rather than by using the evidence provided by representations or descriptions of the gardens and landscapes themselves. These texts, however, make most sense when we consider them within the context of the various 'alternative' styles of gardening that we have just briefly described. Some, indeed, make little sense unless we do so.

The most important of these works is Sir William Chambers's *Dissertation on Oriental Gardening*, published in 1772.[77] Chambers was an interesting figure who was born in Sweden,

spent nine years with the Swedish East India Company (including three trips to China), trained in architecture in Paris with Blondel and spent four years in Italy studying classical architecture before coming to England. It has been suggested that he had a particular antipathy to Brown because he had been beaten by him in securing the commission for rebuilding Claremont House for Lord Clive in 1769, and his *Dissertation*, which appeared only three years later, does appear to include derogatory references to his erstwhile rival, noting for example how 'peasants emerge from the melon ground to take the periwig and turn professor.'[78] Chambers's text is in fact a curious piece of work that purports to provide a description of the practice of landscape design in China in the hope that some of its principles might be adopted in England. He contrasts the variety and excitement of oriental gardens with their dull, repetitive and tame counterparts in England, which provided nothing to 'delight or amuse' or to excite interest or curiosity, consisting as they did largely of placid water and endless vistas of turf, 'smooth and green as a billiard table'.[79] In reality the book reads more like a fantasy novel, with its descriptions of vast gardens containing immense forests and lakes, whole settlements and 'submerged habitations'; its salacious details, such as the pavilions hidden away in thickets occupied by the 'most accomplished concubines' or the tree houses for 'voluptuous pleasure'; and its comic-book images of travellers passing through the most dramatic parts of the gardens, with their 'scenes of terror'.

> Dark passages cut in the rocks, on the sides of which are recesses, filled with colossal figures of Dragons, infernal furies, and other horrid forms . . . with preparations that yield a constant flame; serving at once to guide and to astonish the passenger; from time to time he is surprised with repeated shocks of electrical impulse, with showers of artificial rain . . . or instantaneous explosions of fire.[80]

Superficially this is all rather batty stuff, but when we strip away the more bizarre aspects of Chambers's fantasy gardens we begin to see something more familiar, and rather more English.

> The usual method of distributing gardens in China is to contrive a great variety of scenes, to be seen from certain points of view and at which are placed seats or buildings, adapted to the different purposes of mental or sensual enjoyments. The perfection of their Gardens consists in the number and diversity of these scenes; and in the artful combination of their parts.[81]

The various 'scenes' were designed to stimulate the senses, emotions and imagination, and were connected by wide paths running through 'thickets'. Their key features were cataracts, lakes, inscriptions and sculptures, all intended to 'awaken the mind to pleasing contemplation', and a wide variety of buildings, 'spacious, splendid and numerous'. Chambers described one garden in which there were 400 of these, 'all so different in their architecture, that each seems the production of a different country'.[82] They commonly included hermitages, ruins of castles, temples, 'deserted religious houses', triumphal arches and mausoleums. The separate 'scenes' also included rich and varied planting featuring pines, firs, cedars, evergreen oaks, phillyreas, hollies, yew, juniper and a range of exotic species. Chambers's 'Chinese' gardens, in short, were based around a series of separate experiences, in which mood and emotions were evoked by buildings, structures, planting and texts, and were thus very different from most English gardens, which contained 'little to flatter the senses, and less to touch the passions'. The Chinese, according to Chambers, were thus puzzled by such features of English gardens as circuit walks or drives around the extremities of a piece of open ground, as often found in both pleasure grounds and parks, thinking that the spectator 'would be but moderately entertained by walking several miles with the same objects continually obtruding upon his sight'.[83]

The reader will hopefully recognize in all this, suitably exaggerated, the key elements of the larger Rococo gardens in England, such as Stourhead or Painshill. Indeed, it is noteworthy that, in his criticisms of the dominant mode of English gardening, Chambers acknowledged that there were exceptions to the overall low level of design, but that these were to be found in gardens which had principally been 'laid out by their owners, who are so eminently skilled in Gardening, as in many other branches of polite knowledge'.[84] Exploration and excitement were what Chambers was after, gardens in which the visitor was constantly amazed, interested, shocked. Such gardens could only be laid out by the cognoscenti – by men of genius, experience and knowledge, 'fertile in imagination, and thoroughly versed in all the affections of the human mind'. In contrast, he argues that at present – in what may be another side-swipe at Brown, but is perhaps a more general observation about the subservient role of the gardens to the house in the landscapes of the Capability Men – their design was 'a collateral branch of the Architect's employment'.[85] A recognition that Chambers was advocating, in effect, a version of emblematic or Rococo gardens like Stourhead or Painshill helps to make sense of what might otherwise be a very odd text. Such an enthusiasm may have been fuelled by Chambers's personal antipathy to Brown, but it may also have been encouraged by the fact that many of his commissions were for garden buildings, including no fewer than seventeen in the gardens at Kew alone. It is hardly surprising that he disliked the somewhat empty landscapes of the Capability Men.

If Chambers's objections to the dominant style were primarily focused on its bland character, then those put forward by William Gilpin were rather different. As most readers will be aware, Gilpin was an immensely successful writer on landscape appreciation and the most famous propagator of the notion of Picturesque beauty. He produced a number of popular texts, several of

them published during Brown's lifetime. His first interest was in paintings, and he approached real landscapes in a similar manner – in effect, judging them as visual representations.[86] In particular, as the classic compositions of Poussin and Claude Lorrain, whom he much admired, organized visual space into 'three distances' – a foreground, a middle ground and a distance – he believed that the best real landscapes should display a similar structure. He thus criticized the views around Burford in Oxfordshire because, although they were extensive, 'none of these landscapes however are perfect, as they want the accompaniments of foregrounds'.[87] Gilpin also encouraged the appreciation of rougher and wilder scenery than had hitherto been fashionable, although the extent to which earlier generations had also enjoyed rugged terrain and mountains is often underestimated. It is sometimes assumed that mountainous wildness was the principal concern both of Gilpin himself and of those who – a little later – would come to apply Picturesque principles to the design of landscapes. But in fact, his (and their) aesthetic enthusiasms embraced old trees, forests, exposed roots and rock strata, abandoned quarries, ruined cottages, the characteristic details of local landscapes. He was keenly aware of the particular qualities of places and districts. While landscapes were, in a sense, all to be formed into paintings, following rules of visual composition, this was intended to bring out their peculiar qualities, rather than to negate them.

There would appear to be a number of reasons why Gilpin should have found Brown's landscapes distasteful, as those who further developed his ideas of the Picturesque at the end of the century were certainly to do. Indeed, in a much-quoted passage he attacked aspects of the dominant style: 'How flat, and insipid is often the garden scene, how puerile, how absurd! The banks of the river, how smooth and parallel! The lawn, and its boundaries, how unlike nature.'[88] In fact the situation is more complicated. Gilpin described Brown's landscape at Warwick Castle as 'a paltry work', but only because of the circumscribed nature of the site; he praised his 'masterly' design at Trentham, Staffordshire, calling it a 'scene of great simplicity and beauty'; had few reservations about Caversham, where Brown's 'great merit lay in pursuing the path, which nature had marked out'; and admired both the house and the grounds at Cadland, describing Brown as the 'ingenious improver'.[89] But it is a passage in his *Remarks on Forest Scenery* that explains most clearly his attitude to Brown's style. 'Park scenery' works best, he suggests, on undulating ground, where the somewhat smooth landscapes of the dominant fashion were acceptable because they formed a connection or transition between the irregular landscape of the countryside on the one hand, and the structure and order of the mansion itself on the other. 'Thus as the house is connected to the country through the medium of the park; the park should partake of the neatness of the one, and of the wildness of the other.'[90] Moreover, Gilpin appears to have appreciated and welcomed (in a way that Chambers did not) the paucity of buildings in the landscapes of fashion, commenting that 'In the park-scene we wish for no expensive ornament. Temples, Chinese bridges and all the laboured works of art, suggest inharmonious ideas.' Such erections only worked in the grounds of particularly palatial mansions, otherwise even in pleasure grounds their numbers should be restricted.[91] In much of this, and in such matters as his advocacy of planting clumps

of trees, of carefully concealing the bounds of parks, and of keeping sheep and cattle rather than deer within them, Gilpin was clearly in agreement with Brown.[92] But he was critical of his serpentine drives and uneasy about his artificial lakes, which generally appeared too contrived: 'Mr Brown, I think, has failed more in river-making than in any of his attempts.' While he admitted that Brown's water bodies had 'sometimes a good effect', such artificial creations, imposed on the landscape, could never compete with purely *natural* lakes.[93] That which Brown created at Sandbeck, beside the ruins of Roche Abbey, he elsewhere described as 'too magnificent and too artificial a creation to be in unison with the ruins of an abbey', just as he criticized the smooth lawn which Brown created as a setting for the ruins: 'The ruin stands now on a neat bowling-green, like a house just built, and without any kind of *connection* with the ground it stands on. There is certainly little judgement shewn in this mode of improvement.'[94]

There is a clear sense in Gilpin's comments, not so much that the style of Brown's parks was in itself deficient, but rather that it was applied indiscriminately, regardless of local conditions. Such views were to be further developed after Brown's death, by Uvedale Price and Richard Payne Knight, but do not appear to have been widely shared in the 1770s, and even Gilpin appears, on the whole, to have been surprisingly sympathetic to the dominant fashion.

CHAMBERS, COWPER AND TO some extent Gilpin, as well as other contemporary writers and commentators, thus expressed reservations about or outright hostility towards the landscape style of the Capability Men. But of more importance is perhaps the evidence of the landscape itself, which leaves no doubt that right through the 1760s and '70s a substantial minority of land-owners laid out their grounds along different lines, or at least bought into the new taste but sparingly. There was not a single alternative style, as we have seen; and the alternatives could themselves, to varying degrees, be combined with the dominant fashion of the Capability Men. Nor was there a single reason why particular landowners chose to order their landscapes along alternative lines. Instead – and ignoring those cases where simple limitations of resources or space dictated a different approach – there seem to have been several reasons for resisting Brown's style, reasons that to a significant extent overlap, and which together provide something approaching a coherent critique of the ideological meaning of the landscape park.

First, as Chambers's text indicates, and as the continuing popularity of Rococo gardens testifies, the landscapes of Brown were conceived by many to be bland, repetitive and dull, lacking in excitement and variety. Emblematic gardens in the older style, moreover – or at least, the most famous and influential examples – were the idiosyncratic creations of amateur gentlemen like Southcote or Miller. The Capability Men, in contrast, were generally from more lowly middle-class backgrounds, and supplied a somewhat standardized commercial package. Second, the aesthetics of the dominant style were rooted in the concept that the pure forms of nature inherent in the landscape needed to be brought to the surface by the calculated interventions of the designer. In Whately's words, 'the business of a gardener ... is to shew all the advantages of the place upon which he is employed; to supply its

defects, to correct its faults, and to improve its beauties.' In the writings of Gilpin, as in the comments by Caroline Lybbe Powys quoted earlier, we can see an emerging reaction against such an approach: for the removal of superfluous detail that was required to create such idealized landscape served to negate the particular character of a place, so that everywhere did, indeed, begin to look the same. As Joseph Cradock put it in 1775, 'most of our largest gardens are laid out by some general undertaker, who, regardless of the peculiar beauties of each situation, introduces the same objects at the same distances in all.'[95]

Moreover, the Neoclassical ideal of smooth landforms embraced by Brown and his fellows was more suited to the muted terrain of the southeast and the Midlands than it was to sites in the north or west of the country, and when applied to the latter – as when Brown removed the boulders on the slopes below the castle at Alnwick in Northumberland – appeared to represent the imposition of a kind of Home Counties aesthetic on local topography. The Capability Men thus provided not only a standardized and rather predictable commercial package, but one which symbolized new wealth – and London money. The negation of local character thus expressed both the dominance of the capital in the cultural life of the nation and the increasingly transient character of ownership, as long-established families were replaced by the newly wealthy, with landed property regarded as a commodity. The landowner, in Cowper's words, was now 'but a transient guest, newly arrived./And soon to be supplanted':

Estates are landscapes, gazed upon a while
Then advertised, and auctioneer'd away.[96]

Lastly, the landscape park was too inward-looking for many landowners, turning its back on the working countryside and shunning useful, domestic production. Both the *ferme ornée* and productive walled gardens beneath the main facades expressed a different attitude, of active engagement in agriculture and, by implication, with the life of the local community.

These varied objections did not, we would emphasize again, amount to a single coherent critique of the dominant style – the lover of a landscape like Stourhead would not necessarily have appreciated an old-fashioned walled garden – but there is nevertheless a broad congruence of these various ideas, neatly summarized in Joseph Cradock's *Village Memoirs* of 1765. This describes how Mr Massem, a wealthy Londoner, purchased the estate of Marleston following the death of Mr Arlington, the last of a long-established gentry family. He immediately commissioned 'Mr Lay-out' – 'a designer in taste in gardening' – to improve the grounds of the old manor house, removing what had evidently been some kind of *ferme ornée*, much to the disapproval of his neighbour:

> The alterations already made at Marleston are so great, that I hardly know my own village. Mr Massem every day makes purchases of ground, no matter at what expence, that Mr Lay-out may at least acknowledge he has scope enough for his inventions ... They talk of taste just as if it was to be brought down in a broad-wheeled waggon, and they had nothing to do but scatter it at random. Mr Lay-out thinks there should be a clump, and there is one ... it rather grieves me to find that the grove on the

right-hand, where the rustic seat was ... should be condemned to be cut down, as well as the large one, which Mr Arlington had used to call Shenstone's Grove.[97]

Outside money changed the very character of a place, and 'by what I see of the intended alterations to the water, it is destined to take any course but its own, for the merit of everything seems to consist only in the sum it is to cost'. The neighbour concluded by observing that he would rather 'contemplate nature herself in a simple farm, unbroken in upon by a Mr Lay-out'. While it would be too simple to identify Brown's landscape with a broadly Whig attitude to landscape, and the various alternatives as 'Tory', there is nevertheless a measure of truth in such a characterization. Such objections to Brown's style were to gather pace in the decades following his death. But they were also to take new forms, as patterns of social and economic organization, ideologies and lifestyles all continued to develop, and the landscapes of the wealthy with them.

122, 123 A Neoclassical park in the style of Capability Brown (above) contrasted with one designed in the Picturesque mode (below): illustrations by Thomas Hearne for Richard Payne Knight's *The Landscape* (1794).

Conclusion: Afterlife and Legacy

THE WORK OF LANCELOT BROWN and the Capability Men is sometimes still portrayed as the apogee, the culmination, of the development of English landscape design. But their style was the outcome of specific social and economic circumstances and as these changed, so too did the tastes of patrons and customers. The 'landscape' style did not die a rapid death, of course, with Brown's own demise in 1783. Nathaniel Richmond, 'many years known among the gentlemen of landed property, as an eminent improver of parks and gardens', died the following year; but Richard Woods was still preparing new designs when he died in 1793, while both Thomas White and William Emes produced landscapes in a broadly 'Brownian' style well into the 1790s. But by this time many customers, for a variety of reasons, were looking for something new. Indeed, even Brown's own landscapes were being modified within his memory. At Kimberley in Norfolk, for example, where he worked on the lake as late as 1778, the Wodehouses were already, in 1786, asking the obscure local designer John Hare to prepare a 'Plan for the intended Alterations at the South End of the Lake at Kimberley'.[1]

The later history of the landscapes created by Brown and his fellow designers – their reception and treatment in the nineteenth century – are poorly researched, but matters of some importance: as John Dixon Hunt in particular has emphasized, the 'afterlife of gardens' is in many ways as culturally significant as their creation.[2] But there is insufficient space here to discuss in any detail how, when and why the style of the Capability Men fell from favour; in some respects, as we shall see, it never did. Much attention has been paid by scholars to the attacks made on Brown and his landscapes by the 'prophets of the Picturesque', Uvedale Price and Richard Payne Knight. Both men published texts in 1794 which sought to apply to landscape *design* the principles of landscape *appreciation* earlier propagated by William Gilpin.[3] They hammered home once again the accusation that Brown's style was bland and repetitive, suppressing the characteristics of locality and applying a landscape aesthetic derived, by implication, from the counties in the hinterland of London, to the whole of the country. Knight famously suggested that Brown was the 'Thin, meagre genius of the bare and bald', Price that 'monotony and baldness are the greatest defects of improved places'. Their stated alternative – the creation of landscapes that, in their spatial composition, echoed the paintings of Claude Lorrain and Poussin, and which were characterized by roughness and variety – likewise continued, in many ways, existing undercurrents of opposition to the dominant style (illus. 122, 123). It might be thought that such an emphasis would have encouraged the creation of landscapes organized around a limited number of set views, principally from the house and its immediate vicinity, but in fact the two men advocated designs that were to be explored in order to reveal a succession of interesting details and features. Knight wrote how:

> The stately arch, high rais'd with massive
> stone
> The ponderous flag, that forms a bridge alone;
> The prostrate tree, or rudely propt-up beam,
> That leads the path across the foaming
> stream;
> May each the scene with different beauty
> grace.[4]

Abandoned quarries overgrown with trees, ruined cottages, traces of past human activity of all kinds, provided interest, variety and, above all, a sense of place. Details of the vernacular landscape could, moreover, be augmented with newly constructed features, often in a plain style and using specifically local materials.[5] The grounds of Knight's estate of Downton Castle in Herefordshire contained a whole succession of such things, strung out along the paths winding through the rocky grounds, a landscape of individual stimulation for a society now more interested in emotion and personal experience, as Romanticism supplanted the immutable certainties of Neoclassicism. Yet neither Price nor Knight were professional designers – both were part of the time-honoured tradition of gentleman amateurs – and their

influence on landscape design appears, at least initially, to have been limited. The mainstream was in fact represented by Humphry Repton, who set up in business in 1788 as Brown's self-styled successor (at the same time, as we have seen, acknowledging his debt to Nathaniel Richmond); Payne and Price described his work as 'designed and executed exactly after Mr Brown's receipt, without any attention to the natural or artificial character of a place'. Repton's influence arose in part from the fact that, in marked contrast to Brown, he was the author of no fewer than four well-received books on landscape architecture. And it was under Repton and his contemporaries like John and Lewis Kennedy that the style of the Capability Men was gradually changed, to suit new times.

From the start of his career, Repton tended to deal with smaller properties than Brown, in part because the greatest landscapes in the land had already been extensively 'improved', and the changes he gradually made to the latter's style largely reflected this.[6] He thus criticized Brown's meandering drives, which were clearly unsuitable for smaller park landscapes, and in general relied on subtlety of planting or building, rather than on scale, to produce required effects. If Brown was a cosmetic surgeon, then Repton was a make-up artist. He was, moreover, especially keen on providing ways in which the owners of modest estates could display their status in a locality, suggesting at Livermere in Suffolk in 1790, for example, that all the village fences should be painted the same colour – an approach he described as 'appropriation', and which was robustly ridiculed by Price and Knight.[7] The same interests made Repton an enthusiast for establishing a degree of 'connection' between mansion and estate land, by in particular providing some openings in the perimeter belts of the landscape park. Repton's nostalgic enthusiasm for the role of long-established families in the life of the countryside – his unease about the accelerating eruption of 'upstart wealth' – shaded off into generalized paternalist sentiments, especially as class distinctions and poverty in rural England increased still further during the Napoleonic Wars. In his later works these loom ever larger as an explanation for aspects of his style, and especially for the greater permeability of the bounds of the park, the blurring of the line between the designed and the vernacular countryside: labourers' cottages, for example, if made 'a subordinate part of the general scenery . . . so far from disfiguring it, add to the dignity that wealth can derive from the exercise of benevolence'.[8] The country house should not stand, solitary and isolated, within its private park. Looked at in one way, Repton is Brown with a more Tory face, and by the early nineteenth century the design of landscapes in England often displayed such overtly 'paternalist' aspects. At many country houses, for example, the line of the approach was changed so that the main entrance opened directly onto a village street, with cottages (and in some cases alms-houses) clustering around it deferentially, 'the rich man in his castle/the poor man at his gate'. But for the most part, parks continued to function as exclusive landscapes in a socially polarized countryside.

Over time Repton followed the market, his style changing as – in spite of the economic dislocations of the Napoleonic Wars – industrialization and agricultural growth continued, and focused wealth at ever lower social levels. There was a further expansion in both the numbers, and economic power, of those members of the middling groups in society who could never have been fully accommodated into Georgian notions of the polite. By 1816 Repton was able to describe how

> It seldom falls to the lot of the improver to be called upon for his opinion on places of great extent . . . while in the neighbourhood of every city or manufacturing town, new places as villas are daily springing up, and these, with a few acres, require all the conveniences, comforts and appendages, of larger and more sumptuous, if not more expensive places. And . . . these have of late had the greatest claim to my attention.[9]

It was not, as Repton further explained, by 'adding field to field, or by taking away hedges, or by removing roads to a distance' that the surroundings of a villa were to be improved, but rather by exploiting 'every circumstance of interest or beauty within our reach, and by hiding such objects as cannot be viewed with pleasure'. But with middle-class money now structuring the market, and middle-class attitudes increasingly shaping taste, the garden now returned to prominence, and was gradually reintroduced by Repton and others in front of the country house (illus. 124, 125). By the 1820s, in the designs of men like William Sawrey Gilpin – William Gilpin's nephew – terraces with elaborate parterres were routinely placed below the main facades. The importance of the garden rather than the park was, more generally, advocated in the writings of designers like John Claudius Loudon. By the middle decades of the nineteenth century, especially in the works of William Andrews Nesfield and the architect Charles Barry, complex and substantial architectural terraces were being interposed between house and park (illus. 126). Gardens thus became not only more visually prominent but more structured and geometric, with a return to fashion of parterres, topiary and terraces.[10] They also became, at the larger country houses especially, more horticultural in character and more complex and varied in design, with a proliferation of 'themed' gardens (American gardens, Swiss gardens and the like) and tree collections or arboreta.

Changes in the distribution of wealth, and thus in the arbitration of taste, as England became a fully industrial nation, were a major factor in this decisive shift in taste. Loudon's first major work, published in 1806, was the *Treatise on Farming, Improving and Managing Country Residences*; his last work on the subject of private gardens, published over three decades later, was significantly entitled *The Suburban Gardener and Villa Companion*. But, as in the time of Brown, a myriad of other influences shaped styles of landscape design. In particular, developments in architecture, in domestic planning and in the use of social space continued to be of critical importance. The last decades of the eighteenth century saw the overwhelming dominance of classical styles in country house architecture come to an end. Mansions in a wide range of medieval or pseudo-Elizabethan or Jacobean styles were now erected, while 'Italianate' houses – modelled upon seventeenth-century Italian palace architecture, with balustraded rooflines and (usually) a soaring tower, asymmetrically placed – also became popular. To some extent, as Repton explained when he laid out the grounds of James Wyatt's huge Gothic edifice at Ashridge in Hertfordshire in 1803, a house built in such a

rambling and asymmetrical style required grounds that referenced the medieval past.[11] But more important, perhaps, was the direct impact on gardens of the social forces which were shaping changes in country house design.

Country houses in general grew larger from the end of the eighteenth century. The numbers of servants employed by landowners steadily increased and as roads improved still further and – from the 1840s – the railway network developed, they entertained on a lavish scale, holding house parties at which guests (and their servants) would expect to be put up for several days.[12] Not only did this necessitate greater numbers of bedrooms, it also encouraged a further proliferation of spaces for recreation and entertaining, with the arrival of morning rooms, billiard rooms, smoking rooms and much else. Houses grew larger, and their plans more rambling, for another reason. Increasing agitation for political reform on the part of the wider middle class had encouraged violent criticism, in Girouard's words, 'of the arrogance, immorality and inefficiency of the upper classes who, they considered, ran the country badly and for their own benefit'. During the first half of the nineteenth century, however, 'the upper classes adjusted their image to make it acceptable to middle-class morality. They became . . . more serious, more religious, more domestic, and more moral.'[13] By the 1840s landowners were wanting houses with plans more strongly gendered in character than anything seen in the previous century. Particular rooms were now considered the preserve of particular genders – smoking and billiard rooms for men, drawing rooms for women – and, more importantly, male and female servants were provided with strictly segregated accommodation and working areas, insofar as this was practical, in order to reduce their exposure to moral temptation. This overriding notion of structure, order and morality – of everything in its place and a place for everyone – also infected the grounds of the country house, not only in the development of highly ordered and structured plans for gardens, but in the return of designs in which all was open and everyone visible – on the main lawns or terraces – or, in the case of 'themed' gardens, were at least kept close to the house. The temptations presented by distant pavilions or temples, or by long carriage rides in parks, were now to be avoided.

For a host of reasons, in addition to those already outlined, the style of the Capability Men thus fell from favour. The pure forms of Neoclassicism seemed inappropriate in an age of medieval revival and architectural eclecticism. The kind of complex business model that had ensured the success of Lancelot Brown, moreover, does not seem to have been replicated by late eighteenth- and nineteenth-century designers. It was not so much that large-scale landscaping itself declined, although to some extent it did. As interest in exposing and enhancing natural landforms waned, so too did the need for the teams of labourers laboriously grading the slopes. Nevertheless, in the grounds of the wealthy lakes continued to be constructed, substantial tree-planting schemes were still undertaken and large amounts of materials and labour were required to make elaborate gardens, with terraces, rockworks and the rest. It was rather that leading designers, with national reputations, now kept to the business of design, and seldom got involved in the direct execution of the works themselves. They supplied the plan and if required would inspect the progress of the works, but they would

not contract for the works themselves, this now being the business of 'trade' – a contractor – or of the estate itself. Nurseries continued to supply a 'design and build' service for middle-class customers, but at more exalted social levels this was now seen as inferior to the provision of a design by a professional designer. Repton never seems to have done anything for his clients other than supply a Red Book, and on occasions stake out planting on the ground. Loudon undertook some direct supervision of work in the early years of his career but a major dispute concerning overrun of costs at Stradsett in Norfolk in 1813, which resulted in an expensive court case, seems to have put him off the idea. Leading nineteenth-century garden designers made their money in a range of ways, as well as by advising on specific sites. The massive expansion in literacy, and in the numbers of middle-class gardeners eager for advice, meant that many profited from writing. Repton, as already noted, was a prolific author; Loudon penned eleven books, mostly on gardening, as well as editing (and writing much of) the *Gardener's Magazine*; Edward Kemp was perhaps better known for his book on *How to Lay Out a Garden* than for the actual parks and gardens he designed. Others, like Nesfield, benefited from their close partnership with architectural practices: Joseph Paxton, the famous gardener at Chatsworth, branched out into civil engineering and politics. There was no single model, but there was no replication of Brown's complex and flexible business structure.

In this changed climate the works of Brown and his contemporaries were, through the nineteenth century, often attacked and misunderstood. Brown was castigated as a low-born upstart, a social climber, a vandal, who spawned a mass of 'illiterate followers'. This was the age of the 'hero

124, 125 Before and after views from Humphry Repton's Red Book for Shrubland Park, Suffolk, 1789. This is probably the first time that Repton proposed creating a flower garden immediately below the main facade of a country house. The parkland beyond is broadly 'Brownian' in style, although more open to the surrounding countryside.

126 Shrubland Park, Suffolk: the 'Descent', designed by Charles Barry and constructed in 1852–3, as illustrated in E. Adveno Brooke's 1850s *Gardens of England*. This view, drawn from roughly the same position as illus. 124 and 125, shows the increasingly architectural and monumental quality of gardens in the middle decades of the nineteenth century.

gardener' – of men like Donald Beaton of Shrubland Park in Suffolk – whose horticultural achievements were lauded in the gardening press. But the contribution of such men did not usually extend to the overall *design* of country house grounds. As taste and social attitudes gradually came to be defined by a broad middle-class group, as sharper social boundaries were drawn, the previous generation of 'improvers' were no longer perceived as 'gentlemen', but as 'lowly' gardeners.

Hostility to Brown and his works was not universal. Loudon, a noted critic, recounted a visit he made to Claremont in 1834 (landscaped by Brown in 1769) where the head gardener 'pointed out ... several parts of the original plan of Brown, which he had restored: a mode of improvement highly to be commended'.[14] What Loudon (or the gardener) meant by 'restoration' in this context is unclear, but it is interesting that 65 years after Brown's commission, this particular landscape

was thought to be both in need of it, and worthy of it. Of far greater importance, however, was the fact that the Capability Men bequeathed a more general legacy to the world of the nineteenth century. Although formal gardens now returned to grace the main facades of fashionable mansions they were not – as their seventeenth-century predecessors had been – separated from the park by high walls, pierced only at intervals by gates, but rather by low balustrades, so that uninterrupted prospects over the adjacent parkland could be enjoyed. Brown and his fellows had succeeded in establishing the park, the park without deer, and in particular the park as an artistic landscape, as the indispensable sign of wealth and gentility. And new parks continued to be established right through the nineteenth century, and existing ones to be expanded. While it is true that there were differences in planting and other details between these nineteenth-century creations and those of the eighteenth century, we should not exaggerate their extent. Superficially, Victorians appear to have favoured a much wider planting palette, partly influenced by the belated exercise of Picturesque principles by men like William Sawrey Gilpin, partly by a further increase in the range of plant material brought from distant shores and made available by commercial nurseries. Extensive use was also made of the horse chestnut, copper beech and various native or long-established coniferous species. But as we have suggested, to some extent the apparent scale of the contrast with eighteenth-century practice is misleading. Brown and his contemporaries had also employed horse chestnut, pine, larch and the rest, but the shorter lifespans of these species have ensured that only the plantings of oak, lime, beech and sweet chestnut have survived to the present. It is also true that the nineteenth century saw the reinstatement, on a limited scale, of avenues within parks. Overall, however, it is the continuities rather than the discontinuities which are most striking, and not always perhaps sufficiently emphasized. Lakes pre-dated the time of Brown, but it was he and his collaborators who made them an almost standard feature of designed landscapes, and in the nineteenth century they lost none of their appeal, albeit now often provided with margins more complex and often rugged, and more closely planted, in the hands of men like Gilpin. Other features of the Brownian landscape continued to enjoy popularity, such as planting in clumps. Perimeter belts, enclosing the park from the surrounding countryside, were now if anything an even more prominent feature, in a country still wracked by gross inequalities.

Landscape parks thus survived and flourished as a landscape form until the late nineteenth century, when a wide range of social and economic changes began to render the country house itself an expensive and unnecessary luxury. From the 1880s, a major agricultural depression and the imposition of death duties and other exactions threatened the fortunes of landowners; the costs of labour rose; and a range of political reforms gradually ensured that a mansion set in extensive grounds was no longer the centre of local life, or an indispensable accessory for those seeking political power.[15] Large-scale fellings took place in parklands as financially challenged families cashed in their mature timber to stave off ruin. The trees planted by Brown and his contemporaries would have been over a century old by the early twentieth century, ripe for harvesting anyway. Lilias Rider Haggard described in the 1930s how 'the wholesale cutting of timber all over the country is a sad sight, but often the owner's last desperate bid to enable him to cling to the family acres.'[16] Around a sixth of the large houses which existed in England in 1880 were demolished over the succeeding century and their parks and gardens largely or entirely destroyed; many others were abandoned by their owners to become schools, care homes, hotels or hospitals. Country house grounds, those designed by Brown included, thus slid gradually into neglect or were subject to minimal or inappropriate maintenance, were built over or converted to arable fields or gravel pits. This assault on designed landscapes was itself arrested, and then to an extent reversed, by further phases of economic, political and cultural change in the second half of the twentieth century, but by this stage many had been destroyed or irrevocably damaged.

Brown's own designs have, not surprisingly, survived developments since the late eighteenth century to very varying extents. Even where houses and parks have remained intact, in private or in institutional ownership, his contribution to the landscape has usually been significantly eroded or overwritten by subsequent changes and alterations. Chatsworth in Derbyshire, like a number of major country houses, still remains in the hands of the family who commissioned Brown to modernize their grounds, and the parkland remains unploughed and beautifully maintained to this day (with free public access to most parts of it). But the planting was much augmented in the nineteenth century, and the pleasure grounds extensively remodelled under Joseph Paxton and the sixth Duke, with a formal parterre intruded between the house and park, so that to a large extent the landscape feels more Victorian than Georgian. A similar fate has, albeit to varying degrees, affected all surviving examples of Brown's work, as later owners added to the planting or replaced trees that had grown old and died. The interventions of the Capability Men, as we have emphasized on a number of occasions, usually represented one phase in a longer and more complex history of a landscape, and just as they both removed and reinterpreted what already existed at a place, so too have subsequent designers reused or obliterated their own contribution. Nevertheless, there remain many places – Bowood, Petworth, Burghley and Grimsthorpe among them – where the essence of Brown's design survives intact, where the principal planting has perpetuated the original patterns, and where lakes and landforms remain largely unaltered, although even in these places the pleasure grounds that formed so important an element in these landscapes have been altered beyond recognition.

Even in degraded examples of Brown's works some fragments of interest usually survive. Langley in Norfolk became a school in the 1960s, with much of the outlying parkland reverting to agriculture, but sections of Brown's perimeter belts remain in place, and a few of his specimen trees. At Shortgrove in Essex the house was burned down in 1966 (and the stable block was converted to residential use); large areas of the park, especially in the south, have been ploughed up; and the narrow lake to the west has gone. Yet sections of pasture, with free-standing trees, survive near the site of the house; most of the perimeter belts survive, albeit much replanted; and Brown's entrance drive remains intact, complete with the fine bridge designed by Matthew Brettingham. A surprising number of Brown's parks have become golf courses, the smooth swells of the Neoclassical landscape peculiarly well suited to such a use. At Moor Park in Hertfordshire Brown's planting mounds, so criticized by Walpole, still remain, and some of his trees still stand, amid the greens and bunkers; in the north of the same county, at Ashridge, the 'Golden Valley' survives as a striking feature of the landscape, and the main areas of Brown's woodland are still in place. Substantial fragments of lost Brownian landscapes can be found in surprising places. Digswell House in Hertfordshire still stands but its estate was engulfed by Welwyn Garden City in the middle decades of the twentieth century. An impressive slice of parkland nevertheless survives as an open space among the modern houses, still boasting a number of Brown's original trees ranged either side of a dry valley (illus. 127): the prospect was terminated by one of his lakes, no longer visible and surrounded by secondary woodland, but still surviving and managed as a nature reserve.

127 The remains of the park at Digswell, Hertfordshire, designed by Lancelot Brown in the early 1770s and now largely engulfed in the houses of Welwyn Garden City.

Once again, in the foregoing paragraphs, we have found ourselves focusing on the works of Capability Brown, but a similar range of fates has, of course, befallen the more numerous creations of his less famous contemporaries. Their best-preserved works – places like Ditchingham in Norfolk, noted at the start of this book – can provide a better impression of eighteenth-century landscape design than many of the more mangled examples of Brown's own parklands. But all these landscapes, even those in the care of the National Trust and English Heritage, are to varying degrees still under threat, from over-zealous restoration, age, climate change and rising levels of tree disease. Brown's elms have long gone; his beech trees are all approaching the ends of their natural lives; most of the oaks, sweet chestnuts and elms have reached 'veteran' status and are entering senescence – have grown to an age greater than their planters can ever have envisaged, at a time when most timber trees were felled before they became a century old. There are few places where we can really experience a landscape created by Brown or his fellows in anything like its original condition, or – perhaps more accurately – in anything like the form which they intended the landscape to take, when mature. Even if we could find such a place we could never hope to experience it as their clients would have done, given that the wider physical environment, and our own perceptions of the world, have changed beyond recognition.

Landscapes are at once the most problematic and the most ephemeral of art forms, always growing and changing, always decaying. We may think of these as 'historic landscapes' but unlike the past they are not dead but living – and thus always in the process of changing, and of dying. We should enjoy the much-altered remains, disjointed and uncontextualized for the most part, of Georgian landscapes, and strive to maintain – in something like their pure, unadulterated form – some representative examples, not bothering overmuch, perhaps, whether or not they were designed by Brown himself. But we should not fool ourselves into thinking that any really survive, pristine and unaltered. And we must always remember that, for all their contrived air of timeless nature, the designs of the Capability Men were the product of a specific constellation of social and economic circumstances, which has passed for ever.

REFERENCES

1 The World of Mr Brown

1 N. Pevsner, 'The Genesis of the Picturesque', *Architectural Review*, 96 (November 1944), p. 139.

2 M. Symes, *The Picturesque and the Later Georgian Garden* (Bristol, 2012).

3 C. Hussey, *The Picturesque* (London, 1927), p. 39; C. Hussey, 'Introduction', in D. Stroud, *Capability Brown* (London, 1950), pp. 27–35; C. Hussey, *English Gardens and Landscapes, 1700–1750* (London, 1967).

4 D. Stroud, *Capability Brown* (London, 1975); E. Hyams, *Capability Brown and Humphry Repton* (London, 1971); T. Hinde, *Capability Brown: The Story of a Master Gardener* (London, 1986); R. Turner, *Capability Brown and the Eighteenth-century English Landscape* (London, 1985). Of these books, Stroud's remains the most useful and informative, and where information in this volume remains unreferenced, Stroud is usually the source.

5 J. Brown, *The Omnipotent Magician: Lancelot 'Capability' Brown* (London, 2011); L. Mayer, *Capability Brown and the English Landscape Garden* (Princes Risborough, 2011).

6 S. Shields, '"Mr Brown Engineer": Lancelot Brown's Early Work at Grimsthorpe Castle and Stowe', *Garden History*, XXXIV/2 (2006), pp. 174–91.

7 *Public Advertiser*, 9 September 1772.

8 Stroud, *Capability Brown*, pp. 53–5; Turner, Capability Brown, pp. 57–8.

9 *Public Advertiser*, 9 September 1772.

10 P. Willis, 'Capability Brown's Account with Drummonds Bank, 1753–1783', *Architectural History*, 27 (1984), pp. 382–91.

11 A. Buchan, *Charlecote and the Lucys: The Chronicle of an English Family* (Oxford, 1958), p. 225.

12 J. Gregory, S. Spooner and T. Williamson, 'Lancelot "Capability" Brown: A Research Impact Review', *English Heritage Research Report*, 50 (London, 2015); J. Phibbs, 'A List of Landscapes that have been Attributed to Lancelot "Capability" Brown', *Garden History*, XLI/2 (2013); J. Phibbs, 'A List of Landscapes that have been Attributed to Lancelot "Capability" Brown: Revisions', *Garden History*, XLII/2 (2014).

13 Private collection, Ditchingham Hall, Norfolk.

14 Stroud, *Capability Brown*, p. 224; Turner, *Capability Brown*, p.177.

15 T. Williamson, *The Archaeology of the Landscape Park: Garden Design in Norfolk, England, c. 1680–1840* (Oxford, 1998), pp. 100–103; J.C. Loudon, *The Landscape Gardening and Landscape Architecture of the Late Humphry Repton Esq* (London, 1840), p. 328. The individual concerned was probably Adam Mickle, for whom see below, p. 140.

16 M. Symes, 'David Garrick and Landscape Gardening', *Journal of Garden History*, 6 (1986), pp. 34–49; *Gazetteer and New Daily Advertiser*, 13 December 1780.

17 For Overstone, see Gregory et al., 'Lancelot "Capability" Brown: A Research Impact Review', p. 9.

18 *Public Advertiser*, 6 September 1770.

19 H. Repton, *Sketches and Hints on Landscape Gardening* (London, 1795), p. 110; H. Repton, *An Inquiry into the Changes of Taste in Landscape Gardening* (London, 1806), p. 328.

20 J. Phibbs, 'Groves and Belts', *Garden History*, XIX/2 (1991), pp. 175–86; pp. 181–4; J. Phibbs, 'The Englishness of Lancelot "Capability" Brown', *Garden History*, XXXI/2 (2003), pp. 122–40;

J. Phibbs, 'Projective Geometry', *Garden History*, xxxiv/1 (2006), pp. 1–21; J. Phibbs, 'Point Blank', *Garden History*, xxxv/1 (2007), pp. 110–18; 'The View-point', *Garden History*, xxxvi/2 (2008), pp. 215–28; J. Phibbs, 'Field Sports and Brownian Design', *Garden History*, xl/1 (2012), pp. 56–71.

21 T. Mowl, *Gentlemen and Players: Gardeners of the English Landscape* (Stroud, 2000); T. Mowl, *William Kent: Architect, Designer, Opportunist* (London, 2007).

22 K. Felus, 'Beautiful Objects and Agreeable Retreats: Uses of Garden Buildings in the Designed Landscape in 18th-century England', PhD thesis, University of Bristol, 2009; K. Felus, 'Boats and Boating in the Designed Landscape, 1720–1820', *Garden History*, xxxiv/1 (2006), pp. 22–46; F. Cowell, *Richard Woods (1715–1793): Master of the Pleasure Garden* (Woodbridge, 2009).

23 S. Bending, 'H. Walpole and Eighteenth-century Garden History', *Journal of the Warburg and Courtauld Institutes*, 57 (1994), pp. 209–26; S. Bending, 'A Natural Revolution?', in K. Sharpe and S. Zwicker, *Refiguring Revolutions: Aesthetics and Politics from the English Revolution to the Romantic Revolution* (Berkeley, ca, 1998), pp. 241–66; B. P. Lange, 'The English Garden and Patriotic Discourse', in H. J. Diller et al., *Englishness*, Anglistik & Englischunterricht, 46/47 (Heidelberg, 1992).

24 J. C. D. Clarke, *English Society, 1688–1742: Ideology, Social Structure and Political Practice during the Ancien Regime* (Cambridge, 1980).

25 B. Hill, *The Growth of Parliamentary Parties, 1680–1742* (London, 1976); P. Langford, *A Polite and Commercial People* (Oxford, 1989), pp. 1–58; S. Hoppit, *A Land of Liberty? England, 1689–1727* (Oxford, 2000), pp. 174, 200–205.

26 Langford, *Polite and Commercial People*, pp. 9–58.

27 H. T. Dickinson, *Walpole and the Whig Supremacy* (London, 1973); C. Gerrard, *The Patriot Opposition to Walpole: Politics, Poetry, and National Myth, 1725–1742* (London, 1995).

28 G. Clarke, 'Grecian Taste and Gothic Virtue: Lord Cobham's Gardening Programme and its Iconography', *Apollo*, 97 (1973), pp. 56–67; P. Edwards, 'The Gardens at Wroxton Abbey, Oxfordshire', *Garden History*, 14 (1986), pp. 50–59; A. Hodges, 'Painshill Park, Cobham, Surrey, 1700–1800', *Garden History*, ii/3 (1973), pp. 36–68;

K. Rorsehach, *The Early Georgian Landscape Garden* (New Haven, ct, 1983), pp. 39–46.

29 H. T. Dickinson, 'Tories: 1714–1830', in *Reader's Guide to British History*, ed. D. Loades (London, 2003), vol. ii, p. 1279.

30 A. Smith, *An Inquiry into the Nature and Causes of the Wealth of Nations* [1776], ed. R. H. Campbell and A. S. Skinner, 2 vols (Oxford, 1976); A. Smith, *The Theory of Moral Sentiments* [1759], ed. D. D. Raphael and A. L. Macfie, 2 vols (Oxford, 1976); M. Quinn, ed., *The Collected Works of Jeremy Bentham: Writings on the Poor Laws*, vol. i: *Writings on the Poor Laws* (Oxford, 2001); T. Malthus, *An Essay on the Principle of Population* [1798], ed. J. Bonar (New York, 1966).

31 J. R. McCulloch, *A Discourse on the Rise, Progress, Peculiar Objects and Importance of Political Economy* (Edinburgh, 1824), p. 10.

32 Bending, 'Walpole and Eighteenth-century Garden History'; Bending, 'A Natural Revolution?'; Lange, 'The English Garden and Patriotic Discourse'.

33 N. Everett, *The Tory View of Landscape* (London, 1994), pp. 13–37.

34 G. Claeys, *Utopias of the British Enlightenment* (Cambridge, 1994), p. vii.

35 C. Dudley, 'Party Politics, Political Economy, and Economic Development in Early Eighteenth-century England', *Economic History Review*, 66 (2013), pp. 1084–100.

36 W. Cobbett, *The Parliamentary History of England from the Earliest Period to 1816*, vol. xi (London, 1812), p. 7.

37 L. Colley, *Britons: Forging the Nation, 1707–1837* (revd edn, London, 2009), p. 69.

38 Ibid.

39 S. Drescher, *Econocide: British Slavery on the Eve of Abolition* (Pittsburgh, pa, 1977), p. 27.

40 I. G. Simmons, *An Environmental History of Great Britain, from 10,000 years ago to the Present* (Edinburgh, 2001), p. 142; M. Campbell-Culver, *The Origins of Plants* (London, 2010), pp. 148–81.

41 J. Finch, 'Three Men in a Boat: Biographies and Narratives in the Historic Landscape', *Landscape Research*, xxxiii/5 (2008), pp. 511–30, at p. 516.

42 J. Barnatt and T. Williamson, *Chatsworth: A Landscape History* (Macclesfield, 2005), p. 105.

43 C. Christie, *The British Country House in the Eighteenth Century* (Manchester, 2000), p. 9.

44 B. R. Mitchell and P. Deane, *Abstract of British Historical Statistics* (Cambridge, 1962), pp. 5–6.

45 B. A. Holderness, 'Prices, Productivity and Output', in *The Agrarian History of England and Wales*, vol. VI, ed. G. E. Mingay (Cambridge, 1989), pp. 84–189, 145; J. V. Beckett, *The Agricultural Revolution* (London, 1990), p. 9.

46 M. Overton, *Agricultural Revolution in England* (Cambridge, 1996), pp. 121–8.

47 M. W. Flinn, *The History of the British Coal Industry*, vol. II: *1700–1830* (Oxford, 1984), p. 27.

48 M. Palmer and P. Neaverson, *Industry in the Landscape, 1700–1900* (London, 1994), pp. 94–119.

49 T. Williamson, *The Transformation of Rural England: Farming and the Landscape, 1700–1870* (Exeter, 2002), pp. 155–78; T. Williamson, *An Environmental History of Wildlife in England, 1550–1950* (London, 2013), pp. 73–7.

50 N. Cossons, *The bp Book of Industrial Archaeology* (London, 1987), p. 32.

51 Langford, *Polite and Commercial People*, p. 70.

52 K. Pomeranz, *The Great Divergence: China, Europe, and the Making of the Modern World Economy* (Princeton, NJ, 2001), p. 67.

53 E.A.W. Wrigley, *Continuity, Chance and Change: The Character of the Industrial Revolution in England* (Cambridge, 1988), pp. 54–5.

54 M. Girouard, *The English Town: A History of Urban Life* (London, 1990), pp. 76–7.

55 O. Goldsmith, *The Life of Richard Nash of Bath, Esquire, extracted principally from his Original Papers* (London, 1762), p. 24.

56 A. Smith, *An Inquiry into the Nature and Causes of the Wealth of Nations* [1776], ed. R. H. Campbell and A. S. Skinner, 2 vols (Oxford, 1976), p. 348.

57 Bowood archives, Lady Shelburne's Diary, 17 April 1767, vol. III, p. 173.

58 The best account of social relations in this period remains K. Snell, *Annals of the Labouring Poor: Social Change and Agrarian England, 1660–1900* (Cambridge, 1986).

59 W. Blackstone, *Commentaries on the Laws of England*, vol. III (London, 1765), p. 326.

60 J. Schofield, *London, 1100–1600: The Archaeology of a Capital City* (Sheffield, 2011), p. 343.

61 J. Finch and K. Giles, eds, *Estate Landscapes: Design, Improvement and Power in the Post-medieval Landscape* (Woodbridge, 2007).

62 T. Williamson, 'Archaeological Perspectives on Landed Estates: Research Agendas', in *Estate Landscapes: Design, Improvement and Power in the Post-medieval Landscape*, ed. Finch and

Giles, pp. 1–18; H. Clemenson, *English Country Houses and Landed Estates* (London, 1982), pp. 7–9.

63 Norfolk Record Office, NRS 14625.

64 Bowood archives, Lady Shelburne's Diary, 24 August 1769, vol. V, p. 18.

65 E. Hughes, 'The Eighteenth-century Estate Agent', in *Essays in British and Irish History*, ed. H. Cronne, T. Moody and D. Quin (London, 1949), pp. 185–99; P. Horn, 'An Eighteenth-century Land Agent: The Career of Nathaniel Kent (1737–1810)', *Agricultural History Review*, 30 (1982), pp. 1–16; S. Webster, 'Estate Improvement and the Professionalization of Land Agents on the Egremont Estates in Sussex and Yorkshire, 1770–1835', *Rural History*, 18 (2007), pp. 47–69.

66 Norfolk Record Office, NRS 14625.

67 J. Cradock, *Village Memoirs, in a Series of Letters between a Clergyman and his Family in the Country, and his Son in Town* (London, 1765), p. 126.

68 A. Rowe, A.D.M. MacNair and T. Williamson, *Dury and Andrews' Map of Hertfordshire: Society and Landscape in the Eighteenth Century* (Hatfield, 2015), pp. 148–50.

69 For example A. Bermingham, *Landscape and Ideology: The English Rustic Tradition, 1740–1860* (London, 1987), pp. 9–14.

70 J. C. Loudon, *The Suburban Gardener and Villa Companion* (London, 1838), p. 162.

71 O. Rackham, *The History of the Countryside* (London, 1986), pp. 1–5, 155–80; M. Turner, *English Parliamentary Enclosures* (Folkstone, 1980); J. A. Gelling, *Common Field and Enclosure in England, 1450–1850* (London, 1977); T. Williamson, 'Understanding Enclosure', *Landscapes*, I/1 (2000), pp. 56–79; J. Chapman and S. Seeleger, *Enclosure, Environment and Landscape in Southern England* (Stroud, 2001).

72 T. Williamson, R. Liddiard and T. Pardita, *Champion: The Making and Unmaking of the English Midland Landscape* (Liverpool, 2013), pp. 128–59.

73 Estate map, 1763, Bowood archives: no catalogue number.

74 Williamson, *Transformation of Rural England*.

2 Gardens and Society, 1700–1750

1 D. Jacques, *The Grand Manner: Changing Style in Garden Design, 1660–1735* (London, 1999); J. D. Hunt and E. de Jong, eds, 'The Anglo-Dutch

Garden in the Reign of William and Mary', *Journal of Garden History*, 8 [special issue] (1988).

2 T. Williamson, *Polite Landscapes: Gardens and Society in Eighteenth-century England* (Stroud, 1995), pp. 31–4.

3 Barnatt and Williamson, *Chatsworth*, pp. 80–81.

4 Survey of the manor of Somerleyton, 1652: East Suffolk Record Office (Lowestoft), 295.

5 The Journals of Sir John Clerk of Pennicuik: Scottish Record Office, GD 18/2107.

6 J. James, *The Theory and Practice of Gardening: Wherein is Fully Handled All That Relates to Fine Gardens, Commonly Called Pleasure-gardens . . .* (London, 1712).

7 S. Switzer, *Ichnographia rustica* (London, 1718), vol. 1, p. 34.

8 J. M. Bartos, 'Wilderness and Grove: Gardening with Trees in England, 1688–1750', PhD thesis, University of Bristol, 2013.

9 Switzer, *Ichnographia rustica*, vol. 1, p. 76.

10 J. S. Curl, *Georgian Architecture: The British Isles, 1714–1830* (London, 2014).

11 M. Girouard, *Life in the English Country House: A Social and Architectural History* (London, 1978), pp. 119–60.

12 Ibid., pp. 144–5, 156–8.

13 J. Summerson, *Architecture in Britain, 1530–1830* (London, 1991), p. 28.

14 Ibid., pp. 110, 221–33.

15 R. Browne, *The Architectural Outsiders* (London, 1985).

16 D. Cruickshank, *A Guide to the Georgian Buildings of Britain and Ireland* (London, 1985), pp. 2–23; J. Lees-Milne, *Earls of Creation* (London, 1962).

17 R. Morris, *Lectures on Architecture, consisting of Rules founded upon Harmonick and Arithmetical Proportions in Buildings* (London, 1734), p. 94.

18 Summerson, *Architecture in Britain*, pp. 295–343; H. E. Stutchbury, *The Architecture of Colen Campbell* (Manchester, 1967); R. Wittkower, *Palladio and Palladianism* (New York, 1974); J. Harris, 'The Architecture of the House', in *Houghton Hall: The Prime Minister, the Empress and the Heritage*. ed. A. Moore (London, 1996), pp. 20–24.

19 Cruickshank, *Georgian Buildings*, pp. 2–23.

20 G. Worsley, *Classical Architecture in Britain: The Heroic Age* (London, 1995).

21 T. Friedman, *James Gibbs* (London, 1984); Summerson, *Architecture in Britain*, pp. 324–33.

22 Girouard, *Life in the English Country House*, pp. 158–62.

23 Cruickshank, *Georgian Buildings*, pp. 63–5; J. Cornforth, 'The Genesis and Creation of a Great Interior', in *Houghton Hall: The Prime Minister, the Empress and the Inheritance*, pp. 29–40; at pp. 38–9.

24 L. Schmidt, C. Keller and P. Feversham, eds, *Holkham* (Munich, 2005), pp. 81–102.

25 Girouard, *Life in the English Country House*, p. 194.

26 J. Cornforth, *Early Georgian Interiors* (London, 2004).

27 F. Kimball, *The Creation of the Rococo Decorative Style* (New York, 1980).

28 K. Scott, *The Rococo Interior: Decoration and Social Space in Early Eighteenth-century Paris* (New Haven, CT, 1995); G. Bazin, *Baroque and Rococo* (London, 1998).

29 T. Mowl and B. Earnshaw, *An Insular Rococo: Architecture, Politics and Society in Ireland and England, 1710–70* (London, 1999).

30 Cornforth, *Early Georgian Interiors*, pp. 189–213.

31 Ibid., pp. 253–4.

32 Ibid., pp. 253–72.

33 Mowl and Earnshaw, *Insular Rococo*, p. 89.

34 Ibid., pp. 105–8.

35 O. Goldsmith, *The Life of Richard Nash of Bath, Esquire, extracted principally from his Original Papers* (London, 1762); R. B. Shoemaker, 'Reforming Male Manners: Public Insults and the Decline of Violence in London, 1660–1740', in *English Masculinities, 1660–1800*, ed. T. Hitchcock and M. Cohen (London, 1999), pp. 133–50; E. Foyster, 'Boys Will Be Boys? Manhood and Aggression, 1660–1800', in *English Masculinities, 1660–1800*, ed. Hitchcock and Cohen, pp. 151–66.

36 L. Stone, *The Family, Sex and Marriage in England, 1500–1800* (London, 1977), pp. 217–24; R. Trumbach, *The Rise of the Egalitarian Family: Aristocratic Kinship and Domestic Relations in Eighteenth-century England* (New York, 1977).

37 A. Fletcher, *Gender, Sex and Subordination in England, 1500–1800* (New Haven, CT, and London, 1996), p. 395.

38 Cornforth, *Early Georgian Interiors*, p. 264.

39 M. Laird, *The Formal Garden: Traditions of Art and Nature* (London, 1992), p. 121.

40 Quoted in G. Sheeran, *Landscape Gardens of West Yorkshire* (Wakefield, 1990), p. 23.

41 B. Langley, *Practical Geometry Applied in the Practical and Useful Arts of Building, Surveying, Gardening and Mensuration* (London, 1729); see in particular pp. 32–4.

42 H. Walpole, *Anecdotes of Painting* (London, 1798), p. 484. It was a small world: Langley worked as a garden designer at Twickenham Park for Thomas Vernon, a merchant in the Levant trade and Alexander Pope's landlord.

43 P. Willis, *Charles Bridgeman and the English Landscape Garden* (2nd edn, London, 2002).

44 B. Langley, *New Principles of Gardening* (London, 1728), pp. 203–7; Switzer, *Ichnographia rustica*, pp. 311–17.

45 T. Hamilton (6th Earl of Haddington), *Forest Trees: Some Directions About Raising Forest Trees*, ed. M. L. Anderson (Edinburgh, 1953), p. 58.

46 P. Miller, *The Gardener's Dictionary* (London, 1731); n. pag., under 'GA'.

47 G. Bickham, *The Beauties of Stow* (London, 1750), pp. 66–7; H. Walpole, *History of the Modern Taste in Gardening* (London, 1780), pp. 24–5.

48 'Map of an estate belonging to Jeremy Sambrooke Esq.' Surveyed by Thos. Holmes. Undated, said to be '*c.* 1735': Gloucester Record Office, D1245/FF75.

49 Bodleian Library, MS. Maps Herts. a.1.

50 A. Rowe and T. Williamson, 'New Light on Gobions', *Garden History*, 40 (2012), pp. 82–97.

51 W. Toldervy, *England and Wales Described in a Series of Letters* (London, 1762), pp. 117–22.

52 Holkham Hall archives, map 2/3.

53 A. Fletcher, 'Charles Bridgeman at Tring Park: A Reassessment', in *Hertfordshire Garden History: A Miscellany*, ed. A. Rowe (Hatfield, 2007), pp. 41–8; Hertfordshire Gardens Trust and T. Williamson, *The Parks and Gardens of West Hertfordshire* (Letchworth, 2000), pp. 18, 28–9.

54 Northamptonshire Record Office, H(K) 84.

55 L. Worsley, *Bolsover Castle* (London, 2000); M. Girouard, 'Early Drawings of Bolsover Hall', *Architectural History*, 27 (1984) pp. 510–18.

56 J. D. Hunt, *William Kent, Landscape Garden Designer: An Assessment and Catalogue of His Designs* (London, 1987).

57 T. Williamson, *The Archaeology of the Landscape Park: Garden Design in Norfolk, England, 1680–1840* (Oxford, 1998), pp. 63–70.

58 Schmidt et al., *Holkham*, pp. 154–8.

59 J. D. Hunt, *Garden and Grove: The Italian Renaissance Garden in the English Imagination, 1600–1750* (London, 1986), pp. 180–223.

60 R. Castell, *Villas of the Ancients Illustrated* (London, 1728).

61 G. Clarke, 'Grecian Taste and Gothic Virtue: Lord Cobham's Gardening Programme and Its Iconography', *Apollo*, 97 (1973), pp. 56–67; J. M. Robinson, *Temples of Delight: Stowe Landscape Gardens* (London, 1999); J. Shurmer, *The Stowe Landscape Gardens* (London, 1997); K. Rorschach, *The Early Georgian Landscape Garden* (New Haven, CT, 1983), pp. 27–34.

62 N. Penny, 'The Macabre Garden at Denbies and its Monument', *Garden History*, III/3 (1975), pp. 58–61.

63 T. Richardson, *The Arcadian Friends: Inventing the English Landscape Garden* (London, 2008), p. 13.

64 H. Tromp and E. Newby, 'A Dutchman's Visits to Some English Gardens in 1791', *Journal of Garden History*, 2 (1982), pp. 41–58; at p. 55.

65 J. J. Cartwright, ed., *The Travels through England of Dr Richard Pococke*, 2 vols (London, 1888), vol. II, pp. 137–8.

66 Mowl and Earnshaw, *Insular Rococo*, pp. 73–87.

67 W. and J. Halfpenny, *New Designs for Chinese Bridges, Temples, Triumphal Arches, Garden Seats, Palings, Obelisks, termini etc.* (London, 1751).

68 Quoted in Mowl and Earnshaw, *Insular Rococo*, p. 72.

69 Ibid., p. 80: the authors' chapter on Rococo gardens is the best treatment of the subject.

70 Richardson, *Arcadian Friends*, pp. 420–21.

71 C. Gilbert, *The Life and Works of Thomas Chippendale* (London, 1978), p. 109.

72 C. R. Elrington, *Victoria History of the County of Warwickshire*, vol. IX (London, 1968), pp. 81–6; T. Mowl and D. James, *Historic Gardens of Warwickshire* (Bristol, 2011), pp. 99–100.

73 Alscot House archives, box 2 and box 6.

74 Alscot House archives, box 35.

75 Alscot House archives, map of *c.* 1749, uncatalogued.

76 Mowl and Earnshaw, *Insular Rococo*, pp. 78–9.

77 Alscot House archives, box 42; memoranda book of James West, pp. 58, 64.

78 A. Young, *The Farmer's Tour through the East of England* (London, 1771), vol. I, pp. 36–7.

79 Quoted in Richardson, *Arcadian Friends*, p. 125.

80 Norfolk Record Office, Mf/Ro 219/1.

81 John H. Harvey, 'The Stocks held by Early Nurseries', *Agricultural History Review*, 22 (1974), pp. 18–34; at p. 18.

82 Quoted in J. Harvey, *Early Nurserymen* (London, 1974), pp. 52–3.

83 Switzer, *Ichnographia rustica*, vol. I, p. 81.

84 Ibid., pp. 84–5.
85 F. Thompson, *A History of Chatsworth; being a Supplement to the 6th Duke of Devonshire's Handbook* (London, 1949).
86 Chatsworth House archives, First Series, 70.0.
87 Chatsworth House archives, First Series, 70.1.
88 Chatsworth House archives, First Series, 70.12.
89 Voltaire, *Lettres sur les Anglais*, Letter No. xix, trans. A. Wilson-Green (London, 1931).
90 Switzer, *Ichnographia rustica*, vol. ii, pp. 197–8.
91 Ibid., p. 198.
92 Harvey, *Early Nurserymen* (London, 1974), p. 55.
93 Ibid.
94 Ibid.
95 Switzer, *Ichnographia rustica*, vol. i, p. x.
96 W. A. Brogden, 'Stephen Switzer and Garden Design in Britain in the Early 18th Century', PhD thesis, University of Edinburgh (1973), pp. 4–5.
97 Quoted ibid., pp. 4–5.
98 Ibid., p. 154.
99 V. di Palma, *Wasteland: A History* (New Haven, ct, 2014), p. 203; A. Chilvers, *The Berties of Grimsthorpe Castle* (London, 2010), p. 149.
100 Berkshire Record Office, d/ex 258/9.
101 Charles Bridgeman senior, gardener at Wimpole, died in 1726: Spink-Leger, *Head and Shoulders: Portrait Drawings and Some Small Paintings* (London, 1999), n. pag.
102 P. Willis, *Charles Bridgeman and the English Landscape Garden*, 2nd edn (London, 2002), p. 177.
103 For a full review of Bridgeman's life and works see Willis, *Charles Bridgeman*.
104 *Journals of the House of Commons*, vol. xix (London, 1803), pp. 573–4.
105 K. Harwood, 'Some Hertfordshire Nabobs', in *Hertfordshire Garden History: A Miscellany*, ed. A.Rowe (Hatfield, 2007), pp. 49–77; at pp. 52–3; D. Jacques, 'The Formal Garden', in *Sir John Vanbrugh and Landscape Architecture in Baroque England, 1690–1730*, ed. C. Ridgway and R. Williams (Stroud, 2000), pp. 31–48; at p. 40.
106 Harwood, 'Hertfordshire Nabobs', p. 57; Bodleian Library, Gough Drawings a4. Fo58.
107 Willis, *Charles Bridgeman*, p. 43, fn. 41.
108 Bridgeman drew heavily on still earlier proposals put forward by Nathaniel Kinderley in his 'The Present State of the Navigation of the Towns of Lyn, Wisbech, Spalding and Boston' [1721]. Willis, *Charles Bridgeman*, pp. 35–6.

109 *Gentleman's Magazine*, vol. l (April 1780), p. 203; Warwickshire Record Office, cr125b/419; W. Hawkes, ed., *The Diaries of Sanderson Miller of Radway* (London, 2005), p. 121.
110 See J. D. Hunt, *William Kent, Landscape Garden Designer* (London, 1987), for more on Kent's life and works.
111 A. Tinniswood, *A History of Country House Visiting* (London, 1989), p. 75.
112 Ibid., p. 9.
113 Alscot House archives, box 2.

3 The 'Brownian' Landscape

1 M. Hadfield, *A History of British Gardening* (London, 1960), p. 212.
2 Walpole, *The Connoisseur*, cxcii/773–4 (August 1976), p. 233.
3 T. Turner, *English Garden Design: History and Styles since 1650* (Woodbridge, 1986), p. 97.
4 P. Miller, *The Gardeners Dictionary* (London, 1731), n. pag.
5 West Sussex Record Office, Petworth archives, bills and receipts for work at Shortgrove in Essex: pha/7428.
6 Longleat archives, Thynne papers, Box xxx, vol. lxxvii.
7 West Sussex Record Office, pha/6623.
8 West Sussex Record Office, Add Mss 22.784 (pha 5177).
9 West Sussex Record Office, pha/6623.
10 Chatsworth archives, l/95/8.
11 Chatsworth archives, gardens file, no catalogue number.
12 Longleat archives, Thynne papers, Box xxx, vol. lxxvii.
13 Stroud, *Capability Brown*, p. 85; Plate 5a.
14 H. Leiper, 'Mr Lancelot Brown and his Hertfordshire clients', in *Hertfordshire Garden History, A Miscellany*, ii: *Gardens Pleasant, Groves Delicious*, ed. D. Spring (Hatfield, 2012), pp. 92–120.
15 J. Wright, ed., *The Letters of Horace Walpole, Earl of Orford*, 6 vols (London, 1844), vol. iv, p. 69.
16 T. Whately, *Observations on Modern Gardening* (London, 1770), p. 5.
17 Hertfordshire Archives and Local History d/ep/p22; for Brown's involvement at Cole Green as early 1752 see Leiper, 'Hertfordshire Clients', p. 100. The mounds are also shown on an undated painting,

Hertfordshire Archives and Local History CV HERTING/39.

18 P. Toynbee, ed., *Horace Walpole's Journal of Visits to Country Seats &c.* (Oxford, 1928), p. 24.

19 Hertfordshire Archives and Local History, D/EP/A8.

20 Hertfordshire Archives and Local History, AH 2270.

21 N. Smith, *Wrest Park* (London, 1995); L. Cabe Halpern, 'Wrest Park 1686–1730s: Exploring Dutch Influences', *Garden History*, 30 (2002), pp. 131–52.

22 W. S. Lewis, ed., *The Yale Edition of the Correspondence of Horace Walpole*, vol. I (New Haven, CT, 1937), p. 140.

23 Stroud, *Capability Brown*, p. 53; Whately, *Observations on Modern Gardening*, p. 87.

24 Stroud, *Capability Brown*, p. 56; T. Mowl and D. James, *Historic Gardens of Warwickshire* (Bristol, 2011), pp. 122–4.

25 West Sussex Record Office, PHA/6623; *The Yale Edition of the Correspondence of Horace Walpole*, vol. I (New Haven, CT, 1937), p. 140. The bath house was, in fact, probably designed by Edward Stevens around 1769–71 (English Heritage listing information), and the hermitage perhaps by 'Mr Edwards', but Walpole's comments indicate an assumption that Brown would supply such structures.

26 Plan of Temple Newsham; West Yorkshire Archives, Leeds, 100/EA/20 5A.

27 M. W. Farr, *Victoria County History of Warwickshire*, vol. VIII (London, 1969), pp. 461–5.

28 Royal Commission on Historical Manuscripts, *Report on the Manuscripts of the Earl of Verulam, Preserved at Gorhambury* (London, 1906), pp. 275–7.

29 Stroud, *Capability Brown*, pp. 74–8.

30 L. Dickens and M. Stanton, *An Eighteenth-century Correspondence: being the Letters of Deane Swift – Pitt – the Lytteltons and the Grenvilles – Lord Dacre – Robert Nugent – Charles Jenkinson – the Earls of Guildford, Coventry, & Hardwicke – Sir Edward Turner – Mr. Talbot of Lacock, and others to Sanderson Miller, Esq., of Radway* (London, 1910); Toynbee, ed., *Horace Walpole's Journal of Visits*, p. 59.

31 J. Barnatt and T. Williamson, *Chatsworth: A Landscape History* (Macclesfield, 2005), pp. 104–20.

32 Toynbee, ed., *Horace Walpole's Journal of Visits*, pp. 28–9.

33 Chatsworth House archives, C22, unpaginated; C21, pp. 46–7, 211–15.

34 In 1760–61 alone the estate accounts record the purchase of 71,800 thorns, 15,000 mountain ash and birch, 10,000 oaks and unspecified numbers of spruce. Some of the trees came from local suppliers – the 10,000 oaks came from Matlock – but sometimes the estate was forced to look further afield, as in 1764, when there were payments for 'fetching oaks out of Leicestershire': Chatsworth House archives, C21, pp. 224–5.

35 J. Paine, *Plans, Elevations and Sections, of Noblemen and Gentlemen's Houses* (London, 1767), p. ii.

36 W. Watts, *The Seats of the Nobility and Gentry* (London, 1779), Plate XXV.

37 Stroud, *Capability Brown*, pp. 151–3.

38 Whately, *Observations on Modern Gardening*, p. 118.

39 Cumbria Records Office, D/LONS/L plan 17; Bowood hall, private archive.

40 N. Scarfe, ed., *A Frenchman's Year in Suffolk: French Impressions of Suffolk Life in 1784* (Woodbridge, 1988), p. 142.

41 Staffordshire Record Office, D1287.

42 R. Williams, 'Making Places: Garden-mastery and English Brown', *Journal of Garden History*, 3 (1983), 382–5; at p. 382.

43 Quoted in Stroud, *Capability Brown*, pp. 156–7.

44 Corsham Court archives, Brown's plan of 1761; Bowood House archives, Brown's plan of 1763.

45 Corsham Court archives, Brown's plan of 1761; Bowood House archives, Brown's plan of 1763.

46 F. Cowell, *Richard Woods (1715–1793): Master of the Pleasure Ground* (Woodbridge, 2009), p. 137.

47 T. Whately, *Observations on Modern Gardening* (London, 1770), p. 148.

48 W. Roberts, *Memoirs of the Life and Correspondence of Mrs Hannah More* (London, 1836), p. 267.

49 *Gazetteer and New Daily Advertiser*, 13 December 1780.

50 E. Burke, *A Philosophical Enquiry into the Origin of our Ideas of the Sublime and the Beautiful* (London, 1756), p. 155.

51 Whately, *Observations on Modern Gardening*, p. 146.

52 Stroud, *Capability Brown*; for Lowther: Cumbria Records Office, D LONS/LII/3/1–6; for Peper Harow, Surrey History Centre, 1567/1–3.

53 J. Paine, *Plans, Elevations and Sections, of Noblemen and Gentlemen's Houses*, 2nd edn (London, 1783), p. 19.

54 H. Repton, Red Book for Panshanger, HALS DE/P/P21.

55 Williams, 'Making Places', p. 382.

56 H. Repton, *Observations on the Theory and Practice of Landscape Gardening* (London, 1805), p. 67.

57 Staffordshire Record Office, D1287.

58 Bowood archives, Lady Shelburne's Diary, 13 May 1766, vol. III, p. 57.

59 Plan for the ground at Lowther, Cumbria Records Office D/LONS/L plan 19; Scarfe, *Frenchman's Year in Suffolk*, p. 141.

60 Kimberley Hall, Norfolk, private archives.

61 U. Price, *Essays on the Picturesque*, vol. II (London, 1810), p. 148.

62 M. Laird, *The Flowering of the English Landscape Garden: English Pleasure Grounds, 1720–1800* (Philadelphia, PA, 1999).

63 Scarfe, *Frenchman's Year*, pp. 34–5.

64 As shown on G. Barker, *A Plan of Chatsworth Park, 1770* (Chatsworth archives); and on a roughly contemporary map which survives only as a nineteenth-century copy, probably made by Jeffrey Wyatville (Chatsworth archives, no catalogue number).

65 Chatsworth archives, C21.

66 T. Jefferson, *Memoranda of a Tour of the Gardens of England*: founders.archives.gov/documents/Jefferson/01-09-02-0328, accessed 24 July 2015.

67 Bowood archives, Lady Shelburne's Diary, 30 May 1765, vol. II, p. 12.

68 H. Leiper, 'Mr Lancelot Brown and his Hertfordshire Clients', in *Hertfordshire Garden History, a Miscellany*, II: *Gardens Pleasant, Groves Delicious*, ed. D. Spring (Hatfield, 2012), pp. 92–120.

69 T. Williamson, *The Archaeology of the Landscape Park: Garden Design in Norfolk, England, c. 1680–1840* (Oxford, 1998), pp. 104–9.

70 H. Davis, ed., *Pope: Poetical Works* (Oxford, 1978), p. 316: Epistle to Burlington, line 62.

71 Bowood archives, survey of the park, 1810.

72 O. Rackham, 'Pre-existing Trees and Woods in Country-house Parks', *Landscapes*, V/2 (2004), pp. 1–15; Williamson, *Archaeology of the Landscape Park*, pp. 135–6.

73 S. Petit and C. Watkins, 'Pollarding Trees: Changing Attitudes to a Traditional Land Management Practice in Britain, 1600–1900', *Rural History*, 14 (2003), pp. 157–76.

74 East Sussex Record Office, AMS 6185/242, letter of 1796.

75 W. Gilpin, *Remarks on Forest Scenery; and Other Woodland Views, illustrated by scenes of the New Forest in Hampshire*, vol. I (London, 1791), p. 202.

76 J. Brown, *The Omnipotent Magician: Lancelot 'Capability' Brown* (London, 2011), p. 79.

77 G. Mason, *An Essay on Design in Gardening* (London, 1768), p. 80.

78 E. Hall, '"Mr Brown's Directions": Capability Brown's Landscaping at Burton Constable (1767–82)', *Garden History*, XXIII/2 (1995), pp. 145–74; at p. 170.

79 Hall, '"Mr Brown's Directions"', p. 170.

80 East Sussex Record Office, AMS 6185/242.

81 J. Phibbs, 'Groves and Belts', *Garden History*, XIX/2 (1991), pp. 175–86; pp. 181–4.

82 Hall, '"Mr Brown's Directions"', p. 166.

83 G. Mason, *An Essay on Design in Gardening* (London, 1768), pp. 41–2.

84 H. Repton, Red Book for Honing Hall, Norfolk, 1792; private collection.

85 East Sussex Record Office, AMS 6185/242: letter of 1796.

86 A subject dealt with in Wendy Bishop's forthcoming PhD thesis, University of East Anglia.

87 J. Roberts, 'Well Tempered Clay: Constructing Water Features in the Landscape Park', *Garden History*, XXIX/1 (2001), pp. 12–28.

88 Norfolk Record Office, Chest of Deeds at Seaton Delaval Hall EW21; West Sussex Record Office, PHA/6623; Bowood archives, contact with Lancelot Brown, August 1762.

89 Roberts, 'Well Tempered Clay', pp. 17–18.

90 Bowood house archives, 'designs for dams'.

91 East Sussex Record Office, AMS 6185/242: letter of 1796.

92 Barnatt and Williamson, *Chatsworth*, pp. 113–17, 212.

93 J. Roberts, 'Cusworth Park: The Making of an Eighteenth-century Designed Landscape', *Landscape History*, 21 (1999), pp. 77–93.

94 Roberts, 'Cusworth Park', p. 84.

95 W. Watts, *The Seats of the Nobility and Gentry in a Collection of the Most Interesting and Picturesque Views* (London, 1779).

96 Williamson, *Archaeology of the Landscape Park*, pp. 220–21; R. Haslam, 'Beeston Hall', *Country Life*, 172 (1983), pp. 270–74.

97 The National Archives, Public Record Office, 30/29/2, articles of agreement for Trentham, 1759; Bowood archives, contract with Lancelot Brown, 10 August 1762.

98 Roberts, 'Cusworth Park', p. 87.

99 Barrett and Williamson, *Chatsworth*, pp. 112–13.

100 J. Phibbs, 'Recording What Isn't There: Three Difficulties with 18th-century Landscapes', in *There by Design: Field Archaeology in Parks and Gardens*, ed. P. Pattison (Swindon, 1998), pp. 27–31; p. 31.

101 Bowood archives, Lady Shelburne's Diary, 17 April 1767, vol. III, p. 173.

102 D. Brown, 'Lancelot Brown and his Associates', *Garden History*, XXIX/1 (2001), pp. 2–11; J. Meir, *Sanderson Miller and his Landscapes* (Chichester, 2006), p. 206; Cowell, *Richard Woods*, p. 106.

103 Val Bott, 'The Greenings', http://nurserygardeners.com/?p=92 (2010); accessed 12 July 2015.

104 Thomas Greening was paid £3,000 in 1747–8 for his work on Cumberland Lodge in Windsor Great Park for the Duke of Cumberland: J. Roberts, *Royal Landscapes: The Gardens and Parks of Windsor* (New Haven, CT, 1997), p. 43. See also R. Desmond, *Dictionary of British and Irish Botanists and Horticulturalists: Including Plant Collectors, Flower Painters and Garden Designers* (London, 1994), p. 295; R. Desmond, *Kew: The History of the Royal Botanic Gardens* (London, 1998), pp. 19, 37, 360; Ladd, *Architects at Corsham Court*, p. 70.

105 J. Meir, 'Sanderson Miller and the Landscaping of Wroxton Abbey, Farnborough Hall and Honington Hall', *Garden History*, XXV/1 (1997), pp. 81–106.

106 Meir, *Sanderson Miller and His Landscapes*.

107 H. Bilborough, 'Documents in Record Offices Which Might Affect the Assessment of the Achievement of "Capability" Brown', *Garden History*, I/3 (1973), pp. 16–17; 'A Plan of Normanby Park the Seat of the Honble Charles Sheffield Esqr by Fras. Richardson 1754': North East Lincolnshire Archives, 524/A/7/2; 'Survey of the Park and Gardens at Kirklees by Francis Richardson', 1757; West Yorkshire Archive Service, Calderdale, KM/A/1215; 'A survey of part of Hale the Seat of Thos Blackburn … by Fras Richardson', 1758; Cheshire and Chester Archives and Local Studies Service, DWW/1/299.

108 Bodleian Library, Gough Drawings, a3, fol. 7.

109 S. Markham, ed., *John Loveday of Caversham, 1711–1789: The Life and Tours of an Eighteenth-century Onlooker* (Salisbury, 1984), p. 87.

110 Historic Manuscripts Commission, *Fifteenth Report, Appendix*, Part VI: *The Manuscripts of the Earl of Carlisle Preserved at Castle Howard* (London, 1907), p. 159.

111 Letter from Adam to his brother, cited in Laird, *The Flowering of the English Landscape Garden*, p. 297.

112 Cowell, *Richard Woods*, pp. 12–19.

113 Ibid., pp. 25–36.

114 Norfolk Record Office NRS 21369; N. Kingsley, *The Country Houses of Gloucestershire*, vol. II: *1660–1830* (Chichester, 1992), pp. 46–9; T. Mowl, *Historic Gardens of Gloucestershire* (Stroud, 2002), p. 113.

115 Mowl, *Historic Gardens of Gloucestershire*, pp. 103–5; T. Mowl and D. James, *Historic Gardens of Warwickshire* (Bristol, 2011), pp. 115, 142–3; T. Mowl, *Historic Gardens of Worcestershire* (Stroud, 2006), pp. 91–2.

116 Mowl, *Gloucestershire*, p. 105. The records of Davenport's account with Drummonds Bank records payments from a large number of wealthy clients including the Earl of Darlington, Capt. Thomas Backhouse, Viscount Barrington, the Duchess of Beaufort, Charles Sloane Cadogan (of Caversham Park in Berkshire), Lawrence Dundas (of Moor Park in Hertfordshire), Baron Heathfield, Charles Hamilton (of Painshill, Surrey), Sir John Mordaunt, Sir John Sebright (of Beechwood in Hertfordshiire) and the Hon. Frederick Vane (Selaby Hall, Co. Durham). His plans for Batsford Park are in Gloucestershire Record Office, D1447/5/4; his plans for Croughton, in Warwickshire County Record Office, CR 1998/M/21.

117 E. J. Climenson, ed., *Passages from the Diaries of Mrs Phillip Lybbe Powys, 1756–1808* (London, 1899), p. 25.

118 S. Festing, 'Menageries in the Landscape Garden', *Journal of Garden History*, VIII/4 (1988), pp. 104–17.

119 Stroud, *Capability Brown*; Turner, *Capability Brown*. For Cole Green, see Leiper, 'Hertfordshire Clients', p. 102.

120 Cumbria archives, D/Lons/L plan 19.

121 British Library, Sloane 4078, f. 66.

122 W. J. Withers, 'Geography, Natural History, and the Eighteenth-century Enlightenment: Putting the World in Place', *History Workshop Journal*, 39 (1995), pp. 136–63.

123 E. A. Goodwyn, *Selections from Norwich Newspapers, 1760–1790* (Ipswich, 1972), p. 15; Williamson, *Archaeology of the Landscape Park*, pp. 100–104.

124 B. Cozens-Hardy, *The Diary of Sylas Neville, 1767–1788* (Oxford, 1950), p. 379.

125 H. Repton, Red Book for Holkham Hall, 1789, Holkham Hall archives.

126 K. Felus, 'Boats and Boating in the Designed Landscape, 1720–1820', *Garden History*, XXXIV/1 (2006), pp. 22–46; p. 24.

127 Wendy Bishop, personal communication with the authors, May 2015.

128 Felus, 'Boats and Boating', pp. 34–6.

129 A. Rowe and T. Williamson, *Hertfordshire: A Landscape History* (Hatfield, 2013), p. 234.

130 R. Williams, 'Rural Economy and the Antique in the English Landscape Garden', *Journal of Garden History*, VII/1 (1987), pp. 73–96; at p. 88; T. Mowl, *Gentlemen and Players: Gardeners of the English Landscape* (Stroud, 2000), p. 152; Brown, *Omnipotent Magician*, p. 309.

131 P. B. Munsche, *Gentlemen and Poachers* (Cambridge, 1981).

132 J. Phibbs, 'Field Sports and Brownian Design', *Garden History*, XL/1 (2012), pp. 56–71.

133 C. B. Andrews, ed., *The Torrington Diaries*, vol. 1 (London, 1934), p. 395.

134 Scarfe, *Frenchman's Year*, pp. 40–41.

135 Staffordshire Record Office, D952/5/1/2.

136 D. Hill and P. Robinson, *The Pheasant: Management and Conservation* (London, 1988), pp. 38–45.

137 Anon, *Thoughts on the Present Laws for Preserving Game* (London, 1750); H. Zouch, *An Account of the Present Daring Practices of Night-hunters and Poachers* (London, 1783); Munsche, *Gentlemen and Poachers*, pp. 75–105; H. Hopkins, *The Long Affray* (London, 1985).

138 J. Phibbs, 'The Englishness of Lancelot "Capability" Brown', *Garden History*, XXXI/2 (2003), pp. 122–40; pp. 129–30.

139 T. Williamson, *Polite Landscapes: Gardens and Society in Eighteenth-century England* (Stroud, 1995), pp. 121–4.

140 Rowe and Williamson, *Hertfordshire*, pp. 135–41.

141 J. Lawrence, *The Modern Land Steward* (London, 1801), p. 100.

142 H. Repton, Red Book for Honing Hall (1792), private collection.

143 P. Miller, *The Gardener's Dictionary* (London, 1731); J. Wheeler, *The Modern Druid* (London, 1747); E. Wade, *A Proposal for Improving and Adorning the Island of Great Britain; for the Maintenance of our Navy and Shipping* (London, 1755); W. Hanbury, *An Essay on Planting* (London, 1758).

144 S. Daniels, 'The Political Iconography of Woodland in Later Georgian England', in *The Iconography of Landscape: Essays on the Symbolic Representation,*

Design and Use of Past Environments, ed. D. Cosgrove and S. Daniels (Cambridge, 1988), pp. 43–82.

145 Brown's plan of Kimberley, 1778, Kimberley Hall archives; Longleat archives, Thynne papers, Box XXX, vol. LXXVII; Hertfordshire Gardens Trust and Tom Williamson, *Parks and Gardens of West Hertfordshire*, pp. 40–41; Stroud, *Capability Brown*, p. 107.

146 Stroud, *Capability Brown*, p. 157.

147 As at Belhus, Longleat, Corsham or Sandbeck.

148 Longleat archives, Thynne papers, Box XXX, vol. LXXVII.

149 Norfolk Record Office, contract between Lancelot Brown and Sir Edward Astley Bt for works at Melton Constable Hall; Chest of Deeds at Seaton Delaval Hall, EW 21.

150 Historic Manuscripts Commission, *Manuscripts of the Earl of Carlisle* (1907), p. 159.

151 Stroud, *Capability Brown*; Turner, *Capability Brown*.

152 Norfolk Record Office, Contract between Lancelot Brown and Sir Edward Astley Bt for works at Melton Constable Hall; Chest of Deeds at Seaton Delaval Hall, EW 21.

153 Warwickshire Record Office, CR8/184.

154 Kimberley Hall, private archive.

155 Hall, 'Mr Brown's Directions'; Longleat archives, Thynne papers, Box XXX, vol. LXXVII.

156 H. Repton, *Fragments on the Theory and Practice of Landscape Gardening* (London, 1816), p. 167.

157 C. Muckerji, 'Reading and Writing with Nature: A Materialist Approach to French Formal Gardens', in *Consumption and the World of Goods*, ed. J. Brewer and R. Porter (London, 1993), pp. 439–61; J. Finch, 'Three Men in a Boat: Biographies and Narratives in the Historic Landscape', *Landscape Research*, XXXIII/5 (2008), pp. 511–30; at p. 525.

158 Quoted in Stroud, *Capability Brown*, p. 157.

4 The Brown Connection

1 D. Brown, 'Nathaniel Richmond (1724–1784): "One of the Gentleman Improvers"', PhD thesis, University of East Anglia (2000).

2 Royal Commission on Historical Monuments (England), *An Inventory of the Historical Monuments in the County of Cambridge*, vol. 1: *West Cambridgeshire* (London, 1968), pp. 214–23.

3 P. Willis, *Charles Bridgeman and the English Landscape Garden*, 2nd edn (London, 2002), pp. 436–7; and D. Adshead, *Wimpole: Architectural*

Drawings and Topographical Views (London, 2007) for Bridgeman's drawings of Wimpole.

4 D. Soulden, *Wimpole Hall, Cambridgeshire* (London, 1991), pp. 10–12.

5 F. Cowell, *Richard Woods (1715–1793): Master of the Pleasure Garden* (Woodbridge, 2009), p. 137.

6 Miller also advised on other improvements to the grounds, and surviving correspondence makes it clear that Harwicke had shown him Greening's design in 1752.

7 Letter Lord Hardwicke to Brown, 24 December 1767, British Library, Add. MS 69795, fol. 20.

8 Payments recorded in Drummonds Bank ledgers, account of Lancelot Brown, held at Royal Bank of Scotland.

9 Reference to Wimpole in Brown's account book at the RHS Lindley Library, fol. 59.

10 Essex Record Office, D/P 15/1/2.

11 J. Brown, *The Omnipotent Magician: Lancelot 'Capability' Brown* (London, 2011).

12 Quoted in Stroud, *Capability Brown*, p. 186.

13 H. Leiper, 'Mr Lancelot Brown and his Hertfordshire Clients', in *Hertfordshire Garden History*, vol. II: *Gardens Pleasant, Groves Delicious*, ed. D. Spring (Hatfield, 2012), pp. 92–119; at p. 107.

14 Bowood House archives, letter, 1757.

15 Bowood archives, Lady Shelburne's Diary, 7 August 1765, vol. II, p. 40.

16 S. Johnson, *A Dictionary of the English Language* (London, 1755).

17 J. Dryden, trans., *Virgil's Aeneid* (London, 1697), dedication, p. 42.

18 W. S. Lewis, ed., *The Yale Edition of Horace Walpole's Correspondence*, vol. IX: *Letters to George Montagu* (New Haven, CT, 1941), p. 121.

19 A. M. Suarez Huerta, 'Wilson, Mengs, and Some British Connections', in *Richard Wilson and the Transformation of European Painting*, ed. M. Postle and R. Simon (New Haven, CT, 2014), pp. 107–17: at pp. 112–13.

20 Cowell, *Richard Woods*, pp. 230–35.

21 *Norwich Mercury*, 4 February 1764.

22 K. Goodway, personal communication with the authors, June 1998; *The Times*, 14 April 1794.

23 Adam Mickle junior (1747–1811) made plans for Brancepeth Castle, Northumberland, in 1783, was at Newby Park in 1786, and Tredegar House, Monmouthshire, in 1790. He drew up plans for Piercefield, Monmouthshire, in the 1790s (see D. Jacques, *Georgian Gardens,* p. 62, plate 23) and worked at that time at Corby Castle, Carlisle, and Thirkleby Park, Yorkshire. According to J. C. Loudon in *Encyclopedia of Gardening* (London, 1824), 'the late Mr Meickle' was a 'landscape gardener': pp. 1079, 1081. Correspondence survives in the Bedfordshire and Luton Archives and Record Office between Adam Mickle junior and both Thomas Robinson, 2nd Baron Grantham, and, after his death in 1786, his younger brother Frederick 'Fritz' Robinson regarding the improvements at Newby, near Ripon, Yorkshire: Bedfordshire and Luton Record Office, L30/14/254.

24 W. Hawkes, ed., *The Diaries of Sanderson Miller of Radway* (London, 2005), p. 97.

25 Maltby St Bartholomew Parish Records, Sheffield Archives, PR(M)82.

26 Received payments from Brown, Drummonds account from 3/1/64–1783.

27 D. Coombs, 'The Garden at Carlton House of Frederick Prince of Wales and Augusta Princess Dowager of Wales: Bills in Their Household Accounts, 1728–1772', *Garden History*, XXV/2 (1997) pp. 153–77.

28 John Spyers, A Survey of the Manor of Fenstanton &c. [1777]: Huntingdon Records Office, Map 47. In Brown's surviving account book at the Lindley Library Spyers is named as surveyor at: Warnford Park, Hampshire (early 1770s); Hallingbury, Hertfordshire (?), 1778; Highclere, Hampshire, 1770; Peterborough House, Fulham, 1773; Himley, Staffordshire, 1774; North Stoneham, Hampshire, 1775; Sheffield Place, Sussex, 1776; Cardiff Castle, 1777; Taplow, Buckinghamshire, 1778; Kings Weston, Gloucestershire, 1778; Longford Castle, Wiltshire, 1778; Belvoir, Leicestershire, 1779; Wilton, Wiltshire, 1780; Laleham, Surrey, 1780; Fornham St Genevieve, Suffolk, 1781; Sandleford, Berkshire, 1781; Stanstead Park, Sussex, 1782; Byram, Yorkshire, 1782; Stourton House, Yorkshire, 1782; Woodchester Park, Gloucestershire, 1782. Payments in Samuel Lapidge account at Drummonds of £10 on 18 June 1781 and £10 on 10 July 1781.

29 John Spyers's probate will, The National Archives, PCC PROB 11/1318/339.

30 Elizabeth Spyers's probate will, the National Archives, PCC PROB 11/1318/339.

31 J. Harvey, *Early Nurserymen* (London, 1974), p. 97.

32 F. Cowell, 'Richard Woods (?1716–93): A Preliminary Account, Part 1', *Garden History*, XIV/2 (London, 1986), pp. 85–120: at p. 91.

33 Brown's account book, Lindley Library, Royal Horticultural Society, London.

34 *Morning Post*, 30 March 1784.

35 Holy Trinity, Stratford-upon-Avon, Parish Records, Shakespeare Birthplace Trust, no reference.

36 Canaletto's painting of Warwick Castle of 1748, prior to Brown's work there, clearly shows the formal gardens being removed. The nurseryman, Henry Clark of Gloucestershire, was supplying plant material and labour for planting in 1744/5 (Christine Hodgetts, personal communication with the authors, June 2015), so work was clearly underway at Warwick Castle some years before Brown's arrival. Richmond is recorded as a Master in 1766, The National Archives, IR1/25, Register of Duties Paid for Apprentices' Indentures, Friday, 17 October 1766, [Master] Nath. Richmond of St Mary-le-Bone, Middx., Surveyor, – [Apprentice]: Thos. Snelling.

37 Tardebigge Parish Records, Worcestershire Archive and Archaeology Service, 850 TARDEBIGGE.

38 Hawkes, ed., *The Diaries of Sanderson Miller*, p. 152: 22 July 1750, '5:30. Rode with Lord Cobham, Mr Townsend and Neale round Burton grounds until 10.' Fn. 1 notes, *'Neale'* William Neale, 'yeoman' in the 1750 freeholder list (Warwickshire Record Office QS 7/1/83, fol. 10). There are several more references to Neale in the *Diaries*.

39 Rickmansworth Parish Records, Hertfordshire Archives and Local History, DP 85.

40 Richmond leased his nursery land in 1759 from William Baker of Syon Hill; the two local projects with Brown were active in the 1750s so Richmond's involvement is a distinct possibility.

41 Marylebone Archives, Deed 456. Richmond countersigned the existing lease between William Henry Portman and William Baker. Richmond is first rated at Marylebone for 'Houses and Land' in 1759.

42 Richmond is rated on 13 Bryanston Street from 1780 to 1784.

43 Surrey Record Office 61/3/2.

44 Roger Turner, *Capability Brown* (New York, 1985), p. 185. 'Brown made a plan for the park, but "Mr Richmond" completed his proposals by making series of long serpentine lakes from five existing "quadrilateral" ones.'

45 J. Britton and E. W. Brayley, *The Beauties of England and Wales*, vol. 1 (London, 1801), p. 396.

46 D. Hancock, *Citizens of the World: London Merchants and the Integration of the British Atlantic Community, 1735–1785* (Cambridge, 1995), pp. 217–18.

47 R. W. King, 'Joseph Spence of Byfleet Part IV', *Garden History*, VIII/3 (London, 1980), pp. 77–144; at p. 87.

48 Willis, *Charles Bridgeman*, p. 434.

49 Brown, *Nathaniel Richmond*, p. 130. Calculated from payments recorded in William Drake's bank account with Hoare's Bank.

50 *A Plan of the Alterations at Himley Hall*, Dudley Archives, c396 – the lakes are now part of Baggeridge Country Park.

51 *Morning Post*, 30 March 1784.

52 R. Blunt, *Mrs Montagu, 'Queen of the Blues'* (London, 1923), vol. II, p. 214.

53 Bristol University Library, Letter, Humphry Repton to Revd Norton Nicholls, 26 August 1788.

54 Lamer, Red Book: private collection.

55 G. Jackson-Stops, *Claydon House, Buckinghamshire* (London, 1979), p. 26; the National Archives, Public Record Office, PROB 11/1028/297. Sanderson left money to finance his son's training as an architect: see S. M. Gould, *Biographical Dictionary of Architects at Reading* (London, 1999), p. 161: his son, James Wright Sanderson (1770–1813), entered the Royal Academy Schools in 1788 and won the Silver Medal for architecture in 1790. He was a pupil of James Wyatt from 1788 to 1791 and became a successful architect based in Reading, designing a house for John Walter, the proprietor of *The Times*, at Bearwood and the Mansion House, Prospect Park, in Reading.

56 H. Colvin, *A Biographical Dictionary of British Architects, 1600–1840*, 4th edn (London, 2008); S. and H. Tayler, eds, *Lord Fife and his Factor* (London, 1925), p. 42.

57 *Country Life*, 179 (1940), p. 721.

58 *Dictionary of Scottish Architects*, www.scottisharchitects.org.uk, accessed 15 January 2015.

59 *Caledonian Mercury*, 8 March 1760.

60 *Dictionary of Scottish Architects*, www.scottisharchitects.org.uk.

61 Durham County Record Office, Whorlton Parish Registers.

62 *Caledonian Mercury*, 8 March 1760.

63 National Archive of Scotland, RHP 31443: photocopy of plan for improvement of Careston (Carriston), the seat of George Skene, 1761.

Surveyor: Robert Robinson, architect. National Archives of Scotland, GD248/346/5/50, 6 May 1764, Castle of Banff, plan. National Archive of Scotland, GD248/250/1/15, Letter, Lord Deskfoord to James Grant of Grant, July 10 1764, 'Has been to Castle Grant and made the plan; asks for money.'

64 *Dictionary of Scottish Architects*, www.scottisharchitects.org.uk; also *Caledonian Mercury*, 12 January 1782.

65 Account of Lancelot Brown at Drummonds Bank, RBS Archives: 1759: £170, 1760: £385, 1761: £585, 1762: £590, 1763: £560, 1764: £350, 1765: £325 LB A/C Drummonds.

66 D. Turnbull, 'Thomas White (1739–1811): Eighteenth-century Landscape Designer and Arboriculturist', PhD thesis, University of Hull (1990), p. 5.

67 Ibid.

68 J. C. Loudon, *Encyclopedia of Gardening* (London, 1824), p. 74.

69 Ibid., p. 80.

70 His designs have been mistaken for the work of Brown, as have Richmond's. For a full treatment of the work of White Sr and Jr see Turnbull's Thomas White.

71 Account of Lancelot Brown at Drummonds Bank, RBS Archives; Stroud, *Capability Brown*, p. 207.

72 Hinde, *Capability Brown*, p. 194.

73 G. Lawton, *Collectio rerum ecclesiarum de diœcesi eboracensis* (London, 1840), p. 198.

74 Probate Will of John Ireland, The National Archives, PCC PROB 11/808/167.

75 Bedfordshire and Luton Record Office, R3/2150.

76 D. Brown, 'Lancelot Brown and his Associates', *Garden History*, XXIX/1 (London, 2001), pp. 2–11.

77 Stroud, *Capability Brown*, p. 133.

78 Brown account book at the RHS Lindley Library: A/c Earl of Exeter, accs. 1769–1774, payment to Ireland. A/c Stapleford, 1776, payment to William Ireland. A/c Trentham Hall, 1779, 'work under the direction of Ireland'. After Brown's death he worked with Lapidge at Chalfont House and Bulstrode, Buckinghamshire (Payments, Lapidge A/c at Drummonds, 1783, 1784).

79 J. C. Loudon, 'James Main', *Gardener's Magazine*, IV (9 April 1812), pp. 115–16.

80 Brown's surviving account book at the RHS Lindley Library: *Earl of Coventry, Croome, June, 1760–June, 1765, disbursed by Benjamin Read, £799–8–10*; Stowe Papers in the Huntington Library, Acc.

George Grenville (George Clark via John Phibbs pers comm.); D. Jacques, *Georgian Gardens: The Reign of Nature* (London, 1983), p. 81. For Cole Green see H. Leiper, 'Mr Lancelot Brown and his Hertfordshire Clients', in *Hertfordshire Garden History, A Miscellany*, II: *Gardens Pleasant, Groves Delicious*, ed. D. Spring (Hatfield, 2012), p. 97.

81 Chatsworth House archives C22, unpaginated; C21, pp. 46–7, 211–15; Kew archives, Milliken papers, uncatalogued.

82 Archives of the Royal Botanical Society, Kew, Milliken papers, uncatalogued. Probably refers to 24 September 1769.

83 Williamson, *Archaeology of the Landscape Park*, pp. 100–104.

84 George Bowstreed snr. Probate Will, The National Archives, PCC PROB 11/1025/296.

85 Brown's surviving account book at the RHS Lindley Library: A/c Viscount Spencer, Wimbledon.

86 RBS Archives: Drummonds Bank Ledgers, A/c Charles Ingram, Viscount Irwin, Sandbeck, Yorkshire, in 1764–8. Brown's surviving account book at the RHS Lindley Library: A/c Earl of Scarborough, Sandbeck, *Andrew Gardener . . . £6–5–6, 1766 . . . expenses to & from Sanbeck, time etc.*, *There again in 1768*, *See more money paid by Mr Brown*. He appears to have worked for the Earl of Waldegrave at Navestock, Essex, in 1771 with Brown. A/c Earl of Waldegrave, of Navestock, Essex, at Drummonds Bank, RBS Archives, shows payment of £200 to 'Mr Gardiner' among a series of payments to Brown in 1771.

87 According to Stroud, *Capability Brown*, pp. 206–7, he worked on North Stoneham and Branches. Also, Brown's surviving Account Book in the RHS Lindley Library states for the account of Ambrose Dickens of Branches, Suffolk: 'See the Acct. of the extra work done by Alexander Knox from November the 6 1764 to January the 1, 1765 . . . £58–1–8. Mr. Brown could not get the money for the Extra Work and tore the Acct. before Mr Dickens face & said his say upon that business to him.'

88 Brown's surviving account book at the RHS Lindley Library: A/c Copt Hall, Mr Griffin, £31–10-0; A/c Maiden Early, 'Survey by Griffin'; Brown's surviving account book at the RHS Lindley Library: A/c Earl of Abingdon, Rycote, Oxon. 24 October 1770 – 21 September 1771: Disbursed to James Hope . . . £288–7–1, which correlates well with payments recorded in the Drummonds Bank Ledgers, Brown

account 1770–71; Brown's surviving account book at the RHS Lindley Library: A/c Francis Herne Esq: '1769 . . . Aug the 4 Received by William Horsburgh £20-00', Brown's Drummonds Bank account shows more substantial payments to him 1756–61, 1765–7 and 1769.

89   The National Archives, 30/29/2.

90   Norfolk Record Office, Chest of Deeds at Seaton Delaval Hall EW 21.

91   Chatsworth archives, C22, unpaginated; C21, pp. 46–7, 211–15.

92   R. Brown, *Society and Economy in Modern Britain, 1700–1850* (London, 2002), p. 126.

93   J. Locke, *Some Thoughts Concerning Education* (London, 1693), p. 234.

94   Letter in private collection.

5 Landscape and Modernity

1   H. Walpole, *The History of the Modern Taste in Gardening* (London, 1780).

2   S. Bending, 'A Natural Revolution?', in *Refiguring Revolutions: Aesthetics and Politics from the English Revolution to the Romantic Revolution*, ed. K. Sharpe and S. Zwicker (Berkeley, CA, 1998), pp. 241–66; B. P. Lange, 'The English Garden and Patriotic Discourse' in H.-J. Diller et al., *Englishness, Anglistik & Englischunterricht*, 46/47 (Heidelberg, 1992); T. Turner, *English Garden Design: Landscape and Styles since 1660* (Woodbridge, 1986), pp. 5–37.

3   R. Liddiard, ed., *The Medieval Park: New Perspectives* (Macclesfield, 2007); S. Mileson, *Parks in Medieval England* (Oxford, 2009); J. Fletcher, *Gardens of Earthly Delight: The History of Deer Parks* (Oxford, 2011).

4   T. Whately, *Observations on Modern Gardening* (London, 1770), p. 1.

5   M. Girouard, *Life in the English Country House: A Social and Architectural History* (London, 1978), p. 76.

6   R. North, *A Discourse of Fish and Fish Ponds* (London, 1713).

7   O. Rackham, *The History of the Countryside* (London, 1986), pp. 126–8; O. Rackham, *Woodlands* (London, 2006), pp. 139–41.

8   H. Walpole, *Anecdotes of Painting in England: With Some Account of the Principal Artists . . .* (London, 1762), p. 247.

9   O. Goldsmith, *The Traveller*, ll. 405–6, 404, in A. Friedman, ed., *The Collected Works of Oliver Goldsmith*, vol. IV (Oxford, 1966), pp. 267–8. For a discussion of villages deserted for 'emparking' see T. Williamson, '"At Pleasure's Lordly Call": The Archaeology of Emparked Settlements', in *Deserted Villages Revisited*, ed. C. Dyer and R. Jones (Hatfield, 2010), pp. 162–81.

10   Bowood archives, John Bull's accounts for Cowage, Combe Grove and Mannings Hill, 1765–8; Michaelmas 1765.

11   The National Archives, 30/29/2, articles of agreement for Trentham, 1759.

12   L. Lewis, ed., *Hird's Annals of Bedale* (Northallerton, 1990), stanzas 675–6.

13   Barnatt and Williamson, *Chatsworth*, pp. 105–7; J.M.L. Booker, 'The Essex Turnpike Trusts', PhD thesis, University of Durham (1979), pp. 54–6.

14   S. Spooner, '"A Prospect Two Field's Distance": Rural Landscapes and Urban Mentalities in the Eighteenth-century', *Landscapes*, X/1 (2009), pp. 101–22.

15   Hertfordshire Archives and Local History, D/EX55/E1.

16   *Morning Post*, Tuesday, 30 July 1776.

17   Charles Perry's tour of northern England, Norfolk Record Office, MC 130/49.

18   N. Scarfe, ed., *A Frenchman's Year in Suffolk: French Impressions of Suffolk Life in 1784* (Woodbridge, 1988), p. 35.

19   Chatsworth archives AS/1062 and 1063.

20   D. Defoe, *Tour Through the Whole Island of Great Britain* (Harmondsworth, 1971), pp. 73–4.

21   *Norwich Mercury*, 2 February 1788.

22   A. Young, *General View of the Agriculture of Hertfordshire* (London, 1804), p. 18.

23   P. Toynbee, *Supplement to the Letters of Horace Walpole* (Oxford, 1925), vol. III, p. 5.

24   Red Book for Tewin Water, 1799; Hertfordshire Archives and Local History, D/Z42/Z1.

25   W. Armstrong, *History and Antiquities of the County of Norfolk*, vol. IX: *Taverham Hundred* (Norwich, 1781), p. 15.

26   *Norwich Mercury*, 12 May 1770.

27   *Norwich Mercury*, 28 July 1770.

28   J. Harvey, *Early Nurserymen* (London, 1975).

29   R. L. Winstanley, *Parson Woodforde: Diary of the First Six Norfolk Years* (London, 1984), pp. 78–9.

30   D. Cruickshank, *A Guide to the Georgian Buildings of Britain and Ireland* (London, 1985), pp. 67–74; J. Summerson, *Architecture in Britain, 1530–1830* (London, 1991), pp. 334–53; Girouard, *Life in the English Country House* (London, 1978), pp. 199–202.

31 Girouard, *Life in the English Country House,* p. 210.

32 S. Graig Bell, 'Women Create Gardens in Male Landscapes: A Revisionist Approach to Eighteenth-century English Garden History', *Feminist Studies,* XVI/3 (1990), pp. 471–91.

33 W. Howitt, *Visits to Remarkable Places: Old Halls, Battle Fields &c.* (London, 1842), pp. 210–11.

34 J. A. Home, ed., *The Letters and Journals of Lady Mary Coke* (Oxford, 1966), p. 163; W. Roberts, ed., *Memoirs of the Life and Correspondence of Mrs Hannah More* (London, 1834), vol. II, p. 287.

35 Stroud, *Capability Brown,* pp. 195–7.

36 J. Fletcher, *Gardens of Earthly Delight,* pp. 117–18.

37 K. Thomas, *Man and the Natural World* (London, 1983), p. 202.

38 Anon., *The Ladies Compleat Letter-writer* (London, 1763), p. 234.

39 A. Smart, *The Life and Art of Allan Ramsay* (London, 1952), p. 93.

40 D. Irwin, *Neoclassicism* (London, 1997), pp. 25–35; H. Honour, *Neo-classicism* (London, 1977), pp. 50–62.

41 D. Irvin, *Winckelmann: Writings on Art* (London, 1972).

42 J. Stuart and N. Revett, *The Antiquities of Athens and Other Monuments of Greece* (London, 1762).

43 D. Yarwood, *Robert Adam* (London, 1970), pp. 47–87; J. Fleming, *Robert Adam and his Circle in Edinburgh and Rome* (London, 1962), pp. 170–219.

44 Fleming, *Robert Adam,* p. 218.

45 Ibid.

46 Fleming, *Robert Adam,* p. 219.

47 Fleming, *Robert Adam,* p. 22.

48 Yarwood, *Robert Adam,* pp. 91–138.

49 G. Beard, *Craftsmen and Interior Decoration in England, 1660–1820* (London, 1981), pp. 203–11; G. Beard, *The Work of Robert Adam* (London, 1992); D. Stillman, *The Decorative Work of Robert Adam* (London, 1966).

50 G. Beard, *Craftsmen and Interior Decoration,* p. xxiii.

51 C. Gilbert, *The Life and Works of Thomas Chippendale* (London, 1978), pp. 108–22.

52 Ibid., p. 33.

53 Ibid., pp. 25–8.

54 A. Forty, *Objects of Desire: Design and Society since 1750* (London, 1986), p. 21.

55 Forty, *Objects of Desire,* pp. 22–4.

56 R. Reilly, *Josiah Wedgwood, 1730–1795* (London, 1992), pp. 78–92, 152–6.

57 A. Kelly, *Decorative Wedgwood in Architecture and Furniture* (London, 1965), p. 21.

58 D. King, *The Complete Works of Robert and James Adam* (Oxford, 1991), pp. 105, 124, 179.

59 Stroud, *Capability Brown,* p. 91.

60 E. Meteyard, *The Life of Josiah Wedgwood, from his Private Correspondence and Family Papers,* 2 vols (London, 1866), vol. II, p. 377.

61 Honour, *Neo-classicism,* pp. 101–14.

62 Forty, *Objects of Desire,* p. 24.

63 Quoted in Stroud, *Capability Brown,* p. 157.

64 Switzer, *Ichnographia rustica,* vol. III, p. 5.

65 R. Williams, 'Making Places: Garden-mastery and English Brown', *Journal of Garden History,* 3 (1983), pp. 382–5; at p. 384.

66 H. Young, *The Genius of Wedgwood* (London, 1995), p. 13.

67 Norfolk Record Office, KIM 8/1/3.

68 R. Blunt, ed., *Mrs Montagu, 'Queen of the Blues': Her Letters and Friendships from 1762 to 1800* (London, 1923).

69 F. J. Ladd, *Architects at Corsham Court: A Study in Revival Style Architecture and Landscaping, 1749–1849* (Bradford-on-Avon, 1978).

70 Design by Lancelot Brown, 1761; Corsham Court archives.

71 W. Watts, *The Seats of the Nobility and Gentry in a Collection of the Most Interesting and Picturesque Views* (London, 1779), Plate VI.

72 William Mason, letter to Humphry Repton, 24 April 1792, quoted in H. Repton, *Sketches and Hints on Landscape Gardening* (London, 1795), p. 53.

73 Forty, *Objects of Desire,* p. 15.

74 Honour, *Neo-classicism,* p. 13.

75 Young, *Genius of Wedgwood,* p. 13.

76 Honour, *Neo-classicism,* p. 23.

77 S. Daniels and S. Seymour, 'Landscape Design and the Idea of Improvement, 1730–1814', in *An Historic Geography of England and Wales,* ed. R. A. Dodgshon and R. A. Butlin (London, 1990), pp. 487–519; S. Tarlow, *The Archaeology of Improvement in Britain, 1750–1860* (Cambridge, 2007).

78 K. Woodbridge, 'Stourhead in 1768: Extracts from an Unpublished Journal by Sir John Parnell', *Journal of Garden History,* 2 (1982), pp. 59–70, at p. 62.

79 G. Colman and D. Garrick, *The Clandestine Marriage* (London, 1765), p. 41.

80 Tarlow, *Archaeology of Improvement.*

81 Quoted in Stroud, *Capability Brown,* p. 157.

82 R. North, *A Discourse of Fish and Fish Ponds* (London, 1713), pp. 20–52; Norfolk Record Office, MS 6688 and 6689 6 E. 6 BRA. 63.

83 J. Armstrong, *The Art of Preserving Health: A Poem* (London, 1744), pp. 10 and 12.

84 Ibid., p. 19.

85 L. Dickens and M. Stanton, *An Eighteenth-century Correspondence: Being the Letters of Deane Swift – Pitt – the Lytteltons and the Grenvilles – Lord Dacre – Robert Nugent – Charles Jenkinson – the Earls of Guildford, Coventry, & Hardwicke – Sir Edward Turner – Mr. Talbot of Lacock, and others to Sanderson Miller, Esq., of Radway* (London, 1910), p. 416.

86 Ibid.

87 R. Bradley, *A General Treatise on Husbandry and Gardening* (London, 1727), p. 23; N. Salmon, *The History of Hertfordshire* (London, 1728), p. 1; T. Williamson, *The Transformation of Rural England: Farming and the Landscape, 1700–1870* (Exeter, 1999), pp. 85–90.

88 J. Bettey, 'The Floated Water Meadows of Wessex: A Triumph of English Agriculture', in *Water Meadows: History, Ecology and Conservation*, ed. H. Cook and T. Williamson (Oxford, 2007), pp. 8–22.

89 T. Batchellor, *General View of the Agriculture of Bedfordshire* (London, 1813), p. 487; S. Wade Martins and T. Williamson, 'Floated Water-meadows in Norfolk: A Misplaced Innovation', *Agricultural History Reviews*, 42 (1994), pp. 20–37.

90 Longleat archives, Thynne papers, Box XXX, vol. LXXVII.

91 N. Cossons, *The bp Book of Industrial Archaeology* (London, 1987), pp. 254–8.

92 D. Defoe, *Tour Through the Whole Island of Great Britain* (Harmondsworth, 1971), p. 435.

93 D. Bogart, 'Did Turnpike Trusts Increase Transportation Investment in Eighteenth-century England?', *Journal of Economic History*, LXV/2 (2005), pp. 439–68; W. Albert, *The Turnpike Road System in England, 1663–1840* (Cambridge, 1972).

94 Cossens, *Industrial Archaeology*, pp. 244–5.

95 A. Ingram, *Horse-drawn Vehicles Since 1760* (Blandford, 1977).

6 Alternatives and Oppositions

1 W. S. Lewis, ed., *The Yale Edition of Horace Walpole's Correspondence*, vol. IX: *Letters to George Montagu* (New Haven, CT, 1941), p. 122.

2 J. Sambrook, 'Wooburn Farm in the 1760s', *Garden History*, VII/2 (1979), pp. 82–101; at p. 94.

3 K. Woodbridge, *The Stourhead Landscape* (London, 1982); K. Rorschach, *The Early Georgian Landscape Garden* (New Haven, CT, 1983); T. Mowl, *Gentlemen and Players: Gardeners of the English Landscape* (Stroud, 2000), pp. 144–5.

4 Mowl, *Gentlemen and Players*, p. 144.

5 Ibid., p. 145.

6 Rorschach, *Early Georgian Landscape Garden*, pp. 39–46; Mowl, *Gentlemen and Players*, pp. 141–2.

7 J. Heeley, *A Description of Hagley Park* (London, 1777), p. 45.

8 H. Tromp and E. Newby, 'A Dutchman's Visits to Some English Gardens in 1791', *Journal of Garden History*, 2 (1982), pp. 41–58; at p. 46.

9 G. Jackson-Stops, *An English Arcadia, 1600–1990: Designs for Gardens and Garden Buildings in the Care of the National Trust* (Washington, DC, 2006), pp. 89–91.

10 Tromp and Newby, 'A Dutchman's Visits', p. 44.

11 Hertfordshire Gardens Trust and Tom Williamson, *The Parks and Gardens of West Hertfordshire* (Letchworth, 2000), pp. 46–7; D. Carless Webb, *Observations and Remarks made during four Excursions made to Various Parts of Great Britain . . . in 1810 and 1811* (London, 1812), p. 167; Anon., *The Scotch Hut; A Poem, Addressed to Euphorbus, or the Earl of the Grove* (London, 1779).

12 M. Symes, *The English Rococo Garden* (Princes Risborough, 1991), pp. 35–6.

13 Richard Jago, *Edge-Hill, or, The Rural Prospect Delineated and Moralized* (London, 1767), p. 18.

14 A letter in the Alscot archives (uncatalogued) refers to a visit by a 'Mr Brown' in that year.

15 D. Lysons, *The Environs of London*, vol. II: *The County of Middlesex* (1795), p. 224.

16 W. Angus, *The Seats of the Nobility* (London, 1787), p. 147.

17 Gunnersbury House archive, DP119 Deposition of Benjamin Price, 1786; British Museum Additional Manuscripts MS 33135.

18 W. S. Lewis, ed., *The Yale Edition of Horace Walpole's Correspondence*, vol. XXXI (1941), pp. 146, 178.

19 Historic Manuscripts Commission, *Fifteenth Report, Appendix*, Part VI: *The Manuscripts of the Earl of Carlisle Preserved at Castle Howard* (London, 1907), pp. 143–4.

20 *The World*, 15 (12 April 1753).

21 G. Mason, *An Essay on Design in Gardening* (London, 1768), pp. 48–9.
22 W. Cowper, *The Task* (London, 1785), Book I, p. 19.
23 Mowl, *Gentlemen and Players*, p. 146.
24 F. Cowell, *Richard Woods (1715–1793): Master of the Pleasure Ground* (Woodbridge, 2009), p. 137.
25 Cowell, *Richard Woods*, p. 164.
26 Ibid., pp. 230–36.
27 Tromp and Newby, 'Dutchman's Visits', p. 55.
28 K. Woodbridge, 'Stourhead in 1768: Extracts from an Unpublished Journal by Sir John Parnell', *Journal of Garden History*, 2 (1982), pp. 59–70, at p. 64.
29 H. Repton, *An Enquiry into the Changes of Taste of Landscape Gardening* (London, 1806), p.33.
30 J. Cradock, *Village Memoirs, in a Series of Letters between a Clergyman and his Family in the Country and his Son in Town* (London, 1765), p. 113.
31 Cowper, *The Task*, Book I, p. 18.
32 T. Williamson, 'The Character of Hertfordshire's Parks and Gardens', in *Hertfordshire Garden History: A Miscellany*, ed. A. Rowe (Hatfield, 2007), pp. 1–25: at pp. 18–21.
33 National Archives of Scotland, GD/18/210 7; NRO COL 7/11, Diary of John Price's travels in Suffolk and Norfolk; A. Young, *The Farmer's Tour through the East of England*, vol. I (London, 1771), p. 65; R. W. Ketton-Cremer, *Norfolk Assembly* (London, 1957), pp. 187, 189.
34 'The Book of the Pleser Grownd att Blickling begun to set ought [out] the work May the 4th 1761. With an account of all the work done and cash pd. for itt': Norfolk Record Office, NRS 8869, 21 F4. M. Armstrong, *The History and Antiquities of the County of Norfolk*, vol. III (London, 1781), p. 91.
35 Private collection; quoted in Williamson, *Archaeology of the Landscape Park*, pp. 220–21.
36 H. Walpole, *The History of Modern Taste in Gardening*, p. 143.
37 Norfolk Record Office, NRS 21369; NRS 8373 24 DS.
38 Norfolk Record Office, NRS 8373 2405.
39 Norfolk Record Office, MC 50/25 503 X 7.
40 Cowper, *The Task*, Book III, p. 124.
41 Ibid., p. 120.
42 S. Daniels, *Humphry Repton: Landscape Gardening and the Geography of Georgian England* (London, 1999), p. 152.
43 Cowper, *The Task*, Book III, p. 130.
44 *The Spectator*, 414, Wednesday 25 June 1712.
45 S. Switzer, *Ichnographia rustica; or, The Nobleman, Gentleman, and Gardener's Recreation* (London, 1718), vol. I, p. xvii.
46 Ibid., vol. III, p. 6.
47 R. W. King, 'The "Ferme Ornée": Philip Southcote and the Wooburn Farm', *Garden History*, II/3 (1974), pp. 27–60; J. Sambrook, 'Wooburn Farm in the 1760s', *Garden History*, VII/2 (1979), pp. 82–101; Mowl, *Gentlemen and Players*, pp. 125–30.
48 C. Gallagher, 'The Leasowes: A History of the Landscape', *Garden History*, XXIV/2 (1996), pp. 201–20.
49 Hertfordshire Archives and Local History, D/EP/E20.
50 Hertfordshire Archives and Local History, DE/P/E8.
51 Hampshire Record Office, 9M73/958.
52 T. Whately, *Observations on Modern Gardening* (London, 1770), p. 178.
53 F. Cowell, *Richard Woods (1715–1793): Master of the Pleasure Ground* (Woodbridge, 2009), p. 22.
54 Ibid., pp. 205–6.
55 Ibid., pp. 60, 140, 181–2.
56 Whately, *Observations on Modern Gardening*, p. 94.
57 D. Chambers, *The Planters of the English Landscape Garden: Botany, Trees and the Georgics* (London, 1993), p. 11.
58 Mowl, *Gentlemen and Players*, p. 128.
59 T. Ruggles, 'Picturesque Farming', series in *Annals of Agriculture*, 6 (1786), pp. 175–84; 7 (1787), pp. 20–28; 8 (1787), pp. 89–97; 9 (1788), pp. 1–15.
60 J. Plaw, *Ferme ornée; or, Rural Improvements* (London, 1796).
61 H. Repton, *Observations on the Theory and Practice of Landscape Gardening* (London, 1803), p. 208.
62 S. Wade Martins, *A Great Estate at Work: the Holkham Estate and its Inhabitants in the Nineteenth Century* (Cambridge, 1980), p. 48; T. Williamson, *The Archaeology of the Landscape Park: Landscape Design in Norfolk, England, c. 1680–1840* (Oxford, 1998), pp. 103, 106–8.
63 Williamson, *Archaeology of the Landscape Park*, pp. 101–3.
64 Whately, *Observations on Modern Gardening*, p. 207.
65 Thornham estate map, East Suffolk Record Office, HA 116/8004.
66 Suggested by a later estate map, East Suffolk Record Office, HD 417/31.
67 Benacre estate map, 1778; East Suffolk Record Office T631 (rolls).

68 S. Morris, 'Shropshire Deer Parks, *c.* 1500–1914: Recreation, Status and Husbandry', PhD thesis, University of East Anglia (2015), pp. 163–4.

69 Shropshire Archives 552/18/1/13.

70 Morris, 'Shropshire Deer Parks', pp. 150–51.

71 Shropshire archives, 11/406.

72 Cholmondeley Castle archives, DCH/L/52/4.

73 Cholmondeley Castle archives, DCH/A/397; DCH/4605/1.

74 O. Rackham, *The Last Forest: The Story of Hatfield Forest* (London, 1989), p. 129.

75 E. J. Climenson, ed., *Passages from the Diaries of Mrs Phillip Lybbe Powys, 1756–1808* (London, 1899), p. 175.

76 For more on regional diversity, see S. Spooner, *Regions and Designed Landscapes in Georgian England* (London, 2015).

77 W. Chambers, *A Dissertation on Oriental Gardening* (London, 1772).

78 Stroud, *Capability Brown*, p. 164.

79 Chambers, *Oriental Gardening*, p. vii.

80 Ibid., p. 43.

81 Ibid., p. 21.

82 Ibid., p. 35.

83 Ibid., p. 53.

84 Ibid., p. 10.

85 Ibid., p. iii.

86 W. Gilpin, *An Essay on Prints: Containing Remarks upon the Principles of Picturesque Beauty; The Different Kinds of Prints; and the Characters of the Most Noted Masters* (London, 1768).

87 W. Gilpin, *Observations on the River Wye, and Several Parts of South Wales, etc. Relative Chiefly to Picturesque Beauty; Made in the Summer of the Year 1770* (London, 1782), pp. 3–4.

88 W. Gilpin, *Three Essays on Picturesque Beauty; on Picturesque Travel; and on Sketching Landscape* (London, 1792), p. 57.

89 W. Gilpin, *Observations, Relative Chiefly to Picturesque Beauty; made in the year 1772, on Several Parts of England Particularly the Mountains and Lakes of Cumberland and Westmoreland* (London, 1788), pp. 41, 75; Gilpin, *Observations on the River Wye*, p. 2; Gilpin, *Remarks on Forest Scenery; and Other Woodland Views*, illustrated by scenes of New Forest in Hampshire, vol. 1 (London, 1791), p. 202.

90 *Remarks on Forest Scenery*, vol. 1, p. 184.

91 Ibid., p. 185.

92 Ibid., p. 188.

93 Ibid., p. 187.

94 W. Gilpin, *Observations on Several Parts of Great Britain: Particularly the High-lands of Scotland, Relative Chiefly to Picturesque Beauty, Made in the Year 1776*, vol. 1 (London, 1808), p. 23.

95 Cradock, *Village Memoirs*, p. 119.

96 Cowper, *The Task*, Book II, p. 130.

97 Cradock, *Village Memoirs*, pp. 69–70.

Conclusion: Afterlife and Legacy

1 Kimberley Hall archives.

2 J. Dixon Hunt, *The Afterlife of Gardens* (Philadelphia, PA, 2004).

3 R. Payne Knight, *The Landscape: A Didactic Poem in Three Books, Addressed to Uvedale Price Esq.* (London, 1794); U. Price, *An Essay on the Picturesque, as Compared with the Sublime and the Beautiful* (London, 1794); C. Watkins and B. Cowell, *Uvedale Price (1747–1829): Decoding the Picturesque* (Woodbridge, 2012).

4 Knight, *The Landscape*, p. 51.

5 J. Phibbs, 'The Picturesque Movement', *Architectural Conservation Newsletter*, 3 (1992), pp. 2–5.

6 S. Daniels, 'The Political Landscape', in *Humphry Repton, Landscape Gardener*, ed. G. Carter, P. Goode and K. Laurie (Norwich, 1983), pp. 110–21; S. Daniels, *Humphry Repton: Landscape Gardening and the Geography of Georgian England* (London, 1999).

7 East Suffolk Record Office, P 617/3; Price, *The Picturesque*, p. 217.

8 H. Repton, *Observations on the Theory and Practice of Landscape Gardening* (London, 1803), p. 119.

9 H. Repton, *Fragments on the Theory and Practice of Landscape Gardening* (London, 1816), p. 69.

10 B. Elliott, *Victorian Gardens* (London, 1986).

11 H. Repton, Red Book for Ashridge, Huntingdon Library, San Marino, California.

12 M. Girouard, *The Victorian Country House* (London, 1979).

13 M. Girouard, *Life in the English Country House* (London, 1978), p. 270.

14 J. C. Loudon, *Gardener's Magazine*, vol. X (1834), p. 329.

15 G. Worsley, *England's Lost Houses: From the Archives of Country Life* (London, 2002); J. M. Robinson, *The Country House at War* (London, 1989).

16 L. R. Haggard and H. Williamson, *Norfolk Life* (London, 1943), p. 97.

BIBLIOGRAPHY

Adshead, D., *Wimpole: Architectural Drawings and Topographical Views* (London, 2007)

Albert, W., *The Turnpike Road System in England, 1663–1840* (Cambridge, 1972)

Anderson, M. L., ed., T. Hamilton (6th Earl of Haddington), *Forest Trees: Some Directions About Raising Forest Trees* (Edinburgh, 1953)

Andrews, C. B., ed., *The Torrington Diaries*, 4 vols (London, 1934–8)

Angus, W., *The Seats of the Nobility* (London, 1787)

Anon., *The Ladies Compleat Letter-writer* (London, 1763)

Anon., *The Scotch Hut; a Poem, Addressed to Euphorbus, or the Earl of the Grove* (London, 1779)

Anon., *Thoughts on the Present Laws for Preserving Game* (London, 1750)

Armstrong, J., *The Art of Preserving Health: A Poem* (London, 1744)

Armstrong, M., *The History and Antiquities of the County of Norfolk*, 3 vols (London, 1781)

Barnatt, J., and T. Williamson, *Chatsworth: A Landscape History* (Macclesfield, 2005)

Bartos, J. M., 'Wilderness and Grove: Gardening with Trees in England, 1688–1750', PhD thesis, University of Bristol (2013)

Batchellor, T., *General View of the Agriculture of Bedfordshire* (London, 1813)

Bazin, G., *Baroque and Rococo* (London, 1998)

Beard, G., *Craftsmen and Interior Decoration in England, 1660–1820* (London, 1981)

——, *The Work of Robert Adam* (London, 1992)

Beckett, J. V., *The Agricultural Revolution* (London, 1990)

Bell, S. Groag, 'Women Create Gardens in Male Landscapes: A Revisionist Approach to Eighteenth-century English Garden History', *Feminist Studies*, XVI/3 (1990), pp. 471–91

Bending, S., 'H. Walpole and Eighteenth-century Garden History', *Journal of the Warburg and Courtauld Institutes*, 57 (1994), pp. 209–26

——, 'A Natural Revolution?', in *Refiguring Revolutions: Aesthetics and Politics from the English Revolution to the Romantic Revolution*, ed. K. Sharpe and S. Zwicker (Berkeley, CA, 1998), pp. 241–66

Bermingham, A., *Landscape and Ideology: The English Rustic Tradition, 1740–1860* (London, 1987)

Bettey, J., 'The Floated Water Meadows of Wessex: A Triumph of English Agriculture', in *Water Meadows: History, Ecology and Conservation*, ed. H. Cook and T. Williamson (Oxford, 2007), pp. 8–22

Bickham, G., *The Beauties of Stow* (London, 1750)

Bilborough, H., 'Documents in Record Offices Which Might Affect the Assessment of the Achievement of "Capability" Brown', *Garden History*, I/3 (1973), pp. 16–17

Blackstone, W., *Commentaries on the Laws of England*, vol. III (London, 1765)

Blunt, R., ed., *Mrs Montagu, 'Queen of the Blues': Her Letters and Friendships from 1762 to 1800* (London, 1923)

Bogart, D., 'Did Turnpike Trusts Increase Transportation Investment in Eighteenth-century England?', *Journal of Economic History*, LXV/2 (2005), pp. 439–68

Booker, J.M.L., 'The Essex Turnpike Trusts', PhD thesis, University of Durham (1979)

Bradley, R., *A General Treatise on Husbandry and Gardening* (London, 1727)

Britton, J., and E. W. Brayley, *The Beauties of England and Wales*, vol. I: *Bedfordshire, Berkshire and Buckinghamshire* (London, 1801)

Brogden, W. A., 'Stephen Switzer and Garden Design in Britain in the Early 18th Century', PhD thesis, University of Edinburgh (1973)

Brown, D., 'Nathaniel Richmond (1724–1784): One of the Gentleman Improvers', PhD thesis, University of East Anglia (2000)

——, 'Lancelot Brown and his Associates', *Garden History*, XXIX/1 (2001), pp. 2–11

Brown, J., *The Omnipotent Magician: Lancelot 'Capability' Brown* (London, 2011)

Browne, R., *The Architectural Outsiders* (London, 1985)

Buchan, A., *Charlecote and the Lucys: The Chronicle of an English Family* (Oxford, 1958)

Burke, E., *A Philosophical Enquiry into the Origin of our Ideas of the Sublime and the Beautiful* (London, 1756)

Cabe Halpern, L., 'Wrest Park, 1686–1730s: Exploring Dutch Influences', *Garden History*, 30 (2002), pp. 131–52

Campbell-Culver, M., *The Origins of Plants* (London, 2010)

Cartwright, J. J., ed., *The Travels through England of Dr Richard Pococke*, 2 vols (London, 1888)

Castell, R., *Villas of the Ancients Illustrated* (London, 1728)

Chambers, D., *The Planters of the English Landscape Garden: Botany, Trees and the Georgics* (London, 1993)

Chambers, W., *A Dissertation on Oriental Gardening* (London, 1772)

Chapman, J., and S. Seeleger, *Enclosure, Environment and Landscape in Southern England* (Stroud, 2001)

Chilvers, A., *The Berties of Grimsthorpe Castle* (London, 2010)

Christie, C., *The British Country House in the Eighteenth Century* (Manchester, 2000)

Claeys, G., *Utopias of the British Enlightenment* (Cambridge, 1994)

Clarke, G., 'Grecian Taste and Gothic Virtue: Lord Cobham's Gardening Programme and its Iconography', *Apollo*, 97 (1973), pp. 56–67

Clarke, J.C.D., *English Society, 1688–1742: Ideology, Social Structure and Political Practice during the Ancien Regime* (Cambridge, 1980)

Clemenson, H., *English Country Houses and Landed Estates* (London, 1982)

Cobbett, W., *The Parliamentary History of England from the Earliest Period to 1816*, 36 vols, vol. XI (London, 1812)

Colley, L., *Britons: Forging the Nation, 1707–1837*, revd edn (London, 2009)

Colman, G., and D. Garrick, *The Clandestine Marriage* (London, 1765)

Colvin, H., *A Biographical Dictionary of British Architects, 1600–1840*, 4th edn (London, 2008)

Coombs, D., 'The Garden at Carlton House of Frederick Prince of Wales and Augusta Princess Dowager of Wales: Bills in Their Household Accounts, 1728–1772', *Garden History*, XXV/2 (1997) pp. 153–77

Cornforth, J., 'The Genesis and Creation of a Great Interior', in *Houghton Hall: The Prime Minister, the Empress and the Inheritance*, ed. A. Moore (London, 1996), pp. 29–40

——, *Early Georgian Interiors* (London, 2004)

Cossons, N., *The bp Book of Industrial Archaeology* (London, 1987)

Cowell, F., 'Richard Woods (?1716–93): A Preliminary Account, Part 1', *Garden History*, XIV/2 (London, 1986), pp. 85–120

——, *Richard Woods (1715–1793): Master of the Pleasure Garden* (Woodbridge, 2009)

Cowper, W., *The Task* (London, 1785)

Cozens-Hardy, B., *The Diary of Sylas Neville, 1767–1788* (Oxford, 1950)

Cradock, J., *Village Memoirs, in a Series of Letters between a Clergyman and his Family in the Country, and his Son in Town* (London, 1765)

Cruickshank, D., *A Guide to the Georgian Buildings of Britain and Ireland* (London, 1985)

Daniels, S., 'The Political Iconography of Woodland in Later Georgian England', in *The Iconography of Landscape: Essays on the Symbolic Representation, Design and Use of Past Environments*, ed. D. Cosgrove and S. Daniels (Cambridge, 1988), pp. 43–82

——, *Humphry Repton: Landscape Gardening and the Geography of Georgian England* (London, 1999)

——, and S. Seymour, 'Landscape Design and the Idea of Improvement, 1730–1814', in *An Historic Geography of England and Wales*, ed. R. A. Dodgshon and R. A. Butlin (London, 1990), pp. 487–519

Davis, H., ed., *Pope: Poetical Works* (Oxford, 1978)

Defoe, D., *Tour through the Whole Island of Great Britain* (Harmondsworth, 1971)

Desmond, R., *Dictionary of British and Irish Botanists and Horticulturalists, including Plant Collectors, Flower Painters and Garden Designers* (London, 1994)

——, *Kew: The History of the Royal Botanic Gardens* (London, 1998) di Palma, V., *Wasteland: A History* (New Haven, CT, 2014)

Dickens, L., and M. Stanton, *An Eighteenth-century Correspondence: Being the Letters of Deane Swift – Pitt – the Lytteltons and the Grenvilles – Lord Dacre – Robert Nugent – Charles Jenkinson – the Earls of Guildford, Coventry, & Hardwicke – Sir Edward Turner – Mr Talbot of Lacock, and others to Sanderson Miller, Esq., of Radway* (London, 1910)

Dickinson, H. T., *Walpole and the Whig Supremacy* (London, 1973)

——, 'Tories: 1714–1830', in *Reader's Guide to British History*, ed. D. Loades (London, 2003), vol. II, p. 1279

Drescher, S., *Econocide: British Slavery on the Eve of Abolition* (Pittsburgh, PA, 1977)

Dryden, J., trans., *Virgil's Aeneid* (London, 1697)

Dudley, C., 'Party Politics, Political Economy, and Economic Development in Early Eighteenth-century England', *Economic History Review*, 66 (2013), pp. 1084–100

Edwards, P., 'The Gardens at Wroxton Abbey, Oxfordshire', *Garden History*, XIV (1986), pp. 50–59

Elliott, B., *Victorian Gardens* (London, 1986)

Elrington, C. R., *Victoria History of the County of Warwickshire* (London, 1968)

Everett, N., *The Tory View of Landscape* (London, 1994)

Felus, K., 'Beautiful Objects and Agreeable Retreats: Uses of Garden Buildings in the Designed Landscape in 18th-century England', PhD thesis, University of Bristol (2009)

——, 'Boats and Boating in the Designed Landscape, 1720–1820', *Garden History*, XXXIV/1 (2006), pp. 22–46

Festing, S., 'Menageries in the Landscape Garden', *Journal of Garden History*, 4 (1988), pp. 104–17

Fielding, H., *An Enquiry into the Causes of the Late Increase in Robbers* [1751], ed. M. R. Zirker (Oxford, 1988)

Finch, J., and K. Giles, 'Three Men in a Boat: Biographies and Narratives in the Historic Landscape', *Landscape Research*, XXXIII/5 (2008), pp. 511–30

——, eds, *Estate Landscapes: Design, Improvement and Power in the Post-medieval Landscape* (Woodbridge, 2007)

Fleming, J., *Robert Adam and his Circle in Edinburgh and Rome* (London, 1962)

Fletcher, Alan, 'Charles Bridgeman at Tring Park: A Reassessment', in *Hertfordshire Garden History: A Miscellany*, ed. A. Rowe (Hatfield, 2007), pp. 41–8

Fletcher, Anthony, *Gender, Sex and Subordination in England, 1500–1800* (New Haven, CT, and London, 1996)

Fletcher, J., *Gardens of Earthly Delight: The History of Deer Parks* (Oxford, 2011)

Flinn, M. W., *The History of the British Coal Industry*, vol. II: *1700–1830* (Oxford, 1984)

Forty, A., *Objects of Desire: Design and Society since 1750* (London, 1986)

Foyster, E., 'Boys Will Be Boys? Manhood and Aggression, 1660–1800', in *English Masculinities, 1660–1800*, ed. T. Hitchcock and M. Cohen (London, 1999), pp. 151–66

Friedman, A., ed., *The Collected Works of Oliver Goldsmith*, vol. IV (Oxford, 1966)

Friedman, T., *James Gibbs* (London, 1984)

Gallagher, C., 'The Leasowes: A History of the Landscape', *Garden History*, XXIV/2 (1996), pp. 201–20

Gelling, J. A., *Common Field and Enclosure in England, 1450–1850* (London, 1977)

Gerrard, C., *The Patriot Opposition to Walpole: Politics, Poetry, and National Myth, 1725–1742* (London, 1995)

Gilbert, C., *The Life and Works of Thomas Chippendale* (London, 1978)

Gilpin, W., *An Essay on Prints: Containing Remarks upon the Principles of Picturesque Beauty; the Different Kinds of Prints; and the Characters of the Most Noted Masters* (London, 1768)

——, *Observations on the River Wye, and Several Parts of South Wales, etc. Relative Chiefly to Picturesque Beauty; Made in the Summer of the Year 1770* (London, 1782)

——, *Observations, Relative Chiefly to Picturesque Beauty; Made in the year 1772, on Several Parts of England Particularly the Mountains and Lakes of Cumberland and Westmoreland* (London, 1788)

——, *Remarks on Forest Scenery; and Other Woodland Views*, illustrated by scenes of the New Forest in Hampshire, 2 vols (London, 1791)

——, *Three Essays on Picturesque Beauty; on Picturesque Travel; and on Sketching Landscape* (London, 1792)

——, *Observations on Several Parts of Great Britain: Particularly the High-lands of Scotland, Relative Chiefly to Picturesque Beauty, Made in the Year 1776*, vol. I (London, 1808)

Girouard, M., *Life in the English Country House: A Social and Architectural History* (London, 1978)

——, *The Victorian Country House* (London, 1979)

——, 'Early Drawings of Bolsover Hall', *Architectural History*, 27 (1984), pp. 510–18

——, *The English Town: A History of Urban Life* (London, 1990)

Goldsmith, O., *The Life of Richard Nash of Bath, Esquire, Extracted Principally from his Original Papers* (London, 1762)

Goodwyn, E. A., *Selections from Norwich Newspapers, 1760–1790* (Ipswich, 1972)

Gould, M., *Biographical Dictionary of Architects at Reading* (London, 1999)

Gregory, J., S. Spooner and T. Williamson, 'Lancelot "Capability" Brown: A Research Impact Review', English Heritage Research Report no. 50 (London, 2015)

Hadfield, M., *A History of British Gardening* (London, 1960)

Haggard, L. R., and H. Williamson, *Norfolk Life* (London, 1943)

Halfpenny, W. and J., *New Designs for Chinese Bridges, Temples, Triumphal Arches, Garden Seats, Palings, Obelisks, Termini etc.* (London, 1751)

Hall, E., '"Mr Brown's Directions": Capability Brown's Landscaping at Burton Constable (1767–82)', *Garden History*, XXIII/2 (1995), pp. 145–74

Hanbury, W., *An Essay on Planting* (London, 1758)

Hancock, D., *Citizens of the World: London Merchants and the Integration of the British Atlantic Community, 1735–1785* (Cambridge, 1995)

Harris, J., 'The Architecture of the House', in *Houghton Hall: The Prime Minister, the Empress and the Heritage*, ed. A. Moore (London, 1996), pp. 20–24

Harvey, J., *Early Nurserymen* (London, 1974)

Harwood, K., 'Some Hertfordshire Nabobs', in *Hertfordshire Garden History: A Miscellany*, ed. A. Rowe (Hatfield, 2007), pp. 49–77

Haslam, R., 'Beeston Hall', *Country Life*, 172 (1983), pp. 270–74

Hawkes, W., ed., *The Diaries of Sanderson Miller of Radway* (London, 2005)

Heeley, J., *A Description of Hagley Park* (London, 1777)

Hertfordshire Gardens Trust and T. Williamson, *The Parks and Gardens of West Hertfordshire* (Letchworth, 2000)

Hill, B., *The Growth of Parliamentary Parties, 1680–1742* (London, 1976)

Hill, D., and P. Robinson, *The Pheasant: Management and Conservation* (London, 1988)

Hinde, T., *Capability Brown: The Story of a Master Gardener* (London, 1986)

Hodges, A., 'Painshill Park, Cobham, Surrey, 1700–1800', *Garden History*, 11/3 (1973), pp. 36–68

Holderness, B. A., 'Prices, Productivity and Output', in *The Agrarian History of England and Wales*, vol. VI, ed. G. E. Mingay (Cambridge, 1989), pp. 84–189

Home, J. A., ed., *The Letters and Journals of Lady Mary Coke* (Oxford, 1966)

Honour, H., *Neo-classicism* (London, 1977)

Hopkins, H., *The Long Affray* (London, 1985)

Hoppit, S., *A Land of Liberty? England, 1689–1727* (Oxford, 2000)

Horn, P., 'An Eighteenth-century Land Agent: The Career of Nathaniel Kent (1737–1810)', *Agricultural History Review*, 30 (1982), pp. 1–16

Howitt, W., *Visits to Remarkable Places: Old Halls, Battle Fields &c.* (London, 1842)

Hughes, E., 'The Eighteenth-century Estate Agent', in *Essays in British and Irish History*, ed. H. Cronne, T. Moody and D. Quin (London, 1949), pp. 185–99

Hunt, J. D., *Garden and Grove: The Italian Renaissance Garden in the English Imagination, 1600–1750* (London, 1986)

——, *William Kent, Landscape Garden Designer: An Assessment and Catalogue of his Designs* (London, 1987)

——, *The Afterlife of Gardens* (Philadelphia, PA, 2004)

——, and E. de Jong, eds, 'The Anglo-Dutch Garden in the Reign of William and Mary', *Journal of Garden History*, 8 [special issue] (1988)

Hussey, C., *The Picturesque* (London, 1927)

——, *English Gardens and Landscapes, 1700–1750* (London, 1967)

Hyams, E., *Capability Brown and Humphry Repton* (London, 1971)

Ingram, A., *Horse-drawn Vehicles since 1760* (Blandford, 1977)

Irwin, D., *Winckelmann: Writings on Art* (London, 1972)

——, *Neoclassicism* (London, 1997)

Jackson-Stops, G., *Claydon House, Buckinghamshire* (London, 1979)

——, *An English Arcadia, 1600–1990: Designs for Gardens and Garden Buildings in the Care of the National Trust* (Washington, DC, 2006)

Jacques, D., *Georgian Gardens: The Reign of Nature* (London, 1983)

——, *The Grand Manner: Changing Style in Garden Design, 1660–1735* (London, 1999)

——, 'The Formal Garden', in *Sir John Vanbrugh and Landscape Architecture in Baroque England,*

1690–1730, ed. C. Ridgway and R. Williams
(Stroud, 2000), pp. 31–48

Jago, R., *Edge-Hill, or, The Rural Prospect Delineated and Moralized* (London, 1767)

James, J., *The Theory and Practice of Gardening: Wherein is Fully Handled All That Relates to Fine Gardens, Commonly Called Pleasure-gardens . . .* (London, 1712)

Jefferson, T., *Memoranda of a Tour of the Gardens of England*, founders.archives.gov/documents/Jefferson/01-09-02-0328, accessed 24 July 2015

Johnson, S., *A Dictionary of the English Language* (London, 1755)

Kelly, A., *Decorative Wedgwood in Architecture and Furniture* (London, 1965)

Ketton-Cremer, R. W., *Norfolk Assembly* (London, 1957)

Kimball, F., *The Creation of the Rococo Decorative Style* (New York, 1980)

King, D., *The Complete Works of Robert and James Adam* (Oxford, 1991)

King, R. W., 'The "*Ferme ornée*": Philip Southcote and the Wooburn Farm', *Garden History*, II/3 (1974), pp. 27–60

——, 'Joseph Spence of Byfleet, Part IV', *Garden History*, VIII/3 (1980), pp. 77–144

Kingsley, N., *The Country Houses of Gloucestershire*, vol. II: *1660–1830* (Chichester, 1992)

Ladd, F. J., *Architects at Corsham Court: A Study in Revival Style Architecture and Landscaping, 1749–1849* (Bradford-on-Avon, 1978)

Laird, M., *The Formal Garden: Traditions of Art and Nature* (London, 1992)

——, *The Flowering of the English Landscape Garden: English Pleasure Grounds, 1720–1800* (Philadelphia, PA, 1999)

Lange, B. P., 'The English Garden and Patriotic Discourse', in *Englishness*, ed. H.-J. Diller et al., Anglistik & Englischunterricht 46/47 (Heidelberg, 1992)

Langford, P., *A Polite and Commercial People* (Oxford, 1989)

Langley, B., *New Principals of Gardening* (London, 1728)

——, *Practical Geometry Applied in the Practical and Useful Arts of Building, Surveying, Gardening and Mensuration* (London, 1729)

Lawrence, J., *The Modern Land Steward* (London, 1801)

Lawton, G., *Collectio rerum ecclesiasticarum de diœcesi eboracensis* (London, 1840)

Lees-Milne, J., *Earls of Creation* (London, 1962)

Leiper, H., 'Mr Lancelot Brown and his Hertfordshire Clients', in *Hertfordshire Garden History: A Miscellany*, vol. II: *Gardens Pleasant, Groves Delicious*, ed. D. Spring (Hatfield, 2012), pp. 92–120

Lewis, L., ed., *Hird's Annals of Bedale* (Northallerton, 1990)

Lewis, W. S., ed., *The Yale Edition of Horace Walpole's Correspondence*, 48 vols (New Haven, CT, 1937–83)

Liddiard, R., ed., *The Medieval Park: New Perspectives* (Macclesfield, 2007)

Locke, J., *Some Thoughts Concerning Education* (London, 1693)

Loudon, J. C., *The Suburban Gardener and Villa Companion* (London, 1838)

——, *The Landscape Gardening and Landscape Architecture of the Late Humphry Repton Esq* (London, 1840)

Lysons, D., *The Environs of London*, vol. II: *The County of Middlesex* (London, 1795)

McCulloch, J. R., *A Discourse on the Rise, Progress, Peculiar Objects and Importance of Political Economy* (Edinburgh, 1824)

Malthus, T., *An Essay on the Principle of Population* [1798], ed. J. Bonar (New York, 1966)

Markham, S., ed., *John Loveday of Caversham, 1711–1789: The Life and Tours of an Eighteenth-century Onlooker* (Salisbury, 1984)

Mason, G., *An Essay on Design in Gardening* (London, 1768)

Mayer, L., *Capability Brown and the English Landscape Garden* (Princes Risborough, 2011)

Meir, J., 'Sanderson Miller and the Landscaping of Wroxton Abbey, Farnborough Hall and Honington Hall', *Garden History*, XXV/1 (1997), pp. 81–106

——, *Sanderson Miller and his Landscapes* (Phillimore, 2006)

Meteyard, E., *The Life of Josiah Wedgwood, from his Private Correspondence and Family Papers*, 2 vols (London, 1866)

Mileson, S., *Parks in Medieval England* (Oxford, 2009)

Miller, P., *The Gardener's Dictionary* (London, 1731)

Mitchell, B. R., and P. Deane, *Abstract of British Historical Statistics* (Cambridge, 1962)

Morris, R., *Lectures on Architecture, Consisting of Rules Founded upon Harmonick and Arithmetical Proportions in Buildings* (London, 1734)

Morris, S., 'Shropshire Deer Parks, c. 1500–1914: Recreation, Status and Husbandry', PhD thesis, University of East Anglia (2015)

Mowl, T., and Brian Earnshaw, *An Insular Rococo: Architecture, Politics and Society in Ireland and England, 1710–70* (London, 1999)

—, *Gentlemen and Players: Gardeners of the English Landscape* (Stroud, 2000)

—, *Historic Gardens of Gloucestershire* (Stroud, 2002)

—, *Historic Gardens of Worcestershire* (Stroud, 2006)

—, *William Kent: Architect, Designer, Opportunist* (London, 2007)

—, and D. James, *Historic Gardens of Warwickshire* (Bristol, 2011)

Muckerji, C., 'Reading and Writing with Nature: A Materialist Approach to French Formal Gardens', in *Consumption and the World of Goods*, ed. J. Brewer and R. Porter (London, 1993), pp. 439–61

Munsche, P. B., *Gentlemen and Poachers* (Cambridge, 1981)

North, R., *A Discourse of Fish and Fish Ponds* (London, 1713)

Overton, M., *Agricultural Revolution in England* (Cambridge, 1996)

Paine, J., *Plans, Elevations and Sections, of Noblemen and Gentlemen's Houses* (London, 1767)

Palmer, M., and P. Neaverson, *Industry in the Landscape, 1700–1900* (London, 1994)

Penny, N., 'The Macabre Garden at Denbies and its Monument', *Garden History*, III/3 (1975), pp. 58–61

Petit, S., and C. Watkins, 'Pollarding Trees: Changing Attitudes to a Traditional Land Management Practise in Britain, 1600–1900', *Rural History*, 14 (2003), pp. 157–76

Pevsner, N., 'The Genesis of the Picturesque', *Architectural Review*, 96 (November 1944)

Phibbs, J., 'Groves and Belts', *Garden History*, XIX/2 (1991), pp. 175–86

—, 'Recording What Isn't There: Three Difficulties with 18th-century Landscapes', in *There by Design: Field Archaeology in Parks and Gardens*, ed. P. Pattison (Swindon, 1998), pp. 27–31

—, 'The Englishness of Lancelot "Capability" Brown', *Garden History*, XXXI/2 (2003), pp. 122–40

—, 'Projective Geometry', *Garden History*, XXXIV/1 (2006), pp. 1–21

—, 'Point Blank', *Garden History*, XXXV/1 (2007), pp. 110–18

—, 'The View-point', *Garden History*, XXXVI/2 (2008), pp. 215–28

—, 'Field Sports and Brownian Design', *Garden History*, XL/1 (2012), pp. 56–71

Plaw, J., *Ferme ornée; or, Rural Improvements* (London, 1796)

Pomeranz, K., *The Great Divergence: China, Europe, and the Making of the Modern World Economy* (Princeton, NJ, 2001)

Price, U., *Essay on the Picturesque, As Compared with the Sublime and the Beautiful*, 3 vols (London, 1794)

Quinn, M., ed., *The Collected Works of Jeremy Bentham: Writings on the Poor Laws*, vol. 1: *Writings on the Poor Laws* (Oxford, 2001)

Rackham, O., *The History of the Countryside* (London, 1986)

—, *The Last Forest: The Story of Hatfield Forest* (London, 1989)

—, 'Pre-existing Trees and Woods in Country-house Parks', *Landscapes*, V/2 (2004), pp. 1–15

Reilly, R., *Josiah Wedgwood, 1730–1795* (London, 1992)

Repton, H., *Sketches and Hints on Landscape Gardening* (London, 1795)

—, *Observations on the Theory and Practice of Landscape Gardening* (London, 1805)

—, *An Inquiry into the Changes of Taste in Landscape Gardening* (London, 1806)

—, *Fragments on the Theory and Practice of Landscape Gardening* (London, 1816)

Richardson, T., *The Arcadian Friends: Inventing the English Landscape Garden* (London, 2007)

Roberts, Hon. Jane, *Royal Landscapes: The Gardens and Parks of Windsor* (New Haven, CT, 1997)

Roberts, Judith, 'Cusworth Park: The Making of an Eighteenth-century Designed Landscape', *Landscape History*, 21 (1999), pp. 77–93

—, 'Well Tempered Clay: Constructing Water Features in the Landscape Park', *Garden History*, 11/1 (2001), pp. 12–28

Roberts, W., *Memoirs of the Life and Correspondence of Mrs Hannah More* (London, 1836)

Robinson, J. M., *Temples of Delight: Stowe Landscape Gardens* (London, 1999)

Rorschach, K., *The Early Georgian Landscape Garden* (New Haven, CT, 1983)

Rowe, A., and T. Williamson, 'New Light on Gobions', *Garden History*, XL/1 (2012), pp. 82–97

—, and T. Williamson, *Hertfordshire: A Landscape History* (Hatfield, 2013)

—, A.D.M. MacNair and T. Williamson, *Dury and Andrews' Map of Hertfordshire: Society and Landscape in the Eighteenth Century* (Hatfield, 2015)

Royal Commission on Historical Manuscripts, *Report on the Manuscripts of the Earl of Verulam, Preserved at Gorhambury* (London, 1906)

——, *Fifteenth Report, Appendix*, Part VI: *The Manuscripts of the Earl of Carlisle Preserved at Castle Howard* (London, 1907)

Royal Commission on Historical Monuments (England), *An Inventory of the Historical Monuments in the County of Cambridge*, vol. I, *West Cambridgeshire* (London, 1968)

Ruggles, T., 'Picturesque Farming', series in *Annals of Agriculture*, 6 (1786), pp. 175–84; 7 (1787), pp. 20–28; 8 (1787), pp. 89–97; 9 (1788), pp. 1–15

Salmon, N., *The History of Hertfordshire* (London, 1728)

Sambrook, J., 'Woburn Farm in the 1760s', *Garden History*, VII/2 (1979), pp. 82–101

Scarfe, N., ed., *A Frenchman's Year in Suffolk: French Impressions of Suffolk Life in 1784* (Woodbridge, 1988)

Schmidt, L., C. Keller and P. Feversham, eds, *Holkham* (Munich, 2005)

Schofield, J., *London, 1100–1600: The Archaeology of a Capital City* (Sheffield, 2011)

Scott, K., *The Rococo Interior: Decoration and Social Space in Early Eighteenth-century Paris* (New Haven, CT, 1995)

Sheeran, G., *Landscape Gardens of West Yorkshire* (Wakefield, 1990)

Shields, S., '"Mr Brown Engineer": Lancelot Brown's Early Work at Grimsthorpe Castle and Stowe', *Garden History*, XXXIV/2 (2006), pp. 174–91

Shoemaker, R. B., 'Reforming Male Manners: Public Insults and the Decline of Violence in London, 1660–1740', in *English Masculinities, 1660–1800*, ed. T. Hitchcock and M. Cohen (London, 1999), pp. 133–50

Shurmer, J., *The Stowe Landscape Gardens* (London, 1997)

Simmons, I. G., *An Environmental History of Great Britain, from 10,000 Years Ago to the Present* (Edinburgh, 2001)

Smart, A., *The Life and Art of Allan Ramsay* (London, 1952)

Smith, A., *An Inquiry into the Nature and Causes of the Wealth of Nations* [1776], ed. R. H. Campbell and A. S. Skinner, 2 vols (Oxford, 1976)

——, *The Theory of Moral Sentiments* [1759], ed. D. D. Raphael and A. L. Macfie, 2 vols (Oxford, 1976)

Smith, N., *Wrest Park* (London, 1995)

Snell, K., *Annals of the Labouring Poor: Social Change and Agrarian England, 1660–1900* (Cambridge, 1986)

Soulden, D., *Wimpole Hall, Cambridgeshire* (London, 1991)

Spooner, S., '"A Prospect Two Field's Distance": Rural Landscapes and Urban Mentalities in the Eighteenth-century', *Landscapes*, X/1 (2009)

——, *Regions and Designed Landscapes in Georgian England* (London, 2015)

Stillman, D., *The Decorative Work of Robert Adam* (London, 1966)

Stone, L., *The Family, Sex and Marriage in England, 1500–1800* (London, 1977)

Stroud, D., *Capability Brown* (London, 1975)

Stuart, J., and N. Revett, *The Antiquities of Athens and Other Monuments of Greece* (London, 1762)

Stutchbury, H. E., *The Architecture of Colen Campbell* (Manchester, 1967)

Suarez Huerta, A. M., 'Wilson, Mengs, and Some British Connections', in *Richard Wilson and the Transformation of European Painting*, ed. M. Postle and R. Simon (New Haven, CT, 2014), pp. 107–17

Summerson, J., *Architecture in Britain, 1530–1830* (London, 1991)

Switzer, S., *Ichnographia rustica*, 3 vols (London, 1718)

Symes, M., 'David Garrick and Landscape Gardening', *Journal of Garden History*, 6 (1986), pp. 34–49

——, *The English Rococo Garden* (Princes Risborough, 1991)

——, *The Picturesque and the Later Georgian Garden* (Bristol, 2012)

Tarlow, S., *The Archaeology of Improvement in Britain, 1750–1860* (Cambridge, 2007)

Tayler, S. and H., eds, *Lord Fife and his Factor* (London, 1925)

Thomas, K., *Man and the Natural World* (London, 1983)

Thompson, F., *A History of Chatsworth: Being a Supplement to the 6th Duke of Devonshire's Handbook* (London, 1949)

Tinniswood, A., *A History of Country House Visiting* (London, 1989)

Toldervy, W., *England and Wales Described in a Series of Letters* (London, 1762)

Toynbee, P., ed., *Horace Walpole's Journal of Visits to Country Seats &c.*, Walpole Society (Oxford, 1928)

——, *Supplement to the Letters of Horace Walpole*, 3 vols (Oxford, 1918–25)

Tromp, H., and E. Newby, 'A Dutchman's Visits to Some English Gardens in 1791', *Journal of Garden History*, 2 (1982), pp. 41–58

Trumbach, R., *The Rise of the Egalitarian Family: Aristocratic Kinship and Domestic Relations in Eighteenth-century England* (New York, 1977)

Turnbull, D., 'Thomas White (1739–1811): Eighteenth-century Landscape Designer and Arboriculturist', PhD thesis, University of Hull (1990)

Turner, M., *English Parliamentary Enclosures* (Folkstone, 1980)

Turner, R., *Capability Brown and the Eighteenth-century English Landscape* (London, 1985)

Turner, T., *English Garden Design: History and Styles since 1650* (Woodbridge, 1986)

Wade, E., *A Proposal for Improving and Adorning the Island of Great Britain; for the Maintenance of our Navy and Shipping* (London, 1755)

Wade Martins, S., *A Great Estate at Work: The Holkham Estate and its Inhabitants in the Nineteenth Century* (Cambridge, 1980)

——, and T. Williamson, 'Floated Water-meadows in Norfolk: A Misplaced Innovation', *Agricultural History Reviews*, 42 (1994), pp. 20–37

Walpole, H., *The History of the Modern Taste in Gardening* (London, 1780)

——, *Anecdotes of Painting in England: With Some Account of the Principal Artists . . .* (London, 1762)

Watts, W., *The Seats of the Nobility and Gentry in a Collection of the Most Interesting and Picturesque Views* (London, 1779)

Webb, D. Carless, *Observations and Remarks Made during Four Excursions Made to Various Parts of Great Britain . . . in 1810 and 1811* (London, 1812)

Webster, S., 'Estate Improvement and the Professionalization of Land Agents on the Egremont Estates in Sussex and Yorkshire, 1770–1835', *Rural History*, 18 (2007), pp. 47–69

Whately, T., *Observations on Modern Gardening* (London, 1770)

Wheeler, J., *The Modern Druid* (London, 1747)

Williams, R., 'Making Places: Garden-mastery and English Brown', *Journal of Garden History*, III/4 (1983), pp. 382–5

——, 'Rural Economy and the Antique in the English Landscape Garden', *Journal of Garden History*, VII/1 (1987), pp. 73–96

Williamson, T., *Polite Landscapes: Gardens and Society in Eighteenth-century England* (Stroud, 1995)

——, *The Archaeology of the Landscape Park: Garden Design in Norfolk, England, c. 1680–1840* (Oxford, 1998)

——, 'Understanding Enclosure', *Landscapes*, I/1 (2000), pp. 56–79

——, *The Transformation of Rural England: Farming and the Landscape, 1700–1870* (Exeter, 2002)

——, 'Archaeological Perspectives on Landed Estates: Research Agendas', in *Estate Landscapes: Design, Improvement and Power in the Post-medieval Landscape*, ed. J. Finch and K. Giles (Woodbridge, 2007), pp. 1–18

——, 'The Character of Hertfordshire's Parks and Gardens', in *Hertfordshire Garden History: A Miscellany*, ed. A. Rowe (Hatfield, 2007), pp. 1–25

——, '"At Pleasure's Lordly Call"; The Archaeology of Emparked Settlements', in *Deserted Villages Revisited*, ed. C. Dyer and R. Jones (Hatfield, 2010), pp. 162–81

——, *An Environmental History of Wildlife in England, 1550–1950* (London, 2013)

——, R. Liddiard and T. Pardita, *Champion: The Making and Unmaking of the English Midland Landscape* (Liverpool, 2013)

Willis, P., 'Capability Brown's Account with Drummonds Bank, 1753–1783', *Architectural History*, 27 (1984), pp. 382–91

——, *Charles Bridgeman and the English Landscape Garden*, 2nd edn (London, 2002)

Winstanley, R. L., *Parson Woodforde: Diary of the First Six Norfolk Years* (London, 1984)

Withers, W. J., 'Geography, Natural History, and the Eighteenth-century Enlightenment: Putting the World in Place', *History Workshop Journal*, 39 (1995), pp. 136–63

Wittkower, R., *Palladio and Palladianism* (New York, 1974)

Woodbridge, K., *The Stourhead Landscape* (London, 1982)

——, 'Stourhead in 1768: Extracts from an Unpublished Journal by Sir John Parnell', *Journal of Garden History*, 2 (1982), pp. 59–70

Worsley, G., *Classical Architecture in Britain: The Heroic Age* (London, 1995)

Worsley, L., *Bolsover Castle* (London, 2000)

Wright, J., ed., *The Letters of Horace Walpole, Earl of Orford*, 6 vols (London, 1844).

Wrigley, E.A.W., *Continuity, Chance and Change: The Character of the Industrial Revolution in England* (Cambridge, 1988)

Yarwood, D., *Robert Adam* (London, 1970)

Young, A., *The Farmer's Tour through the East of England*, 4 vols (London, 1771)

——, *General View of the Agriculture of Hertfordshire* (London, 1804)

Young, H., *The Genius of Wedgwood* (London, 1995)

Zouch, H., *An Account of the Present Daring Practices of Night-hunters and Poachers* (London, 1783)

ACKNOWLEDGEMENTS

A large number of people and organizations have helped with this volume over the years, providing advice, information, or access to private archives and landscapes. We would like to thank, in particular, Sally Bate, Liz Bellamy, Wendy Bishop, Robbie and Iona Buxton, Lord Cholmondeley, Fiona Cowell, Patsy Dallas, John Dixon Hunt, Jon Finch, Jon Gregory, Roger Gawn, Kate Harwood, Sue Haynes, Emma Hazell, Christine Hiskey, Christine Hodgetts, Emma Holman-West, Tim Holt-Wilson, Matthew Hume, David Jacques, Jo Johnston, Mark Lamey, Lord Lansdowne, Helen Leiper, Robert Liddiard, Andrew Macnair, Paul Methuen-Campbell, Robert Miller, Sandra Morris, Tim Mowl, the National Trust, Tracey Partida, Anne Rowe, Rachel Savage, Steffie Shields, Sarah Spooner, Anthea Taigel, Robert Tamworth, Jill Tovey, Lisa Voden-Decker, Paul Ware, George West, Jennifer White, Robert Williams, Richard Wilson, Philip Winterbottom, Moor Park Golf Club, and the members of the Hertfordshire Gardens Trust, the Norfolk Gardens Trust and the Warwickshire Gardens Trust. We would also like to thank the staff of the archives at Badminton House, Bedfordshire and Luton Archives and Records Service, Bexley Local Studies and Archive Centres, the Bodleian Library at Oxford, Chatsworth House, Cheshire Archives and Local Studies, Cumbria Archives Centre, East Sussex Record Office, Essex Record Office, Hertfordshire Archives and Local History, Lincolnshire Archives, Longleat House, Norfolk Record Office, the Royal Institute of British Architects, the Royal Bank of Scotland, the Suffolk Record Offices, Staffordshire Record Office, Surrey History Centre, Warwickshire County Record Office, West Sussex Record Office and the Wiltshire and Swindon History Centre.

PHOTO ACKNOWLEDGEMENTS

The authors and publishers wish to express their thanks to the following sources of illustrative material and/or permission to reproduce it. Some locations are also supplied here, not given in the captions for reasons of brevity.

Photographs by or courtesy of the authors: 3, 7, 17, 29, 31, 33, 35, 44, 48, 49, 50, 52, 58, 62, 68, 75, 79, 88, 93, 97, 99, 100, 101, 102, 104, 107, 109, 110, 114, 115, 116, 127; Badminton House Muniments: 42, 43; Bedfordshire and Luton Archives and Records Service, Bedford: 22; Bexley Local Studies and Archive Centre, Kent: 86; Bodleian Library, University of Oxford: 25, 26, 74; from E. Adveno Brooke, *The Gardens of England* (London, 1857–9): 126; Robbie Buxton: 72; from Colen Campbell, *The third volume of Vitruvius Britannicus: or, The British architect: Containing the geometrical plans of the most considerable gardens and plantations; also the plans, elevations, and sections of the most regular buildings, not published in the first and second volumes. With large views, in perspective, of the most remarkable edifices in Great Britain . . .* (London, 1725): 18; from Thomas Chippendale, *The Gentleman and Cabinet Maker's Director: Being a large collection of . . . designs of household furniture in the Gothic, Chinese and modern taste . . .* (London, 1754): 19; The Courtauld Institute, London: 98; Fiona Cowell and the Essex Record Office, Chelmsford: 120; Fiona Cowell and Wiltshire and Swindon Archives: 118; Cumbria Archives Service, Carlisle, and the Lowther Estate Trust: 65, 67; Patsy Dallas: 92; © Devonshire Collection, Chatsworth, and reproduced by permission of the Chatsworth Settlement Trustees: 56, 57, 70; from Robert Dodsley, ed., *The Works in Verse and Prose, of William Shenstone, Esq . . .* (London, 1764): 119; from Andrew Dury and John Andrews, *A Topographical Map of Hart-fordshire* (London, 1766): 46; by permission of the Earl of Leicester and the Trustees of the Holkham Estate: 27, 30; East Sussex Record Office, Brighton: 89, 105, 113; reproduced by permission of English Heritage, © English Heritage: 10, 16, 63, 71; Jon Finch: 4; Gloucestershire Record Office, Gloucester: 24; Jon Gregory and Sarah Spooner: 32, 94, 95; Harewood House, London (reproduced by the kind permission of the Trustees of the 7th Earl of Harewood Will Trust and the Trustees of the Harewood House Trust): 5; Hertfordshire Archives and Local History, Hertford: 23, 45; Tim Holt-Wilson: 64, 78; Horsham Museum and Art Gallery and West Sussex Record Office, Chichester: 106; photo IBM: 13; Ipswich and East Suffolk Record Office, Ipswich: 14; from Johannes Kip and Leonard Knyff, *Britannia Illustrata: or Views of Several of the Queens Palaces as also of the Principal Seats of the Nobility and Gentry of Great Britain Curiously Engraven . . .* (London, 1707): 15, 81; from Richard Payne Knight, *The Landscape: a didactic poem. In three books. Addressed to Uvedale Price, Esq.* (London, 1794): 122, 123; from Batty Langley, *Practical Geometry applied to the Useful Arts of Building, Surveying, Gardening and Mensuration; Calculated for the Service of Gentlemen as well as Artisans . . .* (London, 1729): 21; Robert Liddiard: 11; Lincolnshire Archives, Lincoln, and the Grimsthorpe Estate: 91, 112; Lord Egremont and West Sussex Record Office, Chichester: 53; reproduced by kind permission of Lord Lansdowne and the Trustees of the Bowood Collection, © Trustees of the Bowood Collection: 60, 90; photo Andrew Macnair: 46; courtesy Andrew Macnair: 96 (from Macnair's 2012 digital remastering of Andrew Dury and John Andrews's *Topographical Map of Hart-fordshire* [London, 1766]); courtesy of the National Gallery, London: 1; National Gallery of Art, Washington, DC: 76; courtesy The National Trust: 82, 83, 84, 117; Tracey Partida: 12; private collections: 28, 34, 66, 69, 87, 121;

The Royal Bank of Scotland: 85; Anne Rowe: 20, 103,
108; photo Library of the Royal Institute of British
Architects: 73; courtesy Eric de Saumarez: 124, 125;
Steffie Shields: 59, 111; reproduced by permission of
Shropshire Council, Shropshire Museums, Shrewsbury:
8; Tate Gallery, London: 55; Victoria and Albert Museum,
London (photos © Victoria and Albert Museum): 36,
37; Trustees of the Croome Estate: 51; Warwickshire
County Record Office, Warwick: 80; from William
Watts, *The Seats of the Nobility and Gentry: In a Collection
of the most Interesting & Picturesque Views . . .* (London,
1779-86); 77; Trustees of the Weston Park Foundation
and Staffordshire Record Office, Stafford: 41, 54, 61;
Wiltshire and Swindon Archives: 2; Yale Center for
British Art, New Haven, Connecticut (Paul Mellon
Collection): 38, 39, 40; The Zetland Collection: 47.

INDEX

Illustration numbers are in *italics*.